ORIGINAL NARRATIVES
OF EARLY AMERICAN HISTORY

REPRODUCED UNDER THE AUSPICES OF THE
AMERICAN HISTORICAL ASSOCIATION

GENERAL EDITOR, J. FRANKLIN JAMESON, PH.D., LL.D., LITT.D.

DIRECTOR OF THE DEPARTMENT OF HISTORICAL RESEARCH IN THE
CARNEGIE INSTITUTION OF WASHINGTON

NARRATIVES OF THE INSURRECTIONS

1675—1690

ORIGINAL NARRATIVES
OF EARLY AMERICAN HISTORY

NARRATIVES
OF THE INSURRECTIONS
1675—1690

EDITED BY

CHARLES M. ANDREWS, Ph.D., L.H.D.
FARNAM PROFESSOR OF AMERICAN HISTORY IN YALE UNIVERSITY

WITH THREE FACSIMILES

CHARLES SCRIBNER'S SONS
NEW YORK

CONTENTS

NARRATIVES OF THE INSURRECTIONS

Edited by Charles M. Andrews

v

CONTENTS

CONTENTS

CONTENTS

FACSIMILE REPRODUCTIONS

NARRATIVES OF THE INSURREC-
TIONS, 1675–1691

GENERAL INTRODUCTION

In the year 1676, the date of the first narrative in this volume, the English settlements in America were still in the formative stage of their development. Though ideas and institutions were taking shape, the social order was unsettled and there prevailed a great variety of opinions similar to those held in England and ranging from the conservative belief in passive obedience and the divinity of kings to the radical notions of Levellers and Fifth Monarchy men. As a rule, colonists radical in opinion and restless in spirit crossed the water to America, and naturally the environment into which they entered did little to arouse conservative instincts. Intolerance was a characteristic of those who differed on questions of government and religious faith, and much quarrelling accompanied the establishing of homes in the New World. The colonies were still receiving new accessions of people— English, French, and German—and each newcomer, having fled from persecution or economic distress abroad, added his quota to the stock of varied and often antagonistic opinions on matters of politics and religion.

Among the colonies themselves many diversities appeared. The New Englanders were homogeneous in race, social relations, religion, and methods of government, but to a degree greater than elsewhere were they illiberal toward others and independent of all that concerned the interest and welfare of the mother country. Virginia was largely homogeneous in race but not in class, and in political organization and economic relations was in close accord with the government at home. Maryland, homogeneous in race but not in religion

3

or class, presented conditions very similar to those in Virginia; while in New York, where popular government had not been established, great diversity prevailed in race, religion, and political ideas. In the north there was little discontent due to poverty and suffering; but in the southern colonies social uneasiness, penury, and ignorance were everywhere factors of importance.

Upon a people, sensitive and excitable and reflecting in so many ways the restlessness and discontent prevailing in England during the seventeenth century, every change in the situation at home was bound to make a deep impression. The age was one when men were not content to let sleeping dogs lie. Fears and suspicions were easily aroused; hatred and anger cut deep into men's souls; and trifling incidents were sufficient to arouse doubt and mistrust. Colonial society at this time was in a ferment and quick to respond to outside forces. The fact that during the years from 1676 to 1690 insurrections broke out in nearly all the colonies can be explained only in part by conditions existing in the colonies themselves; for behind the immediate causes lie those remoter influences, largely from outside, which give to the uprisings a common origin and common characteristics. These popular movements were not isolated phenomena; they were manifestations of a general discontent in the larger English world and the result of fears which prevailed in England as well as America, and though not always present in equal measure, or operating with equal effect, were everywhere much the same.

Throughout the colonies bodies of settlers existed holding definite ideas regarding a "free government," or, as the more common phrase had it, a "free parliament." Despite the presence of representative assemblies in all the colonies except New York, the belief widely prevailed that elsewhere than in New England "free parliaments" did not actually exist. Men of the Carolinas, Virginia, and Maryland held this view of the matter, and were in part justified by the facts; for in these colonies the royal or proprietary appointees controlled affairs and often compelled the popular assemblies to follow their lead. In New York, since the days of Governor Nicolls, demands for a representative assembly had been heard, and the Long Island towns had frequently plotted among themselves for a return to the jurisdiction of Connecticut. The New England colonies were content as long as they were let alone, but when they lost their charters and were combined in a Dominion of New England, with a royal governor, they too joined the ranks of those opposed to the preponderant influence of the royal prerogative.

But there is nothing to show that there was any widespread opposition to the connection with England or to the royal or proprietary authority as such. The insurgents of Albemarle, Virginia, and Maryland may have planned to set up popular governors, as in New England, but no colonist at this period would have been so foolhardy as to believe that separation from England was desirable or that English aid or protection could be dispensed with. The enemy that the colonists in America opposed and endeavored to destroy was the same enemy that their fellow Englishmen were fighting— the royal authority as exercised by and under the Stuart kings. In the government of Charles II. and James II. and of all who represented them, the colonists thought they saw a menace to free government. There was much in the royal policy that they neither knew nor understood, but in their eyes the government of the Stuarts was not only harsh and despotic, but wrong, for they believed that it meant the dominance of Roman Catholicism, at this time a terrifying spectre and a fearful menace to Protestantism, and also the possible ascendancy of France, where despotism and Roman Catholicism were wreaking a terrible vengeance on the Protestant Huguenots. Even if a Stuart appointee were an avowed Protestant, he was classed with dogs, rogues, strangers, Irishmen, and Papists, and suspected of plots to bring down the French upon the colony or to carry the colony over to the side of France.

We know that these fears were baseless and irrational, but they were real to many a colonist of this period and were forces that drove men to action. Bad government, heavy taxation, and perverted justice lent evidence and proof; wars and rumors of wars with the Indians on the frontiers gave ample warrant for belief in the machinations of Jesuits and Frenchmen at their doors; and the presence of Roman Catholic governors in Maryland and New York and of Roman Catholic officials in both colonies furnished grounds for belief that conspiracy was fomenting in the midst of the people themselves. Among ignorant and distressed planters and laborers, who, isolated in large part from the world outside, lived in a wilderness as yet untamed, these rumors, elaborated and magnified, assumed startling proportions, and even in towns such as New York and Boston lost few of their terrors. Any examination of the causes of these insurrections becomes a study in human psychology.

How far the revolts were due to England's efforts to enforce her commercial policy, as expressed in the navigation acts, royal proclamations and instructions, and customs officials, it is not easy to determine. In every instance where such influence can be seen, other causes were at work to such an extent as to render it more than doubtful whether the British policy was a serious contributing factor. The uprising in Albemarle was a protest against the attempt of Miller, the collector, to collect the plantation duty, but as Miller was trying to act also as governor, and doing his part very badly, we cannot be sure that the plantation duty alone would have brought about the revolt. Bacon's rebellion in Virginia was supported largely by the poor and discontented planters, but even if the navigation acts can be shown to have been a cause of destitution, they cannot be placed as determining factors in the same class with the heavy taxation and the political misrule. Though the Marylanders had had difficulties with the royal officials, they do not mention the acts in their complaints; and the northern colonists seem to have little to say of them, save that the New England merchants objected to their enforcement by Randolph as interfering with the freedom of their trade. As the acts were largely neglected before 1676, and very inadequately applied until after 1696, I am not inclined to see in them a cause of much importance.

One cannot study the insurrections as a whole without noticing the mutual dependence of one colony upon another. New England sea-captains took part in the Albemarle movement; Albemarle men were at Jamestown and had some place in the Virginia uprising; Virginia and Maryland were so near together that their leading actors were in constant touch and almost mutually interchangeable. Leisler in New York was in correspondence with Maryland, Connecticut, and Massachusetts, while New York and Boston were in close communication, New Yorkers serving as officials under Andros in Boston, Dudley presiding in New York at Leisler's trial, and Leislerian supporters at Boston obtaining the reversal of Leisler's attainder by act of Parliament in England. The measure of these intercolonial relations and their effect upon the insurrectionary movements are difficult to determine, but the fact that such interdependence existed is of considerable moment, and shows that not only were the causes of the movement much the same at bottom, but also that the influence of one revolutionary group on another is a matter not to be disregarded.

C. M. A.

THE BEGINNING, PROGRESS, AND CONCLU-
SION OF BACON'S REBELLION, 1675–1676
[1705]

INTRODUCTION

THE first popular uprising in colonial America took place in Virginia. This movement, commonly called, after its leader, Bacon's Rebellion, was at bottom a protest of the growing middle class in the newer plantations and counties against the political and social monopoly of the aristocrats living in the older settled areas. The number of small planters, poor immigrants, and servants freed from bondage had greatly increased since 1650 and formed a social element easily disturbed by conditions that distressed the colony. Virginia had but one staple, tobacco, and so staked her prosperity on a single commodity that was liable to constant fluctuations in its market value. Her people, despite frequent efforts of those in authority, both in England and in the colony, refused to engage in other staple industries. Government, both local and general, was in the hands of a clique, charged not only with political monopoly but also with favoritism, corruption, and incompetence. Most of the people had no share in political life, for appointments were in the hands of the crown and the governor; the assembly of 1661 sat continuously for fourteen years; and a disfranchising act of 1670 cut off the landless class entirely from the right to vote. Taxation was unjust because the only direct tax was a poll tax, and was heavy owing to levies at this period for certain unusual charges, such as the agency to England for the purpose of obtaining a reversal of the king's iniquitous grant of the Northern Neck to Arlington and Culpeper, and the new forts erected on the upper waters of the rivers for protection against the Indians. The political scandals and the heavy taxes

11

touched very closely a people among whom poverty and ignorance widely prevailed, owing to normal frontier conditions, the falling price of tobacco, and disasters that resulted in heavy local losses.

The burden of England's commercial policy was undoubtedly a grievance temporarily and in certain particular quarters, but it was in no sense a cause of the insurrection. Virginia had been living under the limitations of a restricted market for thirty years, and neither before nor after 1660 had the colonists protested against the requirement that they send their tobacco directly to England. Such protests as exist were individual and not general. Even after 1676, when the people at large had a chance to say what they thought, they scarcely mention this requirement among their grievances. They speak of the bad government, of heavy taxes, of dangers from the Indians, and of the oppressive conduct of individuals, but only in a very few instances of the navigation acts. They ascribed the low price of tobacco to heavy customs dues in England and to excessive planting in the colony.

There are many accounts of Bacon's Rebellion, of which the three selected for insertion here cover in an authoritative and fairly impartial fashion the entire movement.

The narrative of *The Beginning, Progress, and Conclusion of Bacon's Rebellion* was written in 1705 by "T. M." at the request of Secretary Harley, and must have remained for many years in the Harleian library. Though the Harleian collection of manuscripts was sold in bulk to the British Museum in 1753, this particular document, which bears the library numbering, fell in some way into the hands of the trade and was bought, in November, 1801, at a sale of the stock of Collins, bookseller of London, by Rufus King, minister plenipotentiary of the United States at the court of St. James. In December, 1803, he sent it to President Jefferson. The original is now in the Library of Congress. The

Virginia Historical Society has a copy of one of the two transcripts which Jefferson caused to be made; the other was given by him to the American Antiquarian Society and is now in its possession.

The author, "T. M.," is undoubtedly Thomas Mathew, of Cherry Point, in the parish of Boutracy,[1] Northumberland County, in the Northern Neck, Virginia. Mathew was a merchant-planter, having extensive landholdings in Virginia, particularly in those counties where the troubles with the Indians first began, Northumberland and Stafford, at the lower and upper waters of the Potomac. Although he was not interested in the politics of the colony and preferred to restrict himself to mercantile pursuits, yet he served as a county justice in 1672 and 1676, and at his house in 1677–1678 the county court of Northumberland sat as a "court maritime" to try a shipmaster guilty of a breach of the navigation acts. In 1676, though a resident of Northumberland County, he was chosen, with Colonel George Mason, to represent Stafford County in the House of Burgesses, and sat as a member of the Reforming or Baconian Assembly of that year. He took an active part in the work of the session and, as his own account testifies, was a member of influence. But he was not a party man and political responsibilities were irksome to him. He disliked controversy, though he could not avoid it altogether, and he tried to steer a path between the two extremes, committing himself to neither party. He was twice offered a lieutenancy by Bacon, but each time refused.

After the rebellion was over Mathew returned to his mercantile interests, experimented with the manufacture of linen, and came into frequent contact with William Fitzhugh, the well-known planter and letter-writer, who also had lands in

[1] Boutracy has long since disappeared as the name of a parish in Virginia, but it is mentioned in the early Northumberland records.

Stafford County. Later he returned to England, where he lived in Westminster until his death, which took place some time between October, 1705, and February, 1706. He married a sister of Captain John Cralle, and left three children, born in Virginia between 1677 and 1680.

Mathew wrote his account of the rebellion thirty years after the event. From internal evidence it would appear that he had at hand notes made at the time, though there is nothing directly to prove such a statement. He was well fitted to write the account, having lived in the midst of the events he describes and having been an eye-witness of many of them. He drew much information from personal conversation with Bacon, Lawrence, and other leaders, and certainly at first had much sympathy with the cause they represented, though not with its excesses. His narrative is straightforward and concise, such as one would expect from a man of business, and it is manifestly fair and honest. Mathew displayed no partisan interest in the rebellion, but rather a desire to do what he could to protect the country and to further the cause of peace.

The narrative was first printed in the Richmond *Enquirer*, September 1, 5, and 8, 1804, from the copy now owned by the American Antiquarian Society. In 1820, it was printed for the second time, from a copy obtained from the Library of Congress, in the Virginia *Evangelical and Literary Magazine*, III. 128–149. It was issued for the third time by Peter Force in 1836, in his *Collection of Tracts*, vol. I., no. 8, the text being that of the copy possessed by the American Antiquarian Society, and for the fourth time, after the second copy, in the *Virginia Historical Register and Literary Note Book*, III. 61–75, 121–136, in April and July, 1850. A fifth reprint was issued in 1897, by G. P. Humphrey, in *Colonial Tracts*, no. 8. The present text is from the original manuscript in the Library of Congress.

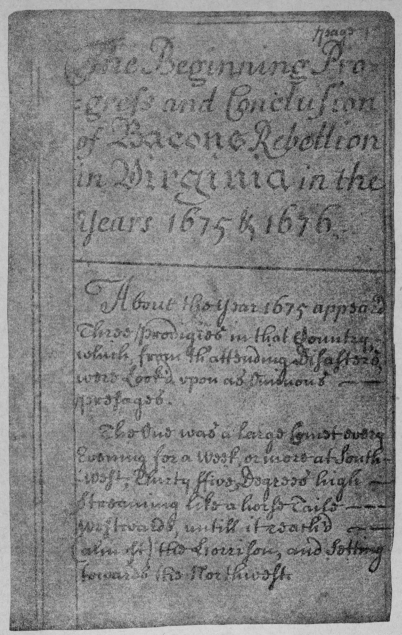

FIRST PAGE OF THOMAS MATHEW'S NARRATIVE

From the original in the Library of Congress

THE BEGINNING, PROGRESS, AND CONCLUSION OF BACON'S REBELLION, 1675–1676

To the Right Honoble Robert Harley, Esqr.[1] Her Majties Principal Secretary of State, and One of her Most Honoble Privy Council.

Sr.

The great Honour of Your Command obliging my Pen to step aside from it's habituall Element of Figures into this little Treatise of History; which having never before Experienced, I am like Sutor ultra crepidam,[2] and therefore dare pretend no more, than (nakedly) to recount Matters of Fact.

Beseeching your honour will vouchsafe to Allow, that in 30 Years, divers occurences are laps'd out of mind, and others Imperfectly retained.

So as the most solemn Obedience Can be now paid, is to pursue the Track of barefac'd Truths, as Close as my Memory can Recollect, to have seen, or believed, from Credible Friends, with Concurring Circumstances;

And whatsoever your Celebrated Wisdom shall find amisse in the Composure my intire dependance is upon your Candour favourably to Accept these most Sincere Endeavours of

Your Honours

Most Devoted humble Servt

T. M.

The 13th. July 1705

The Beginning, Progress and Conclusion of Bacons Rebellion in Virginia in the Years 1675 and 1676.

ABOUT the year 1675 appear'd three Prodigies in that Country, which, from th' attending Disasters, were Look'd upon as Ominous Presages.

The One was a large Comet every Evening for a Week, or

---

[1] The noted statesman of Queen Anne's reign, afterward Earl of Oxford.
[2] The shoemaker away from his last.

more at South-West; Thirty five Degrees high, Streaming like a horse Taile Westwards, untill it reach'd (almost) the Horrison, and Setting towards the Northwest.

Another was, Flights of Pigeons in breadth nigh a Quarter of the Mid-Hemisphere, and of their Length was no visible End; Whose Weights brake down the Limbs of Large Trees whereon these rested at Nights, of which the Fowlers Shot abundance and Eat 'em; This Sight put the old Planters under the more Portentous Apprehensions, because the like was Seen (as they said) in the year 1640 When th' Indians Committed the last Massacre, but not after, untill that present Year 1675.

The Third strange Appearance was Swarms of Flyes about an Inch long, and big as the Top of a Man's little finger, rising out of Spigot Holes in the Earth, which Eat the New Sprouted Leaves from the Tops of the Trees without other Harm, and in a Month left us.

My Dwelling was in Northumberland, the lowest County on Potomack River, Stafford being the upmost;[1] where having also a Plantation, Servant's, Cattle, etc, My Overseer there had agreed with one Robt. Hen to come thither, and be my Herdsman, who then Lived Ten Miles above it; But on a Sabbath day Morning in the summer Anno 1675, People in their Way to Church, Saw this Hen lying th'wart his Threshold, and an Indian without the Door, both Chopt on their Heads, Arms and other Parts, as if done with Indian Hatchetts. Th' Indian was dead, but Hen when ask'd who did that? Answered "Doegs Doegs,"[2] and soon Died, then a Boy came out from under a Bed, where he had hid himself, and told them, Indians had come at break of day and done those Murders.

From this Englishman's bloud did (by Degrees) arise Bacons Rebellion with the following Mischiefs which Overspread all Virginia and twice endangerd Maryland, as by the ensuing Account is Evident.

[1] Of all the counties in Virginia Stafford lay farthest from Jamestown, being a frontier region a hundred miles away by land and much more by water. Northumberland lay on the lower Potomac, forming with Lancaster, Westmoreland, Richmond, and King George, the Northern Neck, that is, the land between the Potomac and Rappahannock Rivers, in width from nine to thirty miles, and in area a scant thousand square miles.

[2] The Doegs were an Indian tribe dwelling in Maryland.

Of this horrid Action Coll: Mason[1] who commanded the Militia Regiment of Foot and Capt. Brent[2] the Troop of Horse in that County, (both dwelling Six or Eight Miles Downwards) having speedy notice raised 30 or more men, and pursu'd those Indians 20 Miles up and 4 Miles over that River into Maryland, where landing at Dawn of Day, they found two small Paths. Each Leader with his Party took a Separate Path and in less than a furlong, either found a Cabin, which they Silently Surrounded. Capt. Brent went to the Doegs Cabin (as it proved to be) Who Speaking the Indian Tongue Called to have a *Matchacomicha Weewhip i. e.* a Councill, called presently Such being the usuall manner with Indians. The King came Trembling forth, and wou'd have fled, when Capt. Brent, Catching hold of his twisted Lock (which was all the Hair he wore) told him he was come for the Murderer of Robt. Hen, the King pleaded Ignorance and Slipt loos, whom Brent shot Dead with his Pistoll. Th' Indians Shot Two or Three Guns out of the Cabin, th' English shot into it, th' Indians throng'd out at the Door and fled, The English Shot as many as they cou'd, so that they Kill'd Ten, as Capt. Brent told me, and brought away the Kings Son of about 8 Years old, Concerning whom is an Observable Passage, at the End of this Expedition; the Noise of this Shooting awaken'd th' Indians in the Cabin which Coll: Mason had Encompassed, who likewise Rush'd out and fled, of whom his Company (supposing from that Noise of Shooting Brent's party to be Engaged) shott (as the Colll: Inform'd me) Fourteen before an Indian Came, who with both hands Shook him (friendly) by one Arm Saying *Susquehanougs Netoughs i. e.* Susquehanaugh friends, and fled, Whereupon he ran amongst his Men, Crying out "For the Lords sake Shoot no more, these are our friends the Susquehanoughs."

This unhappy Scene ended, Collo. Mason took the King of

[1] Colonel George Mason, a native of Staffordshire, England, came to Virginia in 1651, and settled in Stafford County. He filled many public offices, dying in 1686. At this time he was forty-six years old.

[2] Colonel George Brent, of Woodstock or Aquia, was one of the Maryland family of Brents and came to Virginia in 1650. He had lands in Stafford County near those of William Fitzhugh, whose partner he was in the practice of law. His house was on Aquia Creek, where the Potomac bends northward, as one ascends, toward the present Mount Vernon. He was a Roman Catholic.

the Doegs Son home with him, who lay Ten dayes in Bed, as one Dead, with Eyes and Mouth Shutt, no Breath Discern'd, but his body continuing Warm, they believ'd him yett alive; Th' aforenamed Capt. Brent (a Papist) Coming thither on a Visit, and seeing his little Prisoner thus languishing Said "Perhaps He is *pawewawd,*" *i. e.* Bewitch'd, and that he had heard Baptism was an Effectuall Remedy against Witchcraft—Wherefore advis'd to Baptize him. Collo. Mason Answered, No Minister cou'd be had in many Miles; Brent replied, "your Clerk Mr. Dobson may do that Office," which was done by the Church of England Liturgy; Collo. Mason with Capt. Brent Godfather and Mrs. Mason Godmother, My Overseer Mr. Pimet being present, from whom I first heard it, and which all th' other Persons (afterwards) affirm'd to me; The Four Men return'd to drinking Punch, But Mrs. Mason Staying and Looking on the Child, it open'd the Eyes, and Breath'd, whereat she ran for a Cordial, which he took from a Spoon, gaping for more and so (by degrees) recovered, tho' before his Baptism, they had often tryed the same meanes but Coud by no Endeavours Wrench open his Teeth.

This was taken for a Convincing Proofe against Infidelity.

But to return from this Digression, The Susquehanoughs were newly driven from their Habitations, at the head of Chesepiack Bay, by the Cineka[1]-Indians, down to the head of Potomack, where they sought Protection under the Pascataway Indians,[2] who had a fort[3] near the Head of that River, and also were our Friends.

After this unfortunate Exploit of Mason and Brent, one or Two being kill'd in Stafford, Boats of War were Equipt to

---

[1] The Senecas, "the greatest and most considerable nation," were at this time pressing down from the north upon the Susquehannas at the head of Chesapeake Bay.

[2] Piscattaway or Pascattoway Creek flows into the upper Potomac from Maryland. The Piscattoways were one of the smaller tribes of Indians, and their "empress" had married Giles Brent of Maryland.

[3] This was an old fort erected by Maryland for the protection of the frontier. It was attacked at this time by invitation of the Marylanders, as the narrative states, by a joint force of Virginians and Marylanders. The Virginia forces were led by Colonel John Washington, and a deposition of June 14, 1677, shows that the four (five or six) captured Susquehannas were put to death by the Marylanders. (*William and Mary Quarterly,* II. 39–40.)

prevent Excursions over the River, and at the same time Murders being (likewise) Committed in Maryland, by whom not known, on either Side the River, both Countrys raised their Quota's of a Thousand Men, upon whose coming before the Fort, Th' Indians sent out 4 of their great Men, who ask'd the Reason of that Hostile Appearance, What they said more or offered, I Do not Remember to have heard; But our Two Commanders Caused them to be (Instantly) Slaine, after which the Indians made an Obstinate Resistance, Shooting many of our Men, and making frequent, fierce and Bloody Sallyes; and when they were Call'd to, or offerd Parley, Gave no other Answer, than "Where are our four *Cockarouses, i. e.* Great Men?"

At the End of Six Weeks, March'd out Seventy five Indians with their Women Children etc. who (by Moon light) past our Guards, hollowing and firing att Them without Opposition, leaving 3 or 4 Decrepits in the Fort.

The next Morning th' English followed, but could not, or (for fear of Ambuscades), woud not Overtake these Desperate fugitives. The Number we lost in that Siege I Did not hear was published.

The Walls of this fort were high banks of Earth, with Flankers having many Loop Holes, and a Ditch round all, and without this a Row of Tall Trees fastned 3 foot Deep in the Earth, their Bodies from 5 to 8 Inches Diameter, watled 6 Inches apart to shoot through with the Tops twisted together, and also Artificially Wrought, as our Men[1] coud make no Breach to Storm it, nor (being Low Land) coud they undermine it by reason of Water—neither had they Cannon to batter itt, So that 'twas not taken, untill Famine drove the Indians out of it.

These Escap'd Indians (forsaking Maryland,) took their Rout over the Head of that River, and thence over the heads of Rappahannock and York Rivers, killing whom they found of th' upmost Plantations untill they Came to the Head of James River, where (with Bacon[2] and others,) they Slew Mr.

---

[1] "And all so artificially wrought as [that] our men," etc.

[2] Nathaniel Bacon, jr., was the son of Thomas Bacon of Freestone Hall, Suffolk, England. He married in 1670 Elizabeth Duke, daughter of Sir Edward Duke. He and his wife came to the colony in 1674, settling at Curles on the

Bacon's Overseer whom He much Loved, and One of his Servants, whose Bloud Hee Vowed to Revenge if possible.

In these frightfull times the most Exposed small families withdrew into our houses of better Numbers, which we fortified with Pallisadoes and redoubts, Neighbours in Bodies Joined their Labours from each Plantation to others Alternately, taking their Arms into the Fields, and Setting Centinels; no Man Stirrd out of Door unarm'd, Indians were (ever and anon) espied, Three, 4, 5, or 6 in a Party Lurking throughout the Whole Land, yet (what was remarkable) I rarely heard of any Houses Burnt, tho' abundance was forsaken, nor ever, of any Corn or Tobacco cut up, or other Injury done, besides Murders, Except the killing a very few Cattle and Swine.

Frequent Complaints of Bloudsheds were sent to Sr. Wm. Berkeley (then Governour,)[1] from the Heads of the Rivers, which were as often Answered, with Promises of Assistance.

These at the Heads of James and York Rivers (having now most People destroyed by the Indians Flight thither from Potomack) grew Impatient at the many Slaughters of their Neighbours and rose for their own Defence, who Chusing Mr. Bacon for their Leader Sent often times to the Governour, humbly Beseeching a commission to go against those Indians at their own Charge which his Honour as often promis'd but did not send; The Misteryes of these Delays, were Wondred at and which I ne're heard any coud Penetrate into, other than the Effects of his Passion, and a new (not to be mentioned) occasion of Avarice, to both which, he was (by the common Vogue) more than a little Addicted; Whatever were the Popular Surmizes and Murmurings *vizt.*

"That no Bullets woud pierce Bever Skins.

"Rebells forfeitures woud be Loyall Inheritances etc."

During these Protractions and People often Slaine, most or

James, a short distance below Henrico. Of this marriage two daughters were born in Virginia, one of whom died there. Mrs. Bacon, in a letter to her sister-in-law, says that the Indians destroyed "a great stock of cattle and a good cargo that we should have made there." We know that Bacon left his wife very destitute at his death and that she married again, losing her second husband in 1679. William Byrd, who lived near the Bacons, says that Bacon had lost three of his men, one of whom was the overseer, before he took any action.

[1] Berkeley had been governor since 1662, as well as from 1641 to 1652.

all the Officers, Civill and Military, with as many Dwellers next the Heads of the Rivers as made up 300 Men, taking Mr. Bacon for their Commandr. met, and Concerted together, the Danger of going without a Comissn on the one Part, and the Continuall Murders of their Neighbours on th' other Part (not knowing whose or how many of their own turns might be next) and Came to this Resolution *vizt.* To prepare themselves with necessaries for a March, but interim to send again for a Comission, which if could or could not be Obteyned by a certaine day, they woud proceed Commission or no Comission.

This day Lapsing and no Comn. come, They march'd into the Wilderness in Quest of these Indians after whom the Governour sent his Proclamacion, Denouncing all Rebells,[1] who shoud not return within a Limited Day, Whereupon those of Estates obey'd; But Mr. Bacon with 57 Men proceded untill their Provisions were near Spent, without finding Enemy's, when coming nigh a Fort of Friend Indians, on th' other Side a Branch of James River, they desired reliefe offering paymt. which these Indians kindly promised to help them with on the Morrow, but put them off with promises untill the Third day, So as having then Eaten their last Morsells They could not return, but must have Starved in the Way homeward and now 'twas Suspected, these Indians had received private Messages from the Governour and those to be the Causes of these Delusive procrastinations; Whereupon the English Waded Shoulder deep thro' that Branch to the Fort Pallisado's still intreating and tendering Pay, for Victuals; But that Evening a Shot from the Place they left on th' other side of that Branch kill'd one of Mr. Bacons Men, which made them believe, those in the Fort had sent for other Indians to come behind 'em and Cut 'em off.

Hereupon they fired the Palisado's, Storm'd and burnt the Fort and Cabins, and (with the Losse of Three English) Slew 150 Indians. The Circumstances of this expedicion Mr. Bacon Entertain'd me with, at his own Chamber, on a Visit I made him, the occasion whereof is hereafter mencioned.

From hence they return'd home where Writts were come up to Elect Members for an Assembly, When Mr. Bacon was

---

[1] *I. e.,* as rebels.

unanimously Chosen for One, who coming down the River was Commanded by a Ship with Guns to come on board, where waited Major Hone the High Sheriff of James Town ready to Seize him, by whom he was Carried down to the Governour and by him receiv'd with a Suprizing Civillity in the following Words "Mr. Bacon have you forgot to be a Gentleman?" "No, May it please your Honour," Answer'd Mr. Bacon; "Then" replyed the Governour "I'le take your Parol," and Gave him his Liberty. in March 1675–6 Writts came up to Stafford to Choose their Two Members for an Assembly to meet in May; when Collo. Mason, Capt. Brent and other Gentlemen of that County, invited me to stand a Candidate; a Matter I little Dreamt of, having never had Inclinacions to tamper in the Precarious Intrigues of Governt; and my hands being full of my own business; They press't severall Cogent Argumts, and I having Considerable Debts in that County, besides my Plantation Concerns, where (in one and th' other) I had much more severely Suffered than any of themselves by th' Indian Disturbances in the Sumer and Winter foregoing, I held it not (then) Discreet to Disoblige the Rulers of it, so Coll: Mason with my Selfe were Elected without Objection, he at time Convenient went on horseback; I took my sloop and the Morning I arriv'd at James town after a Weeks voyage, was welcomed with the strange Acclamations of "All's over, Bacon is taken," having not heard at home of these southern comotions, other than rumours like idle tales, of one Bacon risen up in rebellion, nobody knew for what, concerning the Indians.[1]

The next forenoon, th' Assembly being met in a chamber over the generall court and our Speaker chosen, the governour

---

[1] "Sherwood's Account" states that Bacon, having been elected burgess for Henrico, went to Jamestown in a sloop with fifty armed men, "with intent that when the house sat to force his way amongst them. It was judged he was not a fit person to sit as burgess, but that he should first be brought to answer the great charge against him. Of this he was informed by some of his faction and endeavors to escape, upon which several boats with armed men were sent to force his submission, and a command from the governor to one Capt. Gardner, whose ship rides at Sandy Point, not to permit him to pass. The small boats pursue him in that ship, by which he is fired at to come to anchor, and so he was taken and with all his men brought to town the 7th instant (June) and delivered to the governor." See below, p. 54.

sent for us down, where his honour with a pathetic Emphasis made a Short abrupt Speech wherein were these Words.

"If they had killed my Grandfather and Grandmother, my father and Mother and all my friends, yet if they had come to treat of Peace, they ought to have gone in Peace," and sat down.

The two chief commanders at the forementioned siege, who Slew the Four Indian great men, being present and part of our Assembly.

The Governour stood up againe and said "if there be joy in the presence of the angels over one sinner that repenteth, there is joy now, for we have a penitent sinner come before us, call Mr. Bacon;" then did Mr. Bacon upon one Knee at the Bar deliver a Sheet of paper Confessing his Crimes, and begging Pardon of God the King and the Governour, Whereto (after a short Pause) He Answered "God forgive you, I forgive you," thrice repeating the same Words; When Collo. Cole[1] (One of the Councill) said, "and all that were with him," "yea," said the Governour "and all that were with him," Twenty or more Persons being then in Irons Who were taken Coming down in the same and other Vessels with Mr. Bacon.

About a Minute after this the Governour, Starting up from his Chair a Third time said, "Mr. Bacon! if you will live Civilly but till next Quarter Court (doubling the Words) but till next Quarter Court, Ile promise to restore you againe to your Place There" pointing with his hand to Mr. Bacons Seat, he having been of the Councill before these troubles, tho' he had been a very short time in Virginia but was Deposed by the foresaid Proclamacion, and in th' afternoon passing by the Court door, in my Way up to our Chamber, I saw Mr. Bacon on his quondam Seat with the Governour and Councill, which Seemed a Marveilous Indulgence to one whom he had so lately Proscribed as a Rebell.

The Governour had Directed us to Consider of Meanes for Security from th' Indian Insults and to Defray the Charge etc. Advising us to beware of Two Rogues amongst us, nam-

[1] Colonel William Cole of Baltrope, Warwick County, was a member of the council, and a supporter of Berkeley.

ing Laurence[1] and Drumond[2] both dwelling at James Town and Who were not at the Pascataway Siege.

But at our Entrance upon Businesse, Some Gentlemen took this opportunity to Endeavour the Redressing severall Grievances the Country then Labour'd under, Motions were made for Inspecting the Publick Revenues, the Collectors Accompts etc. and so far was Proceeded as to name Part of a Committee whereof Mr. Bristol[3] (now in London,) was and my self another, when we were Interrupted by Pressing Messages from the Governour to Medle with nothing, untill the Indian Business was Dispatch't.

This Debate rose high, but was Overruled and I have not heard that those Inspections have since then been Insisted upon, tho' such of that Indigent People as had no benefits from the Taxes groand under our being thus Overborn.

The next thing was a Committee for the Indian Affaires, whereof in appointing the Members, my self was unwillingly Nominated having no knowledge in Martiall Preparations, and after our Names were taken, some of the house moved for sending 2 of our Members to Intreat the governour wou'd please to Assign Two of his Councill to Sit with, and Assist us in our Debates, as had been usuall.

When seeing all Silent looking each at other with many Discontented faces, I adventur'd to offer my humble Opinion to the Speaker "for the Comittee to form Methods as agree-

---

[1] Richard Lawrence, William Drummond, and one Arnold were called "the bell-wethers of the rest during the whole rebellion." Lawrence has generally been considered the chief instigator of the movement. He was an Oxford man and a person of means, who lived at Jamestown, where he had a house. There Bacon, Lawrence, and Drummond conferred for three hours on June 7. See below, p. 114.

[2] William Drummond, a Scotsman, had lived at Jamestown before he was appointed governor of Albemarle County, 1664–1667. Returning to Jamestown, he became one of the chief men of the rebellion, continuing in arms after Bacon's death, until his capture, January 14, 1677. He was hung the same day. His daughter married a son of Colonel Thomas Swann, of Swann's Point, where the commissioners resided and held court in 1677. See below, pp. 98, 103.

[3] Probably Major Robert Bristow, who came to Virginia in 1660 and settled in Gloucester County. He was captured by the insurgents and kept a prisoner until after Bacon's death. He lost heavily by the rebellion in estate and goods. He went to England in October, 1677, where he continued his career as a merchant.

able to the Sense of the house as we could, and report 'em, whereby they woud more clearly See, on what points to Give the Governour and Councill that trouble if perhaps it might bee needfull."

These few words rais'd an Uproar; One party Urging hard "It had been Customary and ought not to be omitted;" Whereto Mr. Presley[1] my Neighbour an old Assembly Man, sitting next me, rose up, and (in a blundering manner replied) "tis true, it has been Customary, but if we have any bad Customes amongst us, We are come here to mend 'em," which Set the house in a Laughter.

This was huddl'd off without coming to a Vote, and so the Committee must Submit to be overaw'd, and have every Carpt at Expression Carried streight to the Governr.

Our Committee being sat, the Queen of Pamunky[2] (Descended from Oppechankenough a former Emperor of Virginia) was Introduced, who entred the Chamber with a Comportment Gracefull to Admiration, bringing on her right hand an Englishman Interpreter, and on the left her Son a Stripling Twenty Years of Age, She having round her head a Plat of Black and White Wampum peague Three Inches broad in imitation of a Crown, and was Cloathed in a Mantle of dress't Deerskins with the hair outwards and the Edge cut round 6

---

[1] William Pressly sat in the Long Assembly, 1662–1676, in the Reforming Assembly, June, 1676, and in the royalist assembly that gathered February 20, 1677, after the rebellion was over.

[2] "Pamunkey" seems to have designated the triangular section of country formed by the two main branches of the York River, with West Point at the apex. The Pamunkey tribes, however, occupied parts of New Kent County also. The queen represented the chiefs of the Powhatan group of Indians, her husband Tottopottomoy (Tatapamoi) having been killed in 1656. She had a son, John West, from whom came the name of the locality West Point. She was a faithful friend to the English, but suffered greatly by Bacon's rebellion, "being driven out into the wild woods and there almost famished. Plundered of all she had, her people taken prisoners and sold, she was also robbed of her rich match-coat for which she had great value and offered to redeem at any price." Among the presents sent to various chiefs from England was a red velvet cap to the Queen of Pamunkey, to which was attached a silver frontlet by chains of the same metal. This frontlet, which is now the property of the Association for the Preservation of Virginia Antiquities, is the only one of these "crowns" known to exist. Whether others were sent is uncertain, as the Virginia Assembly protested against making such regal presents to the Indians.

Inches deep which made Strings resembling Twisted frenge from the Shoulders to the feet; Thus with grave Courtlike Gestures and a Majestick Air in her face, she Walk'd up our Long Room to the Lower end of the Table, Where after a few Intreaties She Sat down; th' Interpreter and her Son Standing by her on either side as they had Walked up, our Chairman asked her what men she would Lend us for Guides in the Wilderness and to assist us against our Enemy Indians, She Spake to th' Interpreter to inform her what the Chairman Said, (tho' we believed She understood him). He told us She bid him ask her Son to whom the English tongue was familiar, and who was reputed the Son of an English Colonel, yet neither woud he Speak to or seem to understand the Chairman but th' Interpreter told us, he referred all to his Mother, Who being againe urged She after a little Musing with an earnest passionate Countenance as if Tears were ready to Gush out and a fervent sort of Expression made a Harangue about a quarter of an hour, often interlacing (with a high shrill Voice and vehement passion) these Words, *Tatapatamoi Chepiack, i. e.* Tatapamoi dead. Coll: Hill[1] being next me, Shook his head. I ask'd him What was the matter, he told me all she said was too true to our Shame, and that his father was Generall in that Battle, where diverse Years before Tatapatamoi her Husband had Led a Hundred of his Indians in help to th' English against our former Enemy Indians, and was there Slaine with most of his men; for which no Compensation (at all) had been to that day Rendered to her wherewith she now upbraided us.

Her Discourse ending and our Morose Chairman not advancing one cold word towards asswaging the Anger and Grief her Speech and Demeanour Manifested under her oppression, nor taking any notice of all she had Said, Neither

---

[1] Colonel Edward Hill, the younger (1637–1700), lived at Shirley (opposite the mouth of the Appomattox), an estate that he received from his father. He was one of the Berkeley adherents, and one thoroughly disliked by the Baconians. The Charles City County grievances were so full of complaints against him in particular that he felt obliged to write an elaborate, but, as it happens, not a very convincing defense, denying all the charges. The commissioners from England, to whom the defense was addressed, characterized him as "a most notorious coward and insolent turbulent fellow," but the indictment is hardly just, though Hill was undoubtedly grasping and oppressive.

Considering that we (then) were in our great Exigency, Supplicants to her for a favour of the same kind as the former, for which we did not Deny the having been so Ingrate, He rudely push'd againe the same Question "What Indians will you now Contribute" etc? of this Disregard she Signified her Resentment by a disdainfull aspect, and turning her head half a side, Sate mute till that same Question being press'd, a Third time, She not returning her face to the board, answered with a low slighting Voice in her own Language "Six," but being further Importun'd She sitting a little while Sullen, without uttering a Word between, Said "Twelve," tho' she then had a hundred and fifty Indian men in her Town, and so rose up and gravely Walked away, as not pleased with her Treatment.

Whilst some daies past in Setling the Quota's of Men Arms and Ammunicion Provisions etc. each County was to furnish, One Morning early a Bruit ran about the Town, "Bacon is fled, Bacon is fled," Whereupon I went Straight to Mr. Lawrence, Who (formerly) was of Oxford University, and for Wit Learning and Sobriety was equall'd there by few, and Who some Years before (as Col: Lee[1] tho' one of the Councill and a friend of the Governours inform'd me) had been partially treated at Law, for a Considerable Estate on behalfe of a Corrupt favourite; which Lawrence Complaining loudly of, the Governour bore him a Grudge and now Shaking his Head, Said, "Old Treacherous Villain," and that his House was Searcht that Morning, at day break, but Bacon was Escaped into the Country, having Intimation that the Governours Generosity in Pardoning him and his followers and restoring him to his Seat in Councill, were no other than Previous Wheadles to amuse him and his Adherents and to Circumvent them by Stratagem, forasmuch as the taking Mr. Bacon again into the Council was first to keep him out of the Assembly, and in the next place the Governour knew the Country People were hastning down with Dreadfull Threatnings to double Revenge all

[1] Colonel Richard Lee was a son of the secretary of state of the colony, who had come to Virginia about 1642, settling first in York and then in Northumberland Counties. He was a strong Berkeleyite, one of the "wicked and pernicious councillors" named by the commissioners, and had suffered at Bacon's hands, having been imprisoned for six weeks, to the injury of health and property.

Wrongs shoud be done to Mr. Bacon or his Men, or whoever shou'd have had the least hand in 'em.

And so much was true that this Mr. young Nathaniel Bacon (not yet Arrived to 30 Yeares) had a Nigh Relation Namely Col: Nathaniel Bacon[1] of Long Standing in the Council a very rich Politick Man, and Childless, designing this Kinsman for his heir, who (not without much Paines) had prevailed with his uneasy Cousin to deliver the forementioned written Recantation at the Bar, having Compiled it ready to his hand and by whose meanes 'twas Supposed that timely Intimation was Convey'd to the Young Gentleman to flee for his Life, And also in 3 or 4 daies after Mr. Bacon was first Seiz'd I Saw abundance of Men in Town Come thither from the Heads of the Rivers, Who finding him restor'd and his Men at Liberty, return'd home Satisfied; a few Daies after which the Governour seeing all Quiet, Gave out Private Warrants to take him againe, intending as was thought to raise the Militia, and so to Dispose things as to prevent his friends from gathering any more into a like Numerous Body and Comming down a Second time to Save him.

In Three or Four daies after this Escape, upon News that Mr. Bacon was 30 Miles up the River, at the head of four hundred Men, The Governour sent to the Parts adjacent, on both Sides James River for the Militia and all the Men could be gotten to Come and Defend the Town. Express's Came almost hourly of th' Army's Approaches, who in less than 4 daies after the first Account of 'em att 2 of the Clock entred the Town, without being withstood, and form'd a Body upon a green, not a flight Shot from the End of the Statehouse, of Horse and Foot, as well regular as Veteran Troops, who forthwith Possest themselves of all the Avenues, Disarming all in Town, and Comming thither in Boats or by Land.

In half an hour after this the Drum beat for the House to meet, and in less than an hour more Mr. Bacon came with a file of Fusileers on either hand near the Corner of the State-

---

[1] Colonel Nathaniel Bacon, the elder, kinsman of the younger Bacon, came to Virginia in 1650 and died childless in 1692. He endeavored to divert his young relative from rebellion by promising "to invest him in a considerable part of his estate at once and to leave him the remainder in reversion after his own and his wife's death." He was a loyal Berkeleyite.

house where the Governour and Councill went forth to him;
We Saw from the Window the Governour open his Breast,
and Bacon Strutting betwixt his Two files of Men with his
Left Arm on Kenbow[1] flinging his Right Arm every Way both
like men Distracted; and if in this Moment of fury, that En-
raged Multitude had fal'n upon the Governour and Council
We of the Assembly Expected the same Immediate fate; I
Stept down and amongst the Crowd of Spectators found the
Seamen of my Sloop, who pray'd me not to Stir from them,
when in Two Minutes, the Governour Walk'd towards his
Private Apartm. a Coits[2] cast Distant at th' other end of the
Statehouse, the Gentlemen of the Council following him, and
after them Walked Mr. Bacon with outragious Postures of
his Head, Arms, Body, and Leggs, often tossing his hand from
his Sword to his Hat and after him came a Detachment of
Fusileers (Musketts not being there in Use)[3] Who with their
Cocks Bent presented their Fusils at a Window of the Assem-
bly Chamber filled with faces, repeating with Menacing Voices,
"We will have it, We will have itt," half a Minute when as
one of our house a person known to many of them, Shook
his Handkercher out at the Window, Saying "You shall have
it, You shall have itt," 3 or 4 times; at these Words they sate
Down their fusils, unbent their Locks and stood Still untill
Bacon coming back, they followed him to their Main Body;
In this hubub a Servant of mine got so nigh as to hear the
Governours Words, and also followed Mr. Bacon, and heard
what he Said, who came and told me, That When the Governour
opened his Breast he Said, "Here! Shoot me, foregod, fair
Mark, Shoot," often Rehearsing the same, without any other
Words; Whereto Mr. Bacon Answer'd "No May it please
your honor, We will not hurt a hair of your Head, nor of any
other Mans, We are Come for a Comission to save our Lives
from th' Indians, which you have so often promised, and now
We Will have it before we go;"

But when Mr. Bacon followed the Governour and Councill
with the forementioned impetuos (like Delirious) Actions whil'st
that Party presented their Fusils at the Window full of Faces,
He said "Dam my Bloud, I'le Kill Governr Councill Assem-

[1] Akimbo.   [2] Quoit's.
[3] The fusil was a flint-lock gun, of lighter construction than the musket.

bly and all, and then Ile Sheath my Sword in my own heart's
bloud"; and afterwards 'twas Said Bacon had Given a Signall
to his Men who presented their fusils at those Gasing out at
the Window, that if he shoud draw his Sword, they were on
sight of it to fire, and Slay us, So near was the Masacre of us
all that very Minute, had Bacon in that Paroxism of Phren-
tick fury but Drawn his Sword, before the Pacifick Handkercher was Shaken out at Window.

In an hour or more after these violent Concussions Mr.
Bacon came up to our Chamber and Desired a Commission
from us to go against the Indians; Our Speaker sat Silent,
When one Mr. Blayton a Neighbour to Mr. Bacon and Elected
with him a Member of Assembly for the same County (Who
therefore durst Speak to him,) made Answer, "'twas not in
our Province, or Power, nor of any other, save the Kings
Vicegerent our Governour"; he press'd hard nigh half an hours
Harangue on the Preserving our Lives from the Indians, Inspecting the Publick Revenues, th' exorbitant Taxes and redressing the Grievances and Calamities of that Deplorable
Country, Whereto having no other Answer, He went away
Dissatisfied.

Next day there was a Rumour the Governour and Councill
had agreed Mr. Bacon shou'd have a Commission to Go Generall of the Forces, We then were raising, Whereupon I being
a Member for Stafford, the most Northern frontier, and where
the War begun, Considering that Mr. Bacon dwelling in the
most Southern Frontier County,[1] might the less regard the
Parts I represented, I went to Coll: Cole (an active Member
of the Councill) desiring his Advise, if Applicacions to Mr.
Bacon on that Subject were then Seasonable and safe, which
he approving and earnestly Advising, I went to Mr. Laurence
who was esteemed Mr. Bacons Principall Consultant, to whom
he took me with him, and there left me where I was Entertained
2 or 3 hours with the particular relacions of diverse before recited Transactions; and as to the matter I spake of, he told
me, that th' Governour had indeed promised him the Command of the forces, and if his Honour shou'd keep his Word
(which he doubted) He assured me the like care shoud be
taken of the remotest Corners in the Land, as of his own Dwell-

[1] Henrico.

ing-house, and pray'd me to Advise him what Persons in those parts were most fit to bear Commands. I frankly Gave him my Opinion that the most Satisfactory Gentlemen to Governour and People, woud be Commanders of the Militia, wherewith he was well pleased, and himself wrote a List of those I Nominated.

That Evening I made known what had past with Mr. Bacon to my Colleague Coll: Mason (whose bottle attendance doubled my Task). the matter he liked well, but questioned the Governours approbacion of it.

I Confess'd the Case required Sedate thoughts, reasoning, that he and such like Gentlemen must either Command or be Commanded, and if on their denials Mr. Bacon shoud take distast, and be Constrained to Appoint Commanders out of the Rabble, the Governour himself with the Persons and Estates of all in the Land woud be at their Dispose, whereby their own Ruine might be owing to themselves; In this he agreed and said "If the Governour woud give his own Commission he woud be Content to Serve under Generall Bacon, (as now he began to be Intituled,) but first would Consult other Gentlemen in the same Circumstances; who all Concur'd 'twas the most safe barrier in view against pernicious Designes, if such shoud be put in Practice; With this I acquainted Mr. Laurence who went (rejoicing) to Mr. Bacon with the good tidings, that the Militia Commanders were inclined to serve under him, as their Generall, in Case the Governour woud please to Give them his own Commissions.

Wee of the House proceeded to finish the Bill for the War which by the Assent of the Governour and Councill being past into an Act the Governour sent us a Letter Directed to his Majesty, wherein were these Words "I have above 30 Years Governed the most flourishing Country the Sun ever Shone over, but am now Encompassed with Rebellion like Waters in every respect like to that of Massanello[1] Except their Leader," and of like Import was the Substance of that Letter, But We did not believe his Honour Sent us all he Wrote to his Majesty.

Some judicious Gentlemen of our house likewise penn'd a

[1] The fisherman who led the revolt of the populace of Naples in 1647. See below, p. 323, note 2.

Letter or Remonstrance to be sent his maj'tie Setting forth the
Gradations of those Erupcions, and Two or Three of them
with Mr. Mings[1] our Clerk brought it me to Compile a few
Lines for the Conclusion of it, which I did, tho' not without
regret in those Watchfull times, when every Man had Eyes on
him, but what I wrote was with all possible Deference to the
Governour and in the most Soft terms My Pen cou'd find the
Case to Admit.

Col: Spencer[2] being my Neighbour and Intimate friend,
and a prevalent Member in the Council I pray'd him to Intreat the Governour we might be Dissolved, for that was my
first and shoud be my last going astray from my wonted
Sphere of Merchandize and other my private Concernments
into the dark and Slippery Meanders of Court Embarrass-
ments; He told me the Governour had not (then) Determined
his Intention, But he wou'd Move his Honor about itt, and in
2 or 3 dayes we were Dissolved, which I was most heartily
Glad of, because of my getting Loose againe from being ham-
pered amongst those pernicious Entanglements in the Laby-
rinths and Snares of State Ambiguities, and which untill then
I had not seen the practice nor the dangers of, for it was
Observ'd that severall of the Members had secret badges of
Distinction fixt upon 'em, as not docill enough to Gallop the
future Races, that Court seem'd dispos'd to Lead 'em, whose
maximes I had oft times heard Whisper'd before, and then
found Confirm'd by diverse Considerate Gentlemen _vizt._ "That
the Wise and the Rich were prone to Faction and Sedition
but the fools and poor were easy to be Governed."

Many Members being met One Evening nigh Sunsett, to
take our Leaves each of other, in order next day to return
homewards,[3] came Genll. Bacon with his hand full of unfolded

[1] James Minge, clerk of the House of Burgesses in 1676, was a signer of the
grievances of Charles City County, which were so strongly directed against
Colonel Edward Hill.

[2] Colonel Nicholas Spencer was one of the leading men of the colony, representing with the Ludwells and Lee the landed aristocracy. He held the office
of secretary for a number of years and was one of the judges appointed for the
trial of Drummond. He died in 1689.

[3] This assembly, commonly called the Reforming or Bacon's Assembly, met
at Jamestown, June 5, and sat until June 25, the day before Bacon marched out
of town. All the acts of this assembly were afterward declared void both by

Papers, and overlooking us round, walking in the Room Said "Which of these Gentlemen shall I Intreat to write a few Words for me," where every one looking aside as not willing to Meddle; Mr. Lawrence pointed at me Saying "That Gentlemen Writes very well," Which I Endeavouring to Excuse, Mr. Bacon came stooping to the ground and said "Pray Sr. Do me the Honour to write a Line for me."

This Surprizing Accostment Shockt me into a Melancholy Consternation, dreading upon one hand, that Stafford County woud feel the smart of his Resentment, if I shoud refuse him whose favour I had so lately sought and been generously promis'd on their behalf; and on th' other hand fearing the Governours Displeasure who I knew woud soon hear of it; What Seem'd most Prudent at this Hazadous Dilemma, was to Obviate the present impending Peril; So Mr. Bacon made me Sit the Whole Night by him filling up those Papers, which I then Saw were blank Commissions[1] Sign'd by the Governour incerting such Names and Writing other matters as he Dictated; which I took to be the happy Effects of the Consult before mentioned, with the Commanders of the Militia, because he gave me the Names of very few others to put into these Commissions, and in the Morning he left me with an hours worke or more to finish, when Came to me Capt. Carver,[2] and said he had been to wait on the Generall for a Comission, and that he was resolved to adventure his old Bones against the Indian Rogues with other the like discourse, and at length told me that I was in mighty favour—and he was bid to tell me, that whatever I desir'd in the Generals power, was at my Service, I pray'd him humbly to thank his Honour and to acquaint him I had no other Boon to Crave, than his promis'd

royal instruction and proclamation, and by formal act of the assembly which met at Green Spring, February 20, 1677. (*Calendar of State Papers, Colonial*, 1674–1676, § 1223.)

[1] Bacon took the title "General of the Virginia War" and issued commissions to his followers, authorizing them "to impress horse, armes, and furniture for and in order to their present march," July, 1676. Many who accepted commissions went vigorously to work to aid him, until the commission was rescinded by Berkeley, when they withdrew.

[2] Captain William Carver of Lower Norfolk County, merchant and mariner and high sheriff, sided with Bacon. He was captured and put to death and his estate confiscated in January, 1677.

Kindnesse to Stafford County, for beside the not being worthy, I never had been Conversant in Military matters, and also having lived tenderly, my Service cou'd be of no benefit because the hardships and fatigues of a Wilderness Campaigne woud put a speedy Period to my daies, little Expecting to hear of more Intestine Broiles, I went home to Patomack, where Reports were afterwards various; We had Account that Generall Bacon was March'd with a Thousand Men into the Forest to Seek the Enemy Indians, and in a few daies after our next News was, that the Governour had Summoned together the Militia of Glocester and Middlesex Counties to the Number of Twelve Hundred Men, and proposed to them to follow and Suppress that Rebell Bacon; whereupon arose a Murmuring before his face "Bacon Bacon Bacon," and all Walked out of the field, Muttering as they went "Bacon Bacon Bacon," leaving the Governour and those that came with him to themselves, who being thus abandon'd Wafted over Chesepiacke Bay 30 Miles to Accomack where are two Counties of Virginia.[1]

Mr. Bacon hearing of this Came back part of the Way, and sent out Parties of Horse Patrolling through every County, Carrying away Prisoners all whom he Distrusted might any more molest his Indian Prosecucion, yet giving liberty to such as Pledg'd him their Oaths to return home and live quiet; the Copies or Contents of which Oaths I never Saw, but heard were very Strict, tho' little observed.

About this time was a Spie Detected pretending himself a Deserter who had twice or thrice Come and gone from Party to Party and was by Councill of Warr sentenced to Death, after which Bacon Declared openly to him, That if any one Man in the Army wou'd Speak a Word to save him, he shou'd not suffer, which no man appearing to do, he was Executed. Upon this Manifestation of Clemency Bacon was applauded for a Mercifull Man, not willing to Spill Christian Bloud, nor indeed was it said, that he put any other Man to Death in Cold Bloud, or Plunder any house; Nigh the same time came Majr. Langston with his Troop of horse and Quartered Two Nights at my house who (after high Compliments from the

[1] While at Accomac Berkeley lived in the house of Colonel John Custis, who offered to advance £1,000 to victual the king's ships. The two Eastern Shore counties were Accomac and Northampton.

Generall) told me I was desired to Accept the Lieutenancy for preserving the peace in the 5 Northern Counties betwixt Patomack and Rappahanock Rivers. I humbly thank'd his Honour Excusing my self; as I had done before on that Invitation of the like Nature at James Town, but did hear he was mightily offended at my Evasions and threatened to Remember me.

The Governour made a 2d. Attempt comming over from Accomack with what men he coud procure in Sloops and Boats, forty Miles up the River to James Town, which Bacon hearing of, Came againe down from his Forest Persuit, and finding a Bank not a flight Shot long, Cast up thwart the Neck of the Peninsula there in James Town,[1] He Stormed it, and took the Town, in which Attack were 12 Men Slaine and Wounded But the Governour with most of his followers fled back, down the River in their Vessells.

Here resting a few daies they Concerted the Burning of the Town, wherein Mr. Laurence and Mr. Drummond owning the Two best houses save One, Set fire each to his own house, which Example the Souldiers following Laid the whole Town (with Church and Statehouse) in Ashes, Saying, The Rogues shoud harbour no more there.

On these reiterated Molestacions Bacon Calls a Convention at Midle Plantation[2] 15 miles from James Town in the Month of August 1676, Where an Oath with one or more Proclamations were formed, and Writts by him Issued for an Assembly; The Oaths or Writts I never Saw, but One Proclamation Commanded all Men in the Land on Pain of Death to Joine him, and retire into the Wildernesse upon Arivall of the forces Expected from England, and oppose them untill they shoud propose or accept to treat of an Accommodation, which we who lived Comfortably coud not have undergone, so as the whole Land must have become an Aceldama[3] if Gods exceeding Mercy had not timely removed him.

[1] The scene of the siege and sally was the neck of land formed by Powhatan Creek and James River, where the glass factory had formerly stood, the chimney of which still remained. This point was a clearing of forty-four acres, which had been purchased by Colonel Francis Moryson and was known as his plantation. It was also called Paspahegh Old Fields, from the fact that it had been formerly occupied by the Paspahegh Indians. Jamestown was burned September 19, 1676.

[2] Where Williamsburg was afterward founded

[3] Acts i. 19.

During these Tumults in Virginia a 2d Danger menaced Maryland by an Insurrection in that Province, Complaining of their heavy Taxes etc. Where 2 or 3 of the leading Malecontents (Men otherwise of Laudable Characters) were put to death which Stifled the father Spreading of that flame, Mr. Bacon (at this time) press't the best Ship in James River Carrying 20 Guns and putting into her his Lieutenant-Generall Mr. Bland[1] (a Gentleman newly come thither from England to possesse the Estate of his Deceased Uncle late of the Council) and under him the forementioned Capt. Carver formerly a Commander of merchants Ships with men and all necessaries, he sent her to ride before Accomack to Curb and Intercept all small Vessells of War Comission'd by the Governour Coming often over and making Depredations on the Western Shoar, as if we had been Forreign Enemies, which gives occasion in this place to Digresse a few Words.

Att first Assembly after the Peace came a Message to them from the Governour for some Marks of Distinction to be set on his Loyal friends of Accomack, Who received him in his Adversity which when came to be considr'd Col: Warner[2] (then Speaker) told the House "Ye know that what Mark of Distinction his Honour coud have sett on those of Accomack unlesse to give them Earmarks or Burnt Marks for Robbing and Ravaging honest People, who Stay'd at home and Preserv'd th' Estates of those who ran away, when none intended to hurt 'em."

Now returning to Capt. Carver the Governour sent for him to come on Shoar, promising his peaceable return, Who Answer'd, he could not trust his Word, but if he woud send his hand and Seal, he wou'd adventure to Wait upon his Honour. which was done, and Carver went in his Sloop well Armed and

---

[1] Giles Bland, only son of John Bland, was sent to Virginia, in 1671, to manage certain plantations there, known as Kymages, in the parish of Westover. He was a man of hot temper and resentful disposition, and having become involved in a quarrel with Thomas Ludwell, was removed as collector and fined. He took sides with Bacon, was captured by Thomas Ludwell's brother Philip, and hung, March 15, 1677, at "Bacon's Trench," near Jamestown. The vessel seized was that of Captain Larrimore, which was converted from a merchant ship into a man-of-war by the addition of guns and men and then sent to Accomac to capture Berkeley.

[2] For Colonel Augustine Warner, see below, p. 72, note 1.

Man'd with the most trusty of his Men, where he was Caress'd with wine etc. and large promises, if he woud forsake Bacon, resigne his Ship or joine with him; to all which he Answer'd that If he served the Devill he woud be true to his Trust, but that He was Resolved to go home and live quiet.

In the time of this Recepcion and Parley, an Armed Boat was prepared with many Oars in a Creek not far off, but out of Sight, which when Carver Sail'd, Row'd out of the Creek, and it being almost Calm the Boat outwent the Sloop whilst all on board the Ship were upon the Deck, Staring at both, thinking the Boats Company comming on board by Carvers Invitation to be Civilly Entertained in requitall of the Kindness they Supposed he had received on Shoar, untill Comming under the Stern, those in the Boat Slipt Nimbly in at the Gun Room Ports with Pistols etc. when one Couragious Gentleman ran up to the Deck, and Clapt a Pistoll to Blands Breast, Saying you are my Prisoner, the Boats Company Suddainly following with Pistolls Swords etc. and also Capt. Larimore (the Commander of the Ship before she was prest) having from the highest and hindmost Part of the Stern Interchang'd a Signal from the Shoar, by flirting his handkercher about his Nose, his own former Crew had laid handspikes ready, which they (at that Instant) Caught up etc. So as Bland and Carvers Men were Amazed and Yielded.

Carver seeing a hurly Burly on the Ships Deck, woud have gone away with his Sloop, but having little Wind and the Ship threatning to Sink him, he tamely Came on Board, where Bland and he with their Party were Laid in Irons, and in 3 or 4 daies Carver was hang'd on Shoar, which Sr. Henry Chicheley[1] the first of the Councill then a Prisoner (with diverse other Gentlemen) to Mr. Bacon, did afterwards Exclaime against as a most Rash and Wicked Act of the Governour, He (in particuler) expecting to have been treated by way of Reprizall, as Bacons friend Carver had been by the Governour.

---

[1] Sir Henry Chicheley, son of Sir Henry Chicheley of Wimple, Cambridgeshire, had served in the royal army during the Civil War in England. He came to Virginia in 1649, served as burgess and councillor, and in 1675 was commander-in-chief against the Indians. He was commissioned deputy governor, 1673–1674, and acting governor, 1678–1680. He lived at Rosegill, Middlesex County, and died in 1682.

Mr. Bacon now returns from his last Expedicion Sick of a Flux, without finding any Enemy Indians, having not gone far by reason of the Vexations behind him, nor had he one dry day in all his Marches to and fro in the Forrest whilst the Plantations (not 50 Miles Distant) had a Summer so dry as stinted the Indian Corn and Tobacco etc. Which the People Ascribed to the *Pawawings, i. e.* the Sorceries of the Indians, in a While Bacon dyes[1] and was succeeded by his Lieutenant Genll. Ingram, who had one Wakelet next in Command under him, Whereupon hasten'd over the Governour to York River, and with him they Articled for themselves and whom else they Could, and so all Submitted and were Pardoned Exempting those Nominated and otherwise Proscribed, in a Proclamacion of Indempnity, the principall of whom were Lawrence and Drummond.

Mr. Bland was then a Prisoner having been taken with Carver, as before is noted, and in few daies Mr. Drumond was brought in, when the Governour being on board a Ship came Immediately to Shore and Complimented him with the Ironicall Sarcasm of a low Bend, saying "Mr. Drumond! You are very welcome, I am more Glad to See you, than any man in Virginea, Mr. Drumond you shall be hang'd in half an hour;" Who Answered "What your honour pleases," and as soon as a Council of War cou'd meet, his Sentence be dispatcht and a Gibbet erected, (which took up near Two houres) He was Executed.

This Mr. Drumond was a sober Scotch Gentleman of good repute with whome I had not a particuler acquaintance, nor do I know the Cause of that rancour his honour had against him, other than his Pretensions in Common for the publick but meeting him by Accident the Morning I left the Town, I advis'd him to be very Wary, for he saw the Governour had put a brand upon him. He (gravely expressing my Name) Answered, "I am in over Shoes, I will be over Boots," which I was sorry to heare and Left him.[2]

---

[1] Bacon died in October (two dates are given, 18th and 26th) at the house of Pate in Gloucester County. The identity of Pate is uncertain. He may have been either John Pate, or his nephew, Thomas Pate. For Ingram, see below, p. 78, note 1.

[2] After Drummond's death, his wife, an energetic and persistent woman, with five children dependent on her, applied for her husband's pay as burgess,

The last Account of Mr. Laurence was from an uppermost plantation, whence he and Four others Desperado's with horses pistolls etc. March'd away in a Snow Ancle Deep, who were thought to have Cast themselves into a Branch of some River, rather than to be treated like Drummond.

Bacons Body was so made away, as his Bones were never found to be Exposed on a Gibbet as was purpos'd, Stones being laid in his Coffin, Supposed to be done by Laurence.

Near this time Arrived a small Fleet with a Regiment from England Sr. John Berry Admirall, Col: Herbert Jefferies Commander of the Land forces and Collo. Morrison[1] who had One Year been a former Governour there, all Three Joined in Commission with or to Sr. William Barclay,[2] Soon after when a Generall Court and also an Assembly were held, where some of our former Assembly (with so many others) were put to Death, diverse whereof were Persons of honest reputations and handsome Estates, as that the Assembly Petitioned the Governour to Spill no more bloud, and Mr. Presley at his Coming home told me, he believed the Governour would have hang'd half the Countrey, if they had let him alone. The first was Mr. Bland whose Friends in England had procured his pardon to be sent over with the Fleet, which he pleaded at his Tryall, was in the Governours Pocket, (tho' Whether 'twas so, or how it Came there, I know not, yet did not hear 'twas openly Contradicted,) But he was Answered by Collo. Morrison that he Pleaded his pardon at Swords point, which was look'd upon an odd Sort of Reply, and he was Executed (as was talked) by private Instructions from England, The Duke of York having Sworn "By God Bacon and Bland shoud Dye."

The Governour went in the Fleet to London, (whether by

and for reinstatement in his property, a small plantation. She also demanded compensation for certain goods, including pipes of wine and casks of brandy that had been seized for the king's use by Sir John Berry, one of the English commissioners. She also brought suit against Lady Berkeley for property confiscated by the governor, her son-in-law, Swann, appearing in her behalf. The Lords of Trade declared her case to be "very deplorable and a fit object of his Majesty's compassion," and, as her cause was upheld by the commissioners, she obtained restitution of nearly all that she sought for.

[1] For Berry, Jeffreys, and Moryson, the royal commissioners, see below, pp. 101, 102.

[2] Berkeley, then commonly pronounced Barkley.

Command from his Majesty or Spontaneous I did not hear)
Leaving Col: Jefferyes in his Place, and by next Shipping Came
back a Person who waited on his Honour in his Voyage, and
untill his Death, from whom a report was Whisper'd about,
that the King did Say "That old fool has hang'd more men in
that naked Country, than he had done for the Murther of his
Father," whereof the Governour hearing dyed soon after
without having seen his Majesty; Which shuts up this Tragedy.

Appendix.

To avoid Incumbring the Body of the foregoing little dis-
course, I have not therein mentioned the received Opinion in
Virginia, which very much Attributed the promoting these
Perturbacions to Mr. Laurance, and Mr. Bacon with his other
Adherents were esteemed, as but Wheels agitated by the
Weight of his former and present Resentments, after their
Choler was raised up to a very high Pitch, at having been (so
long and often) trifled with on their humble Supplications to
the Governour for his immediate taking in hand the most
speedy meanes towards stopping the Continued Effusions of
so much English Bloud, from time to time by the Indians;
Which Common Sentiments I have the more reason to believe were not altogether groundlesse, because my self have
heard him (in his familiar discourse) Insinuate as if his fancy
gave him prospect of finding (at one time or other,) some
expedient not only to repaire his great Losse, but therewith to
See those abuses rectified that the Countrey was oppress'd
with through (as he said) the frowardness avarice and french
Despotick Methods of the Governour and likewise I know
him to be a thinking Man, and tho' nicely honest, affable,
and without Blemish, in his Conversation and Dealings, yet
did he manifest abundance of uneasiness in the Sense of his
hard Usages, which might prompt him to Improve[1] that Indian Quarrel to the Service of his Animosities, and for this the
more fair and frequent opportunities offered themselves to
him by his dwelling at James Town, where was the Concourse
from all Parts to the Governour and besides that he had Married a Wealthy Widow who kept a large house of publick

[1] Make use of.

Entertainment unto which resorted those of the best quality, and such others as Businesse Called to that Town, and his Parts with his even Temper made his Converse Coveted by Persons of all Ranks; So that being Subtile, and having these advantages he might with lesse Difficulty discover mens Inclinations, and Instill his Notions where he found those woud be imbib'd with greatest Satisfaction.

As for Mr. Bacon fame did lay to his Charge the having run out his Patrimony in England Except what he brought to Virginia and of that the most Part to be Exhausted, which together made him Suspected of Casting an Eye to Search for Retrievment in the troubled Waters of popular Discontents, wanting Patience to wait the Death of his oppulent Cousin, old Collo. Bacon, Whose Estate he Expected to Inherit.

But he was too young, too much a Stranger there, and of a Disposition too precipitate, to Manage things to that length those were Carried, had not thoughtfull Mr. Laurence been at the Bottom.

THE HISTORY OF BACON'S AND INGRAM'S REBELLION, 1676

INTRODUCTION

The History of Bacon's and Ingram's Rebellion, though of
unknown origin, was written by a resident of Virginia, as the
text of the narrative shows. The author speaks of Jamestown
as "our Metropolis," calls the Virginians "our deare Bretheren
and countrymen," and refers to Major Page as "once my servant." That he was familiar with the course of the rebellion
is evident from the narrative itself; and that he obtained a
part of his evidence at first hand appears from his references
to Captain Grantham and from the elaborate abstracts of
documents given in the text. Though the style is verbose
and involved, the general treatment shows the writer to have
been of a literary turn of mind, well read, proficient at cards,
sport, and astronomy, and possessed of an unusual sense of
humor. The manuscript is undoubtedly contemporary with
the events described and was sent to some one not named,
probably in Virginia, as it was in Virginia that it was discovered.

Toward the close of the eighteenth century, Captain Nathaniel Burwell, hearing that the manuscript was in the hands
of an "old and respectable" family of the Northern Neck of
Virginia, secured it as a work of value for the history of the
colony. The Hon. William A. Burwell, a member of Congress
from Virginia, finding the history among his relatives' papers,
sent it to the Hon. Josiah Quincy, a representative in Congress from Massachusetts in 1812, with permission to print,
after which the original manuscript was to be returned to the
owner. The work appeared in the first volume of the second series of the *Collections* of the Massachusetts Historical
Society (1814), pp. 27–80, but through a misunderstanding the

original was retained in the archives of the society.   In 1856, Conway Robinson, chairman of the executive committee of the Virginia Historical Society, wrote to Massachusetts asking for the return of the manuscript, but the society, after consulting with Mr. Quincy, at that time advanced in years and failing in memory, declined to comply with Mr. Robinson's request, on the ground that the document was the property of the society.

In 1866, the original letter written by Burwell to Quincy having come to light, the members of the society learned for the first time of the conditions under which the manuscript had been placed in their hands and determined to return it to Virginia.   Finding, however, that the earlier printed version was very imperfect, as it contained many errors in the text and was incomplete, the society decided to reprint the manuscript and did so in the *Proceedings* for August, 1866, pp. 299–342.   The original was then returned to Virginia and is today among the Burwell manuscripts in the custody of the Virginia Historical Society.

The volume is "in the form of a small octavo, the text, with the heading, measuring five and a half by three and a half inches, not paged.   The portion which remains contains fifty-two pages.   The chirography is remarkably distinct.   Several leaves being destroyed at the beginning and end, there is no title, except the running headings on each page.   Many of the remaining leaves are much injured by time." (*Proceedings*, Massachusetts Historical Society, 1866, p. 342, note.)

THE HISTORY OF BACON'S AND INGRAM'S REBELLION, 1676

The Indians Proseedings.

.   .   .   .

for there owne security.[1] They found that there store was too short to indure a long Seige with out makeing emty belles, and that emty belies makes weake hearts, which all ways makes an unfit Serving Man to wate upon the God of war. Therefore they were resalve, before that there spirits were downe, to doe what they could to keepe there stores up; as oppertunity should befriend them. And all though they were by the Law of Arms (as the case now stood) prohibited the hunting of wilde Deare, they resalved to see what good might be don by hunting tame Horsses. Which trade became their sport soe long, that those who came on Horsback to the seige, began to feare the should be compeld to trot hom a foot, and glad if they scap'd so too : for these belegured blades made so many salleys, and the beseigers kep such neglegent gards, that there was very few days past without som remarkeable mischeife. But what can hould out all ways? even stone walls yeilds to the not to be gaine-saide summons of time. And all though it is saide that the Indians doth the least minde their Bellies (as being content with a litle) of any people in the world, yet now there bellies began to minde them, and there stomacks too, which began to be more inclineable to peace, then war; which was the cause (no more Horss flesh being to be had) that they sent out 6 of their Werawances (cheife men) to commence a treaty. What the Artickles were, that they brought along with them, to treate of, I do not know; but certainly they were so unacceptable to the English, that they caused the Commissioners braines to be knock'd out, for dictateing so badly to there tongues; which yet, 'tis posible, ex-

[1] The narrative opens with the siege of the Indian fort on the upper waters of the Potomac, Maryland side. See pp. 18, 19.

prest more reason then the English had to prove the lawfull-
ness of this action, being Diametrecall to the Law of Arms.

This strange action put those in the Fort to there trumps,
haveing thus lost som of their prime court cards, without a
faire dealeing. They could not well tell what interpretation
to put upon it (nor indeed, nobody ells) and very faine they
wo[uld] . . . . . . why those, whom they sent out with a [view]
to suplicate a peace should be worss delt with then [those who]
were sent out with a sword to denounce a war; but, [no one]
could be got to make inquirye into the reason of this . . . . . .
which put them upon a ressalution to forsake there [station,
and] not to expostulate the cause any further. Haveing [made]
this resalution, and destroyed all things in the fort, that might
be servisable to the English, they bouldly, undiscovered, slip
through the Leagure¹ (leaveing the English to prossecute the
seige, as Schogin's wife brooded the eggs that the Fox had
suck'd)² in the passing of which they knock'd ten men o'th
head, who lay carelessly asleep in there way.

Now all though it might be saide that the Indians went
there ways emty handed, in regard they had left all there
plunder and welth behinde them in the fort, yet it cannot be
thought that they went away emty hearted: For though that
was pritty well drained from it's former curage, through those
inconvenencies that they had bin subjected to by the seige,
yet in the roome thereof, rather then the venticles should lie
voide, they had stowed up so much mallize, entermixt with a
ressalution of revenge, for the affrunt that the English had
put upon them, in killing there messingers of peacè, that they
resalved to commence a most barberous and most bloody
war.

The Beseigers haveing spent a grate deale of ill imployed
time in pecking at the huske, and now findeing the shell open,
and mising the expected prey, did not a litle woonder what
was be com of the lately impounded Indinans, who, though at
present the could not be seene, yet it was not long before that
they were heard off, and felt too. For in a very short time
they had, in a most inhumane maner, murthered no less then

¹ Leagure, probably for "leaguer," the besieging camp of the enemy.
² An allusion to *Scoggan's Jests* (1626 and later editions), a seventeenth-
century "Joe Miller."

60 innocent people, no ways guilty of any actuall injury don to these ill disarning, brutish heathen. By the blood of these poore soules, they thought that the wandering ghosts of those there Commissioners, before mentioned, might be atton'd, and lade downe to take there repose in the dismall shades of death, and they, at present, not obliged for to prossecute any further revenge. Therefore to prove whether the English was as redy for a peace, as themselves, they send in there remonstronce in the name of there [Chief, (ta]ken by an English interpreter,) unto the Governour [of Verg]inia, with whom he expostulates in this sort. Wh[at was it] that moved him to take up Arms, against him, his pr[ofessed] friend, in the behalfe of the Mary-landers, his profes[sed ene]mies, contrary to that league made betwene [him] and himselfe? Declares as well his owne as su[bjects] greife to finde the Verginians, of Friends, without any cause given, to becom his foes, and to be so eager in their groundless quarill, as to persew the chase into anothers domin-ions: Complaines, that his mesingers of peace were not oneley murthered by the English, but the fact countinanced by the Governour's Connivance: For which, seeing no other ways to be satisfied, he had revenged him self, by killing 10 for one of the Verginians, such being the disperportion betwene his grate men murther'd, and those, by his command, slane. That now, this being don, if that his honour would alow him a valluable satisfaction for the damage he had sustained by the war, and no more concerne himselfe in the Marylanders quarill, he was content to renew and confirm the ancient league of amety; other ways him selfe, and those whom he had ingaged to his intress (and there owne) were resalved to fite it out to the last man.

These proposealls not being assented to by the English, as being derogetory and point blanke, both to honour and in-tress, these Indians draw in others (formerly in subjection to the Verginians) to there aides: which being conjoyned (in seperate and united parties) they dayly commited abundance of ungarded and unrevenged murthers, upon the English; which they perpretated in a most barberous and horid maner. By which meanes abundance of the Fronteare Plantations became eather depopulated by the Indians cruletys, or de-sarted by the Planters feares, who were compelled to forsake

there abodes, to finde security for there lives; which they
were not to part with, in the hands of the Indiands, but under
the worst of torments. For these brutish and inhumane brutes,
least their cruilties might not be thought cruill enough, they devised a hundred ways to torter and torment those poore soules
with, whose reched fate it was to fall in to there unmercyfull
hands. For som, before that they would deprive them of
there lives, they would take a grate deale of time to deprive
them first of there skins, and if that life had not, throug[h the
ang]uish of there paine, forsaken there tormented bodyes,
they [with] there teeth (or som instrument,) teare the nailes
of [their fingers and their] toes, which put the poore sufferer
to a wo[ful condition. One was prepared for the fla]mes at
James Towne, who indured [much, but found means] to escape.
Those who had the . . . . . . another world, was to have . . . . . .
to be attributed to . . . . . . there more then can . . . . . . xpire
with . . . . . . or other wayes to be slane out rite, for least that
there Deaths should be attributed unto som more mercyfull
hands then theares, for to put all out of question, they would
leave som of there brutish Markes upon there fenceless bodies,
that might testifye it could be none but they who had commited the fact.

And now it was that the poore distresed and dubly afflicted
Planters began to curss and execrate that ill manidged buisness
at the Fort. There cryes were reitterated againe and againe,
both to God and man for releife. But no appeareance of long
wish'd for safety ariseing in the Horrison of there hopes, they
were redy, could they have tould which way, to leave all and
forsake the Collony, rather then to stay and be expos'd to the
crewiltys of the barberous heathen.

At last it was concluded, as a good expedient for to put the
countrey in to som degree of safety, for to plant Forts upon the
Fronteres,[1] thinkeing there by to put a stop unto the Indians
excurssions: which after the expence of a grate deale of time
and charge, being finished, came short of the designed ends.
For the Indians quickly found out where about these Mouse
traps were sett, and for what purpose, and so resalved to keepe
out of there danger; which they might easely ennough do, with
out any detriment to there designes. For though here by

[1] For the forts, see p. 108.

they were compeld (tis posible) to goe a litle about, yet they never thought much of there labour, so long as they were not debar'd from doing of Mischeife; which was not in the power of these forts to prevent: For if that the English did, at any time, know that there was more ways in to the wood then one, to kill Deare, the Indians found more then a thousand out of the wood, to kill Men, and not com neare the danger of the forts neather.

The small good that was by most expected, and now by [them expe]rienc'd from these useless fabricks (or castells, if a . . . . . . a marvellous discontent amongst the people . . . . . . the charge would be grate, and the benifitt . . . . . . arise out of these wolfe-pi . . . . . . came every day losers; and . . . . . . Banke, if it do not inc . . . . . . to cast about for so . . . . . . lost. It vext t[he hearts of many that they should] be compeld to worke all the day, (nay all the yeare), for to reward those Mole-catchers at the forts, (no body knew for what,) and at night could not finde a place of safety to lie downe in, to rest there wery bones, for feare they should be shatter'd all to peices by the Indians; upon which consideration they thought it best to petition the downe fall of these useless (and like to be) chargeable fabricks, from whose continuance they could neather expect proffitt nor safety.

But for the effecting of this buisness, they found them selves under a very grate disadvantage. For though it may be more easier to cast downe, then irect, well cemented structurs, yet the rule doth not hould in all cases. For it is to be understood that these Forts were contrived, eather by the sole command of the Governour, or other ways by the advice of those whose judgments, in this affaire, he approved off; eather of which was now, they being don, his owne emediate act, as they were don in his name; which to have undon, at the simple request of the people, had bin, in efect, to have undon that Repute he all ways held, in the peoples judgment, for a wise Man; and better that they should suffer som small inconvenencies, then that he should be counted less diserning then those, who, till now, were counted more then halfe blinde. Besides, how should he satisfie his honour with the undertakers of the worke? If the peoples petition should be granted, they must be disapointed, which would have bin litle less then

an undoeing to them allsoe, in there expectation of proffitt to
be raised from the worke. Here by the people quickly found
them selves in an errour, when that they apprehended what a
strong foundation the Forts were irected upon, honour and
proffitt, against which all there saping and mineing had no
power to over turne; they haveing no other ingredience to
makeing up there fire works with but prayers, and miss spent
teares and intreties; which haveing vented to no purpose, and
finding there condition every whit as bad, if not worse since,
as before, the forts were made, they resalved . . . . . . le patience
was set to worke.

. . . . . . many to hope in the countin- . . . . . . of no long
being in the cou- . . . . . . state; and nerely related to one . . . . . .
gnity. A Man[1] he was of larger . . . . . . hich rendred him in-
deared (if not . . . . . . not for any thing he had yet don, as the
cause of there affections, but what they expected he would
doe to disarve there devotion; while with no common zeale,
they send up there reitterated prayers, first to him self, and
next to Heaven, that he may becom there Gardian Angle, to
protect them from the cruilties of the Indians, against whom
this Gent:man had a perfect antipothey.

It seemes, in the first rise of the War, this Gent:man had
made som overtures unto the Governour for a Commission, to
go and put a stop to the Indians proseedings. But the Governour, at present, eather not willing to commence the quarill
(on his part) till more suteable reasons prisented, for to urge
his more severe prosecution of the same, against the heathen:
or that he douted Bacons temper, as he appear'd Populerly
inclin'd; A constetution not consistant with the times, and
the peoples dispossitions; being generally discontented, for
want of timely provissions against the Indians, or for Annuall
impositions lade upon them, too grate (as they saide) for them
to beare, and against which they had som considerable time
complained, without the least redress. For these, or som
other reasons, the Governour refused to comply with Bacon's
proposalls. Which he lookeing upon as an undervalluing as
well to his parts, as a disperidgment to his pretentions, hee in
som elated and passionate expressions sware, Commission or
no Commission, the next man or woman that he heard of that

_____
[1] "A Man" refers to young Nathaniel Bacon.

should be kild by the Indians, he would goe out against them, though but 20 men would adventure the servis with him.   Now it so unhappylie fell out, that the next person that the Indians did kill, was one of his owne Familey.   Where upon haveing got together som 70 or 80 persons, most good Howsekeepers, well armed, and seeing that he could not legally procure a Commission (after som struglings with the Governour . . . . . . Scuffell) and som of his best friends, co . . . . . . terprise, he applyes hi . . . . . . his oath, and so forth . . . . . . ans.

The Governour could not . . . . . . this insolent deportment of Bac . . . . . . ed at his proseedings.   Which . . . . . . insteade of seekeing meanes to appease his anger, they devised meanes to increase it, by frameing specious pretences, which they grounded upon the bouldness of Bacons actions, and the peoples affections.   They began (som of them) to have Bacons Merits in mistrust, as a Luminary that thretned an eclips to there riseing gloryes.   For though he was but a yong man, yet they found that he was master and owner of those induments which constitutes a Compleate Man (as to intrincecalls), wisdom to apprehend and descretion to chuse.   By which imbelishments (if he should continue in the Governours favour) of Seniours they might becom juniours, while there younger Brother, through the nimbleness of his wit, might steale away that blessing, which they accounted there owne by birthright. This rash proseedings of Bacon, if it did not undo himselfe, by his faileing in the enterprise, might chance to undo them in the affections of the people; which to prevent, they thought it conduceable to there intress and establishment, for to get the Governour in the minde to proclame him a Rebell; as knowing that once being don, since it could not be don but by and in the Governours name, it must needs breed bad blodd betwene Bacon and Sir William, not easely to be purged.   For though Sir William might forgive what Bacon, as yet, had acted; yet it might be questionable whether Bacon might forget what Sir William had don: However, according to there desires, Bacon and all his adhereance was proclamed a Rebell, May the 29, and forces raised to reduce him to his duty.   With which the Governour advanced from the Midle Plantation to finde him out, and if neede was to fight him, if the Indians had not knock'd him, and those with him, on the head, as som were in hope they had don, and which by som was ernistly desired.

After som few days the Governour retracts his march (a jurnye of som 30 or 40 miles) to meet with the Assembley,[1] now redy to sit downe at our Metropollis, while Bacon in the meane time meets with the Indians, upon whom he falls with abundance of ressalution and gallentrey (as his owne party relates it) in there fastness; killing a grate many, and blowing up there Magazene of Arms and Pouder, to a considerable quantity . . . . . . y his self, no less then 4000 weight. This [being done, and all his] Provissions spent, he returns hom to his . . . . . . e, where he submits him selfe to be chosen Bur[gess of t]he County in which he did live, contrary to his qualifications, take him as he was formerly one of the Councell of State, or as hee was now a proclamed Rebell. How ever, he applyes him selfe to the performance of that trust reposed in him, by the people, if he might be admited into the Howse. But this not fagging[2] according to his desire, though according to his expectation, and he remaneing in his sloope (then at Ancor before the Towne) in which was about 30 Gent: men besides himselfe, he was there surprised with the rest, and made prissoner, som being put into Irons: in which condition they remaned som time, till all things were fitted for the triall. Which being brought to a day of heareing, before the Governour and Councell, Bacon was not onely acquited and pardoned all misdemeniors, but restored to the Councell Table as before; and not onely, but promised to have a Commission signed the Monday following (this was on the Saterday) as Generall for the Indian war, to the universall satisfaction of the people, who passionately desired the same; witnessed by the ginerall acclameations of all then in towne.

And here who can do less then wonder at the muteable and impermenent deportments of that blinde Godes Fortune; who in the morning loades Man with disgraces, and ere night crownes him with honours: Somtimes depressing, and againe ellivateing, as her fickle humer is to smile or frowne, of which this Gent: mans fate was a kinde of an Epittemey, in the sev-

---

[1] The assembly met on June 5; on the 7th Bacon came to Jamestown in his sloop; and on the 10th he was promised the commission.

[2] Developing.

erall vicissetudes and changes he was subjected to in a very
few dayes. For in the morning, before his triall, he was, in
his Enimies hopes, and his Friends feares, judged for to receve the Gurdian due to a Rebell (and such hee was proclamed to be) and ere night, crowned the Darling of the Peoples hopes and desires, as the onely man fitt in Verginia, to
put a stop unto the bloody ressalutions of the Heathen: And
yet againe, as a fuller manifestation of Fortune's inconstancye,
with in two or three days, the peoples hopes, and his desires,
were both frusterated by the Governours refuseing to signe the
promised Commission. At which being disgusted, though at
present he desembled . . . . . . so well as he could, (and tis supposed that w . . . . . . he beggs leave of the Governour for to
be despence . . . . . . his servis at the Councell table, to vissit
his L . . . . . . he saide, had informed him, was indisposed,[1] as
to her . . . . . . which request the Governour (after som contest with his owne thoughts) granted, contrary to the advise
of som about him, who suspected Bacons designes, and that it
was not so much his Lady's sickness, as the distempers of a
troubled minde, that caused him to with draw to his owne
house, and that this was the truth, with in a few days was
manifested, when that he returned to Towne at the head of
500 Men in Arms.

The Governour did not want intillegence of Bacons designes, and therefore sent out his summons for Yorke Traine
Bands to reinforce his gards, then at Towne. But the time
was so short (not above 12 howers warning) and those that
appeared at the Randevouze made such a slender number,
that under 4 Insignes there was not mustered above 100
Soulders, and not one halfe of them sure neather, and all so
slugish in there march, that before they could reach towne,
by a grate deale, Bacon had enter'd the same, and by force
obtained a Commition, calculated to the hight of his owne
desires. With which Commission (such as it was) being invested, hee makes redy his provissions, fills up his Companies
to the designed number (500 in all) and so applies him selfe to
those servises the Countrey expected from him. And, first,
for the secureing the same from the excursions of the Indians,

---

[1] Bacon desired to return to Henrico to visit his wife, who, he declared,
was sick.

in his absence (and such might be expected) he commissionated severall persons (such as he could confide in) in every respective county, with select companies of well armed men, to range the Forists, swomps, thickits, and all such suspected places where the Indiands might have any shelter for the doeing of mischeife. Which proceedings of his put so much curage into the Planters, that they began to applye them selves to there accustomed imployments in there plantations: which till now they durst not do, for feare of being knock'd on the head, as, God knowes, too many were, before these orders were observed.

While the Generall (for so was Bacon now denominated by vertue of his Commission) was sedulous in these affaires, and fitting his provissions, about the head of Yorke River, in order to his advance against the Indians,[1] the Governour was steareing quite contrary courses. He was once more perswaded (but for what reasons not visible) to proclaime Bacon a Rebell againe, And now since his absence afforded an advantage, to raise the countrey upon him, so soone as he should returne tired and exhausted by his toyle and labour in the Indian war. For the puting this councell in execution, the Governour steps over into Gloster County, (a place the best replenished for men, arms, and affections of any County in Verginia), all which the Governour summons to give him a meeteing at a place and day assigned, where being met, according to the summons, the Governours proposalls was so much disrellished, by the wholl convention, that they all disbanded to there owne aboades, after there promise past to stand by, and assist the Governoure, against all those who should go about to rong, eather his parson,[2] or debase his Authority; unto which promise they annext, or subjoyned severall reasons why they thought it not, at present, convenient to declare them selves against Bacon, as he was now advanceing against the common enimy, who had in a most barberous maner murthered som hundreds of our deare Breatheren and Countrey Men, and would, if not prevented by God, and the endeviours of good

---

[1] Bacon marched on Jamestown Thursday, June 22; the commission was drawn up on the 23d and delivered on the 24th. On the 25th the assembly broke up, and on the 26th Bacon began his march against the Indians.
[2] Person.

men, do there utmost for to cut of the wholl Collony. Therefore they did thinke that it would be a thing inconsistant
with reason, if that they, in this desperate conjunture of time,
should go and ingage themselves one against another; from the
result of which proseedings, nothing could be expected but
ruing and destruction unto both, to the one and the other
party, since that it might reasonably be conceved, that while
they should be exposeing there brests against one anothers
wepons, the barberous and common enimy (who would make
his disadvantages [*sic*] by our disadvantages) should be upon
there backs to knock out there brains. But if it should so
hapen (as they did hope it would never so hapen) that the
Generall after the Indian war was finished, should attempt any
thing against his Hon'rs person or Goverment, that then they
would rise up in arms, with a joynt consent, for the prisarvation of both.

Since the Governour could obtaine no more, he was, at
present, to rest himselfe contented with this, while those who
had advised him to these undertakeings, was not a litle dis-
satisfide to finde the event not to answer there expectations.
But he at present, seeing there was no more to be don, since
he wanted a power to have that don, which was esteemed the
maine of the affaires, now in hand to be don, namely, the gaine-
ing of the Gloster men, to do what he would have don, he
thought it not amiss to do what he had a power to do, and that
was once more to proclame Bacon a Tratour, which was performed in all publick places of meetings in these parts. The
noyse of which proclameation, after that it had past the admireation of all that were not aquainted with the reasons
that moved his honor to do what he had now don, soone
reached the Generall eares, not yet stopt up from lisning to
apparent dangers.

This strange and unexpected news put him, and som with
him, shrodely[1] to there trumps, beleveing that a few such
deales, or shuffles (call them which you please) might quickly
ring the cards, and game too, out of his hand. He perceved
that he was falne (like the corne betwene the stones) so that
if he did not looke the better about him, he might chance to
be ground to powder. He knew that to have a certaine enimy

[1] Shrewdly.

in his frunt, and more then uncertaine friends in his reare, portended no grate security from a violent death, and that there could be no grate differance betwene his being wounded to death in his brest, with bows and Arows, or in the back with Guns and Musquit bullits.   He did see that there was an abseluted necessity of destroying the Indians, for the prisarvation of the English, and that there was som care to be taken for his owne and soulders safety, otherways that worke must be ill don, where the laberours are mad criples, and compeld, insteade of a sword, to betake themselves to a c[ru]tch.   It vext him to the heart (as he was heard to say) f[or] to thinke, that while he was a hunting Wolves, Tygers and Foxis, which dayly destroyed our ha[r]mless Sheep and Lamb[s,] that hee, and those with him, should be persued in the re[are], with a full crye, as a more salvage or no less rave[nous] beast.   But to put all out of doubt, and himselfe into . . . . . . gree of safety, since he could not tell but that som [whom] he had left behinde, might not more desire his de[ath,] then to here that by him the Indians were dest[royed, he] forth with (after a short consultation held with [som of his soulde]rs) countermarcheth his Army, and in a trice [   ] with them at the midle Plantation, a place sit[uated in the] very heart of the Countrey.

The first thing that Bacon fell upon (after [that he had] setled himselfe at the Midle Plantation) was [to prepare] his Remonstrance, and that as well against [the Governo]urs Paper of the 29 of May,[1] as in answer to th[e Governours pro]clamation.   Puting both papers upon these D[eclarations, he asks] Whether Parsons wholly devoted to there Kin[g and coun]trey, haters of all sinester, and by respects, am[ing on]ly at the Countreys good, and indeviouring to th[e utmost of there] power, to the haserd of there lives and fortunes, ... destroy those that are in Arms against King and . . . . . . that never plotted, contrived, nor indevioured . . . . . . ion, detrement or rong of any of his Majesties [subjects, in] there lives, names, fortunes, or estates, can desarve the appellations of Rebells and Traters?   He cites the wholl country to testifye his and his soulders peaceable behaviours; upbrades som in Authorety with the meaness of there parts; others, now

---

[1] The "paper of the 29 of May" was Berkeley's third proclamation declaring Bacon a rebel.   It is printed in Neill, *Virginia Carolorum*, p. 351.

welthey, with the meaness of there estates, when the came
first in to the Country; and questions by what just ways, or
meanes, they have obtained the same; and whether they have
not bin the spunges that have suck'd up and devoured the
common tresurye? Questions what Arts, Ciences, Schooles
of learning or Ma[n]ufacteres hath bin promoted by any now
in Authorety? Justifyes his averssion (in generall) against
the Indians; Upbrades the Governour for manetaineing there
quarill (though never so unjust) against the Christians rites
and intress; His refuseing to admit an English man's oath
against an Indian, when that an [In]dians word shall be a
sufficient proofe against an [En]glish Man: Saith som thing
against the Governour [con]cerning the Beaver trade, as not
in his power to de . . . . . . off, as being a Monopley appertaine-
ing to the Cro[wn]: Questions whether the Traders at the heads
of the . . . . . . s do not buy and sell the blood of there deare
Brther . . . . . . untrey men: Araignes one Coll: Coles[1] ascer-
tion [for sayi]ng that the English are bound to protect the
Ind[ians] . . . . . . or to the haserd of there blood; and so con-
clu[des with a]n appeale to King and Parliament, where he
[has no doubt] but that his and the Peoples cause will be
im[partially h]eard.

[After this manner] the Game beginns, in which (though
never so . . . . . . the one side must be, undoutedly, losers.
This . . . . . . nce of Bacons was but the Præludum (or rath
. . . . . . e) to the following Chapter; without which the . . . . . . t
(in peoples mindes) be subject to rong interpre . . . . . . other
ways look'd upon to be, at best, but Hetro . . . . . . he inditers
good meaneing.

. . . . . . his next worke was to invite all that had [any
regar]d to themselves, or love to there Countrey, the . . . . . .
Children, or any other relations; to give [him a meeting] in
his Quarters, at a day named, then and the[re to consu]lt how
to put the countrey in to som degree of safety, and to indevoure
for to stop those imminent dangers, now thretning the destruction of the wholl Collony, through the bloody proseedings of
the Indians; and (as he said) by Sir William B. doteing and

---

[1] For Colonel William Cole, see p. 23, note 1. The text here is an abstract
of Bacon's manifesto, issued from Middle Plantation. See *Virginia Magazine
of History*, I. 55–63.

ireguler actings.   Desireing of them not to sit still, in this
common time of callamitye, with there hands in there bosums;
or as unconcer'd spectaters, stand gazeing upon their approcheing ruinys, and not lend a hand to squench those flames now
likely to consume them and theres to ashes.

According to the summons, most of the prime Gent: men
in these parts (where of som were of the Councell of State)
gave Bacon a meeteing in his quarters, at the assigned time.
Where being met (after a long Harange by him made, much
of the nature of, and to explane the summons) he desired them
to take the same so far in to there consideration, that there
might, by there wisdom, som expedient [be] found out, as well
for the countryes securytie against Sir Williams Ireguler proseedings, as that hee, and Armye, might unmollest prossecute
the Indian war.   Ading, that neather him selfe, nor those
under his command, thought it a thing consisting with reason,
or common sence, to advance against the common Enimy, and
in the meane time want insureance (when they had don the
worke abrode) not to have their throtes cut, when they should
return hom, by those whoe had set them to worke: being con-
fident that Sir William and som others with him, through a
sence of their unworantable actions, would do what was posible to be don, not onely to destroy himself, but others (privie
to their knavereys) now ingaged in the Indian servis with him.

After that Bacon had urg'd, what he thought meet for the
better carying on of those affaires, now hammering in his head,
it was concluded by the wholl Convention, that for the establishing the Generall, and Army, in a consistancy of safety,
and that as well upon his march against the Indians, as when
that he should returne from the servis, and allso for the keepeing the Countrey in peace, in his absence, that there should be
a test, or recognition,[1] drawne, and subscribed by the wholl
Countrey, which should oblige them and every of them, not
to be aideing nor assisting to Sir Will. Berkley (for now he
would not afford him the title of Governour) in any sorte, to
the molestation, hinderance or detriment of the Ginerall and
Army.   This being assented to, the Clarke of the Assembley was
ordred to put the same in to forme; which while he was a
doeing, the Generall would needs have another branch added

---

[1] The oath of August 3.   See pp. 35, 122.

to the former, *viz.* That the people should not onely be obliged not to be aideing unto Sir W: B. against the Generall, but that by the force of this Recognition, they should be obliged to rise in Arms against him, if he with armed forces should offer to resist the Generall, or desturb the Countries peace, in his absence: and not onely so, but (to make the ingagement Al-a-mode Rebellion) he would have it added, that if any forces should be sent out of England, at the request of Sir William, or other ways to his aide, that they were likewise to be aposed, till such time as the Countrys cause should be sent hom, and reported to his most Sacred Majesty.

These two last branches of this Bugbeare did marvellously startle the people, especially the very last of all, yet for to give the Generall satisfaction how willing they were to give him all the security that lay in there power, they seemed willing to subscribe the two first, as they stood single, but not to any, if the last must be joyned with them. But the Generall used, or urged, a grate many reasons for the signeing the wholl ingagement, as it was presented in the three conjoyned branches, other ways no securitye could be expected, neather to the Countrey, Armye, nor himselfe: therefore he was resalved, if that they would not do, what hee did judg soe reasonable, and necessary to be don, in and about the premises, that he would surrender up his Commission to the Assembley, and let the countrey finde som other servants to goe abrode and do there worke.

For, sath he, it is to be considered, that Sir William hath allredy proclamed me a Rebell, and it is not unknowne to himselfe that I both can, and shall charge him with no less then Treason. And it is not my selfe onely, that must and is concerned in what shall be charged against him, but severall Gent: men in the countrey, besides; who now are, and ever will be against his intress, and of those that shall adhere to his ilegall proseedings: of which he being more then ordnarely senceable, it cannot in common reason be otherways conceved, but that he being assisted by those forces, now imploied, that they shall not be wholly imploied to the destruction of all those capeable to frame an accuseation against him, to his sacred Majesty. Neather can it reasonably be apprehended, that he will ever condesend to any friendly accomadation wth

those that shall subscribe to all, or any part of this ingagement, unless such or such persons shall be surrendred up to
his marcy, to be proseeded against, as he shall thinke fitt: and
then how many, or few, those may be, whom he shall make
choyce of, to be sent into the tother world, that he may be
rid of his feares in this, may be left to consideration.

Many things was (by many of those who were at this meeting) urged pro and con, concerning the takeing or not takeing
of the ingagement: But such was the ressalute temper of the
Generall, against all reasoning to the contrary, that the wholl
must be swollowed, or ells no good would be don.   In the urging of which he used such specious and subtill pretences; som
times for the pressing, and not to be despenced with necessity,
in regarde of those feares the wholl Collony was subjected to
through the daly murthers perpetrated by the Indians, and
then againe opening the harmlesness of the Oath, as he would
have it to be, and which he manidged solely against a grate
many of those counted the wisest men in the Countrey, with
so much art and sophisticall dixterety, that at length there
was litle said, by any, against the same: Especially when that
the Guner of York Fort[1] arived, imploreing aide to secure the
same against the Indians; ading that there was a grate many
poore people fled into it for protection, which could not be,
unless there was som speedy course taken to reinforce the said
Fort, with Munition and Arms, other ways it, and those fled
to it, would go nere hand to fall in to the power of the Heathen.

The Generall was som what startled at this newes, and
accordingly expostulated the same, how could it posible be
that the most conciderablest fortris in the countrey, should
be in danger to be surprised by the Indians.   But being tould
that the Governour, the day before, had caused all the Arms
and Amunition to be convayed out of the Fort into his owne
vessell, with which he was saled forth of the Countrey, as it
was thought, it is strange to thinke, what impressions this
Story made upon the peoples apprehentions.   In ernist this
action did stager a grate many, otherways well inclined to Sir
William, who could not tell what constructions to put upon
it.   How ever, this was no grate disadvantage to Bacons de-

---

[1] One of the forts ordered by the assembly in March, 1676, to be built for
defense against the Indians.

signes; he knew well enough how to make his advantages out
of this, as well as he did out of the Gloster buisness, before
mentioned, by frameing and stomping out to the peoples apprehentions what commentaries, or interpretations, he pleased,
upon the least oversight by the Governour commited; which
hee managed with so much cuning and subtillety, that the
peoples minds became quickly flexable, and apt to receve any
impression, or simillitude, that his Arguments should represent
to there ill disarneing judgments; in so much that the Oath
became now more smooth, and glib, to be swollowed, even by
those who had the gratest repugnancy against it; so that there
was no more descorses used neather for restrictions nor in-
largements; onely this salvo was granted, unto those who
would clame the benifit of it (and som did soe) yet not exprest
in the writen copey (*viz.*) That if there was any thing in
the same of such dangerous consequence that might tant the
subscribers Alegence, that then they should stand absalved
from all and every part of the sd oath; unto which the Generall gave his consent (and certainely he had too much cuning
to denye, or gaine say it) saying God forbid that it should
be other ways ment, or intended; adding that himselfe (and
Armye by his command) had som few days before taken the
Oath of Alegience, therefore it could not Rationally be im-
magined that eather him selfe, or them, would goe about to
act, or do, any thing contrary to the meaneing of the same.

Bad Ware requires a darke store, while Sleeke and Pounce
inveagles the Chapmans judgment. Though the first subscribers were indulged the liberty of entering there exceptions,
against the strict letter of the oath, yet others who were to
take the same before the respective justices of peace in their
severall juridictions, were not to have the same lattitude.
For the power of affording cautions and exceptions was solely
in the imposer, not in those who should here after administer
the oath, whereby the aftertakers were obliged to swollow the
same (though it might haserd there choakeing) as it stood in
the very letter thereoff. Neather can I apprehend what benifit could posible accrew more unto those who were indulged
the fore sd previlidg, then to those who were debard the same;
since both subscribed the ingagement as it stood in the letter,
not as it was in the meaneing of the subscriber. It is trew,

before God and there owne consciences, it might be pleadeable, but not at the Bar of humane proseedings, with out a favourable interpretation put upon it, by those who were to be the judges.

While Bacon was contriving and imposeing this Illegall Oath, for to secure him selfe against the Governour, the Governour was no less sollicious to finde out meanes to secure him selfe against Bacon. Therefore, as the onely place of securytie within the Collony, to keep out of Bacons reach, he sales over to Accomack. This place is sequestered from the mane part of Verginia through the enterposition of the grate Bay of Cheispiock, being itselfe an Isthmus, and commonly called the Eastern shore. It is bounded on the East with the maine oacian, and on the Sowth west with the afore sd Bay, which runs up into the countrey navigable for the bigest Ships more then 240 miles, and so consequently, not approcheable from the other parts of Verginia but by water, without surrounding the head of the sd Bay: A labour of toyle, time, and danger, in regard of the way, and habitations of the Indians.

It was not long before Bacon was inform'd where the Governour had taken Santuary; neather was he ignorant what it was that moved him to do what he had don: He did all so apprehend that, as he had found the way out, he could (when he saw his owne time) finde the way in againe; and though he went forth with an emty hand he might return with a full fist. For the preventing of which (as he thought) he despach'd away one Esqr Bland, a Gent: man of an active and stiring dispossition, and no grate admirer of Sir Williams goodness; and with him, in Commission, one Capt. Carver, a person aquainted with Navigation, and one (as they say) indebted to Sir W. (before he dyed) for his life, upon a duble account, with forces in two ships, eather to block Sir William up in Accomack, or other ways to inveagle the inhabitants (thinkeing that all the countrey, like the Friere in the Bush, must needs be soe mad as to dance to there Pipe) to surrender him up in to there hands.

Bacon haveing sent Bland, and the rest, to doe this servis, once more re-enters upon his Indian march; after that he had taken order for the conveineing an Assembley, to sit downe on the 4 of September, the Summons being Authentick'd, as they would have it, under the hands of 4 of the Councell of

State; and the reason of the Convention to manidge the affaires
of the Countrey in his absence; least (as he saide) while hee
went abrode to destroy the Wolves, the Foxes, in the meane
time, should com and devoure the Sheepe. Hee had not
march'd many miles from his head quarters, but that newes
came post hast, that Bland and the rest with him were snapt
at Accomack; betrade (as som of there owne party related)
by Capt. Carver: but those who are best able to render an
acount of this affaire do aver, that there was no other Treason
made use of but there want of discretion, assisted by the juce
of the Grape: had it bin other ways the Governour would
never rewarded the servis with the gift of a Halter, which he
honoured Carver with, sudenly after his surpriseall. Bland
was put in Irons, and ill intreated, as it was saide; most of the
soulders owned the Governours cause, by entering them selves
in to his servis; those that refused were made prissoners, and
promised a releasement at the price of Carvers fate.

The Governour being blest with this good servis, and the
better servis, in that it was efected with out blood shed, and
being inform'd that Bacon was entred upon his Indian March,
ships him selfe for the western shore, being assisted with 5
ships and 10 sloops, in which (as it is saide) was about a thousand soulders. The newes where of outstriping his canvis
wings soone reach'd the eares of those left by Bacon, to see
the Kings peace kep, by resisting the Kings vice gerent. For
before that the Governour could get over the Water, two
fugetives was got to land, sent (as may be supposed) from som
in Accomack, spirited for the Generalls quarill, to inform those
here, of the same principles, of the Governours strength, and
upon what terms his soulders were to fight. And first they
were to be rewarded with those mens estates who had taken
Bacons Oath, catch that catch could. Secondly that they,
and there heirs, for 21 years should be discharged from all
impossition, excepting Church dues, and lastly 12 pence per
day, dureing the wholl time of servis. And that it was further
decreed that all Sarvants, whose masters were under the Generall Collours, or that had subscribed the ingágement, should
be set free, and injoy the fore mention'd benifits, if that they
would (in Arms) owne the Governours cause. And that this
was the wholl truth, and nothing but the truth, the two men

be fore mention'd, deposed before Capt. Thorp one of the Just-asses of the peace, for York County, after that one Collonell Scarsbrooke[1] had more prudently declined the admiting these two scoundrills to the test. Whether these Fellows were in the right, or in the rong, as to what they had narated, I know not, but this is certaine, whether the same was trew, or false, it produced the efects of truth in peoples mindes; who hereby became so much destracted in there ressalutions, that they could not tell, at present, which way to turn them selves; while there tongues expresed no other language but what sounded forth feares, wishes, and execrations, as their apprehentions, or affections, dictated: All lookeing upon them selves as a people utterly undon, being equally exposed to the Governours displeasure, and the Indians bloody cruillties; Som cursing the cause of there approcheing destruction, lookeing upo the Oath to be no small ingredient, helping to fill up the measure of there Miserys: Others wishing the Generalls presence, as there onely Rock of safety, while other look'd upon him as the onely quick sands ordained to swollow up and sinke the ship that should set them on shore, or keep them from drownding in the whirle poole of confuseion.

In the midest of these feares and perturbations, the Governour arives with his Fleet of 5 ships and 10 sloopes, all well man'd (or appear'd to be soe) before the Towne; into which the Governour sends his summons (it being possest by 7 or 800 Baconians) for a Rendition; with a free and ample pardon to all that would decline Bacons intress, and owne his, excepting one Mr. Drummond and one Mr. Larance a Collonell, and both active promoters of Bacons designes: Which is a most apparent argument, that what those two men (before mentioned) had sworn to, was a mere pack of untruths. This his Honours Proclamation was acceptable to most in Towne; while others againe would not trust to it, feareing to meet with som after-claps of revenge: Which diverseity of opinions put them all into a ressalution of diserting the place, as not Tenable (but indeed had it bin fortifyed, yet they had no Commission to fight) while they had the liberty of so doeing,

---

[1] Colonel Edmund Scarborough of Northampton County. See Wise, *The Early History of the Eastern Shore of Virginia.*

before it should be wholly invested; which that night, in the darke, they put in execution, every one shifting for him selfe with no ordnary feare, in the gratest hast posible, for fere of being sent after: And that som of them was posses'd with no ordnary feare, may be manifested in Collonell Larence, whose spirits were so much destracted, at his apprehentions of being one excepted in the Governours act of grace, that he forsooke his owne Howse with all his welth and a faire Cupbord of Plate intire standing, which fell into the Governours hands the nex Morning.

The Towne being thus forsaken, by the Baconians, his Honour enters the same the next day, about noone; where after he had rendred thanks unto God for his safe arivall (which he forgot not to perform upon his knees, at his first footeing the shore) hee applyes himselfe not onely to secure what he had got possesion of, but to increace and inlarge the same to his best advantage. And knowing that the people of ould useally painted the God of war with a belly to be fed, as well as with hands to fight, he began to cast about for the bringing in of provissions for to feed his soulders; and in the next place for soulders, as well to reinforce his strength with in, as to inlarge his quarters abrode: But as the saying is, Man may propose, but God will dispose; when that his hon'r thought him selfe so much at liberty, that he might have the liberty to go when and where he pleased, his expectations became very speedily and in a moment frusterated.

For Bacon haveing don his buisness against the Indians, or at least so much as he was able to do, haveing marched his men with a grate deale of toyle and haserd som hundreds of miles, one way and another, killing som and takeing others prissoners, and haveing spent his provissions, draws in his forces with in the verge of the English Plantations, from whence he dismiseth the gratest part of his Army to gether strength against the next designed March, which was no sooner don but he incounters the newes of the Governours being arived at town. Of which being informed he with a marvellous cellerity (outstriping the swift wings of fame) marcheth those few men now with him (which hee had onely resarved as a gard to his parson) and in a trice blocks up the Governour in Towne, to the generall astonishment of the wholl Countrey;

especially when that Bacons numbers was knowne; which at
this time did not exseed above a hundred and fifty, and these
not above two thirds at worke neather. An action of so
strange an Aspect, that who ever tooke notis of it, could not
chuse but thinke but that the Accomackians eather intended
to receve their promised pay, without disart; or other ways
to establish such signall testimonies of there cowerdize or disaffections, or both, that posterity might stand and gaze at
there reched stupidety.

Bacon soone perceved what easey worke he was likely to
have, in this servis, and so began to set as small an esteeme
upon these mens curages, as they did upon there owne credits.
Hee saw, by the Prolog, what sport might be expected in the
play, and soe began to dispose of his affaires accordingly.
Yet not knowing but that the paucity of his numbers being
once knowne, to those in Towne, it might raise there hearts
to a degree of curage, haveing so much the ods, and that mani-
times number prevales against ressalution, he thought it not
amiss, since the Lions strength was too weake, to strengthen
the same with the Foxes Braines: and how this was to be
efected you shall heare.

For emediately he despacheth two or three parties of Horss,
and about so many in each party, for more he could not spare,
to bring in to the Camp some of the prime Gent: Women,
whose Husbands were in towne. Where when arived he sends
one of them to inform her owne, and the others Husbands,
for what purposes he had brought them into the camp, namely,
to be plac'd in the fore frunt of his Men, at such time as those
in towne should sally forth upon him.

The poore Gent:Women were mightely astonish'd at this
project; neather were there Husbands voide of amazements
at this subtill invention. If Mr. Fuller[1] thought it strange,
that the Divells black gard should be enrouled Gods soulders,
they made it no less wonderfull, that there innocent and harm-
less Wives should thus be entred a white garde to the Divell.
This action was a Method, in war, that they were not well
aquainted with (no not those the best inform'd in millitary
affaires) that before they could com to pearce their enimies
sides, they must be obliged to dart there wepons through there

---

[1] Rev. Thomas Fuller (1608–1661), the witty author.

wives brest: By which meanes though they (in there owne parsons) might escape without wounds; yet it might be the lamentable fate of there better halfe to drop by gunshott, or other ways be wounded to death.

Whether it was these Considerations, or som others, I do not know, that kep their swords in there scabards: But this is manifest, That Bacon knit more knotts by his owne head in one day, then all the hands in Towne was able to untye in a wholl weeke: While these Ladyes white Aprons became of grater force to keepe the beseiged from salleing out then his works (a pittifull trench) had strength to repell the weakest shot, that should have bin sent into his Legure, had he not made use of this invention.

For it is to be noted that rite in his frunt, where he was to lodge his Men, the Governour had planted 3 grate Guns, for to play poynt blank upon his Men, as they were at worke, at about 100 or a 150 paces distance; and then againe, on his right hand, all most close aborde the shore, lay the ships, with ther broade sides, to thunder upon him if he should offer to make an onslaute: this being the onely place, by land, for him to make his entry, into the Towne: But for your better satisfaction, or rather those who you may show this Naritive to, who have never bin upon the place, take this short description.

The place, on which the Towne is built, is a perfict Peninsulla, or tract of Land, all most wholly incompast with Water. Haveing on the Sowth side the River (Formerly Powhetan, now called James River) 3 miles brode, Incompast on the North, from the east point, with a deep Creeke, rangeing in a cemicircle, to the west, with in 10 paces of the River; and there, by a smalle Istmos, tacked to the Continent. This Iseland (for so it is denominate) hath for Longitud (east and west) nere upo 2 miles, and for Lattitude about halfe so much, beareing in the wholl compass about 5 miles, litle more or less. It is low-ground, full of Marches and Swomps, which makes the Aire, especially in the Sumer, insalubritious and unhelty: It is not at all replenish'd with springs of fresh water, and that which they have in ther Wells, brackish, ill sented, penurious, and not gratefull to the stumack; which render the place improper to indure the commencement of a seige.

The Towne is built much about the midle of the Sowth line,
close upon the River, extending east and west, about 3 quarters
of a mile; in which is comprehended som 16 or 18 howses,
most as is the Church, built of Brick, faire and large; and in
them about a dozen Familles (for all the howses are not inhabited) getting there liveings by keepeing of ordnaries, at
exstreordnary rates.[1]

The Governour understanding that the Gent: Women, at
the Legure, was, by order, drawne out of danger, resalved, if
posible, to beate Bacon out of his trench; which he thought
might easely be performed, now that his Gardian Angles had
forsaken his Camp. For the efecting of which he sent forth
7 or (as they say) 800 of his Accomackians, who (like scholers
goeing to schoole) went out with hevie harts, but returnd
hom with light heeles; thinkeing it better to turne there backs
upon that storme, that there brests could not indure to strugle
against, for feare of being gauled in there sides, or other parts
of there bodys, through the sharpness of the wether; which
(after a terable noyse of thunder and lightning out of the Easte)
began to blow with a powder (and som leade too as big as mus-
quitt boolitts) full in there faces, and that with so grate a
violence, that som off them was not able to stand upon there
leggs, which made the rest betake them selves to there heeles,
as the onely expedient to save there lives; which som amongst
them had rather to have lost, then to have own'd there safty
at the price of such dishonourable rates.

The Governour was exstremly disgusted at the ill management of this action, which he exprest in som passionate terms,
against those who merited the same. But in ernist, who could
expect the event to be other ways then it was, when at the
first notis given, for the designed salley to be put in execution,
som of the officers made such crabed faces at the report of the
same, that the Guner of Yorke Fort did proffer to purchase,
for any that would buy, a Collonells, or a Captains, Commission, for a chunke of a pipe.

The next day Bacon orders 3 grate Guns to be brought
into the Camp, two whereof he plants upon his trench. The

[1] The topography may be followed by means of Mr. Samuel H. Yonge's *The Site
of Old "James Towne,"* enlarged edition (Richmond, 1907), or President Lyon G.
Tyler's *The Cradle of the Republic* (Williamsburg, second ed., 1906) and their maps.

one he sets to worke (playing som calls itt, that takes delight
to see stately structurs beated downe, and Men blowne up
into the aire like Shutle Cocks) against the Ships, the other
against the enterance into Towne, for to open a pasage to his
intended Storm, which now was resalved upon as he said,
and which was prevented by the Governours forsakeing the
place, and shiping himselfe once more to Accomack; takeing
along with him all the Towne people, and there goods, leaveing
all the grate Guns naled up, and the howses emty, for Bacon
to enter at his pleasure, and which he did the next morning
before day: Where, contrary to his hopes, he met with nothing
that might satisfie eather him selfe or soulders desires, except
few Horses, two or three sellers of wine, and som small
quantety of Indian Corne with a grate many Tan'd hides.

The Governour did not presently leave James River, but
rested at an Ancor som 20 miles below the Towne, which made
Bacon entertaine som thoughts, that eather hee might have a
desire to re-enter his late left quarters, or return and block
him up, as he had Sir William. And that there was som prob-
abillety Sir W. might steare such a course was news from Potomack (a province within the North Verge of Verginia) that
Collonell Brent[1] was marching at the head of 1000 Soulders
towards Towne in vindication of the Governours quarill. The
better to prevent Sir Williams designes (if he had a desire to
returne) and to hinder his Conjuntion with Brent (after that
he had consulted with his Cabinett Councell) he in a most
barberous maner converts the wholl Towne into flames, cin-
ders and ashes, not so much as spareing the Church, and the
first that ever was in Verginia.

Haveing performed this Flagitious, and sacralidgious action (which put the worst of Sperits into a horid Consternation,
at so in-humane a fact) he marcheth his men to the Greene
spring (the Governours howse soe named)[2] where haveing
stade (feasting his Army at the Governours Cost) two or 3
days, till he was inform'd of Sir Williams Motion, he wafts
his soulders over the River, at Tindells point,[3] in to Glocester

[1] Colonel Giles Brent, p. 123, note 2.
[2] Three miles above Jamestown. Its brick walls are still standing.
[3] Tindall's Point, now Gloucester Point, opposite Yorktown (Brown, *Genesis
of the United States*, no. XLVI).

County: takeing up his head quarters at Collonell Warners;[1] from whence hee sends out his Mandates, through the wholl County, to give him a Meeting at the Court howse; there to take the ingagement, that was first promoted at the Midle Plantation: for as yet, in this County, it was not admited. While he was seduliously contriveing this affaire, one Capt. Potter arives in post haste from Rapahanock, with news that Coll: Brent was advanceing fast upon him (with a resalution to fight him) at the head of a 1000 men, what horss what foote, if hee durst stay the commencement. Hee had no sooner red the Letter, but hee commands the Drums to beate, for the gathering his soulders under there Collours; which being don hee aquaints them with Brents numbers and resalutions to fight, and then demands theres; which was cherefully answered in the affirmetive, with showtes and acclemations, while the Drums thunders a March to meet the promised conflict. The Soulders with abundance of cherefullness disburthening them selves of all impediments to expedition, order, and good de-cipling, excepting there Oathes, and Wenches: the first whereof they retain'd in imitation of there Commanders; the other out of pitty to the poore whores; who seeing so many Men going to kill one another, began to feare that if they staide behinde, for want of doing they might be undon (there being but a few left at hom, excepting ould men, to sett them on worke,) and so chose rather to dye amongst the soulders, then to be kep from there labour, and so dye for want of exercize. Besides they knew if fortune cast them into there enimys hands, they had nothing to be plundred of but there honisty; and that, as too grate a burthen, and not fitt to be worn in a Camp, they had left at hom, thereby to be found the more light, and fit for the servis they were destinated to. And then againe they had heard a pritty good carrecter of Brent, and they could not tell but that all or most of his Men might be as good as him selfe; so that let the world go which way it would (Stand still with Ptollomye, or turne rownd like a

---

[1] Colonel Augustine Warner of Gloucester, councillor and speaker of the House, whose residence in Abingdon parish, Gloucester County, was at this time (September, 1676) forcibly entered by Captain William Byrd, acting under Ba-con's orders. Damage was done to the extent of £1000, the amount for which Warner afterward obtained a judgment against Byrd.

whorlegigg with Copernicus) they were likely to com of with
a saveing cast, they being onely to change there Masters, not
the trade they were bound prentis to.

Bacon had not marched above 2 or 3 days jurney (and
those but short ones too, as being loth to tire his Laberours
before they came to there worke) but he meets news in post
hast, that Brents Men (not soulders) were all run away, and
left him to shift for him selfe. For they haveing heard that
Bacon had beate the Governour out o'th Towne they began
to be afeard (if they should com with in his reach) that he
might beat them out of there lives, and so resolved not to
come nere him. Collonell Brent was mightily astonish'd at
the departure of his followers, saying that they had forsaken
the stowtest man, and ruing'd the fairest estate in Verginia;
which was by there cowerdize, or disaffections, expos'd to the
mercy of the Baconians. But they being (as they thought)
more obliged to looke after their owne concernes and lives,
then to take notis, eather of his vallour, or estate, or of there
owne Credits, were not to be rought upon by any thing that
he could do, or say, contrary to there owne fancies.

This buisness of Brents haveing (like the hoggs the devill
sheard) produced more noyse then wooll, Bacon, according to
the Summons, meets the Gloster men at the Court howse:
where appeard som 6 or 7 hundred horss and foot, with there
Arms. After that Bacon, in a long Harage, had tendred them
the ingagement (which as yet they had not taken, and now
was the onely cause of this Convention) one Mr. Cole offered
the sence of all the Gloster men, there present: which was
sum'd up in there desires, not to have the oath imposed upon
them, but to be indulged the benifitt of Neutralitie: But this
he would not grant, telling off them, that in this there request
they appear'd like the worst of sinners, who had a desire to be
saved with the righteous, and yet would do nothing whereby
they might obtaine there salvation; and so offering to go away,
one Coll: Gouge (of his party) calls to him and tould him, that
he had onely spoke to the Horss (meaneing the Troopers)
and not to the foote. Bacon, in som passion, replide, he had
spoke to the Men, and not to the Horss; haveing left that servis
for him to do, because one beast best would understand the
meaneing of another. And because a minister, one Mr.

Wading,[1] did not onely refuse to take the Ingagement, but incouraged others to make him there example, Bacon commited him to the Gard; telling off him that it was his place to Preach in the Church, not in the Camp: In the first he might say what he pleased, but in the last, he was to say no more then what should please him; unless he could fight to better purpose than he could preach.

The Gloster men haveing taken the ingagement, (which they did not till another meeteing, and in another place) and all the worke don on this side the Western Shore, Bacon thought it not a miss, but worth his labour, to go and see how the Accomackians did. It must be confest that he was a Gent: man of a Liberall education, and so consequently must be replenish'd with good maners, which inables and obligeth all civell parsons both to remember, and repay, receved curtesies: which made him not to forget those kindenesses the Accomackians bestow'd, in his absence, on his friends, and there nighbours, the Verginians: and so now he resalved (since he had nothing ells to do) for to go and repay there kinde hearted vissitt. But first he thought good to send them word of his good meaneing, that they might not pleade want of time, or want of knowledg, to provide a reception answerable to his quallety, and attendance. This was pritty faire play, but really the Accomackians did not halfe like it. They had rather his Honour would have had the patience to have stade till he had bin invited, and then he should have bin much more wellcom. But this must not hinder his jurnye; if nothing ells enterveine they must be troubled, with a troublesom guest, as well as there neighbours had bin, for a grate while together, to their exstreordnary charge, and utter undoeing. But there kinde and very mercyfull fate, to whom they and their Posteritye, must ever remane indebted, observeing there cares and feares, by an admireable and ever to be cellibrated providence, removed the causes. For

Bacon haveing for som time bin beseiged by sickness, and now not able to hould out any longer, all his strength, and provissions being spent, surrendred up that Fort he was no longer able to keepe, into the hands of that grim and all conquering Captaine, Death; after that he had implor'd the assistance

[1] Rev. James Wadding, of Petsworth parish in Gloucester County.

of the above mentioned Minester, for the well makeing his Artickles of Rendition. The onely Religious duty (as they say) he was observ'd to perform dureing these Intregues of affaires, in which he was so considerable an actor, and soe much consearn'd, that rather then he would decline the cause, he became so deeply ingaged in, in the first rise there of, though much urged by arguments of dehortations, by his nearest Relations and best friends, that he subjected him selfe to all those inconvenences that, singly, might bring a Man of a more Robust frame to his last hom. After he was dead he was bemoned in these following lines (drawne by the Man that waited upon his person, as it is said) and who attended his Corps to there Buriall place: But where depossited till the Generall day, not knowne, onely to those who are ressalutly silent in that particuler. There was many coppes of Verces made after his departure, calculated to the Lattitude of there affections who composed them; as a relish taken from both appetites I have here sent you a cuple.

Bacons Epitaph, made by his Man.

Death why soe crewill! what, no other way
To manifest thy splleene, but thus to slay
Our hopes of safety; liberty, our all
Which, through thy tyrany, with him must fall
To its late Caoss? Had thy riged force
Bin delt by retale, and not thus in gross
Griefe had bin silent: Now wee must complaine
Since thou, in him, hast more then thousand slane
Whose lives and safetys did so much depend
On him there lif, with him there lives must end.
 If't be a sin to thinke Death brib'd can bee
Wee must be guilty; say twas bribery
Guided the fatall shaft. Verginias foes,
To whom for secrit crimes just vengance owes
Disarved plagues, dreding their just disart
Corrupted Death by Parasscellcian[1] art
Him to destroy; whose well tride curage such,
There heartless harts, nor arms, nor strength could touch.
 Who now must heale those wounds, or stop that blood

---

[1] Medical or alchemical; from Paracelsus, the celebrated physician (1493–1541).

The Heathen made, and drew into a flood?
Who i'st must pleade our Cause? nor Trump nor Drum
Nor Deputations; these alass are dumb,
And Cannot speake. Our Arms (though nere so strong)
Will want the aide of his Commanding tongue,
Which Conquer'd more than Ceaser: He orethrew
Onely the outward frame; this Could subdue
The ruged workes of nature. Soules repleate
With dull Child could[1], he'd annemate with heate
Drawne forth of reasons Lymbick. In a word
Marss and Minerva both in him Concurd
For arts, for arms, whose pen and sword alike,
As Catos did, may admireation strike
In to his foes; while they confess withall
It was there guilt stil'd him a Criminall.
Onely this differance doth from truth proceed:
They in the guilt, he in the name must bleed,
While none shall dare his Obseques to sing
In disarv'd measures, untill time shall bring
Truth Crown'd with freedom, and from danger free,
To sound his praises to posterity.
   Here let him rest; while wee this truth report,
Hee's gon from hence unto a higher Court
To pleade his Cause: where he by this doth know
Whether to Ceaser hee was friend, or foe.

Upon the Death of G: B.

Whether to Ceaser he was Friend or Foe?
Pox take such Ignorance, do you not know?
Can he be Friend to Ceaser, that shall bring
The Arms of Hell, to fight againt the King?
(Treason, Rebellion) then what reason have
Wee for to waite upon him to his Grave,
There to express our passions? Wilt not bee
Worss then his Crimes, to sing his Ellegie
In well tun'd numbers; where each Ella beares
(To his Flagitious name) a flood of teares?
A name that hath more soules with sorow fed,
Then reched[2] Niobe single teares ere shed;
A name that fil'd all hearts, all eares, with paine,
Untill blest fate proclamed, Death had him slane.

---

[1] Chilled cold. In the next line, Lymbick for alembic.   [2] Wretched.

Then how can it be counted for a sin
Though Death (nay though my selfe) had bribed bin,
To guide the fatall shaft? we honour all
That lends a hand unto a T[r]ators fall.
What though the well paide Rochit soundly ply
And box the Pulpitt in to flatterey;
Urging his Rethorick, and straind elloquence,
T' adorne incoffin'd filth and excrements;
Though the Defunct (like ours) nere tride
A well intended deed untill he dide?
'Twill be nor sin, nor shame, for us, to say
A two fould Passion checker-workes this day
Of Joy and Sorow; yet the last doth move
On feete impotent, wanting strength to prove
(Nor can the art of Logick yeild releife)
How Joy should be surmounted, by our greife.
Yet that wee Grieve it cannot be denide,
But 'tis because he was, not cause he dide.
So wep the poore destresed Ilyum Dames[1]
Hereing those nam'd, there Citty put in flames,
And Country ruing'd; If wee thus lament
It is against our present Joyes consent.
For if the rule, in Phisick, trew doth prove,
Remove the cause, th' effects will after move,
We have outliv'd our sorows, since we see
The Causes shifting, of our miserey.
  Nor is't a single cause, that's slipt away,
That made us warble out a well-a-day.
The Braines to plot, the hands to execute
Projected ills, Death Joyntly did nonsute
At his black Bar.   And what no Baile could save
He hath commited Prissoner to the Grave;
From whence there's no repreive.   Death keep him close
We have too many Divells still goe loose.

Ingrams Proceedings.

The Lion had no sooner made his exitt, but the Ape (by indubitable right) steps upon the stage.   Bacon was no sooner removed by the hand of good providence, but another steps in, by the wheele of fickle fortune.   The Countrey had, for som time, bin guided by a company of knaves, now it was to

[1] Dames of Ilium (Troy).

try how it would behave it selfe under a foole. Bacon had not long bin dead, (though it was a long time before som would beleive that he was dead) but one Ingram[1] (or Isgrum, which you will) takes up Bacons Commission (or ells by the patterne of that cuts him out a new one) and as though he had bin his natureall heire, or that Bacons Commission had bin granted not onely to him selfe, but to his Executors, Administraters and Assignes, he (in the Millitary Court) takes out a Probit of Bacons will, and proclames him selfe his Successer.

This Ingram, when that he came first into the Countrey, had gott upon his Back the title of an Esquire, but how he came by it may pussell all the Herolds in England to finde out, u[n]till he informs them of his right name: how ever, by the helpe of this (and his fine capering, for it is saide that he could dance well upon a Rope) he caper'd him selfe in to a fine (though short liv'd) estate: by marying, here, with a rich Widow, vallued at som hundreds of pounds.

The first thing that this fine fellow did, after that he was mounted upon the back of his Commission, was to Spur, or Switch, those who were to pay obedience unto his Authorety, by geting him selfe proclaimed Generall of all the forces, now raised, or here after to be raised, in Verginia: Which while it was performing at the head of the Army, the Milksop stoode with his hatt in his hand, lookeing as demurely as the grate Turks Muftie, at the readeing som holy sentance, extracted forth of the Alchron.[2] The Bell-man haveing don, he put on his hat, and his Janessarys threw up there Caps, crying out as lowde as they could Bellow, "God save our new Generall," hopeing, no dout, but he, in imitation of the grat Sultaine, at his election, would have inlarged there pay, or ells have given them leave to have made Jewes of the best Christians in the Countrey: but he being more than halfe a jew him self, at present forbad all plundrings, but such as he him selfe should be parsonally at.

---

[1] Of Laurence Ingram, who became leader of the movement after Bacon's death, almost nothing is known, beyond what is stated in the narrative. He had recently come to Virginia, apparently with Captain Grantham, on one of the latter's various voyages. Isgrum, or Isengrim, is the wolf, in the old beast-epic of *Reynard the Fox*.

[2] Alkoran.

It was not long before the Governour (still at Accomack) had intimation of Bacons death. He had a long time bin shut up in the Arke (as we may say) and now thought good to send out a winged Messinger to see, if happely the Delluge was any whit abated; and whether any dry-ground emerg'd its head, on which, with safety, he might sett his foot, without danger of being wetshod in blood, which accordingly he effected, under the command of one Maj. Beverly,[1] a parson calculated to the Lattitude of the Servis, which required descretion, Courage, and Celerity, as qualetys wholly subservant to millitary affares: And all though he returnd not with an Olive branch in his Mouth, the Hyrogliph of peace, yet he went back with the Laurell upon his browes, the emblim of Conquest and tryumph, haveing snapt up one Coll: Hansford[2] and his

---

[1] Major Robert Beverley, sr., one of the ruling faction with Berkeley, the Ludwells, Hill, and Hartwell, came to Virginia in 1663 and settled in Middlesex County. He was deemed by Bacon one of the chief enemies of the popular cause and was named in the Declaration of the People. He accompanied Berkeley to the Eastern Shore, but was sent back with troops to suppress the insurrection. In this work, particularly after Bacon's death in October, he was successful, and accomplished his end with so much energy as to call forth charges of oppression. The commissioners were hostile to Beverley and he was afterward removed from the council, but reinstated on the arrival of Governor Culpeper. The commissioners reported him as saying in the presence of Wiseman, their secretary, that he had not plundered enough, and that the rebellion was ended too soon for his purpose. They also charged him with "fomenting the ill-humours" between Governor Berkeley and Colonel Jeffreys, and with refusing to honor their demand, made upon him, April 19, 1677, as clerk of the House, to deliver the journal of the session beginning February 20. In the latter case, the commissioners were compelled to seize the journals, thus committing "a great violation of their privileges," as the House claimed. Beverley was a vigorous but harsh man, hostile to the commissioners, though in his way loyal to the colony. His son, Robert Beverley, jr., was the author of a *History of Virginia*.

[2] Captain Thomas Hansford was one of the most active of Bacon's followers, and is characterized by Mr. Bruce as a man of "high and noble spirit," "the noblest of all the victims of Berkeley's insane wrath." One of his fingers was cut off by Captain William Digges, son of Governor Edward Digges, who in consequence had to flee across the Potomac to St. Mary's, Maryland, where he became one of Lord Baltimore's chief supporters, and took a prominent part in opposing the uprising of 1689. Hansford was captured about the middle of November, 1676, and, with four others, executed at Accomac, by martial law, as a rebel. The commissioners declared that this execution was illegal, as Hansford had had "no tryal or conviction by lawful jury."

party, who kep garde at the Howse where Coll: Reade[1] did
once live. It is saide that Hansford at (or a litle before) the
onslaut, had forsaken the Capitole of Marss, to pay his obla-
tions in the Temple of Venus; which made him the easiere
preay to his enimies; but this I have onely upon report, and
must not aver it upon my historicall reputation: But if it
was soe, it was the last Sacryfize he ever after offred at the
Shrine of that Luxurious Diety, for presently after that he
came to Accomack, he had the ill luck to be the first Verginian
borne that dyed upon a paire of Gallows. When that he came
to the place of Execution (which was about a Mile removed
from his prisson) he seemed very well resalved to undergo the
utmost mallize of his not over kinde Destinie, onely Com-
plaineing of the maner of his death: Being observed neather
at the time of his tryall (which was by a Court Martiall) nor
afterwards, to suplicate any other faviour, then that he might
be shot like a Soulder, and not to be hang'd like a Dog. But
it was tould him, that what he so passionately petitioned for
could not be granted, in that he was not condem'd as he was
merely a Soulder, but as a Rebell, taken in Arms against the
King, whose Laws had ordaind him that death. Dureing the
short time he had to live, after his sentance, he approved to
his best advantage for the well fare of his soule, by repentance
and contrition for all his Sinns, in generall, excepting his Re-
belellion, which he would not acknowledg; desireing the People, at the place of execution, to take notis that he dyed a
Loyall Subject, and a lover of his Countrey; and that he had
never taken up arms, but for the destruction of the Indians,
who had murthered so many Christians.

The buisness being so well accompish'd, by those who had
taken Hansford, did so raise there Spirits, that they had no
sooner deliver'd there Fraight at Accomack, but they hoyse
up there sailes, and back againe to Yorke River, where with
a Marvellous celerity they surprise one Major Cheise-Man[2]
and som others, amongst whom one Capt. Wilford, who (it
is saide) in the bickering lost one of his eyes, which he seem'd
litle concern'd at, as knowing, that when he came to Accomack,

---

[1] Probably the house of Colonel George Reade, on the site of Yorktown.

[2] Of Major Thomas Cheeseman little more is known than is stated in the
text. For Farlow, whose niece was the "loving wife" mentioned below, see p. 138.

that though he had bin stark blinde, yet the Governour would take care for to afford him a guide, that should show him the way to the Gallows. Since he had promised him a hanging, long before, as being one of those that went out with Bacon, in his first expedition against the Indians, without a Commission.

This Capt. Wilford, though he was but a litle man, yet he had a grate heart, and was knowne to be no Coward. He had for som yeares bin an Interpreter betwene the English and the Indians, in whose affaires he was well aquainted, which rendred him the more acceptable to Bacon, who made use of him all along in his Indian War. By birth he was the Second Son of a Kt., who had lost life and estate in the late Kings quarill, against the surnamed long Parliament, which forst him to Verginia (the onely Citty of Refuge left in his Majesties dominians, in those times, for destresed Cavallers) to seeke his fortunes, which through his industerey began to be considerable, if the kindness of his fate had bin more perminent, and not destin'd his life to so reched a death. Major Cheisman, before he came to his triall, dyed in prisson, of feare, Greife, or bad useage, for all these are reported: and so by one death prevented another more dredfull to flesh and blood.

There is one remarkeable passage reported of this Major Cheismans Lady, which because it sounds to the honour of her Sex, and consequent[l]y of all loveing Wives, I will not deny it a roome in this Narrative.

When that the Major was brought in to the Governors presence, and by him demanded, what made him to ingage in Bacons designes? Before that the Major could frame an Answer, to the Governours demand, his Wife steps in and tould his honour that it was her provocations that made her Husband joyne in the Cause that Bacon contended for; ading, that if he had not bin influenc'd by her instigations, he had never don that which he had don. Therefore (upon her bended knees) she desired of his honour, that since what her Husband had don was by her meanes, and so, by Consequence, she most guilty, that shee might be hang'd, and he pardon'd. Though the Governouer did know, that what she had saide, was neare to the truth, yet he saide litle to her request, onely telling of her that she was a W——. But his honour was angrey, and therefore this expression must be interpreted the efects of his passion, not his meaneing: For it is to be understood in reason, that there is not any Woman, who hath soe small affection for her Husband, as to dishonour him by her dishonisty, and yet retaine such a degree of love, that rather then he should be hang'd, shee will be content to submit her owne life to the Sentance, to keep her husband from the Gallows.

Capt. Carver and Capt. Farlow was now (or about this time) Executed, as is before hinted. Farlow was related to Cheisman, as he had maried Farlows Neice. When that he went first into the servis (which was presently after that Bacon had receved his Commission) he was Chosen Commander of those recrutes sent out of Yorke County, to Make up Bacons Numbers, according to the Gage of his Commission, limited for the Indian Servis; and by Sir William (or som one of the Councell) recommended to Bacon, as a fitt parson to be Commander of the saide party. These terms, by which he became ingaged, under Bacons Commands, he urged in his pley,[1] at his triall: Ading, that if he had, in what he had don, denyed the Generalls orders, it was in his power to hang him, by the judgment of a Court Martiall; and that he had acted nothing but in obedience to the Generalls Authority. But it was replide, against him, that he was put under Bacons command for the servis of the Countrey, against the Indians, which imploy he ought to have kep to, and not to have acted by yond his bounds, as he had don: And Since he went into the Army under the Governours orders, he was required to Search the Same, and see if he could finde one that Commissionated him to take up Arms in oppossition to the Governours Authority and parson: Neather had Bacon any other power by his Commission (had the same bin never so legally obtained) but onely to make war upon the Indians. Farlow rejoyned, that Bacon was, by his Commission, to see that the Kings peace was kep, and to Suppress those that should indeviour to Perturbe the same. It was reply'd, this might be granted him, and he might make his advantage of it, but was required to consider, whether the Kings peace was to be kep in resisting the Kings emediate Governour, soe as to levy a War against him; and so commanded him to be silent, while his sentance was pronounced.

[1] Plea.

This man was much pittied by those who were aquainted with him, as one of a peaceable dispossition, and a good scholer, which one might thinke should have inabled him to have taken a better estimate of his imployment, as he was acquainted with the Mathamaticks: But it seems the Asstrolabe, or Quadrant, are not the fitest instruments to take the altitude of a Subjects duty; the same being better demonstrated by practicall, not Speculative observations.

The nimble and timely servis performed by Major Beverly (before mentioned) haveing opened the way, in som measure, the Governour once more sallyeth out for the Westerne Shore, there to make triall of his better fortune; which now began to cast a more favourable Aspect upon him and his affaires, by removeing the maine obstickles out of the way, by a Death, eather Natureall, or violent, (the one the ordnary, the other the exstreordnary workings of providence) which had with such pertinances, and violent perstringes, aposed his most Auspicious proceedings.   The last time he came, he made choyce of James River; now he was resalved to set up his Rest in Yorke, as havein the nearest Vicinety to Gloster County (the River[1] onely enterposeing betwene it and Yorke) in which, though the Enimy was the strongest (as desireing to make it the Seate of the Warr, in regard of severall locall covenencies) yet in it he knew that his friends was not the weakest, whether wee respect number, or furniture.   It is trew they had taken the ingagement (as the rest had) to Bacon; but hee being dead, and the ingagement being onely personall, was lade in the Grave with him; for it was not made to him selfe, his heires, Executors, administrater, and Assignes; if other ways, it might have bin indued with a kinde of immortallety; unless the Sword, or juster (or grater) power might hapen to wound it to death.   But how ever, Bacon being Dead, and with him his Commission, all those, who had taken the ingagement, were now at liberty to go and chuse them selves another Master.

But though his honour knew that though they were discharged from the bindeing power of the oath, yet they were not free from the Commanding power of those Men that was still in Arms, in persuance of those ends for which the ingage-

[1] York River.

ment was pretended to be taken: And that before this could be effected, those Men must first be beaten from there Arms, before the other could get there heeles at liberty, to do him any servis, Therefore he began to cast about how he might remove those Blocks which stoode in the Gloster Mens way: which being once don, it must take away all Pretences, and leave them with out all excuse, if they should offer to sitt still, when he, and his good providence together, had not onely knock'd off there shackles, but eather imprisson'd there Jaylers, or tide them up to the Gallows.

He had with him now in Yorke River 4 Shipps besides 2 or 3 Sloopes. Three of the Ships he brought with him from Accomack: the other (a Marchantman, as the rest were) was som time before arived out of England, and in these about 150 Men, at his emediate command; and no more he had when he came into Yorke River: Where being setled in Consultation with his friends, for the Manageing of his affaires, to the best advantage; he was informed that there was a party of the Baconians (for so they were still denominated, on that side, for destinction sake) that had setled them selves in there winter quarters, at the howse of one Mr. Howards, in Gloster county.

For to keepe these Vermin from breeding, in there warme Kenill, he thought good, in time, for to get them ferited out. For the accomplishment of which peice of servis, he very secritly despacheth away a select number under the Conduct of Major Beverly, who very nimbly performed the same, haveing the good fortune (as it is saide) to catch them all a sleepe. And least the Good man of the Howse should forgett this good servis, that Beverly had don him, in removeing his (to him) chargable gues[t]s, with these sleepers, he convayes a good quantety of there Landlords goods aborde: the Baconians (where of one a Leift. Collonell) to remane prissoners, and the goods to be devided amongst those whose servis had made them such, according to the Law of Arms; which Howard will have to be the Law of *Harms*, by placeing the first letter of his name before the vowill A.

But in ernist (and to leave jesting) Howard did really thinke it hard measure, to see that go out of his store, by the Sword, which he intended to deliver out by the Ell, or yard.

Neather could his Wife halfe like the Markitt, when she saw the Chapmen carey her Daughters Husband away Prissoner, and her owne fine Cloathes goeing into Captivity, to be sould by Match and pin,[1] and after worne by those who (before these times) was not worth a point;[2] Yet it is thought, that the ould Gent:Woman, was not so much concern'd that her Son in Law was made a prissoner, as her Daughter was vext, to see they had not left one Man upon the Plantation, to comfort neather herself nor Mother.

This Block (and no less was the Commander of the fore mention'd sleepers) being removed out of the way, the Gloster Men began to stir abrode: Not provoked thereto out of any hopes of geting, but through a feare of loseing. They did plainely perceve that if they them selves did not goe to worke, sombody ells would, while they (for there neglegence) might be compeld to pay them there wages; and what that might com to they could not tell, since it was probable, in such Servises, the Laberours would be there owne Carvers; and it is commonly knowne, that Soulders makes no Conscience to take more then there due.

The worke that was now to be don, in these parts (and further I cannot go for want of a guide) was cut out into severall parcells,[3] according as the Baconians had devided the

---

[1] *I. e.*, by a form of auction in which a pin was stuck through a piece of slow-match cord, which was then lighted, and bidding could continue till the fire reached the pin, and the pin dropped.

[2] A point was a small appliance for fastening clothing; equivalent to, not worth a pin.

[3] The insurgents were divided into five chief groups. One under Ingram was at West Point, at the junction of the Pamunkey and Mattapony Rivers. The second was at Green Spring, Berkeley's old residence, under Captain Drew. The third was at the house of Nathaniel Bacon, sr., on King's Creek, York County, under Major Whaly. The fourth, with Drummond and Lawrence, remained at the brick house in New Kent County, opposite West Point, until Christmas time, when all who were there moved up the river to the house of Colonel Henry Gooch, where Whaly joined them. A fifth centre of resistance was in Nansemond County, behind Warrascoyack Bay, under Captain Catlin and Colonel Groves (*Calendar of State Papers, Colonial*, 1674–1676, p. 453). These bodies of men lived chiefly from hand to mouth, foraging and plundering where they could. Such a rough commissariat system helps to explain the desolation of the country on the arrival of the commissioners. Nathaniel Bacon, sr., claimed that he had lost £1000 sterling in stock and goods by Whaly's occupation of his house.

same. And first At Wests Point (an Isthmos which gives the Denomination to the two Rivers, Pomunkey and Mattapony (Indian Names) that branch forth of York River, Som 30 Miles above Tindells point) there was planted a garde of about 200 Soulders. This place Bacon had designed to make his prime Randevouze, or place of Retreat, in respect of severall locall Convenencis this place admited off, and which hee found fitt for his purpose, for sundry reasons. Here it was, I thinke, that Ingram did cheifely reside, and from whence he drew his recruts, of Men and Munition. The next Parcell, considerable, was at Green-spring (the Governours howse) into which was put about 100 Men, and Boys, under the Command of on Capt. Drew; who was ressalutely bent (as he sade) to keep the place in spite of all opposition, and that he might the better keepe his promise he caused all the Avenues and approaches to the same to be Baracado'd up, and 3 grate Guns planted to beate of the Assalents. A third parcell (of about 30 or 40) was put in to the Howse of Collonell Nath: Bacons (a Gent:Man related to him deceased, but not of his principles) under the Command of one Major Whaly, a stout ignorant Fellow (as most of the rest) as may be seene here after; these were the most considerablest parteys that the Gloster Men were to deale with, and which they had promised to reduce to obediance, or other ways to beate them out of there lives, as som of them (perhaps not well aquainted with Millitary affairs, or too well conseated of there owne vallour) bosted to doe.

The Parson that, by Commission, was to perform this worke, was one Major Lawrence Smith (and for this servis so intitled, as it is saide) a Gent:Man that in his time had hued out many a knotty peice of worke, and soe the better knew how to handle such ruged fellowes as the Baconians were famed to be.

The place for him to Congregate his men at (I say Congregate, as a word not improper, since his second in dignity was a Minester, who had lade downe the Miter and taken up the Helmett) was at one Major Pates (in whose Howse Bacon had surrendred up both Life and Commission; the one to him that gave it, the other to him that tooke it) where there apeared men ennough to have beaten all the Rebells in the

Countrey, onely with there Axes and Hoes, had they bin led on by a good overseer.

I have eather heard, or have read, That a Compleate Generall ought to be owner of these 3 induments: Wisdom to foresee, Experience to chuse, and Curage to execute. He that wants the 2 last, can never have the first; since a wise Man will never undertake more then he is able to perform; He that hath the 2 first, wanting the last, makes but a lame Commander; since Curage is an inseperable Adjunct to the bare name of a Soulder, much more to a Generall: He that wants the second, haveing the first and the last, is no less imperfict then the other; since without experience, wisdom and curage (like yong Docters) do but grope in the darke, or strike by gess.

Much about the time that the Gloster Men Mustred at M. Pates, there was a riseing in Midlesex, upon the same acount: Who were no sooner gott upon ther feet, but the Baconians resalves to bring them on there knees. For the efecting of which Ingram speeds away one Walklett, his Leift. Generall, (a Man much like the Master) with a party of Horss, to do the worke. M. L. Smith was quickly inform'd upon what arend[1] Walklett was sent, and so, with a Generous ressalution, resalves to be at his heeles, if not before hand with him, to helpe his friends in there destress. And because he would not all together trust to others, in affaires of this nature, he advanceth at the head of his owne Troops, (what Horss what Foote for number, is not in my intillegence) leaveing the rest for to fortify Major Pates howse, and so speeds after Walklet who, before Smith could reach the required distance, had performed his Worke, with litle labour, and (hereing of Smiths advance) was prepareing to give him a Reception answerable to his designements: Swareing to fight him though Smith should out number him Cent per cent; and was not this a dareing ressalution of a Boy that hardly ever saw Sword, but in a Scaberd?

In the meane time that this buisnes was a doeing, Ingram, understanding upon what designe M. L. Smith was gon about, by the advice of his officers strikes in betwene him and his new made (and new mand) Garisson at M. Pates. He very nimbly

[1] Errand.

invests the Howse, and then summons the Soulders (then under the command of the fore said Minester) to a speedy rendition, or otherways to stand out to Mercy, at there utmost perill. After som toos and froes about the buisness (quite beyond his text) the Minester accepts of Such Articles, for a Surrender, as pleased Ingram and his Mermidons to grant.

Ingram had no sooner don this jobb of jurnye worke (of which he was not a litle proud) but M. L. Smith (haveing retracted his March out of Midle-sex, as thinkeing it litle less then a disparagement to have any thing to doe with Walklett) was up on the back of Ingram, before he was aware, and at which he was not a litle daunted, feareing that he had beate Walklett to peices, in Midlesex. But he perceveing that the Gloster Men did not weare (in there faces) the Countinances of Conquerers, nor there Cloathes the marks of any late ingagement (being free from the honourable Staines of Wounds and Gun shott) he began to hope the best, and the Gloster men to feare the worst; and what the properties of feare is, let Feltham[1] tell you, who saith, That if curage be a good Oriter, feare is a bad Counceller, and a worss Ingineare. For insteade of erecting, it beates and batters downe all Bullworks of defence: perswadeing the feeble hart that there is no safety in armed Troops, Iron gates, nor stone walls. In oppossition of which Passion I will appose the Properties of it's Antithesis, and say That as som men are never vallent but in the midst of discourse, so others never manifest there Courage but in the midst of danger: Never more alive then when in the jawes of Death, crowded up in the midst of fire, smoke, Swords and gunns; and then not so much laying about them through despareation, or to save there lives, as through a Generosety of Spirit, to trample upon the lives of there enimies.

For the saveing of Pouder and Shott (or rather through the before mentioned Generossety of Curage) one Major Bristow[2] (on Smiths side) made a Motion to try the equity and justness of the quarill, by single Combett: Bristow proffering him selfe against any one (being a Gent.) on the other side; this was noble, and like a Soulder. This Motion (or rather

---

[1] Owen Feltham, author of *Resolves, Divine, Moral, and Political* (1620, and many other editions).

[2] For Major Bristow, see p. 24, note 3.

Challenge) was as redely accepted by Ingram, as proffer'd by Bristow; Ingram Swareing the newest Oath in fashion, that he would be the Man; and so advanceth on foot, with sword and Pistell, against Bristow; but was fetch'd back by his owne men, as douteing the justness of there cause, or in Consideration of the desparety that was betwene the two Antagonist. For though it might be granted, that in a private Condition Bristow was the better man, yet now it was not to be alowed, as Ingram was intitled.

This buisness not fadging, betwene the two Champions, the Gloster men began to entertaine strange and new Ressalutions, quite Retrogade to there pretentions, and what was by all good men expected from the promiseing asspects of this there Leagueing against a usurping power. It is saide that a good Cause and a good Deputation is a lawfull Authorety for any Man to fight by; yet neather of these, joyntly nor Severally, hath a Coercive power, to make a Man a good Soulder: If he wants Courage, though he is inlisted under both, yet is he not starling quoyne:[1] he is at best but Coper, stompt with the Kings impress, and will pass for no more then his just vallew. As to a good Cause, doutless they had Satisfied themselves as to that, ells what were they at this time a Contending for, and for whom? And as for a good Deputation, if they wanted that, where fore did they so miserably befoole them selves, as to run in to the mouths of there enimies, and there to stand still like a Company of Sheep, with the knife at there throtes, and never so much as offer to Bleat, for the saving of there lives, liberties, Estates, and what to truly vallient men is of grater vallew then these, there Creditts? all which now lay at the Mercy of there enimies, by a tame surrender of there Arms and Parsons in to the hands of Ingram (with out Strikeing one Stroke) who haveing made all the cheife Men prissoners (excepting those who first run away) he dismist the rest to there owne abodes, there to Sum up the number of those that were eather slane or wounded in this Servis.

Much about this time of the Gloster buisness, his honour sends abrode a party of Men, from off aboarde, under the Command of one Hubert Farrill, to feritt out a Company of

---

[1] Sterling coin.

the Rebells, who kep Gard at Coll. Bacons, under the power
of Major Whaly, before mentioned. Coll. Bacon himselfe,
and one Coll : Ludwell, came along with Farrill, to see to the
Management of the enterprise; about which they tooke all
posible care, that it might prove fortunate. For they had no
sooner resolved upon the onsett, but they consult on the Maner,
which was to be effected by a Generossety paralell with the
designe; which required Curage, and expedition : and so con-
cludes not to answer the Centreys by fireing, but to take,
kill, or drive them up to there Avenues, and then to enter
pell mell with them in to the howse : this Method was good
had it bin as well executed as Contrived. But the Centrey
had no sooner made the Challinge, with his mouth, demanding
who Coms there? but the other answer with there Musquits
(which seldom Speakes the language of friends) and that in
soe loud a Maner, that it alarum'd those in the howse to a
defence, and then into a posture to salley out. Which the
other perceveing (contrary to there first orders) wheeles of
from the danger, to find a place for there securytie, which they
in part found behinde som out buildings, and from whence
they fired one upon the other, giveing the Bullits leave to grope
there owne way in the dark (for as yet it was not day) till the
Generall was shot through his loynes; and in his fate all the
soulders (or the grater part) through there hearts, Now sunke
in to there heels which they were now makeing use of instead
of there hands, the better to save there jackits, of which they
had bin Certainely Stript, had they Com under there enimies
fingers, who knowes better how to Steale then fight, not with-
standing this uneven Cast of Fortunes Mallize, Being a Conflict, in which the losers have cause to repent, and the winers
Faith to give God thanks; unless with the same devotion
Theives do when that they have stript honist Men out of there
Mony. Here was none but there Generall kild, whose Commission was found droping-wett with his owne blood, in his
pockitt; and 3 or 4 taken prisoners; what wounded not knowne,
if any; in there backs, as there enimies say, who glory'd more
in there Conquest then ever Scanderbeg[1] did for the gratest
victory he ever obtained against the Turkes. If Sir Williams
Cause were no better then his fortunes, hither to, how many

[1] Albanian leader (1403-1467), rebel against the Turks.

prossellites might his disasters bring over to the tother side? but God forbid that the justice of all quarills should be estimated by there events.

Yet here in this action (as well as som other before) who can chuse but deplore the strange fate that the Governour was subjected to, in the evill choyce of his cheife-commanders, for the leadeing on his Millitary transactions; that when his cause should com to a day of heareing, they should want Curage to put in there pleay of defence, against there Adverssarys arguments; and pittyfully to stand still and see themselves nonsuted, in every sneakeing adventure or Action that cal'd upon there Generossety (if they had had any) to vindicate there indubitable pretences against a usurped power.

It is trew Whalys Condition was desperate, and hee was resalved that his Curage should be conformable and as desperate as his Condition. He did not want intilligence how Hansford, and Som others, was sarved at Accomack; which made him thinke it a grate deale better to dye like a Man, then to be hang'd like a Dogg, if that his Fate would but give him the liberty of picking as well as he had taken the liberty of stealeing, of which unsoulder-like quallety he was fowly guilty. But let Whaleys condition be never so desperate, and that he was resalvd to Manage an oppossition against his Assalent according to his condition, yet those in the Howse with him stoode upon other terms, being two thirds (and the wholl exseeded not 40) prest into the Servis, much against there will; and had a grater antipethy against Whaly then they had any cause for to feare his fate, if he, and they too, had bin taken. As for that Objection, that Farrill was not, at this time, fully cured of those Wounds he receved in the Salley at Towne, which in this action proved detrimentall both to his strength and curage: Why then (if it was so) did he accept of this imploy (he haveing the liberty of refuseing) since none could be better aquainted with his owne Condition (eather for Strength or Courage) better then him selfe? Certainely in this particuler, Farills foolish ostentation was not excuseable, nor Sir William with out blame, to Complye with his ambition, as he had no other parts to prove himselfe a Soulder, then a haire brain'd ressalution to put him selfe forward in those affaires he had no more aquaintance with then what he had heard people talke off; For the falure of this enterprise (which must wholly be refer'd to the breach he made upon their sedulous determinations) which was (as is intimated before, to croude in to the Howse with the Centrey) was not onely injurious to there owne party, by leting slip so faire an occasion to weaken the power of the enimy, by removeing Whaly out of the way, who was esteemed the Most Considerablest parson on that side; but it was, and did prove of bad cosequence to the adjacent parts, where he kep gard: For whereas before he did onely take ame where he might do mischeife, he now did mischeife without takeing ame: before this unhapie conflict, he did levie at this or that particuler onely, but now he shott at Rovers, let the same lite where it would he matter'd nott.

Capt. Grantham[1] had now bin som time in Yorke River, A man unto whom Verginia is very much beholden for his neate contrivance in bringing Ingram (and som others) over to harken to reason. With Ingram he had som small aquaintance, for it was in his Ship that he came to Verginia; and so resalved to try if he might not doe that by words, which others could not accomplish with Swords. Now all though he knew that Ingram was the Point where all the lines of his contrivance were for to Center, yet he could not tell, very well, how to obtaine this point. For all though he did know that Ingram, in his private Condition, was accostable enough; yet since the Tit Mouse (by one of Fortunes figaryes)[2] was becom an Elliphant, he did not know but that his pride might be as immence as his power: since the Peacock (though bred upon a Dunghill) is no less proud of his fine fethers then the princely Eagle is of his noble curage. What Arguments Grantham made use of, to ring the Sword out of Ingrams hand, to me is not visable, more then what he tould me of; which I thinke was not Mercuriall[3] enough, against an ordnary Sophester. But to speake

---

[1] Captain Thomas Grantham, afterward knighted, was a merchant captain who chanced to be in Virginia at this time, and played a loyal but mediating part. Some account of Bacon's rebellion, and of his own life, is given, from documents furnished by him, in the rare little book, *An Historical Account of some Memorable Actions, [Particularly in Virginia*, 2d ed.] *by Sir Thomas Grantham, Kt.* (London, 1714, 1716; reprinted, Richmond, 1882).

[2] Vagaries.

[3] Alluding to Mercury as the god of eloquence.

the truth, it may be imagin'd that Grantham (at this time) could not bring more reasons to Convince Ingram, then Ingram had in his owne head to Convince him selfe; and so did onely awate som favourable overtures (and such as Grantham might, it is posible, now make) to bring him over to the tother side. Neather could he apprehend more reason in Granthams Arguments, then in his owne affaires, which now provok'd him to dismount from the back of that Horss which he wanted skill and strength to Manidge; especially there being som, of his owne party, wateing an opertunity to toss him out of the Sadle of his new mounted honours; and of whose designes he wanted not som intilligence, in the Countinances of his Mermidons; who began for to looke a skew upon this, there Milksopp Generall, who they judged fitter to dance upon a Rope, or in som of his wenches lapps, then to caper, eather to Bellonies[1] Bagpipe, or Marsses whisle.

But though Ingram was won upon to turn honist in this thing (thanks to his necessitye, which made it an act of Compultion, not a free will offering) yet was the worke but halfe don, untill the Soulders were wrought upon to follow his example. And though he him selfe, or any body ells, might command them to take up there Arms, when any mischeife was to be don: yet it was a question whether he, or any in the Countrye, could command them to lay downe there Arms, for to efect or do any good. In such a case as this, where Authority wants power, descretion must be made use of, as a vertue Surmounting a brutish force. Grantham, though he had bin but a while in the Countrey, and had seene but litle, as to mater of Action, yet he had heard a grate deale; and So Much that the name of Authority had but litle power to ring the Sword out of these Mad fellows hands, as he did perceve. And that there was more hopes to efect that by smoothe words, which was never likely to be accomplish'd by rough deeds; there fore he resalved to accoste them, as the Divell courted Eve, though to a better purpose, with never to be performed promises: counting it no sin to Ludificate those for there good, that had bin deceved by others to there hurt. He knew that Men were to be treated as such, and Children according to there childish dispossitions: And all though it was not with

---

[1] Bellona's.

both these he was now to deale, yet he was to observe the severall tempers of those he was to worke upon.

What number of Soulders was, at this time, in Garrisson
at West Point, I am not Certane: It is saide about 250, sum'd
up in freemen, searvants and slaves; these three ingredience
being the Compossition of Bacons Army, ever since that the
Governour left Towne. These was informed (to prepare the
way) two or three days before that Grantham came to them,
that there was a treaty on foote betwene there Generall and
the Governour; and that Grantham did manely promote the
same, as he was a parson that favoured the cause, that they
were contending for.

When that Grantham arived amongst these fine fellowes,
he was receved with more then an ordnary respect; which he
haveing repade with a suteable deportment, he aquaints them
with his Commission, which was to tell them, that there was
a peace Concluded betwene the Governour and there Generall;
and since him self had (in som measures) used his indeviours,
to bring the same to pass, hee beg'd of the Governour, that he
might have the honour to com and aquaint them with the
terms; which he saide was such, that they had all cause to
rejoyce at, then any ways to thinke hardly of the same; there
being a Compleate satisfaction to be given (by the Articles of
agreement) according to every ones particuler intress; which
he sum'd up under these heads. And first, those that were
now in Arms (and free Men) under the Generall, were still to
be retained in Arms, if they so pleased, against the Indians.
Secondly, And for those who had a desire for to return hom,
to there owne abodes, care was taken for to have them satisfide, for the time they had bin out, according to the alowance
made the last Assembley. And lastly, those that were sarvants in Arms, and behaved them selves well in there imployment, should emediately receve discharges from there Inden-
tures, signed by the Governour, or Sequetary of State; and
there Masters to receve from the publick a valluable Satisfaction, for every Sarvant so set free (Marke the words) propor-
tionally to the time that they have to serve.

Upon these terms, the Soulders forsake West-Point, and
goe with Grantham to kiss the Governours hands (still at
Tindells point) and to receve the benifitt of the Articles men-

tioned by Grantham; where when they came (which was by water, them selves in one vessill, and there Arms in another; and so contrived by Grantham, as he tould me him selfe, upon good reason) the Sarvants and Slaves was sent hom to there Masters, there to stay till the Governour had leasure to signe there discharges, or to say better, till they were free, according to the Custom of the Countrey;[1] the rest was made prissoners, or entertain'd by the Governour, as hee found them inclin'd.

Of all the obstickles, that hath hitherto lane in the Governours way, there is not one (which hath falne with in the Verge of my intilligence) that hath bin removed by the Sword; excepting what was performed under the Conduct of Beverly: How this, undertaken by Grantham, was effected, you have heard; though badly (as the rest) by me Sum'd up. The next, that is taken notis of, is that at Greene Spring (before hinted) under the Command of one Capt. Drew, formerly a Miller (by profession) though now Dignifide with the title of a Capt. and made Governour of this Place by Bacon, as he was a person formerly behoulden unto Sir William, and soe, by way of requiteall, most likely to keepe him out of his owne Howse, This Whisker of Whorly-Giggs, perceveing (now) that there was More Water coming downe upon his Mill then the Dam would hould, thought best in time, to fortifye the same, least all should be borne downe before he had taken his toule.[2] Which haveing effected (makeing it the strongest place in the Country what with grate and small Gunns) he stands upon his gard, and refuseth to Surrender, but upon his owne terms; Which being granted, he secures the place till such time as Sir William should, in parson, com and take possesion of the same: And was not this pritely, honestly, don, of a Miller.

The gratest difficulty now to be performed, was to remove Drummond and Larance out of the way. These two Men was

---

[1] Indented servants who had not taken the precaution to secure a written contract defining the terms of their service were obliged to serve "according to the custom of the country." Laws for their protection defined this. Thus, in Virginia at this time, by act of 1643, servants over twenty years old at the time of indenture had to serve four years; if between twelve and twenty, five years; if under twelve, seven years.

[2] Toll.

excepted out of the Governours pardon, by his Proclamation
of June last, and severall papers since, and for to dye without Marcy, when ever taken, as they were the cheife Incen-
diarys, and promoters to and for Bacons Designes; and by
whose Councells all transactions were, for the grater part,
managed all along on that Side.   Drummond was formerly
Governour of Carolina,¹ and all ways esteemed a Parson of
such induments, where Wisdom and honisty are contending
for supriority; which rendred him to be one of that sort of
people, whose dementions are not to be taken by the line of
an ordnary Capassety.   Larance was late one of the Assembley, and Burgis for Towne, in which he was a liver.   He was
a Parson² not meanely aquainted with such learning (besides
his natureall parts) that inables a Man for the management
of more then ordnary imployments, Which he subjected to an
eclips, as well in the transactings of the present affaires, as in
the darke imbraces of a Blackamoore, his slave: And that in
so fond a Maner, as though Venus was cheifely to be wor-
shiped in the Image of a Negro, or that Buty consisted all together in the Antiphety of Complections: to the noe meane
Scandle and affrunt of all the Vottrisses in or about towne.

When that West point was surrendred, and Greene Spring
secur'd for the Governour, these two Gent: was at the Brick-
howse,³ in New Kent: a place Situate allmost oppossitt to
West point, on the South side of York River, and not 2 Miles
removed from the said point, with som Soulders under there
Command, for to keepe the Governours Men from landing on
that Side; he haveing a Ship, at that time, at Ancor nere the
place.   They had made som attempts to have hindred Granthams designes (of which they had gain'd som intilligence)
but there indeviours not fadging, they sent downe to Coll.
Bacons to fetch of the Gard there, under the Command of
Whaley, to reinforce there owne strength.

---

¹ Governor of the Albemarle settlement (North Carolina), 1664–1667.
² Person.
³ An old brick house, built about 1660, on the south side of York River,
opposite West Point.   The house is still standing and is known as "Bacon's
Castle."   It was fortified by Captain William Rookins and others during the
rebellion.   Rookins was condemned to death afterward by martial law, but died
in prison.   He was of Surry County.

Whaly was quickly won to obay the commands of his Masters, especially such in whose servis he might expect to receve good Wages: forthwith drawing ou[t] his Men, amongst whom was Som Boys, all laden with the goods and last remanes of Coll. Bacons Estate, an[d] with all posible Speed (after a March of 30 Miles,) joyne[d] with Larance; where they Mustred in all (besides Co[n]cubines and Whores, Whaley haveing added his to the r[est]) about 300 Men and Boys. With which number, being [too] weake for to desend downe in to the heart of the Coun[trey,] (now clear'd of the Baconians, or possest by the other [par]ty) they march up higher in to New Kent, as far [as] Coll: Gouges, thinking (like the snow ball) to incr[ease by] there rouleing. But finding that in stead of increas[ing] there number decreast, and that the Moone of there fortune was now past the full, they broke up how[se-]keeping, every one shifting for him selfe, as his ta[ste?] or feares directed; Whaly and Larance makein[g a] cleare escape; but which way, or to what place, not knowne. Coll. Gouge and the rest went to there own[e?] Howses, from whence they were brought upon there [tri]all, aborde a Ship, at Tindells point; and from thence ([all] that were condem[ned]) sent to the place of Execution. [A]mongst which (of those that Suffer'd) were one Mr. H[all] Clarke of New Kent Court, a parson of Neate Ingenuo[us] parts, but adicted to a more then ordnary prying in[to] the Secrits of State affaires, which som yeares las[t pa]st wrought him in to the Governours [dis]pleasure. A[nd] which (tis posible) at this time was [not] forgott, [but] was lade to his charge upon his tria[ll(] which w[as by] a Court Martiall) to me is not visa[ble]. He nev[er hav]ing appear'd as a Soulder publickly, [yet] was co[ndemn'd] to be hang'd with 3 others by Coll: [Bacons?]s howse, [viz.] Major Page, (once My Sarvant, at his [fir]st coming [into] the Countrey), Capt. Yong, and one [Harris] . . . . . . rtiall to Bacons Army.

This execution being over, the Govern[our] began to be wery of the Water: and findeing that he be[g]an to gether Strength, resalves to go a shore. There w[as] Considerable Cordialls administred to him, in litle more then a weekes [ti]me, which he found had don him a grate deale of [g]ood; the Surrender of Wests point, Green spring, and [t]he death of the fore Mentioned Men. The place where [he] went on Shore,

was at Coll: Bacons, now clear'd [of] the Rebells by the hapey
removeall of Whally, after [he] had (by the aideing helpe of
his party) devouered [no] less then 2000 pounds (to my certaine
knowledg) [of] Coll. Bacons estate, the grater part in Store
goods.   [Here] he meets with Mr. Drummond, taken[1] the day
be[fore] in New Kent, where he had absconded, ever since [th]e
brakeing up howse keepeing at Coll: Gouges.   The [Govern]our
. . . . . . a more then ordnary gladness for to [see h]im, which
(as he saide) did him more good then the [sigh]t of his owne
Brother.   If the Governour was soe [glad] to see Drummon,
Drommon was no less sad to see [his h]onour, the sight of
whom (with out the help of an As[trol]egr) might inform him
what death he should [die,] and that he had not many days to
live.   That night [he] was sent aborde a Ship in Irons, while
the Governour [re]moved the next day in his Coach to Mr Brays,
a [jour]nye of some 5 Miles.   The next day after, being Sater-
[day,] Drummond was, by a party of Horss (who recev[ed him]
at Coll: Bacons) convayed to his tryall: In his way [thi]ther
he complained very much that his Irons hurt [him], and that
his fine Cloake, as he called it, a green- . . . . . . for the H[a]ng-
man had taken his fur'd Coate from [him,] (a bad presage) did
much hinder him in his way.   [When?] proffer'd [a h]orss, to
ride, he refused, and sade he [would] com to . . . . . . e to his
port before he was preparde [wi]th his Anc[hor]: ading that he
did very much feare [Sir Wil]liam w[ould] not al[low h]im time
to put of his dir[ty cl]othes b[efore] he went to lye downe upon
his ev[en]ing b[e]d.   [He s]aide, welcom be the grace of God,
for [it would clea]nse him from all his filth and pollution.   He
ex[pressed] abundance of thankes for being permitted to res[t
hi]m selfe upon the Roade, while he tooke a pipe of Tobacco.
He discoursed very much with that parson who comm[anded]
his gard concerning the late troubles, affirming that he was
wholly innocent of those. . . . . .[2]

[1] Drummond was taken January 14, 1677.

[2] By the 24th the rebellion was entirely suppressed, and Berkeley was back
at Green Spring before the 27th. On the 29th the English commissioners, Berry
and Moryson, arrived on the *Bristol* in James River.

A TRUE NARRATIVE OF THE LATE REBELLION IN VIRGINIA, BY THE ROYAL COMMISSIONERS, 1677

INTRODUCTION

THE news of the uprising in Virginia reached England in September, 1676, and immediately steps were taken to meet the emergency. At first, the plans of the British authorities went no further than the recall of Berkeley, and the appointment of a successor with power to exercise martial law and grant pardons. But soon it became evident that a special commission must be sent over to settle the affairs of the colony; and as disturbing rumors of the extent of the rebellion continued to come in, the decision was reached to send over also a body of English troops. The members of the commission, as finally made up, were Captain Sir John Berry, in charge of the fleet, Colonel Herbert Jeffreys, in command of the troops, with a commission to succeed Berkeley as governor, and Francis Moryson, a former acting governor of the colony and at this time its agent in England.

Captain Sir John Berry (1635–1690) was a Devonshire man who went to sea early in the merchant service, and in 1663 entered the navy. He served in the West Indies, 1665–1668; in the Mediterranean against the Barbary pirates, 1668–1671; he was knighted in 1672, and rose to the rank of vice-admiral in 1683. Later he became one of the Navy Commissioners.

Colonel Herbert Jeffreys was a relative of Alderman John Jeffreys, of Bread Street Ward, London. The alderman was a friend of Sir Joseph Williamson, secretary of state, and, though not a relative, had aided young George Jeffreys, later the chief justice and chancellor, when a struggling barrister in London. As the Duke of Monmouth was at this time captain-general of the forces, it is quite possible that Herbert

Jeffreys owed his advancement as colonel and commander of the land forces to these connections. He was accompanied to Virginia by his son, John Jeffreys, as ensign in one of the companies. His commission as governor was dated November 11, 1676, and he succeeded Berkeley on the latter's departure in April, 1677. He died December 17, 1678.

Francis Moryson served as major in the royal army during the Civil War, and came to Virginia in 1649. He was speaker of the House of Burgesses, 1655–1656, and on July 10, 1661, was chosen by governor and council to take Berkeley's place on the latter's departure for England. This position as acting governor he held until Berkeley's return in November, 1662. During the following year he was commander of the fort at Point Comfort, after which he was granted leave of absence for three years. With Thomas Ludwell and Major-General Robert Smith he was sent to England to secure the repeal of the grant to Arlington and Culpeper, and to obtain a charter for the colony. He returned to Virginia as one of the commissioners in January, 1677, but left the colony permanently in July of the same year. He was a grandson of Thomas Moryson, of Tooley Park, Leicestershire, and a nephew of Fynes Moryson, the traveller. His father, Sir Richard Moryson, had a long and honorable career in Ireland.

Instructions to the commissioners were issued October 3 and repeated November 11, but the business of gathering and victualling the troops and of providing for their transportation to Virginia was long delayed.

The fleet consisted of three ships of war, the *Bristol*, *Rose*, and *Dartmouth*, and eight hired merchantmen, carrying altogether more than eleven hundred officers and men, chiefly land forces. Sir John Berry and Francis Moryson finally got away with the *Bristol* on November 24, the *Dartmouth* and the merchant ships followed on Sunday, December 3, and the *Rose*, delayed by running aground and damaging her rudder, left a day later. After a tedious voyage of ten weeks, the *Bristol* arrived in James River, January 29, 1677, the *Dartmouth*, February 1, and the others between that date and the 14th.

Berry and Moryson at first issued their instructions from the *Bristol*, but some time before February 11, after Berkeley had refused to receive them into his house, they took up their residence with Colonel Thomas Swann, at Swann's Point, nearly opposite the ruins of Jamestown. There was no other house within four or five miles. They had already communicated from the *Bristol* with Governor Berkeley, whom they visited formally on the 12th, and had sent orders to the sheriffs to obtain from the localities statements of complaints and grievances. Sessions were held on Mondays, Wednesdays, and Fridays for receiving and examining these statements, which were to be sent sealed and signed by such as had taken oath and were prepared to prove their charges. On February 29 the commissioners sent a letter to the House of Burgesses, which had assembled at Green Spring on the 20th, urging peace with the Indians, curtailment of salaries and other public expenses, and a lowering of charges by keepers of ordinaries. They also interrogated many private individuals who came to Swann's Point, established a commission for inquiring into delinquents' estates, sat as a court of oyer and terminer for the trial of the most notorious rebels, and in May met the Indian chiefs at the soldiers' camp in Middle Plantation (now Williamsburg) and made treaties with them. They also provided for the soldiers, a difficult matter as the country was desolate and ruined, the ground in February covered with snow, and the people of the colony wholly averse to any system of quartering.

The relations of the commissioners with Berkeley, at first moderately friendly, eventually became very strained. The old governor, after many delays, sailed for England, probably on April 20, with Captain Larrimore in the *Rebecca*, and after a disagreeable voyage, which undoubtedly had a disastrous effect on the condition of his health, reached England, where he died in August of the same year. The animosity which Berkeley felt for the commissioners was shared by his friends, Philip Ludwell, Hill, Beverley, and Hartwell, all of whom were more or less the objects of attack in the local complaints. Notwithstanding a manifest desire of the commissioners to be fair, their letters and reports reveal their dislike of these men and their conviction that all of them were either responsible for the revolt or had taken advantage of its failure to wreak a harsh vengeance on members of the defeated party.

The final report of the commissioners was drawn up in England after the return of Berry and Moryson, in July, and was presented to the Privy Council in October. Two copies of this report exist, one among the Colonial Office Papers in the Public Record Office, *C. O.* class 5: 1371, and the other in the Pepysian Library, Magdalene College, Cambridge, among the manuscripts of Samuel Pepys, who as secretary to the Board of Admiralty had much to do with the despatch of the expedition. Both are in the handwriting of the secretary of the commission, Samuel Wiseman. The volumes in which these copies are to be found contain, in addition, large numbers of copies of letters and papers written or received by the commissioners, and therefore constitute a kind of entry book of business done. Though in arrangement and content these two volumes differ somewhat, the most important item, "A Narrative of the Rise, Progress, and Cessation of the late Rebellion in Virginia, by His Majesty's Commissioners," is the same in both. This narrative has been printed in the *Virginia Magazine of History and Biography*, IV. 119–154, from a copy of the version in the Public Record Office. This printed text has been at certain points compared with the copy in the Pepysian Library for the purpose of this work.

A TRUE NARRATIVE OF THE LATE REBELLION IN VIRGINIA, BY THE ROYAL COMMISSIONERS, 1677

A True Narrative of the Rise, Progresse, and Cessation of the Late Rebellion in Virginia, Most Humbly and Impartially Reported by his Majestyes Commissioners Appointed to Enquire into the Affaires of the Said Colony.

In all due observance of his Most Sacred Majesties commands, wee have imployed our best endeavours to informe ourselves (for his Royal Satisffaction) by the most knowing, credible and indifferent Persons in Virginia of the true state of affairs in that his Majestyes Colony, and of such other matters as occasioned the late unhappy Divisions, Distractions and Disorders among the People there; which as farr as wee can possibly collect from a strict Inquiry, observation, examination and the most probable impartial Reports by us made and received during our stay upon the Place, seems to take its original Rise, as followeth, *vizt*:

Few or none had bin the Damages sustained by the English from the Indians, other than occasionally had happen'd sometimes upon private quarells and provocations, untill in July, 1675, certain Doegs and Susquahanok Indians on Maryland side, stealing some Hoggs from the English at Potomake on the Virginia shore (as the River divides the same), were pursued by the English in a Boate, beaten or kill'd and the hoggs retaken from them; whereupon the Indians repairing to their owne Towne, report it to their Superiors, and how that one Mathewes (whose hoggs they had taken) had before abused and cheated them, in not paying them for such Indian trucke as he had formerly bought of them, and that they took his hogs for Satisfaction. Upon this (to be Reveng'd on Mathews) a warr Captain with some Indians came over to Potomake

105

and killed two of Mathewes his servants, and came also a
second time and kill'd his sonne.

It happen'd hereupon that Major George Brent and Col.
George Mason pursued some of the same Indians into Maryland, and marching directly up to the Indian Towne with a
Party of 30 Virginians came to a certaine House and there
killed an Indian King and 10 of his men upon the place; the
rest of the Indians fled for their lives. On this occasion the
Governor of Maryland writes a Letter to Sir Wm. Berkeley,
complayning of this rash action and intrusion of the Virginians
on his Province without his leave or knowledge, the Indians
and them being at that time in Peace. By what authority
Brent and Mason went over into Maryland and kill'd those
Indians is an Article of Inquiry in the Rappahanock Grievances and the supposed originall cause of the many murders
that ensued in that county as themselves complaine.

The Indians persisting to Revenge themselves Inforted[1]
in Maryland and now began to be bold and formidable to the
English who Besieged them; their Boldness and daring behavior of late tymes and their promptnesse to Fire arms,
being (indeed) wonderfull, over what they seem'd formerly
indued with, which doubtlesse was of some advantage extraordinary to them considering their Small Body, the Virginians
and Marylanders that Besieged them being said to make a
neer a thousand men. The siege held 7 weekes, during which
tyme the English lost 50 men, besides some Horses which
the Indians tooke, and serv'd themselves to subsist on. But
Provisions growing very scarce with them during this siege
the Indians sent out 5 greate men to Treate of Peace, who were
not Permitted to return to the Fort, but being kept Prisoners
Some tyme were at last murdered by the English.

At length (whether through negligence or cowardize) the
Indians made theire escape through the English, with all
their wives, children and goods of value, wounding and killing some at their sally and going off. After which the English
returning (as Report Saith), the Marylanders composed a
Peace with the Salvages, and soe diverted the warr from themselves.

As yet the General Peace and Government of Virginia

[1] Built themselves a fort.

continued undisturb'd, onely some ignorant People grumbl'd at the 60 *lb*. of Tob. p. pole,[1] that necessary Tax, raised at two paym'ts to take off the Patents granted to the Lord Arlington and Lord Culpepper and the Earl of St. Albans and Lord Berkly etc.

But about the beginning of January, 1675–6, a Party of those abused Susquahanocks in Revenge of the Maryland businesse came suddainly down upon the weak Plantations at the head of Rappahanock and Potomaque and killed at one time 36 persons and then immediately (as their Custome is) ran off into the woods.

Noe sooner was this Intelligence brought to the Governour but he immediately called a court and ordered a competent force of horse and foot to pursue the Murderers under the Comand of Sir Henry Chicheley and some other Gentlemen of the County of Rappahanock, giving them full Power by Comission to make Peace or Warr. But the men being ready to march out upon this Service the Governor on a suddaine recalls this comission, Causes the men to be disbanded, and without any effectual course being taken for present Preservation, referrs all to the next assembly; in the meantime leaving the Poore Inhabitants under continual and deadly feares and terrors of their Lives.

In soe much that in the upper Parts of the Parish of Citternborne[2] in Rappahanock w'ch consisted of 71 Plantations, on the 24th of Jan., 1675–6, by the 10th of Febr following was reduced to eleven what with those that ran away into the heart of the country, and such as stay'd and were cut off by the Enemy.

The assembly mett to consult for the Safety and defence of the Country ag't the Incursions and destructions of the Indians, dayly Comitted upon the Inhabitants of Virginia, there

[1] A poll-tax was the chief form of direct taxation in the colony. By the poorer class of the population it was deemed unjust, as bearing more heavily on them than on the rich landowners. The tax here referred to was levied to meet the expenses of the agents sent to England in 1675. The patents alluded to are that of 1669, granting the Northern Neck, or region between the Potomac and the Rappahannock, to the Earl of St. Albans, John Lord Berkeley, and others, and that of 1672, granting all Virginia for thirty-one years to Lords Arlington and Culpeper.

[2] Sittingbourne.

having beene within the space of about 12 months before, neer 300 Christian persons murder'd by the Indians Enemy. What care the Assembly tooke to prevent these massacres was onely to build Forts[1] at the heads of each River and on the Frontiers and confines of the country, for erecting of w'ch and maintaining Guards on them a heavie leavy was laid by act of Assembly on the People; throughout the country universally disliked before the name of that Imposture Bacon was heard of, as being a matter from which was expected great charge and little or noe security to the Inhabitants, the Scituation of the Virginian Plantations being invironed with thick woods, swamps and other covert, by the help of which the enemy might at their Pleasure make their approaches undiscover'd on the most secure of their habitations, as they have often done not onely on the Frontiers but in the very heart and centre of the country, their sculking nature being apt to use these advantages.

The Murders, Rapines and outrages of the Indians became soe much the more Barbarous, fierce and frequent, by how much the more they perceived the Public Preparations of the English against them, Prosecuting their mischiefs upon the extreem Plantations thereby forcing many to dessert them to their Ruines, and destroying those that adventur'd to stay behind.

The unsatisfied People finding themselves still lyable to the Indian Crueltyes, and the cryes of their wives and children growing grievous and intollerable to them, gave out in Speeches that they were resolved to Plant tobacco rather than pay the Tax for maintaining of Forts, and that the erecting of them was a great Grievance, Juggle and cheat, and of no more use or service to them than another Plantation with men at it, and that it was merely a Designe of the Grandees to engrosse all their Tobacco into their owne hands.

Thus the sense of this oppression and the dread of a comon approaching calamity made the giddy-headed multitude madd,

---

[1] In 1675–1676 a series of forts was erected at the upper waters of the rivers, along the frontier. Beginning with Stafford County on the Potomac, the forts, seven in all, extended southeasterly to the Nansemond. The expense and uselessness of these forts constituted a wide-spread grievance (*Cal. St. P. Col.*, 1674–1676, §§ 909, 939).

and precipitated them upon that rash overture of Running out upon the Indians themselves, at their owne voluntary charge and hazard of their Lives and Fortunes, onely they first by Petition humbly craved leave or comission to be ledd by any comander or comanders as the Governor should please to appoint over them to be their Chieftaine or Generall. But instead of Granting this Petition the Governor by Proclamation under great Penalty forbad the like Petitioning for the future.

This made the People jealous that the Governor for the lucre of the Beaver and otter trade etc. with the Indians, rather sought to protect the Indians than them, Since after publick Proclamation prohibiting all trade with the Indians (they complaine) hee privately gave comission to some of his Friendes to truck with them, and that those persons furnished the Indians with Powder, Shott etc. soe that they were better provided than his Majestye's Subjects.

The People of Charles City County (neer Merchants Hope) being denyed a Commission by the Governor although he was truly informed (as by a Letter of his to his Ma'tie he confesseth) of Several formidable Bodies of Indians coming downe on the heads of James River within 50 or 60 miles of the English Plantations, and knew not where the Storme would light, they begin to beat up drums for Volunteers to goe out against the Indians and soe continued Sundry dayes drawing into armes, the Magistrates being either soe remise or of the Same faction, that they suffered this disaster without contradiction or endeavouring to prevent soe dangerous a begining and going on.

The Rout being got together now wanted nor waited for nothing but one to head and lead them out on their design. It soe happen'd that one Nathaniel Bacon Junr, a person whose lost and desperate fortunes[1] had thrown him into that remote part of the world about 14 months before, and fram'd him fitt for such a purpose, as by the Sequel will appeare, which may make a short character of him no impertinent Digression.

[1] Very little is known of Bacon's earlier career, but some color is given to the statement regarding his "lost and desperate fortunes" by a suit brought in England after his death for the recovery of certain mortgaged properties. The papers in this suit are printed in the *Virginia Magazine*.

Hee was a person whose erratique fortune had carryed and shewne him many Forraigne Parts, and of no obscure Family. Upon his first comming into Virginia hee was made one of the Councill, the reason of that advancement (all on a suddain) being best known to the Governour, which honor made him the more considerable in the eye of the Vulgar, and gave some advantage to his pernicious designes. Hee was said to be about four or five and thirty yeares of age, indifferent tall but slender, blackhair'd and of an ominous, pensive, melancholly Aspect, of a pestilent and prevalent Logical discourse tending to atheisme in most companyes, not given to much talke, or to make suddain replyes, of a most imperious and dangerous hidden Pride of heart, despising the wisest of his neighbours for their Ignorance, and very ambitious and arrogant. But all these things lay hidd in him till after hee was a councillor, and untill he became powerfull and popular.

Now this man being in Company with one Crews,[1] Isham[2] and Bird,[3] who growing to a highth of Drinking and making the Sadnesse of the times their discourse, and the Fear they all lived in, because of the Susquahanocks who had settled a little above the Falls of James River, and comitted many murders upon them, among whom Bacon's overseer happen'd to be one, Crews and the rest persuaded Mr. Bacon to goe over and see the Soldiers on the other Side James river[4] and

[1] Captain James Crews, part owner of Turkey Island, was one of Bacon's most loyal friends. He was hanged at the site of the glass factory by Berkeley's order, January 24, 1677, after a trial by court martial at Green Spring.

[2] Henry Isham, jr., was the son of Henry Isham, who came to Virginia in 1656. He does not appear to have taken part in the rebellion, as he returned to England, where he died in 1679. He had a plantation in Charles City County called Doggams.

[3] William Byrd, son of John Byrd, a London goldsmith, came to Virginia shortly before the rebellion to take charge of property left him by his uncle, Thomas Stegg, a short distance below the Falls (Richmond). He was a neighbor of Bacon's, sympathized with him, and, as the text shows, urged him to take command of the insurgents at Jordan's Point. He wrote a brief account of the rebellion, defending Bacon. He was the father of a more famous son, Colonel William Byrd, of Westover.

[4] The people of Charles City County, terrified by the Indian attacks, sent a delegation to Governor Berkeley asking for permission to go out against the Indians. Berkeley refused the request. Angered at this refusal, a large body of volunteers of the county came together and encamped at Jordan's Point, below

to take a quantity of Rum with them to give the men to drinke, which they did, and (as Crews etc. had before laid the Plot with the Soldiers) they all at once in field shouted and cry'd out, a Bacon! a Bacon! a Bacon! w'ch taking Fire with his ambition and Spirit of Faction and Popularity, easily prevail'd on him to Resolve to head them, His Friends endeavouring to fix him the Faster to his Resolves by telling him that they would also goe along with him to take Revenge upon the Indians, and drink Damnation to their Soules to be true to him, and if hee could not obtain a Comission they would assist him as well and as much as if he had one; to which Bacon agreed.

This Forwardnesse of Bacons greatly cheer'd and animated the People, who looked upon him as the onely Patron of the Country and preserver of their Lives and Fortunes.

For he pretended and bosted what great Service hee would doe for the country, in destroying the Comon Enemy, securing their Lives and Estates, Libertyes, and such like fair frauds hee subtily and Secretly insinuated by his owne Instruments over all the country, which he seduced the Vulgar and most ignorant People to believe (two thirds of each county being of that Sort) Soe that theire whole hearts and hopes were set now upon Bacon.   Next he charges the Governour as negligent and wicked, treacherous and incapable, the Lawes and Taxes as unjust and oppressive and cryes up absolute necessity of redress.

Thus Bacon encouraged the Tumult and as the unquiet crowd follow and adhere to him, he listeth them as they come in upon a large paper, writing their name circular wise, that their Ring-Leaders might not be found out.

Having conjur'd them into this circle, given them Brandy to wind up the charme, and enjoyn'd them by an oth to stick fast together and to him, and the othe being administered, he went and infected New Kent County ripe for Rebellion.

Bacon having gott about 300 men together in armes prepared to goe out against the Indians, the Governour and his Friends endeavour to divert his designes, but cannot.

the mouth of the Appomattox. When Bacon accepted the leadership of this band he took the first important step in the rebellion. This event occurred in April, 1676.

Hee Proclames Bacon and his Followers Rebells and Muti-
neers for going forth against the Indians without a Commission, and (getting a company of Gentlemen together) the
Governor marcheth up to the Falls of James River to pursue
and take Bacon, or to Seize him at his Returne; but all in
vaine, For Bacon had gott over the River with his Forces and
hastning away into the woods, went directly and fell upon the
Indians and killed some of them who were our best Friends of
Indians and had fought ag't the Susquahanocks enemyes to
the English.

The Governour having issued forth a Proclamation importing noe commerce with the reputed Indian Enemyes, Besides
the cloggs and conditions w'ch were put on the Garrisons
placed or to be Placed in the new erected Forts, enjoyning
them not to make any attempt upon the Indians untill they
should first give the Governor an account thereof, and receive
orders from him therein, Put many to a stand, made the People expostulate and say how shall wee know our enemyes from
our Friends, are not the Indians all of a colour, and if wee must
not defend ourselves before they oppose us, they may take
their usual advantage of surprize, and soe destroy us ere wee
are capable of making any resistance; Soe that after all that
charge in erecting of Forts, after all the Troubles of the Con-
gresse[1] of our forces, after all their toyle and diligence used
in discovering the enemy (who are seldome to bee dealt with
but in their owne way of surprize) the very point of Execution
was to be determined of by a person residing in all likelihood
at least a 100 miles distant from the Place of action, to the
losse of opportunityes and utter discouragement of the soldiers and ourselves. Besides of what Security were these
Forts like to be, when the Indians cutt off and destroy'd divers
people within a small distance of the Forts and some of the
very Soldiers in them, and they not daring to stir out to relieve any that were in danger and distresse, themselves being
scarce secure upon the Place they were Posted on. Nor would
the people understand any distinction of Friendly Indians and
Indian Enemyes, for at that tyme it was impossible to distinguish one nation from another, they being deformed with
Paint of many colors, and at best (say they) who is hee that

[1] Bringing together.

can doe it, for there was never any open or free Trade among us that we might know them, But the whole Trade monopolized by the Governour and Grandees.

Soe the common cry and vogue of the Vulgar was, away with these Forts, away with these distinctions, wee will have warr with all Indians which come not in with their armes, and give Hostages for their Fidelity and to ayd against all others; we will spare none. and[1] wee must bee hang'd for Rebells for killing those that will destroy us, let them hang us, wee will venture that rather than lye at the mercy of a Barbarous Enemy, and be murdered as we are etc. Thus went the ruder sort raging and exclaiming agt. the Indians, expressing the calamity that befell New England by them.[2] While the Governour was in the Upper Parts to wait Bacon's returne the people below began to draw into armes, and to declare against the Forts. Hee to appease the comotions of the People leaves off that designe and comes immediately back to his own house, and caused at his returne the Surry and other Forts to be forthwith dismantled, and dissolving the assembly[3] that enacted them, gave the country a free new election, which new assembly were to be for the Settlement of the then distracted condition of Virginia.

At this new election (such was the Prevalency of Bacon's Party) that they chose instead of Freeholders, Free men that had but lately crept out of the condition of Servants[4] (which were never before Eligible) for their Burgesses and such as were eminent abettors to Bacon, and for faction and ignorance fitt Representatives of those that chose them.

At the Same time Bacon being come back from his Indian march with a thousand braging lyes to the credulous Silly People of what feats he had perform'd, was by the Inhabitants

[1] The old "an," meaning "if."

[2] King Philip's War, 1675–1676.

[3] This assembly was dissolved March 7, 1676. The new assembly met on June 5. After it broke up on June 25, Bacon planned to call another to meet September 4, but this plan he never carried out.

[4] Until 1670 all freemen had a right to vote, but in that year the franchise was restricted to freeholders and housekeepers. Before 1676 a few indentured servants, having served their time and acquired a small property, had become freeholders and sat in the House of Burgesses, so that the statement in the text is incorrect.

of the county of Henrico chosen a Burgess, as was also Crews for the Same county.

The assembly being mett Bacon comes down in a sloope to James Towne. But the People being very Fond of him, would not trust his person without a Guard, fearing some violence should be offered him by the Governour for what hee had already acted against his will, and Soe sent Forty armed men along in the Sloope with Bacon, coming somewhat neerer to Towne than Swanns Point dropt anchor and sent (as tis said) on Shore to the Governour to know if he might in safety come on shore, and sett as a Member etc. What answer was return'd we have not heard, onely what the Governor caused to be given him from the great guns that fired at the Sloope from the Towne Fort, soe that having gott his Sloope out of Gunshott, he lay higher up the River, and in the night tyme with a party of his men ventured on shore, and having had some conference (at Laurances house) with Laurance and Drumond came off again undiscovered. Several Propositions were made and some boats sent off to apprehend him but could effect nothing. Bacon endeavours to make his Escape up the River. In this Juncture Capt. Thomas Gardner[1] Master of the Ship *Adam and Eve* being at Towne, having an order from the Governor to pursue and seize him, imediately got on Board his ship, and as Bacon returned up the River comanded his Sloope in by Firing at him from on Board, and soe tooke him and all his men Prisoners and brought them away to the Governor at Towne.

Bacon being delivered up Prisoner to the Governor[2] by Capt. Gardner, the Governor lifting up his hands and eyes said in the hearing of many people, "Now I behold the greatest

---

[1] Captain Thomas Gardner played an important part in upholding Berkeley's authority, as the continuation of the narrative shows. The action of the assembly in fining him £70 for seizing Bacon, and so violating the privilege of a burgess, and for causing the loss of Bacon's sloop, "which perished on shore by the neglect of others," and in throwing him into jail where he remained until Berkeley returned from Accomac, was not approved by the Privy Council. The latter body not only authorized the Admiralty to pay Gardner's claim of £567 for freight, wages, and victuals, and a bonus of £50 as a reward for his services, but also recommended him for employment in the naval service on the first suitable occasion. (*Acts of the Privy Council, Colonial*, I., §§ 1183, 1186, 1253, 1286.)

[2] Bacon was delivered to the governor on June 8.

Rebell that ever was in Virginia," who (with a dejected look) made noe Reply, till after a short pause the Governour ask'd Bacon these words: "Sir, doe you continue to be a Gentleman, and may I take your word? if soe you are at Liberty upon your owne parrol."

Bacon feignes a most deep sense of shame and sorrow for his Guilt, and expresses the greatest kind of obligacion to Gratitude towards the Governour imaginable. And to make it looke the more reall and sincere drew up an humble Submission for and acknowledgem't of his soe late crimes and disobedience, imploring thereby the Governor's Pardon and Favor, which Bacon being in readynesse to Present on his coming before the Governor hee told the Councill then Sitting, "Now you shall see a Penitent Sinner."

Whereupon Bacon in very humble manner and with many low bowings of his Body approacht the Governor and on his knee gave up his Parasiticall Paper into the Governor's hands, and soe withdrew himself.

After a short while hee was sent for in againe and had his pardon confirmed to him, Is restor'd into favor and readmitted into the councell, to the wonder of all men.

Now Capt. Gardner instead of a Reward for the Service hee performed in taking and bringing away Bacon Prisoner was suffered to be fined 70 lb. damage for seizing him and the Sloope, although Capt. Gardner had discharged himself of her, the sd sloope being afterwards by a storme drove on shore and lost.*

However soe powerfull (it seems) was Bacon's interest in this new assembly that he procured a Public order to passe ag't Gardner for the payment of the 70 lb. where upon he threw Gardner into goale till he found Security for his Enlargement. But when they understand that the Governor had not onely sett him free, but readmitted him into the Councill, with Promise also of a commission to be given him to goe out against the Indians, the People were so well pacified for the present as that every man with great gladnesse return'd to his owne home.

* It is a wonder Sir Wm. Berkeley (being then in Towne) did not protect or preserve a Person he had imploy'd in so signal a Service. (Marginal note in original.)

Bacon attending at Towne for a Comission (w'ch the Governor is said to have promised him) and being delayed or putt off, was secretly whispered to by some of his Friends that those delayes would endanger his Life, and that if speedily he endeavour'd not to prevent it, there was a conspiracy to murder him on such a night; upon w'ch hee privately leaves the Towne.   Now whether this was onely a rais'd rumor of Bacon's, or a reall truth wee cannot determine, but being rais'd after Bacon was gone we suppose it false.

Hee no sooner was come to the upper Parts of James River, but the impatient people run to him to ask how affairs Stood, exclaiming still more and more against the Indians, and desired to know if he had yet a comission, and understanding he had or could not obtaine any, they began to sett up their throats in one comon kry of othes and curses and cry'd out aloud that they would either have a comission for Bacon that they might serve under his conduct or else they would pull downe the Towne or doe worse to some if they had it not, and if Bacon would goe but with them they would gett him a commission.   Thus the Raging Tumult came downe to Towne (Sitting the assembly) and Bacon at the head of them, having entred the Towne, hee Seises and secures the Principal Places and avenues, setts Sentinells and sends forth scouts, so that noe Place could bee more Securely guarded.

Having soe done, hee drawes up all his men in armes against the State house where the Governour councell and Burgesses were then assembled and Sitting, and sends in to the Assembly to know if now they would grant him a commission, which Sr. Wm. Berkeley utterly refused, and rising from his chair of judicature came downe to Bacon, and told him to his Face and before all his men that hee was a Rebell and a Traytor etc. and should have noe commission, and uncovering his naked Bosome before him, required that some of his men might shoot him, before ever he would be drawne to signe or consent to a commission for such a Rebell as Bacon, "Noe" (said the Governor) "lett us first try and end the difference singly between ourselves," and offer'd to measure swords with him; all the answer Bacon gave the Governor was, "Sir, I came not, nor intend to hurt a haire of your honor's head, and for your sword your Honor may please to putt it up, it shall rust in the scab-

bard before ever I shall desire you to drawe it. I come for a
commission against the Heathen who dayly inhumanely murder us and spill our Brethrens Blood, and noe care is taken to
prevent it," adding, "God damne my Blood, I came for a commission, and a commission I will have before I goe," and turning to his soldiers, said "Make ready and Present," which they
all did. Some of the Burgesses looking out at the windows and
seeing the soldiers in that posture of Firing cry'd out to them,
"For God's sake hold your handes and forebear a little, and
you shall have what you please."[1] Much hurrying, solicita-
tion and importunity is used on all sides to the Governor to
grant Bacon a commission. At last the Governor consents,
a commission is drawne up and sent him, he dislikes it, they
pray him to draw or direct one himself and the Governour
should signe it. Whereupon Bacon drawes up the contents
of a commission according to his owne mind, and returnes it
to the Clerke, to prepare one by, which is done, liked of and
received.

After the Governor had signed the Principall Commission
to Bacon, hee is also pleas'd to signe 30 commissions more
[Blanke] for officers that were to serve under him.

But Bacon finding occasion for more, sent to Sir William
Berkley to signe others also, who said hee had signed enough
already, and bid him signe the rest himself if hee would.

The assembly also passe orders to raise or presse 1000 men,
and to raise Provisions etc. for this intended service ag't the
Indians wherein severell of the councell and assembly-members
were concern'd and acted in the promoting this designe, encouraging others to list themselves into Bacon's service, and
particularly one Ballard[2] who endeavoure'd to perswade some

---

[1] This dramatic scene took place on Saturday, June 24. On the Monday
following Bacon and his men marched out of town.

[2] Colonel Thomas Ballard, of Jamestown. He is described by Jeffreys as
"a fellow of a turbulent, mutinous spirit, yet one that knows how to be as humble
and penitent as insolent and rebellious, and for these virtues is called by Sir
William Berkeley his Mary Magdalene, but was before Bacon's chief trumpet,
parasite, subscriber, and giver of his unlawful oath and an eminent abetter of the
late rebellion" (Cal. St. P. Col., 1677–1680, § 293). Ballard seems to have been
particularly influential in persuading the people to take Bacon's "unlawful"
oath of August 3. He was a councillor in 1670 and 1677, was excluded in the
latter year, but became speaker in 1680 and 1684.

(who scrupled the Legality of Bacon's commission) that it was fairly and freely granted by Governor, Councill and Burgesses, this Ballard being one of the councill, and of those that both tooke and administer'd Bacon's Oath.

There was also an act of Indempnity pass'd to Bacon and his party who committed the offence on the assembly, and a Publick Letter of applause and approbation of Bacon's actions and Loyalty writ to the King and signed by the Governor and assembly. Which upon the Breaking up of this Session were sent abroad and read among the Ignorant People who believ'd thereby that all was well and nothing coming forth of a long time to quash, contradict or disowne this Commission, Indempnity, Lre etc. granted to Bacon, But on the contrary other comissions of the Governors own signing and seal'd with the Publick seal of the Colony coming to them, they were the more easily inclined to swallow down so fair a bait not seeing Rebellion at the end of it, and most men grew ambitious of the service as thinking it both safe and for the Publick good as having the approbation of the Governor and assembly, at least there yet appeared nothing to the contrary nor of a good while after.

Severall Volunteers and Reformadoes come in to list themselves under Bacon, and many were press'd into this service, till at last having his complement of men, and all things else being in readynesse according as the Assembly had provided for this expedition, A general Rendezvous is appointed by Bacon at the Falls of James River, where all things being well appointed for the march, Bacon makes a speech to his men, Assuring them all of his Loyalty to his Prince, declaring to them that his designe was no other than merely to serve his King and country and to cleere all suspicion of the contrary (if any were amongst them) by what had bin by him already acted or Proclamed against him, as also of what he said about the procuring his comission; hee urges to them the reasons that induced it, the necessity of that tyme that compell'd him, the negligence and coldnesse of others that hated him and the cryes of his Brethrens blood that alarm'd and waken'd him to this Publique revenge, using what motives hee could to raise up the spirits of his men. And finally before them all tooke the oath of allegiance and supremacy, willing his soldiers also to doe the like, which having freely comply'd with Hee drew up an oath of Fidelity to himselfe, which hee (as their head and Generall) required them to take; it comprehended the following contents or heads:

That they should not conceale any Plot or conspiracy of hurt against his Person, but immediately reveale the same to him or such others by whome he might come to the knowledge of it.

That if any harme or damage was intended towards any of his men, whether by surprizal or otherwise, or any conference used, or councell kept about the Same, to discover it.

That noe commerce or correspondence should be had with the Heathen, and if any knowne, to discover it.

That no news or information should be sent out least himself or army by such intelligence should be endanger'd either in Repute or otherwise.

All Councells, Plotts and conspiracyes known of the Heathen, to discover them, etc.

Just now (even on the very night before their going out on the intended march ag't the Indians) a messenger comes Post from Gloster Countyes bringing Intelligence to Bacon, that the Governor was there endeavouring to raise Forces to come and surprize him and his men and that hee was resolved by Force to take his extorted commission away from him, For that the whole county had Petitioned ag't him as a Rebell and a Traytor etc.

This amusing[1] message was noe sooner brought to Bacon, but immediately he causes the Drums to Beat and Trumpett to Sound for calling his men together to whome he spake after this manner:

Gentlemen and Fellow Soldiers: The Newes just now brought mee may not a little startle you as well as myselfe. But seeing it is not altogether unexpected, wee may the better beare it and provide our remedies. The Governour is now in Gloster County endeavouring to raise Forces against us, having Declared us Rebells and Traytors: if true, crimes indeed too great for Pardon; our consciences herein are our best witnesses, and theres soe conscious, as like cowards therefore they will not have the courage to face us. It is Revenge that hurryes them on without regard to the Peoples Safety,

---

[1] "Amusing" in the old sense of "misleading."

and had rather wee should be murder'd and our ghosts sent to our Slaughter'd country-men by their actings, than wee live to hinder them of their Interest with the heathen, and preserve the remaining part of our Fellow Subjects from their crueltyes. Now then wee must bee forced to turne our swords to our owne defence, or expose our-selves to their Mercyes, or Fortune of the woodes, whilest his majes-tyes country here lyes in Bloode and Wasting (like a candle) at both ends. How Incapable wee may be made (if wee should proceede) through Sicknesse, want of Provisions, Slaughter, wounds lesse or more, none of us is void of the Sense hereof.

Therefore while wee are sound at heart, unwearyed and not receiving damage by the fate of Warr, lett us descend to know the reasons why such Proceedings are used against us, That those whome they have raised for their Defence, to Preserve them against the Fury of the Heathen, they should thus seeke to Destroy, and to Betray our Lives whome they raised to Preserve theirs. If ever such Treachery was heard of, such wickednesse and inhumanity (and call all the former ages to Witnesse) and if any, that they suf-fered in like nature as wee are like by the sword and Ruines of warr.

But they are all damn'd Cowards, and you shall see they will not dare to meete us in the Field to try the Justnesse of our cause and soe wee will downe to them etc.

To which they all cry'd "Amen, amen, wee are all ready and will rather die in the Field than be hang'd like Roges, or Perish in the woods, expos'd to the Favours of the mercylesse Indians."

How unhappy, unsuccessfull and how fatale this avocation prov'd the consequence will but too Plainly Shewe. For Bacon (then the hopes of the People) was just upon the Point of marching out, and nothing could have call'd him back, or turn'd the sword of a civil warr into the heart and bowels of the country but soe ill-tymed a Project as this Prov'd.

And although it is asserted by some that at this tyme there was a Paper publickly read to the People that the Governor designed onely to raise a Partie to goe out against the Indians and not against Bacon offering not onely their Estates, But by a solemne oath to bind and confirme this Pretention to the People, yet this did noe feates with the People, or tooke any other impression on them, save onely that it still more con-firmed that Bacons cause was not onely as Good as the Gov-ernors (when their Pretensions were now equally ag't the Indians) But also that the commission granted him was faire and legall, seeing he protested not to prosecute or goe against him for it.

Now in vaine the Governor attempts raising a force against Bacon, and although the Industry and endeavors hee used to effect it was great, yet at this Juncture it was impossible, for Bacon at this tyme was so much the hopes and Darling of the people that the Governor's interest prov'd but weake, and his Friends so very few that he grew sick of the Essay and with very Griefe and sadnesse of Spirit for soe bad successe (as is said) Fainted away on Horseback in the Field,* and hearing of Bacons being on his march to Gloster, hee was feigne to fly thence to Accomack, leaving now the Seat of the Government lyable to the Usurpation of that Rebell who had then also the Militia of the country in his hands to inforce his owne arbitrary Impositions on the People, as hee afterwards did at his coming to Gloster. Where being arrived with his Forces, hee findes the Governour fled, and (without more adoe) the Field his owne; soe leading his men to Middle-Plantacion (the very heart and centre of the country) hee there for some time Quarters them. Then issues forth Proclamation inviting the Gentlemen of Virginia to come in and consult with him for the present Settlement of that his Ma'tyes distracted Colony to Preserve its future Peace, and advance the effectual Prosecuting of the Indian warr. Severall gentlemen appearing on this Summons of Bacons at Middle-Plantation, mett him at one Capt. Thorps,[1] where (under a great guard) were Severall persons confin'd. After a long debate, pro and con, a mischievous writing was drawne up and produced by Bacon, unto

---

* By this it is plain that the Governor was put upon this successless Essay by the few contrivers of Gloster Petition, for had it been the address of the whole county (as pretended) they would doubtlesse all have own'd it and stood by the Governor and not so basely abandoned him and his cause, but there was not one subscriber to this Petition. (Marginal note in the original.)

[1] Captain Otho Thorp of York County was a justice in 1674, and a major in the militia in 1680. He afterward returned to England, where he died in 1687. At his house in Middle Plantation Bacon held his convention of August 3, which marked the beginning of the actual rebellion against Berkeley's authority, and there, too, was held the assembly that met on February 20, 1677. Thorp suffered much from the rebellion. At first he identified himself with the movement, by signing a paper, declared to have been "extracted by menaces and obtained

which (the doors of the house being fast lock'd on them) many by threats, Force and Feare were feigne to subscribe. The tenor of the oath[1] is as follows:

1. You are to oppose what Forces shall be sent out of England by his Majesty against mee, till such tyme I have acquainted the King with the state of this country, and have had an answer.

2. You shall sweare that what the Governor and councill have acted is illegal and destructive to the country, and what I have done is according to the Lawes of England.

3. You shall sweare from your hearts that my comission is lawfull and legally obtained.

4. You shall sweare to divulge what you shall heare at any time spoken against mee.

5. You shall keepe my secrets, and not discover them to any person.

Copyes of this oath are sent to all or most of the countyes of Virginia, and by the Magistrates and others of the respective Precincts administered to the People, which none (or very few) for feare or Force durst or did refuse. To Perfect all at once, and to make all secure, which soe long as the Governour was at Liberty they thought could not bee, But that hee would still seeke means whereby to regaine his Place and authority, and not to be soe basely extruded that high Trust lawfully residing in him, They take Capt. Larrimore's ship by surprize, man her with 200 men and Guns to goe to Accomack and seize the Governour, Pretending to send him home Prisoner to his Ma'tie for to receive Tryall of his demeritts towards his Majesties subjects of Virginia, and for the likely losse of that Colony for want of due and tymely care for the Preservation of it against the dayly Incursions and Encroachments of the Native Salvages, who had destroy'd and laid wast the

by Giles Bland, when Thorp was by drink bereaved of his common reason," but afterward refused to take up arms in the insurgent cause. As a result he and his wife were imprisoned by Bacon and plundered of property worth £1200, while Berkeley stripped him of the remainder of his estate (*Virginia Magazine*, V. 67; *Acts P. C. Col.*, I., § 1189).

[1] Three oaths were exacted by Bacon: one shortly after June 25 at the rendezvous, Falls of James River, just before the march against the Indians; the second, the "illegal" oath, at Middle Plantation; and the third, the same as the second, taken by the Gloucester men at Tindall's Point in October.

Plantations and cutt of many of the Familyes of the English etc.

The Comand of which charge was by Bacon comitted to one Carver a valient, Stout seaman and Gyles Bland (both since executed) onely Mr. Bacon Putting more confidence in Carver had chiefly intrusted Carver on this designe by a Private Comission w'ch Bland knew not of but supposed they had both equal Power.

Things thus agitated Bacon reassumes his first designes of marching out against the Indians, Imprisoning some before hee went out, others hee had of a long continuance in hold, who in the beginning thought and try'd to divert his designes; othersome hee Subtly brought over to his Side and such whose liberty (if left behind) hee jealously suspected might raise any party ag't him in his absence, hee tooke along with him.

Bacon goes up again to the Falls of James River, where hee bestirs himself lustily in order to a speedy march against the Indians, in prosecution of his first pretentions w'ch were ag't the Occannechees and Susquahannocks. From the Falls of James River hee marcheth over to the Freshes of Yorke[1] to pursue the Pamunkey Indians, whose propinquity and neighbourhood to the English and courses among them, was a Pretended reason to render the Rebells Suspicious of them, as being acquainted and knowing both of the manners, customes, and nature of our People, and the Strength, Situation and advantages of the country, and soe capable of doing of hurt and damage to the English, although it was well knowne to the whole country that the Queene of Pamunkey and her People had nere at any time betray'd or injuryed the English. But among the Vulgar it matters not whether they be Friends or Foes Soe they be Indians. Bacon being here mett with all the Northern Forces from Potomack, Rappahanock and those Parts under the comand of Col. Brent,[2] they joyne together and marching to the highest Plantations seated upon Yorke River, were there detained by a day or two's Raine, and for

---

[1] The parts of York River above tide-water.

[2] Giles Brent, a cousin of George Brent of Woodstock, was of Retirement plantation in Stafford County. He was the son of Giles Brent of Maryland and the "empress" of the Piscattoway Indians and he claimed the title to his mother's crown and sceptre. He received a captain's commission from Bacon,

fear of want of Provisions Bacon addresseth himself to the
Army and Speakes to them after this manner:

That hee feared the badnesse of the weather (which was like
to continue) would much hinder their expectations of meeting with
the enemy soe soone as otherwise they might the weather being good,
which would cause a second losse not to be helped or prevented at
present which hee feared would be in the want of Provisions. To
help which in tyme, and to lett them all know, for the future hee
would order but allowances, soe that (being not far out of the reach
of the settl'd Plantations) all those he gave full leave to returne, the
heate of whose courage and resolutions for the Suppressing of the
heathen, and revenge the Bloods of their Friends and acquaintances
they had shed, were not above and more than the particular regard
and care they had for theire Belly. Bidding them draw forth if any
such were, and be gone, for I am sure (said hee) where there shal be
occasion for such a fright, I shall find them the worst of cowards,
serving for number but not for service, and starve my best men,
who would beare the Brunt of all, and dishearten others of half
mettle from freely engaging etc.

Amongst which onely 3 withdrew, soe they were disarm'd
and sent in.

The bad weather abating he proceeds on his march and in
a short time falls into a Path of the Indians which lead to a
maine one which made him imagine himself to be neere their
main camp; but by the Scouts sent out for discovery, hee found
nothing more yet, than a continued large Path and woods,
which made them break the order of marching, and for expedition and conveniency to march at randome, soe continuing
all along till this Path brought them to a Point, on each Side
whereof and before it was a swamp; upon which Point the
Pamunkey Indians had severall cabbins.

Some Indian Scouts were sent out before for discovery (w'ch
were about 10 Indians for the service of Bacon's army) who
being espied by the contrary Party of Indians they lett them
come up soe nigh as to fire at them, which gave the alarme to

though but twenty-four years old, and accompanied him on his first expedition
against the Indians. Afterward, however, he withdrew with his body of four
hundred men and returned to the plantations. There he raised a force of a
thousand men and marched to Berkeley's assistance when besieged at Jamestown.

the English, who riding downe in great disorder and hast to
the Point (being about half a miles distance off) the Indians
broke to the very edge of the swamp, which prov'd so mirey
that Bacon and his men were presently at a ne plus ultra, so
that the mighty deale that was done at this tyme was onely
the taking of a little Indian child, and the killing an Indian
woman.

It chanced that the Queene of Pamunkey with severall of her
Principall Indians and others was not far off when this onset
happen'd and had notice of Bacon's approach on her Track of
which her owne scouts had made discovery to her, who leaving behind her all her goods and Indian corne vessels etc., and
as much as shee could to decline all occasion of offending the
English whom she ever so much loved and reverenced, privately obscured from them, charging her own Indians that if
they found the English coming upon them that they should
neither fire a gun nor draw an arrow upon them.

It soe happened in the Stieffling Pursuit that they light on
an old Indian woman that was the Queen's nurse, whom they
took Prisoner and hoped Shee would be their Guide to find out
those Indians that fled. But instead of directing them that
way she led them quite contrary, Soe that following her the
remainder of that and almost another day, perceiving themselves mislead by her and little likelihood of meeting with
them, Bacon gave command to his Soldiers to knock her in
the head, which they did, and they left her dead on the way.

They marching after this at random (yet hoping and aiming still to find them out) at last met with an Indian Path
against which led them to a main Swamp, where several nations of Indians lay encamped, and striking through Straight
of one of them fell in upon them, where the first that was taken
was a young woman belonging to the Nanjaticoe Indians, half
starved, and so not able to escape. The main of them fled
and upon search made after them they discovered and killed
two or three Indian men and as many women.

The tyme of the meeting of the new assembly (called
Bacon's assembly) now drawing nigh, he thought it expedient
to give the Starved and languishing expectations of the People a little relief and send some on purpose to give them an
account of their Proceedings and the hopes that they had of

destroying the Heathen, and that he would be with them with all possible Speede.

Now Bacon's high Pretences raised the People's hopes to the highest pitch and at the same time put him on a necessity of doing Something before he returned, which might not altogether fall short of his own Vaunting, but being hitherto disappointed, his army tyred, Murmuring, impatient, half starved, dissatisfied, he gives liberty to as many as would to return in with the foot he had ordered to march in before him, giving them two days' provisions to reach (if they could) the English Plantations; those that were dismissed being the Northern forces commanded by Colo. Brent. (The whole being now 400 men) with the rest he moves on hunting and beating the Swamps up and down, at last meets with an opening of a tract upon high land, which he follows so long that almost all his Provisions were spent, and forced to come to quarter allowances, and having led them far into the woods he makes a short halt and speaks thus to them:

Gentlemen,
The indefatigable Paines which hitherto wee have taken doth require abundantly better success than as yett wee have mett with. But there is nothing soe hard, but by Labour and Industry it may bee overcome, which makes me not without hope of obtaining my desires against the heathen in meeting with them to quit Scores for all their Barbarous crueltyes done us.

I had rather my carcase should lye rotting in the woodes, and never see English mans face againe in Virginia, than misse of doing that service the country expects from me, and I vowed to performe against these heathen, which should I returne not succesfull in some manner to damnifie and affright them wee should have them as much animated as the English discouraged, and my adversaryes to insult and reflect on mee; that my Defence of the country is but Pretended and not Reall and (as they already say) I have other Designs and make this but my Pretense and cloke. But that all shall see how devoted I am to it, considering the great charge the country is at in fitting mee forth and the hopes and expectation they have in mee, All you gentlemen that intend to abide with mee must resolve to undergoe all the hardshipps this wilde can afforde, dangers and successes and if need bee to eate chinkapins[1] and horseflesh before hee

---

[1] The chincapin is the dwarf chestnut.

returns. Which resolve I have taken therefore desire none but those which will so freely adventure, the other to Returne in, and for the better knowledge of them I will separate my campe some distance from them bound home.

Which done, and the next morning by an hour and half of the sun, the one marching on towards the Plantation, and the other on the Indian designe. They were not three hours seperated before the Rebell Bacon falls upon the Pamunkey Indians, who lay incamped beyond a small branch of a swamp or Run of water, having a swamp on the right hand, and a small swamp or run on the left of them, betweene which was a fine piece of champion[1] land, but full of thickett, small oke, saplings, chinkapin Bushes and Grape vines, which the Indians made their covert. As the onsett was given they did not at all oppose, but fled, being followed by Bacon and his Forces killing and taking them Prisoners, and looking for the Plunder of the Field which was Indian matts, Basketts, matchcotes, parcells of wampampeag and Roanoke (w'ch is their money) in Baggs, skins, Furrs, Pieces of Lynnen, Broad cloth, and divers sorts of English goods (w'ch the Queene had much value for),* 45 captives which upon sound of Trumpett was brought together and delivered in by order of Bacon; the Plunder and captives estimated noe lesse worth than 6 or 700, the Goodes being 3 horse loades.

The good Queen of Pamunky during this attaque to save her Life betooke herselfe to flight with onely one little Indian Boy of about 10 yeares old along with her, and when she was once coming back with designe to throw herself upon the mercy of the English, Shee happened to meet with a deade Indian woman lying in the way being one of her own nation; which struck such terror in the Queene that fearing their cruelty by that gastly example shee went on her first intended way into wild woodes where shee was lost and missing from her owne People fourteen dayes, all that tyme being Sustained alive onely by gnawing sometimes upon the legg of a terrapin,

[1] Champaign, level.

* The Indian Prisoners were some of them sold by Bacon and the rest disposed of by Sr. Wm. Berkeley, all but five w'ch were restored to the Queen by Ingram who was Bacon's Gen'll. (Marginal note in original.)

which the little Boy found in the woods and brought her when she was ready to dye for want of Foode, and of a great while had not Provisions for her support but noe necessity could incline her to adhere to Bacon's overtures.   While Bacon continued out upon this Indian Enterprize the Governour had the good fortune to retake Larrimore's Shipp from the Rebells with which they designed to seize the Governor and carry him home Prisoner to England; the manner of this reprisal was thus:

Carver with a party of men being gone on shore to treat with the Governor at Accomack, before w'ch Larrimore's ship lay, (the comand whereof Carver had usurped) and leaving onely Bland on board with a number of men to w'ch the seamen of the shipp were not inferior, Larrimore Sends a Letter to the Governour, to acquaint him how things stood on Board, and that if hee could send him off a party of Gentlemen in Boates hee would enter them all at the Gun room Ports, where having already secur'd the Enemyes armes, hee doubted not but to surprize the men and retake the shipp.

The Governor privately ordered off a party of his owne under the command of Col. Philip Ludwell[1] while he capitulated with Carver in dilatory manner to give his owne party tyme to get on Board, which they did, all things succeeding answerable to the design, Bland being taken together with the rest of the Rebells; soone after Carver parting with the Governor rowes on Board, they permitt the Boat to come so neere as that they might fire directly downe upon her, and soe they also comanded Carver on Board and secur'd him.   When hee saw this surprize hee storm'd, tore his haire off and curst, and exclaim'd at the cowardice of Bland that had betray'd and lost all their designes.

The Governor having regain'd this ship goes on Board and

[1] Colonel Philip Ludwell, brother of Thomas Ludwell, lived at Richneck, in James City County, near Middle Plantation. He came to Virginia about 1664 and soon rose to prominence, becoming one of the Green Spring faction of Berkeleyites.   His intimacy with the governor appears from the fact that he married (as her third husband) Berkeley's widow, Lady Frances, who had abetted her husband, the governor, against the English commissioners in 1677. Ludwell was of a hot temper, "rash and fiery," and was excluded from the council in 1679. He became governor of Carolina, 1689–1694, returned to England afterward, and died there.

in company with the ship *Adam and Eve* Capt. Gardner Comander 16 or 17 Sloopes and about 600 men in armes goes up to James Towne, which hee fortifies as well as he could and again Proclames Bacon and his Party Rebells and Traytors, threatening them with the utmost severityes of Law.

Upon this Bacon calls his few men together which upon a muster made a little after the last skirmish with the Indians (with Baggatiers[1] and all) were but 136 tyr'd men, and told them how the Governor intended to proceed against him and them.

But this rather animated and provoked new courage in them than any wise daunted them, soe that among other cheerfull expressions they cry'd out they would stand by him their Generall to the last.

He hearing such hearty expressions from tyred soldiers who embraced his service and refused the Plunder hee now offer'd them, was highly pleased and said to them:

Gentlemen and Fellow Soldiers, How am I transported with gladnesse to find you thus unanimous, Bold and daring, brave and Gallant; you have the victory before you fight, the conquest before battle. I know you can and dare fight, while they will lye in their Place of Refuge and dare not soe much as appeare in the Field before you: your hardynesse shall invite all the country along as wee march to come in and second you.

The Indians wee beare along with us shal be as soe many motives to cause Reliefe from every hand to be brought to you. The Ignomy of their actions cannot but soe reflect upon their spirits, as they will have noe courage left to fight you. I know you have the Prayers and wellwishes of all the People in Virginia, while the other are loaded with their curses.

Bacon in most incens'd manner Threathens to be revenged on the Governor and his party, swearing his soldiers to give noe quarter and professing to scorne to take any themselves, and soe in great fury marches on towards James Towne,[2] onely

---

[1] "Baggage-carriers," apparently.

[2] Bacon marched from New Kent County down the left bank of the Chickahominy to Green Spring, where Berkeley's house stood, and thence south to the clearing formerly known as Argall's Gift or Town, about a mile northwest of Jamestown. The lower half of this clearing was called Paspahegh Old Fields, and there Bacon made his last halt preparatory to attacking Jamestown.

halting a while about New Kent to gain some fresh Forces, and sending to the upper parts of James River for what they could assist him with.

Having increased his number to about 300 in all, hee proceeds directly to Towne, as hee marcheth the People on the high wayes coming forth Praying for his happiness and railing ag't the Governour and his party, and seeing the Indian captives which they led along as in a shew of Tryumph, gave him many thankes for his care and endeavours for their Preservation, bringing him forth Fruits and Victualls for his Soldiers, the women telling him if hee wanted assistance they would come themselves after him.

Intelligence coming to Bacon that the Governour had good in Towne a 1000 men well arm'd and resolute, "I shall see that," saith hee, "for I am now going to try them." Being told that there was a party of Horse of the Governors of abt. 60 Scouting out to observe his motion, hee smilingly answer'd hee feared them not coming soe neere him as to know how he did. But hee not too heedlesse of all reports nor in him Selfe to sure of their cowardice, drawes up his men in Green Spring Old Fields, hee tells them that if ever they will fight they will doe it now, before (saith hee) "I march up to their workes, having all the advantages of ground, places retreats, their men fresh and unwearied and what not advantages" (Saith Bacon) "to us soe few weake and Tyr'd.

"But I speake not this to discourage you, but to acquaint you (as you shall finde) what advantages they will neglect and loose, which" (sayes he) "if they had the courage to maintain that which they declare against us as Rebells, Traytors, etc., their allegiance would be but faintly Defended to lett us take that which they might command; come on, my hearts of gold, hee that dyes in the field lyes in the Bedd of honour." *

In the evening Bacon with his Small tyr'd Body of men, his Forlorne[1] marching some distance before, comes into Paspahayes old Fields and advancing on horseback himselfe on the Sandy Beech before the Towne comands the Trumpet to

---

* September 13th, 1676. The siege of James Towne. Note that Bacon's men had march'd that day betwixt 30 and 40 miles to come to James Towne. (Marginal note in original.)

[1] Vanguard.

sound, Fires his carbyne, dismounts, surveys the Ground and orders a French worke to be cast up.

All this night is spent in failing of Trees, Cutting of Bushes and throwing up Earth, that by the help of the moone light they had made their French before day, although they had but two axes and 2 spades in all to performe this work with.

About day-break next morning six of Bacons Soldiers ran up to the Pallasadees of the Towne and fired briskly upon the Guard, retreating Safely without any damage at first (as is reported) the Governor gave Comand that not a Gun should be fir'd ag't Bacon or his party upon paine of death, pretending to be loath to spill bloode and much more to be Beginner of it, Supposing the Rebells would hardly be soe audacious as to fire a gun against him, But that Bacon would rather have sent to him and sought his Reconciliation soe that some way or other might have bin found out for the Preventing of a Warr, to which the Governour is said to have shewne some Inclination upon the account of the service Bacon had performed (as he heard) against the Indian Enemy, and that he had brought severall Indian Prisoners along with him, and especially for that there were severall Ignorant People which were deluded and drawne into Bacon's Party and thought of noe other designe than the Indian Warr onely, and so knew not what they did.

But Bacon (pretending distrust of the Governor) was soe farr from all thought of a Treaty that hee animates his men against it, telling them that hee knew that party to be as Perfidious as cowardly, and that there was noe trust to be reposed in such, who thinke it noe Treachery by any wayes to Suppresse them, and for his tendernesse of Shedding Blood which the Governor pretends, and preventing a warr, sayes Bacon, "There are some here that know it to be no longer since than last weeke that hee himself comanded to be Fired against us by Boats which the Governor sent up and downe to places where the country's Provisions were kept for mainteinance of the Indian Warr, to fetch them away to support a warr amongst ourselves, and wounded some of us (which was done by Sorrell) which were against the designe of converting these stores to soe contrary a use and intention of what they were raised for by the People." Bacon moving downe towards the Towne

and the Shipps being brought before the Sandy Beach the
better to annoy the enemy in case of any attempt of theirs to
storme the Palassadoes, upon a signall given from the Towne
the Shipps fire their Great Gunns, and at the same tyme they
let fly their Small-shot from the Palassadoes. But that small
sconce[1] that Bacon had caused to be made in the night of
Trees, Bush and Earth (under w'ch they lay) soe defended
them that the shott did them noe damage at all, and was return'd back as fast from this little Fortresse. In the heat of
this Firing Bacon commands a party of his men to make every
one his Faggott and put it before his Breast and come and
lay them in order on top of the Trench on the outside and at
the end to enlarge and make good the Fortification, which
they did, and orders more spades to be gott, to helpe to make
it yet more defensible, and the better to observe their motion
ordered a constant sentinel in the daytime on top of a Brick
Chimney* (hard by) to discover from thence how the men in
Towne mounted and dismounted, Posted and reposted, drew
on and off, what number they were, and how they moved.
Hitherto their happen'd noe other action, than onely Firing
great and small Shott at distances.

But by their movings and drawings up about Towne,
Bacon understood they intended a Sally and accordingly pre-
pares to receive them, draw up his men to the most advantageous places he could, and now expected them (but they observ'd
to draw off againe for some tyme) and was resolved to enter
the Towne with them, as they retreated, as Bacon expected
and foretold they would do. In this Posture of expectation Bacon's Forces continued for a hour till the watchman
gave notice that they were drawne off againe in Towne, soe
upon this Bacon's Forces did soe too. Noe sooner were
they all on the Rebells Side gone off and squandered but all
on a sudden a Sally is made by the Governor's Party, yett in
this great hurry and disorder on t'other side they soe received
them as that they forced them to retreat in as much confusion
as they found them, to the shame of their braging Pretences

---

[1] Sconce, an outlying rampart for defense.
* On Col. Morysons Plantation that was. (Marginal note in original.)
This was the chimney of the old glass factory, the factory itself having long
since disappeared.

of valour, courage and Resolution at their undertaking this at-
tacque and of the cause they defended who yet call themselves
the Loyall party, and yet dessert the Governour, and now
begin to importune him to quit the Towne. But wee cannot
give a better account, nor yet a truer (soe far as wee are informed) of this action than what this Letter of Bacon's relates:

From the Camp at SANDY BEACH,
S'ber the 17th, 1676.

Capt. Wm. Cookson[1] and Capt. Ed'w Skewon :

Before wee drew up to James Towne a party of theirs fled before
us with all hast for Feare: with a small party of horse (being darke
in the Evening) wee rode up to the Point at Sandy Beach, and
sounded a Defiance which they answered, after which with some
difficulty for want of materialls we entrenched ourselves for that
night, our men with a great deal of Bravery ran up to their works
and fir'd Briskly and retreated without any losse.

The next morning our men without the workes gave them some
Braves and contempts to try their mettle, upon w'ch they fir'd their
great guns with Small shott to cleere their workes, but our men
Recovered the workes, and wee are now entrenched very secure both
from the Shipps and Towne. Yesterday they made a Sally with
horse and Foote in the Van, the Forlorne being made up of such men
as they had compell'd to serve; they came up with a narrow Front,
and pressing very close upon one anothers shoulders that the Forlorne might be their shelter; our men received them soe warmly
that they retired in great disorder, throwing downe theire armes,
left upon the Bay, as also their Drum and dead men, two of which
our men brought into our Trenches and Buried with severall of their
armes. This day wee shewed them our Indian captives upon the
workes, the People come in from all parts most bravely, and wee are
Informed that great multitudes of men are up for us in the Isle of
Wight and Nancymond, and onely expect orders, as also all the
South side of the River over against us in great numbers. They
shew themselves such Pitifull cowards, contemptable as you would
admire[2] them. It is said that Hubert Farrell[3] is shot in the Belly,

---

[1] Captain William Cookson was "condemned at my house and executed
when Bacon lay before Jamestown" (Berkeley's report, *Cal. St. P. Col.*, 1677–
1680, § 303). His estate was confiscated. The name of Captain Edward
Skewon does not appear in any of the lists.

[2] *I. e.*, so contemptible that you would wonder at them.

[3] Captain Hubert Farrill was one of those named in Bacon's Declaration
against the government. Later, in company with Ludwell and the elder Bacon,

Hartwell [1] in the Legg, Smith in the head, Mathewes [2] with others, yet as yet wee have noe certaine account. They tooke a solemne oath when they Sallyed out either to Rout us, or never Returne; But you know how they use to keepe them: I believe the Shipps are weary of their Bargaine finding their shotts all inconsiderable. This is our present Intelligence; be sure to take care of the Upper Parts against the Pyrats, and bid the men be courageous for that all the country is bravely Resolute.

I had almost forgot to tell you that Chamberlaine[3] out of a Bravado came with a Sloope, and lay under our workes, and with abundance of vaunting and railing Expressions, Threatned great things, but finding it too warme was feigne to take his Boate and leave his Sloope; Wee guesse hee was wounded by his ceasing to Baule (being much jeer'd by our men) which you know hee is not us'd to doe.

Be sure you encourage the Soldiers in the Upper Parts and lett them know what a Pitifull Enemy wee have to deale with. Wee have just now two great Guns come for one Battery, which they are much affraid off as I am informed. This is the most of our present Newes, of other Passages by the Messenger you may be informed.

Your reall Friend,

NATH: BACON.

After this succeslesse Sally the courages and numbers of the Governor's party abated much, and Bacons men thereby became more bold and daring in soe much that Bacon could Scarce keepe them from immediately falling to storme and enter the Towne; but hee (being as wary as they rash) perswaded them from the attempt, Bidding them keepe their courages untill such tyme as hee found occasion and opportunity to make use of them, telling them that hee doubted not to take

he led a party of men against the insurgents quartered at the house of the latter in York County under Major Whaly. There Farrill was killed. See pp. 89–92.

[1] Captain William Hartwell, brother of Henry Hartwell, joint author with Blair and Chilton of *The Present State of Virginia, 1697–1698*, took a leading and oppressive part in putting down the rebellion, and many complaints against his high-handed proceedings were sent to the commissioners, March–May, 1677.

[2] The identity of Smith and Mathewes is doubtful.

[3] Probably Captain Thomas Chamberlaine of Henrico, whose house was plundered by Bacon's troops. He was "cursed with a passionate temper that brooked neither opposition nor restraint. His native want of self-control was accentuated by a strong taste for liquor, the consequence of which was that he found himself constantly involved in quarrels and brawls." (Bruce, *Institutional History of Virginia*, I. 507.)

the Towne without losse of a man, and that one of their Lives was of more value to him than the whole world.

Having planted his great Guns, hee takes the wives and female Relations of such Gentlemen as were in the Governor's Service against him (whome hee had caused to be brought to the workes) and Places them in the Face of his Enemy, as Bulworkes for their Battery, by which Policy hee promised himself (and doubtlesse had) a goode advantage, yet had the Governors party by much the odds in number besides the advantage of tyme and Place.

But soe great was the Cowardize and Basenesse of the Generality of Sir William Berkeley's Party (being most of them men intent onely upon plunder or compell'd and hired into his service) that of all, at last there were onely some 20 Gentlemen willing to stand by him, the rest (whome the hopes or promise of Plunder brought thither) being now all in hast to be gone to secure what they had gott; soe that Sir Wm. Berkeley himselfe who undoubtedly would rather have dyed on the place than thus deserted it, what with importunate and resistlesse Solicitations of all, was at last over persuaded, nay hurryed away against his owne Will to Accomack and forced to leave the Towne to the mercy of the enemy.

Soe fearfull of Discovery they are, that for secrecy they imbarque and weigh anchor in the night and silently fall downe the River, thus flying from the Face of an enemy that during this siege (which lasted one whole weeke) lay exposed to much more hardships, want and inaccommodation than themselves, besides the fatigue of a long march at their first coming to Towne, for this very service was supposed to be the Death of Bacon, who by lying in a wett Season in his Trenches before Towne contracted the Disease whereof hee not long after dyed.

Bacon haveing early Intelligence of the Governor and his Party's Quitting the Towne the night before, enters it without any opposition, and soldier like considering of what importance a Place of that Refuge was, and might againe bee to the Governor and his Party, instantly resolves to lay it level with the ground, and the same night he became poses'd of it, sett Fire to Towne, church and state house (wherein were the Countryes Records which Drummond had privately convey'd thense and preserved from Burning). The towne consisted of 12 new brick Houses besides a considerable number of Frame houses with brick chimneys, all which will not be rebuilt (as is computed) for fifteen hundred pounds of Tobacco.[1]

Now those who had so lately deserted it, as they rid a little below in the River in the Shipps and Sloopes (to their shame and regret) beheld by night the Flames of the Towne, which they soe basely forsaking, had made a sacrifice to ruine.

Bacon goes next to Greene Spring, and during his stay thereabouts draws a protest or oath against the Governor and his Party, which is said to be imposed on the People and taken by above 600 at once in Gloster County, and also forced upon others in several parts of the Country and is as follows:

Bacons Oath of Fidelity.

Whereas Sir William Berkeley Knight, late Governor of Virginia hath in a most Barbarous and abominable manner exposed and betrayed our lives, and for greediness of sordid Gaine did defer our just defence and hinder all the Loyall endeavours of his Majesties faithfull subjects; and further when the Country did raise a sufficient Force for the effectual proceeding against the Indian Enemy, he did, contrary to all Equity and Justice and the tenors of his commission, endeavour to oppose the said Forces by himself and the Assembly sett forth: of which attempts being severall tymes defeated by the Peoples abhorrence of soe Bloody a design he left the country in a small vessell, it being unknown to all People to what parts of the world he did repair, and whereas as our army upon his departure betaking themselves to the care of the Frontiers did march out against the Indians and obtain soe great a victory, as hath in a manner finished all the disaster and almost Resettled the country in a happy Peace, yet notwithstanding Sir Wm. Berkeley with Forces

---

[1] For recent excavations on the site of old Jamestown, see Samuel H. Yonge, *Site of Old "James Towne," 1607–1698*, enlarged edition (Richmond, 1907). Jamestown was destroyed September 19, 1676. Lawrence, the first to act, set fire to his own house "with all its welth and a faire cupbord of plate"; Bacon with his own hand set fire to the church, the first there built. Other houses and goods burned belonged to Colonel Thomas Swann, Major Theophilus Hone, and William Sherwood. Berkeley in his "Vindication" mentions houses of his own burned at Jamestown. A number of the houses destroyed were unoccupied at the time.

raised in Accomack, did invade the country with acts of hostility, with all intentions to persecute the said Army with these aforsaid reasons, as also having betray'd his Trust to the king by flying from his seate of Judicature, and acting wholly contrary to his comission, We protest against him unanimously as a Traytor and most pernitious Enemy to the Publick, and further we sweare that in all places of his Majestyes Colony of Virginia wee will oppose and prosecute him with all our Endeavours by all acts of hostility as occasion shall present, and further whereas Plotting and wishing in his heart a totall Ruine and Destruction of this Poore colony he hath Endeavoured to set the heart of our Soveraigne against us by false Information and Lyes, requesting Forces of his Majestie wherewith to compell and subdue us, hindering, intercepting and preventing all our Remonstrances for Peace, which might have gone home in our Justification, as also hindering of our sending home of agents in the Peoples behalf which was the most humble and earnest request of the People at first, We doe further declare and sweare that wee think it absolutely consisting with our allegiance and Loyalty to treat with and discourse with the said Forces and commissioners with all submission to his Majesty. But otherwise if it shall soe prove that notwithstanding all intreaties and offers wee shall make, they shall offer to land by Force, in our owne Defense to fly together as in a common calamity and jointly with the present army now under the command of General Bacon, to stand or fall in the Defense of him and the country in soe just a cause, and in all places to oppose their Proceedings (onely untill such time as his Majesty by our agents shall fully understand the miserable case of the country, and the Justice of our Proccedings) Which most just request if they shall refuse and by force endeavour to enter the country, wee are resolv'd to uphold the country as long as we can and never to absent and joyne with any such army whatever, and lastly in case of utmost extremity rather than submit to any soe miserable a slavery (when none can longer defend ourselves, our lives and Liberties) to acquit the colony rather than submitt to soe unheard of Injustice, and this wee all sweare in the presence of Almighty God as unfeignedly and freely as ever wee desire of him for happiness to come.

By the General.

The Governor and his Forces being gone Bacon orders the shore to be Guarded all along to observe their motions, and as they moved to follow them and prevent them from landing, or having any provisions sent on board them.

Bacon now begins to show a more mercelesse severity and

absolute authoity than formerly, Plundering and imprisoning many and condemning some by power of martial law.[1]

But among all made onely one exemplary (to witt) one James Wilkenson that had fled from his Collours, who (with one Mr. Clough[2] Minister of James Towne) was condemned to dye, but the first onely was executed; which (as a soldier) wee look on to be more an act of his Policy than cruelty, to prevent and awe others from disserting him, wee not observing him to have bin Bloodely inclined in the whole progresse of this Rebellion.

Intercession being made for Mr. Clough Captain Hawkins[3] and Major West,[4] Bacon purposed to accept of Bland, Carver and Farloe[5] in exchange for them, neverthelesse none of the first three were put to death by Bacon.

Now Bacon finding that his Soldiers Insolences growing soe great and intolerable to the People (of whom they made noe due distinction) and finding their actings to reflect on himself, he did not onely betake himself to a strict Discipline over his men but also to more moderate courses himself, Releasing some Prisoners, Pardoning others that were condemned, and calling those to account against whom any complaints came for seisures or Plundering their Estates without his order or knowledge.

This Prosperous Rebell, concluding now the day his owne, marcheth with his army into Gloster County, intending to visit all the northern part of Virginia to understand the state of them and to settle affairs after his own measures, in which (wee are informed) he proposed this method.

1. One committee for settling the south side of James River and inquiring into the spoiles that had been comitted there.

[1] Nearly all those executed for participation in the rebellion were condemned by courts martial, though in a few cases trials seem to have been held before a court of oyer and terminer.

[2] The Rev. John Clough, minister of Jamestown and afterward of Southwick parish, Surry, was an active supporter of Berkeley. He died January 15, 1684, and his tombstone is still in the churchyard.

[3] Thomas Hawkins, jr., of Rappahannock.

[4] Captain John West of New Kent.

[5] George Farlow, "one of Cromwell's soldiers, very active in this rebellion, and taken with forty men coming to surprise me at Accomack." (Berkeley's report.)

2. Another committee to be always with the Army, to inquire into the cause of all seisures, and to give orders for doing the same, and to regulate the rudenesse, disorder, spoile and waste of the soldiers, as they had formerly comitted.

3. And another committee to be appointed onely for the management and proceding for the Indian warr and giving Dispatches for affairs relating to it.

But before he could arrive to the Perfection of his designes (w'ch none but the eye of omniscience could Penetrate) Providence did that which noe other hand durst (or at least did) doe and cut him off.

Hee lay sick at one Mr. Pates in Gloster County of the Bloody Flux, and (as Mr. Pate himself affirms) accompanyed with a Lousey Disease; so that the swarmes of Vermyn that bred in his Body he could not destroy but by throwing his shirts into the Fire as often as he shifted himself.

Hee dyed much dissatisfied in minde inquiring ever and anon after the arrival of the Friggats and Forces from England,[1] and asking if his Guards were strong about the House.

After Bacon's Death one Joseph Ingram a stranger in Virginia and came over but the year before this Rebellion, under whose conduct the Faction began to fall into several parties and opinions, which gave Sir Wm. Berkely's party opportunity by these divisions to surprise the Rebels in small Bodyes as they sculked up and down the country.

But the maine service that was done for the reducing the Rebells to their obedience was done by the Seamen and com-

---

[1] Bacon's anxiety regarding the forces from England was in part due to the terms of the oath of August 3 (p. 60) and in part to his determination to resist the British troops when they came. Mr. Bruce quotes Thomas Ludwell as saying that "Bacon and his followers had formed 'vain hopes of taking the country wholly out of his Majesty's hands into their own'" (*Inst. Hist.*, II. 281–282), and there is reason to think that the malcontents of Virginia, Maryland, and Albemarle were in collusion to drive out the governors and to set up popular governors of their own. This determination was the subject of a dialogue reported by John Coode of Maryland (p. 313, note 1) as having taken place between himself and Bacon, September 2, 1676 (*Cal. St. P. Col.*, 1677–1680, § 27), and we know that Albemarle men were in Jamestown and that letters were exchanged between the two colonies (p. 145; *Colonial Records of North Carolina*, I. 317).

manders of Shipps then[1] riding in the Rivers especially the
Generall Surrender at Wests Point of those headed by Ingram
and Wacklute,[2] w'ch was managed and concluded by Capt.
Grantham,[3] to the disgust of those Gentlemen of the Governor's Party, because Sir Wm. Berkeley had not made them concerned in soe considerable a Piece of Service.

After Ingram had submitted to the Governor (who lay then
on Board Martyn's Ship in Yorke River), Laurance that notorious Rebell fled, who was the first man that sett fire to James
Towne by burning his owne house, some others were taken
Prisoners after they had lay'd downe their armes, and the rest
went home in Peace. About the 16th of January, 1676-7, the
whole country had submitted to the Governour and the two
and twentyeth hee came home to his house at Greene Spring,
and had issued out new writts of summons for the convening
of a free assembly at his owne house, the State house being
ruined with the rest of James Towne.

The Particulars of this foregoing Narrative being what wee
could collect or observe from the most credible disinterest'd
Persons, most authentique Papers, Records, Reports and the
Publick Grievances of the respective countyes of Virginia, wee
have, with all integrity of mind and the best of our understanding, without favor or partialty, selected and sett downe
what wee thought most consonant to Truth and Reality, and

---

[1] The share taken by the captains of merchant vessels at this time in Virginia in helping to suppress the rebellion became the subject of a special inquiry
before the Privy Council in 1679. The English commissioners had reported
"that the main service for reducing the rebels to their obedience was done by the
seamen and commanders of ships then riding in the rivers," particularly Captains
Morriss, Consett, Grantham, Prinne, and Gardner. The Privy Council recommended to the Admiralty that these captains should be reimbursed for what they
had spent, should be granted rewards, and should be selected for employment
in the navy (see also *Cal. St. P. Col.*, 1674–1676, § 1035).

[2] Governor Notley of Maryland spoke of Lawrence Ingram as the "titular
general, who succeeded Bacon," and of Walklett as "his lieutenant general."
After the rebellion was suppressed in January, 1677, Walklett offered to come to
Gloucester with a good troop of horse and arms. Captain Grantham encouraged him to do so, and advised him to "declare for the King's Majesty, the governor, and country," promising to assist him. Berkeley offered him both pardon and plunder. Though there is no direct evidence to show that Walklett
accepted these offers, it is probable that he did so.

[3] For his service Captain Grantham was given a reward of £200.

on the other hand rejected whatever wee found or suspected to be false or improbable. And doe here according to his Majestye's Royall commands and our own Dutyes most humbly leave it to his Majestye's most Prudent consideration and Judgement.

JOHN BERRY,
FRANCIS MORYSON.

NARRATIVES OF THOMAS MILLER, SIR PETER
COLLETON, AND THE CAROLINA PROPRI-
ETORS, 1680

INTRODUCTION

ALBEMARLE COUNTY, North Carolina, the scene of one of the minor uprisings of this period, is some sixty or seventy miles below the mouth of the James River. Probably a land trail ran along the route afterward followed by the highway from Jamestown to Edenton, but in the seventeenth century, because of swamps and hostile Indian tribes, the region between the two colonies was difficult of passage and communication was largely by water. However, as this highway crossed Nansemond County, the seat of one of the insurgent movements in Virginia after Bacon's death, which was suppressed in January, 1677, and as the uprising in Pasquotank district, Albemarle, broke out the following December, it is difficult not to see a connection between the two events. Men from Albemarle had been in communication with William Drummond, and we know that John Culpeper, one of the leaders of the Albemarle movement, was at Jamestown in May, 1676. There is reason to believe, also, that Bacon had had negotiations with the discontented representatives of both Carolina and Maryland and that some sort of an understanding had been reached regarding action against the governors of the three colonies. Albemarle was known as "a subterfuge to the late rebels, traitors, and deserters of Virginia (as it hath been and still is [1677])," and Governor Culpeper of Virginia in 1681 called it "the refuge of our renegades." This northern region of Carolina, which at that time contained about a thousand white taxable inhabitants, remained in an unsettled condition for many years, and in 1702 Robert Quary reported that the people were "uneasy and discontented," that there was "no settled militia nor any foundation of government," and that "the proprietors have taken no notice of them for above seven years past."

The trade of the colony was in provisions and tobacco, the latter of which was taken off by New Englanders, whose light craft could pass the shoals and sand-bars shutting in Albemarle Sound, and carried to Boston, Salem, Gloucester, or Newfoundland, whence it was in part transshipped to English or European ports. Very little North Carolina tobacco was taken to England by any one except New Englanders, for English merchant ships were too large to enter through Roanoke Channel, and export by way of Virginia was forbidden by Virginia law. According to the parliamentary act of 1672, tobacco not shipped directly to England was to pay at the port of clearance a duty of a penny a pound, the plantation duty, and because of the continued ignoring of this act by the colonies in general, a royal proclamation was issued in 1675, and stringent instructions were sent to the governors to enforce the act. The situation in Albemarle was made somewhat more serious than in other southern colonies because of the known fondness of the New Englanders for illicit trading.

As one of the results of the more rigorous policy of the home government in 1675 and the years that followed, the Lords Proprietors of Carolina despatched to the colony in 1676 a new governor, Thomas Eastchurch, and the commissioners of the customs sent a collector, Thomas Miller. Attempts by Miller to enforce the act and to control the New England trade were the immediate causes of the revolt, in which New England ship-captains took a prominent part. There were probably other causes, for the proprietors asserted that Miller, who, having left Eastchurch at Bermuda, came to Albemarle with powers as governor and commander-in-chief, "did many extravagant things, making strange limitations for the choice of the parliament, getting power in his hands for laying fines, which 'tis to be feared he neither did nor meant to use moderately, sending out strange warrants to bring some of the most considerable men of the country, alive or dead, before him, setting a sum of money upon their heads." Behind the rage stirred by these actions may have lain a deeper desire for independence of all English control, either royal or proprietary.

The narratives here printed are to be found among the Colonial Office Papers in the Public Record Office, London, having been originally prepared for the use of the Lords of Trade in the trial of John Culpeper for high treason. Their present location is in *Colonial Office*, class 1, vol. 44, nos. 20 (iv), 22 (i), and vol. 45, no. 79. With other papers bearing on the movement, they have been printed in the *Colonial Records of North Carolina*, I. 228–333, 350–352, the pages of the three documents in question being 278–283, 286–289, and 326–328.

Thomas Miller was an apothecary of Albemarle County, who in November, 1673, had been charged with uttering words of blasphemy and treason. He was tried before Governor Berkeley and council at Jamestown and acquitted. Immediately he sailed for England where he obtained his appointment as collector, November 16, 1676. With Eastchurch, the proprietary governor, he returned in 1677, reaching Bermuda some time before May 20. There Eastchurch dallied, sending Miller ahead with powers that the proprietaries afterward declared were illegal. Miller sailed from Bermuda for Albemarle May 20, arriving July 9, and immediately began to exercise the functions of acting governor and collector.

On December 3 the rebellion broke out. Miller and others were seized and imprisoned, he being confined finally in a log house up the Pasquotank River. Escaping in August, 1679, he reached England in December and at once brought suit against Culpeper and Gillam (below, p. 151), both of whom were, at that time, in England. Gillam was never brought to trial, and Culpeper, although at first declared guilty of treason by the Privy Council, was eventually acquitted, largely through the influence of the Earl of Shaftesbury, one of the proprietors of Carolina, who stated that Miller's actions were without legal warrant.

During 1679 and 1680 Miller lived on the bounty of the Treasury and his fees as witness. The Treasury allowances were charged up against the customs account, for Miller was still collector, with Robert Holden deputy in Albemarle. But he soon after lost the collectorship, and all his efforts to obtain its renewal or to secure further employment from the proprietaries or the commissioners of customs failed. The cause may have been his bad habits, for he was known to be a hard drinker.

NARRATIVES OF THOMAS MILLER, SIR PETER COLLETON, AND THE CAROLINA PROPRIETORS, 1680

Affidavit of Thomas Miller concerning the Rebellion of Carolina.

THE affidavit of Tho. Miller aged 31 years or thereabouts saith—That in or about the middle of July 1677 hee arrived in Albemarle County in Carolina with Sundry Commissions Instructions and other Instruments of writing from the Right Hon'ble the Lords Prop'rs of the sd Province under their Lor'ps handes and seales for this deponent to be Register (w'ch then was in the stead of Secretary) of that County aforesaid and also to personate one of their Lor'ps in Councill there and other Commissions and Instruments of writing from the then Gov'r *vid.*[1] Thom. Eastchurch Esqr,[2] for this deponent to preside in Councill and to bee Command'r of the military forces of sd County afores'd during his the sd Gov'rs absence and also a Commission from the hon'ble the Commiss'rs of his Majestyes Customes for this deponent to bee Collector there with sundry Instructions to act by. In pursuance whereof, after having (by the advice of the then Councill there) setled the Lords Prop'rs affaires relating to their governm't, reduced the Indians, who the year before (as was manifested to the deponent) *vid.*, in 76 had committed sundry murders and dep-

---

[1] *Videlicet*, to wit.

[2] Thomas Eastchurch had been speaker of the House of Commons in Albemarle. Going to London in 1676, he was appointed governor by the Lords Proprietors November 21 of that year. Having lingered in England until the following March or April, he sailed for Albemarle with Miller, but for reasons stated in the text remained in Bermuda until late autumn, when he went to Virginia instead of to Albemarle. There he issued a proclamation against the insurgents in North Carolina and endeavored to enlist the support of the English soldiers and of volunteers in Virginia for the purpose of putting down the rebellion. While engaged in this undertaking he died of fever, five weeks after his arrival.

149

redations upon some of the inhabitants, and had brought the people, who in the sd year of 76 (as did appear to the deponent) and then also were in a miserable confusion by reason of Sundry factions amongst them, to a reasonable good conformity to his Majestyes and the Lords Prop'rs Laws and authority and (as then seemed) to the generall satisfaction of the inhabitants. The deponent then setled his Majestyes affaires in reference to the Customes and for the better managing and collecting the same had appointed deputyes and other sub officers[1] in each precynct, And had together with his sd Deputyes gotten into their hands (for his Maj'tyes use) from the former Collector appointed by the Country and part received themselfes as much of the Kings Concerns in bonds for tobbacco and tobbacco received as amounted in the whole to 327068 pounds w'ch in hogsheads allowing 400 pounds to one hogshead comes to about 817 hogsheads as by account will appear, and in sundry other bonds for money, as also in severall seizures of European goods judged illegally imported and of a vessell called the *Patience* for importing some of the sd goods made by him and his deputy and in goods received in lieu of tobbacco for the Kings Customes as amounted to the value of 1242£ 18s. 01d. sterling, as by account will also appear, the product and effect whereof (his salary excepted) hee had taken care for transportation that very year, according to the hon'ble the Commiss'rs of the Customs Orders, as will partly appear by Mr Henry Hudson[2] and Mr Tymothy Biggs,[3] but was hindred therefrom by reason of an Insurrection and (as the

[1] Summers's petition to the Treasury throws light on Miller's method of enforcing the navigation act. From July 9 to December 4, Summers and his men were employed by Miller to prevent frauds, their duty being "to attend the new inlet of the said county, from whence petitioner brought up sundry New England vessels coming thither to trade, in order to their fair entry with the said collector." For this service he claimed to be out of purse £84, and "so has suffered damage and prejudice to himself and family."

[2] Henry Hudson was Miller's deputy in Currituck precinct and was one of the witnesses against Culpeper at his trial in England.

[3] Captain Timothy Biggs had been in Charleston in 1672 but later went to Albemarle. In 1676 he was appointed deputy to the Earl of Craven and received the post of deputy collector under Miller, with an office at Little River Point. Later, September 28, 1678, he was made comptroller and surveyor-general of customs in Albemarle, "where no surveyor hath been yet established." Under the administration of Governor Harvey, 1679, he retired with a number of other Quakers to Virginia.

deponent humbly conceives) a rebellion which violently broke out in that Country 10ber[1] 77 and hath to this day continued without any effectuall restraint and suppression, notwithstanding all the endeav'rs of the Lords Prop'rs in commissionating and appointing Seth Sothel[2] Esq'r to be Gov'r and to reduce the same, w'ch was contrived and carried on then and since by Richard Foster, John Jenkins,[3] George Durant,[4] John Willoughby,[5] Wm. Craford,[6] Patricke White, James Blunt, Capt. Zach. Gillam,[7] John Culpeper,[8] with other their Con-

[1] December.

[2] For Sothell, see below, p. 160.

[3] Lieutenant-Colonel John Jenkins as president of the council was acting governor of the colony in 1676. For reasons not clearly stated, he was thrust out of his place and imprisoned by the assembly in the same year. There seems to have been no acting governor of the colony from that time (May, 1676) until the arrival of Miller (July, 1677), who according to the proprietors had no legal right to exercise the functions of governor. Shaftesbury was, therefore, justified in saying that there was no settled government in the colony until the arrival of Harvey in August, 1679.

[4] George Durant, whose house was the rendezvous of the insurgents, was one of the most influential planters in Albemarle County. He had extensive dealings with the New Englanders and was one of the chief instigators of the rebellion. While in England in 1677 he told the Lords Proprietors that Eastchurch never should be governor. Arriving in the colony about December 1, 1677, in the *Carolina*, with Captain Gillam, he set on foot the insurrection that broke out two days afterward.

[5] Captain John Willoughby, who had got into trouble with Eastchurch and been summoned before the palatine court, refused to attend; and having been declared guilty of contempt, fled to Virginia.

[6] The house of William Crawford, on Albemarle Sound, was a meeting-place of the insurgents, and there Miller was confined immediately after his seizure.

[7] Captain Zachariah Gillam, "old Zach," as he was called, lends picturesqueness to the story of the revolt. He was the son of Benjamin Gillam, who, with an elder son Benjamin, constituted the mercantile firm of Gillam and Company, a prominent trading house in Boston. In 1668 Zachariah co-operated with Radisson and Groseilliers in the opening of Hudson Bay to trade and was a factor in the founding of the Hudson's Bay Company (May 2, 1670). He remained in the service of the company until 1674 and then returned to his former trading activities, going to Albemarle for tobacco in 1676, 1677, and 1678. With him was his son Benjamin, a lad but fourteen years old. In 1682 Zachariah was again in Hudson Bay and was drowned there, in Nelson River, in 1683. His son, who was there at the same time on an interloping expedition, was captured by Radisson, who had returned to the French interests, but afterward was released and went back to Boston. He is not to be identified with the pirate James Gillam.

[8] John Culpeper went from Barbadoes to Charleston in March, 1671. There he was appointed surveyor and surveyor-general. He was deemed "a very able artist," and proved his ability by making maps of Ashley River, "the Lords

federates and New England traders, w'ch Culpeper (by the encouragement and aid of the sd Gillam and the rest of their adherents) assuming the title and office of his Maj'tyes Collector violently seized the premises out of his and his deputyes hands, most cruelly imprisoning them, and disposed of the King concerns according to their own will and pleasure, overthrowing the governm't, imprisoning all or most in authority and office besides and committing sundry other outrages upon all other the inhabitants that would not joyne with them in these exorbitancyes committed in this Insurrection, w'ch was begun and carried on after this manner following: Upon the 4th day of 10ber 1677 and 3 dayes after Capt. Zach. Gillam's arrivall there, a parcell of men to the number of 30 or 40 of the precinct of Pasquotank in the aforesd County, being set on by the fores'd Culpeper, Craford, and encouraged by the example (w'ch 2 of the Lords Prop'rs Deputyes complayned of to this Deponent) as well as assistance with armes of the sd Gillam, and headed by one Valentine Bird[1] and Edward Wells, did without making any addresse, complaint, or information to the deponent or any else in authority, and without any lawfull warrant or order, with force and arms *vid.* swords, guns, and pistolls, violently rush into the house where the deponent and 2 more of

Proprietors Plantations," etc.   In 1672 he was chosen a member of the assembly, but his natural disposition led him to take part in an uprising, and he only escaped hanging for endeavoring "to set the poor to plunder the rich" by fleeing to Albemarle.   He was a restless, discontented colonist, and seems to have been concerned in factious movements elsewhere than in Charleston and Albemarle. He was in Jamestown in May, 1676, and after the Albemarle revolt went to New England in Benjamin Gillam's ship.   Thence he sailed for England, probably in 1679, where, as has already been stated, he was tried for treason and acquitted.   Of his life in New England nothing is known, but a "representation" presented to the proprietors speaks of his plotting there "with some of the discontented traders."   (*Colonial Records of North Carolina*, I. 259.)

[1] Valentine Byrd was a man of wealth and influence in the colony, having filled the office of collector before Miller's arrival.   There is, however, no record of his having been commissioned by the Treasury, just as there is no evidence that Copley and Birch, who were commissioned in 1674, ever actually served. It would appear, therefore, that Miller was the first regular appointee that held the office of collector.   This fact may account for the looseness with which the parliamentary act of 1672 was observed and for the passage by the assembly of an act authorizing Byrd to take a farthing instead of a penny as plantation duty.   It is said that Byrd allowed much tobacco to leave the colony as "bait for New England fishermen."

the Lords Prop'rs Deputyes were present and seized us as their
prisoners and then went to searching over the publique records
and other of the deponents writings, w'ch the sd party had
brought with them, having the day before violently entred one
Mr Tymothy Biggs his house, and there breaking open sundry
the deponents locks, seized the said Records and whatever
other of the deponents writings were then to bee found, having
also in this action sent abroad up and down the Country their
seditious libells drawn by the sd Culpeper to put all in a flame,
and on the sd 4th of 10ber a little after the deponent and the
other 2 Deputyes afores'd were seized their prisoners, some of
the ringleaders _vid_. Bird, Craford, Wells, and others went on
board the sd Gillam's shipp (w'ch in all these confusions rid
with Jack, Ensign, Flag and Penon[1] flying while wee were
prison'rs at Pasquotanck) where on board there was the sd
Gillam the afores'd Culpeper and Durant and after about one
houres or thereaboutes staying on board they came ashoar
again with fresh new Curtleaxes[2] for themselves and many of
the rest of their gang and then altering their first pretences they
searched the deponents and his deputy Mr Biggs pockets and
took away all our publique and private writings and pocket
books w'ch they found about us and then the sd Culpeper
writt another seditious letter w'ch the deponent saw and w'ch
was signed by the afores'd Bird and Craford directed to the
afores'd Mr Foster in the Lower Precinct of that County called
Corrituck, giving him account of what they had done and how
they succeeded and withall requiring or directing him there
to seize Henry Hudson my deputy Collector for that precinct
and all papers about him relating to the Kings affaires and to
bring him prison'r with him and his Company at the Generall
Meeting which they proposed to bee at the fores'd George
Durant's house, and about 2 days after the said Culpeper went
up into the Upper parts of the County called Chowan (as was
given out by himselfe and the rabble) where the like distur-

---

[1] The jack, or union jack, was the chief official naval flag of Great Britain,
bearing on a blue ground the red cross of St. George, superimposed on the white
cross of St. Andrew. The ensign was a large red, white, or blue flag, bearing
in the upper corner next the staff a "canton" of white with the red cross of St.
George.

[2] Curtal-axes, cutlasses.

bance was begun and more violently agitated by the sd Culpeper and where they had seized the Marshall of the County with all his papers relating to his Maj'tys and Lords Prop'rs affaires, and then after that the sd Culpeper returned and in his return seized the deponents Clerk a prisoner, and a little after the sd Culpepers return there followed a party of men in arms from that precinct of Chowan bringing the sd Marshall with them a prisoner. Their main guard then at the fores'd Craford's house w'ch was forced in at Pascotank. Then (after some 14 or 15 dayes keeping the deponent and the other Lords deputys which they had taken close prisoners) the said Craford vowing and swearing that if any came to oppose them or relieve us that they would stand by each other to the last dropp of blood and that if any dyed to bee sure wee that were their prison'rs to dy first, They carried this deponent and their other prison'rs round by water in hostile manner to the fores'd Durant's house and there in the middle of a guard of 60 or 70 men in arms kept us close from all humane converse or accesse of friends, neither would they admitt us the speech of one another. The next day after our being brought to Durant's as afores'd they sent a party of soldiers headed by the afores'd Mr Bird to search for the deponent's box wherein was all his Commissions, Instructions, his Maj'tys printed Proclamations, and letter, and all other bills, bonds, accounts, and other papers relating to the King's, the Lords Prop'rs, the former Gov'rs and this deponent, together with the Lords' great seal of the County and many other books and things of value, w'ch box the sd party soon found (though hid in a tobbacco hogshead) and carried it to the sd Durants house where in presence of the said Culpeper, Craford, Durant, and the rest of the Ringleaders then met, it was broken open and all things therein contained Havocked at their pleasure as the deponent saw openly and then afterwards on the very same day, by the instigation of the said Culpeper (who was the cheife scribe that writt the paper or accusation), Craford, Bird, Durant, and others, they did cause the depon't by beat of Drum and a shout of one and all of the rabble to bee accused of blasphemy, treason and other crimes, and so, upon a shout of one and all of the sd rabble, was the deponent ordered to bee clapt in Irons, w'ch was accordingly done. Then were the stocks and pillory overturned and throwne into the river by this rabble, part of the deponents magazine and estate in whatever specie, wherever to bee found, Havocked at their pleasure, and the rabble being still influenced by the sd Culpeper, Craford, Durant, Jenkins, etc. (the fores'd Gillam being alsoe there countenancing this rout with his drink and presence) they upbraided his Maj'tys proclamations and L'ds Prop'rs authority, and there Lordshipps much threatened also by the sd Culpeper, Durant, Craford. Especially the said Craford said (which this deponent heard with his owne ears) that if the Gov'r came among them there, or the Lords either, they would serve them the same sauce, or words to that purpose, and at this stand the rabble stood (onely still sending out scouts and partyes, either to threaten, seize, disarm, imprison or chase out of the Country all in authority or office or any else that would not Joyn with them) till about 4 or 5 days after up came the afores'd Foster with his party from the Lower precinct called Carituck, bringing with them as their prisoner the afores'd Mr Henry Hudson, Dep'ty Collector for his Maj'tye there, upon whose coming they suddenly elected a parliament out of this medley as a confused rabble (making their drummer one of the burgesses) consisting of about 18 persons. This parliam't seperated 5 of the members *vid:* the fors'd Jenkins, Blunt, Craford, White and Bird (since deceased), to Joyne with the afors'd Foster to make up one Juncto or Court, and this Court so called took upon them Judiciall authority and sate as the supream Court upon 2 of the L'ds Prop'rs deputyes *vid:* Capt Tymothy Biggs, deputy for the right hon'rble the Earle of Craven, whom they accused of murder, and Mr John Nixon Deputy to Sir Peter Colleton, whom they also accused of treason, and then brought the deponent before them in Irons, pulling of his hat, and then upon him impanelled a Jury (as they called it) out of this rabble, the foreman whereof was one Mordslay Bouden, a New England trader and one much indebted to his Majesty, the rest scarce 4 of them could read or write, and this Jury without any law or statute with them were sent out with such articles and Inditements as John Culpeper, their Cheif Councillour and scribe, and George Durant, their Atturney generall, had contrived ag'st the deponent w'ch Jury quickly returned again with what the sd

Culpeper had ordered him to do, as the foreman openly blurted out in their Court, and upon this they ordered their sheriffe to impannell a petty Jury, who being stark drunk as the deponent himself saw, went about summoning of them hee intended should have been the Jurors on the deponents life, who were both scandalous, infamous, and illiterate persons and were resolved then (as the deponent conceives) to have taken away his life, for little else could the deponent hear from them but the threats, vows, and bloody oathes of stabbing, hanging, pistolling, or poysoning; but notwithstanding all this was then prevented by the coming in of the Governr's proclamation, which hee from Virginia (being there arrived some 8 or 9 dayes before) at the very nick of tyme sent in, although it was by the sd Culpeper corruptly abbreviated and transcribed and so by him published to the rabble, the originall (w'ch was under the sd Gov'rs hand and seale) not suffered to bee seen or published to the Inhabitants, and then they took order and sent a guard of the soldiers to oppose the Gov'r coming in and to dispose of the Kings Concernes, making the sd Culpeper Collector, and to committ the deponent close prisoner in Irons as hee was and the rest *per* the authority also prisoners to severall places apart.   The fors'd Court and Parliam't broke of for that tyme and went to their homes, and thereupon immediately as some were going in their way they were highly entertained by the sd Gillam on board his shipp, the sd Gillam very joyfully fireing of severall great guns to accommodate the frolick.   Amongst the rest the deponent saw the sd Foster, Craford, Culpeper with the sd Gillam in a boat together going on board the sd Gillam's shipp, and suddaenly after this the sd Gillam (when hee saw what was done about the governor) opened store and traded with the Insurrectors chiefly; and further the deponent saith that the Gov'r afores'd was kept out till hee dyed in Virginia, w'ch was about 4 or 5 weeks after, upon whose death the sd Insurrectors called the parliament again, but now to bee held at one Jenkins his house, where was present also Capt. Zach. Gillam among them, together with the sd Culpeper, George Durant, John Willoughby, Richard Foster, James Blunt, Wm. Craford and the rest, where (as it after appeared by the manifestation of their actions) it was by them decreed, to build a Loghouse 10 or 11 foot square to inclose the deponent and to keep him from pen, ink, and paper and all accesse of friendes, and then to supervise the Records and the deponents papers w'ch they had in custody embezeling what they pleased of them and then to send 2 Agents, as they called them, to England, and one forthwith, by reason Capt. Tym. Biggs, Deputy for the Earle of Craven, had made an escape for England, w'ch agent (as the sd Craford and others informed the deponent) was credited by the sd Capt. Gillam with money by bills of exchange to carry on the businesse till hee came home with George Durant, the other Agent, whom hee then carryed with him; and in the mean tyme to put their Country in a military posture, to oppose all till the return of the agents afores'd, and thus affaires have been carryed on, to the great damage of his Maj'ty, the Lords Prop'rs, and sundry of his Majestyes Leige subjects both there and in the neighbouring Plantations, by reason sundry fugitives have been entertained among the Albemarle Insurrectors etc.   And further saith not.

THO: MILLER.

1679-80

Jur:[1] 31. die Januar 1679
   coram[2]
      W. MOUNTAGU.

The Case between Thomas Miller Collector of His Maj'ts Customes and Capt. Zachariah Gilham, Culpeper, Durant, Craford and others, principal Autors and Actors in the late Commotion and Disturbances that were in the Northern Part of the Province of Carolina.

MR CARTWRIGHT[3] (who was related to Mr Vice Chamberlaine, one of the Proprietors) being Governor of the Northern part of Carolina and being returned for England and having left the Governm't there in ill order and worse hands, the Proprietors resolved to send another Governor and such a one,

---

[1] For *juratum*, sworn to.   [2] In the presence of.

[3] Peter Carteret (a kinsman of the vice-chamberlain, Sir George Carteret, one of the Lords Proprietors) came to the colony in 1664.   On the death of Samuel Stephens in 1669, he was commissioned governor and served until May, 1673, when he left the colony, and was succeeded by Jenkins, president of the council.

if they could be fortunate in their choyce, as would put in execution their Instructions orders and designes, The former Governor having very much failed them especially in 2 poynts— The first was the incouraging of the New England Trade there —The 2d was their discouraging the planting on the south side of the river Albemarle. The latter was extreamely the interest of the Proprietors, but crost allwayes by the Governors and some of the cheife of the Country, who had ingrosit the Indian trade to themselves and feared that it would be intercepted by those that should plant farther amongst them. The illness of the harbours was the cause that this Northern part of Carolina had no other vent for their Comodityes but either by Virginia, where they paid dutyes to the Governm't, or to New England, who were the onely imediate Traders with them; And ventur'd in, in small Vessells, and had soe manadg'd their affayres that they brought their goods att very lowe rates, eate out and ruin'd the place, defrauded the King of his Customes and yet govern'd the people ag't their owne Interest. To cure those evills the Prop'rs made choyce of one Mr Eastchurch to be their Governor, a Gent'n of a good fame and related to the Lord Trea'r Clifford,[1] who had recommended him to the Prop'rs formerly for that place and had the promise of severall of us. In Summer 1677 we dispatched away the sd Mr Eastchurch, together with Mr Miller, who was the Kings officer and made by us one of our Deputyes. It happen'd soe that they went not directly for Virginia, but took their passage in a ship bound for Nevis,[2] where Mr Eastchurch, lighting upon a woman that was a considerable fortune, took hold of the oppertunity, marryed her, and dispatched away Mr Miller for Carolina to settle affayres against his comeing, who carryed with him the Commission of the Lds Prop'rs to their Deputyes and Commission from Mr Eastchurch himself that made Miller Presid't of the Councill untill his arrival and

---

[1] Lord Clifford, lord high treasurer 1672–1673, had died in the latter year.
[2] It has been commonly assumed that Eastchurch found his wife in Nevis, but Solomon Summers says in his affidavit before the Lords of Trade (*N. C. Rec.*, I. 296) and in his petition to the Treasury (*Cal. of Treasury Books*, VI. 806–807) that Miller sailed with him as master in the small shallop *Success* from Bermuda. We must believe, therefore, that the proprietaries were wrong in their statement and that neither Eastchurch nor Miller got farther than Bermuda.

gave him very full and ample powers. Miller, arriveing in Carolina with these Commissions, is quyetly received into the Governm't, and submitted to not onely as Gov'r but the King's Collector, in the discharg of w'ch duty as Collector he made a very considerable progress. But as Governor he did many extravagant things, making strange limitations for the choyce of the Parliam't, gitting power in his hands of laying fynes, w'ch tis to be feared he neither did nor meant to use moderately, sending out strange warrants to bring some of the most considerable men of the Country alive or dead before him, setting a summe of money upon their heads: these proceedings having startled and disaffected the people towards him, there arrives Capt. Zachariah Gilham with a very pretty vessell of some force, and together with him Durant, and about the same time Culpeper. They brought with them severall Armes, w'ch were for Trade in the Country, and findeing that Miller had lost his reputation and interest amongst the people, stirr'd up a Commotion, seized him and all the writings belonging to the Prop'rs, and all the Tobacco and writings belonging to the Kings Customes, imploying the Kings Tobacco towards the charge of maintaining and supporting their unlawful actions, And, w'ch aggravated the matter very much, Durant had in England sometyme before this Voyage declared to some of the Prop'rs that Eastchurch should not be Governor and threatened to revolt. Capt. Gilham was a fitt man for his turn, having been turn'd out by some of the Prop'rs of a considerable imploym't in Hudson's Bay, wherein he had very much abused them.

Culpeper was a very ill man, having some tyme before fled from South Carolina, where he was in danger of hanging for laying the designe and indeavouring to sett the poore people to plunder the rich. These, with Crafurd and some other New England men, had a designe (as we conceive) to gitt the trade of this part of the Country into their hands for some years att least, And not onely defraud the King of all his Customes but buy the goods of the Inhabitants att their owne rates, for they gave not to them above halfe the vallue for their goods of w'ch the Virginians sold theirs for.

Not long after this imprisonment of Miller and that these generall men had formed themselves into what Mr Culpeper calls the Govern't of the Country by their owne authority and according to their owne modell, Mr Eastchurch arrives in Virginia, whose authority and Commission they had not the least colour to dispute and yet they kept him out by force of armes, soe that he was forced to apply to the then Governr of Virginia for aid and assistance from him to reduce them, w'ch had been accordingly donne, but that Eastchurch unfortunately dyes of a feavour. Presently after this these Gentlemen that had usurped the Govern't and cast of and imprisoned our Deputyes that would not comply with them, sends over 2 Commiss'rs in their names to promise all obedience to the Lds Propr's, but insisting very highly for right against Miller. The Prop'rs perswaded one of their owne Members, Mr Southwell,[1] to goe over and be Governor himselfe, to whome they promised the utmost submission (he being a very sober discreet gentleman) and was allsoe authorized from the Commiss'rs of the Customes to take care of the Kings concerns there, which wee conceive he would have settled in very good order but that he was unfortunately taken by the Turks in his passage thither, And upon whome the settlem't of the place very much depends, it being a very difficult matter to gitt a man of worth and trust to go thither. His redemption is every day expected, and in the meanewhile we have dispatched one Mr Holden[2] with Comissions and Deputations for the Gov-

---

[1] Seth Sothell, having purchased the share of Lord Clarendon, became one of the "true and absolute lords of the province," holding the office of "Admiral," with the right to appoint a provost marshal. The first plan of the proprietaries was to send him to Albemarle to serve as deputy in Miller's place, the deputation to cease should Miller "be thought fit to be sent back"; but in 1678 the plan was changed, and Sothell was commissioned governor. On his way to the colony he was taken by Algerine cruisers and carried to Algiers, but two or three years later he obtained his release by paying a large ransom. (*Documents relative to the Colonial History of New York*, III. 717.) At this time the Algerines were particularly aggressive, Virginia traders reporting them as "very strong" and "coming into the [English] channel," and Boston merchants declaring that they infested the seas and were a great obstruction to trade (*Cal. St. P. Col.*, 1677–1680, pp. 361, 530).

[2] Robert Holden was appointed instead of Sothell to collect for the proprietors the quit-rents and other proprietary dues and droits, at a ten-per-cent commission. He was also appointed deputy collector on the same terms as in Sothell's case, that is, until it was decided whether or not Miller should be sent back. As the customs board decided against Miller's return, Holden became

ernor to those that we did imadgine would manage it with
most moderation, who sends us word that all is now quyett
and peaceable. But his Maj'ty ought to have an exact acc't
and reparation for the damadges donne in his Customes, and
his officers repayed, the charge of w'ch ought in reason to fall
principally upon those that have been the cheife Actors in it.

[*Indorsed:*] The Case of T. Miller, Z. Gilham, etc. concerning The Rebellion of Carolina. Rec'd from Sir P. COLLETON
the 9th of Feb'ry, 1679–80.

Answer of the Lords Proprietors of Carolina, read the 20 Nov.
1680.

IN obedience to your Ld'ps command in your order of the
19th of July we have perused the petitions of Mr Thomas
Miller and Mr Timothy Biggs and some of the Inhabitants
of Albemarle in Carolina, and according to the best information we can att present gett finde the matter of fact they complaine of to be as followeth:

Mr Thomas Miller *without any legall authority* gott possession of the government of the County of Albemarle in Carolina in the yeare 1677, and was for a tyme quyetly obeyed, but
doeing many illegall and arbitrary things and drinking often
to excess and putting the people in generall by his threats and
actions in great dread of their lives and estates, and they as
we suppose getting some knowledge that he had no legall
authority, tumultuously and disorderly imprison him, and
suddainly after Mr Biggs and Mr Nixon, for adhering to Mr
Miller and abetting him in some of his actions, and revive an

collector in Albemarle, serving as deputy from 1679 to 1680 and as principal
from 1680 to 1684. No collector's name for Albemarle is entered on the customs rolls after 1684, until that of Thomas Paice, in 1697. Miller, who was
naturally hostile to Holden not only for taking his place as collector but also
for having acted as secretary of the "Grand Council" held in Albemarle, November, 1679, to try him for treason and blasphemy, asserted that Holden was
"one of the persons condemned as a ringleader in the late rebellion in Virginia";
but I can find no further proof of this statement. Holden was the first collector
in Albemarle to return to the British exchequer any money from the plantation
duty, and after his name disappears in 1684, nothing whatever is recorded from
Albemarle until 1697. This fact furnishes an interesting commentary on the
customs situation in North Carolina.

accusation against Mr Miller of treasonable words for which he had been formerly imprison'd *but never tryed*, And appoynt Mr Culpeper to receive the Kings Customes dureing the imprisonment of Mr Miller, and did many other tumultuous and irregular things.   Mr Bigs makes his escape and comes home to England and gives us information of these disorders, upon w'ch we gott one Mr Seth Sothell, who is interested with us, to undertake the Government, who being a sober moderate man and no way concerned in the factions and animosityes of the place, we doubt not but would settle all things well there, and to whome we gave Instructions to examine into the past disorders and punish the offenders.   And the Comiss'rs of his Maj'ts Customes gave him also a Commission to be Collector of his Maj'ts Customes in Albemarle, but Mr Southell in his voyage thither was taken by the Turks and carryed into Argiers.[1]

As soone as we heard of Mr Sothell's misfortune we sent a Comission to one Mr Harvey[2] to be Gov'r untill Mr Sothel's arrivall there, whose release we speedily expected.   With this Comission went Mr Robert Holden, whoome the Comisioners of the Customes had appoynted Collector of his Maj'tes Customes in Albemarle in the roome of Mr Sothell; both these Comissions as we are informed were quyetly and cherefully obeyed by the people, and Mr Holden hath without any disturbance from the People collected his Maj'tes Customes there and sent part of it home to the Comissioners here, and part of the Customes having been made use of by the people in the tyme of the disorders, they have laid a Taxe upon themselves for the repaying it to Mr Holden the present Collector.

Not long after the settlem't of the Governm't in Mr Harvey, he and the Council (as we are informed) did committ Mr Miller againe, in order to the bringing him to a Tryall for the treasonable words he had formerly spoken, But Mr Miller breakes prison and comes for England.   And not long after Mr Bigs (who is by the Comisioners of the Customes appoynted Surveyor of his Ma'tys dues in Albemarle) and Mr

[1] Algiers.

[2] Governor John Harvey was appointed in February, 1679, to hold office until Sothell should be released.   He died in office in the summer of the same year.

Holden the Collector quarrell among themselves, and Mr Bigs withdrawes himself from the Councill and perswades James Hill, the Duke of Albemarle's Deputy, to doe the same, hopeing thereby as we conceive to make a disturbance in the Governm't. Since then Mr Harvey is dead, and the Councill have chosen Col. Jenkins to execute the place of Governor untill we shall appoynt another, and all things, as we are informed by letters from thence beareing date May, June, and July last, are in quyet, and his Maj'tyes Customes quyetly paid by the People, though Mr Bigs hath endeavoured to interrupt the same together with some others, who being, as we are informed, prosecuted for ayding Mr Miller in his escape and other misdemeanors, are withdrawn into Virginia, and which we conceive are the persons whose names are to the Petition presented to his Majesty. And this is the truest acc'tt we are able to give your Lordships, how the cases of Mr Miller and Mr Bigs appeares to us. And to prevent the like disorders for the future, which hath been in great measure occasioned by factions and animosityes, in which most or all of the Inhabitants have been engaged,

We are sending Capt. Wilkinson[1] thither Governor, to whoome we shall give Instructions to examine into the past disorders, and who being a Stranger and not concerned in the factions and animosityes, we have reason to hope will manage things with moderation and doe equall justice to all partyes, and we undertake will take care so to settle all things that his Maj'tes Customes shall be duely paid to whomsoever shall be appoynted to collect the same.

Notwithstanding, we think it our dutye to informe your Lordships that we are of opinion Mr Miller, being deeply ingaged in the Animosityes of the place and having by divers unjustifyable actions as we are informed (besides Indictments

---

[1] How little is commonly known of Wilkinson's connection with the colony is evident from Ashe's belief, expressed in his *History of North Carolina*, that Wilkinson actually served as governor (I. 138). It is true that Wilkinson was appointed and made all preparations to sail, hiring a vessel and placing family, servants, and goods on board, but before he could depart, he was arrested and thrown into "the Compter in Wood Street," one of the two prisons for the confinement of those who were arrested within London and the liberties. He never went to the colony.

found against him) renderd himself lyable to the sutes of per-
ticular persons for Injuryes donne them, from which he cannot
by Law be protected, That a Stranger will doe his Maj'tye
better service in that Imployment than Mr Miller, and more
conduce to the continuation of the quyet of the place, which
we submit to your Lord'ps great prudence, and rest

Your L'd'ps most humble Serv'ts

CRAVEN.

SHAFTESBURY.

P. COLLETON.

BYFIELD'S ACCOUNT OF THE LATE
REVOLUTION, 1689

INTRODUCTION

THE "great and glorious" revolution that made an end of the reign of the Stuarts in England and placed William of Orange on the throne occurred in November, 1688. Rumors of the projected invasion had come to Boston as early as December, and reports of its success had reached the ears of the people there during the March following. Full details were not available, however, until the arrival of two ships from London, May 26 and 29, 1689, bearing the official confirmation in the form of royal proclamations intrusted for transmission to Sir William Phips.

But on April 4, eight weeks before, John Winslow, arriving from Nevis, had brought written copies of the Declaration issued from Holland, October 10, by the Prince of Orange and printed in translation early in November, instructing "all magistrates who have been unjustly turned out" to resume "their former employments" (*House of Commons Journal*, X. 4). Though this Declaration in no way applied to the colonies, the paper was speedily printed as a broadside, and its contents were made known to the people of the town. On April 18 the uprising took place in Boston and the government of Andros was overthrown. Whether the magistrates and heads of the old order had made any preparations in anticipation of success in England is uncertain. Hutchinson (*History of Massachusetts Bay*, I. 373) says that they "silently wished and secretly prayed" but determined "quietly to await the event." That they had considered plans in private is more than likely, and that in the two weeks between the receipt of the Declaration and the actual uprising something definite

167

had been done seems manifest from the machine-like precision with which the revolution moved and from the fact that the revolution took place on April 18 for no other reason than that preparations were complete (*cf. The Andros Tracts*, II. 195). But of organized conspiracy there is no certain proof, as no papers or other evidence of an incriminating character have come to light, except such as are contained in the statements of those whose interest it was to view the uprising as a movement long maturing (pp. 196–199, 257).

During the two years following the revolution a great amount of pamphlet and other literature came into existence for the purpose of justifying or condemning the event. First among the pamphlets in point of time was the account written by Nathaniel Byfield, who was then residing at Bristol, Rhode Island, and who seized the favorable opportunity of a ship bound for London that had unexpectedly put in at Bristol. Byfield despatched a narrative, composed on April 29, only eleven days after the event, in the form of a letter to Doctor Increase Mather and the other agents and friends in London. It was printed in London the following June and reprinted in Edinburgh the same year. With the narrative Byfield despatched a broadside, entitled *Declaration of the Gentlemen, Merchants, and Inhabitants of Boston and the Country Adjacent*, containing a summary of grievances against the Andros government, which had been drawn up, probably on the day of the revolt, by Increase Mather's son, Cotton Mather, then but twenty-six years old, read from the balcony of the town house to the crowd below, and, a few days afterward, printed in enlarged form as a broadside for distribution.

Byfield's narrative is not the account of an eye-witness but is made up from letters and other forms of advice received from Boston. Nevertheless, it was written by one thoroughly conversant with affairs in Massachusetts, for Byfield had come to the colony in 1674, at the age of twenty-one, and had resided much of the time at Boston, engaging in business as a merchant. Apart from his connection with the militia, which gave him his title of captain, he had as yet taken little part in the government of the colony. After 1689 he became a member of the General Court (legislative assembly) and in 1693 was made speaker. His most important post was that of judge of the court of vice-admiralty, to which he was first appointed in 1699; and, though superseded by Wait Winthrop before he entered on the office, he was reappointed and continued to serve at varying intervals until his death in 1733. Toward the end he was characterized as a "poor, superannuated gentleman, near eighty years old, who already distinguished himself very partial to the country." He became one of the proprietors of Bristol, purchasing the peninsula of Poppysquash, and in 1706 was honored by the selection of his name for the territorial parish of "Byfield," which included the present towns of Newburyport and Haverhill.[1] He was a church elder and deacon and a true New Englander, and his narrative, though naturally favorable to the colony, is straightforward and impartial, substantially correct in all its details.

Byfield's *Narrative* was reprinted in the *Historical Magazine*, January, 1862, and again by Sabin in his Quarto Series, no. 1 (1865). Three years afterward it was again printed by Whitmore as the first of *The Andros Tracts* (1868). An abstract will be found in the *Calendar of State Papers, Colonial*, 1689–1692, § 96. The accompanying *Declaration* was first printed as a broadside at Boston by Samuel Green, a few days after the revolution. It is embodied in all the reprints of the narrative mentioned above and has been reprinted separately by Neal in his *History of New England*. A copy of the broadside is in the Public Record Office.

---

[1] J. L. Ewell, *The Story of Byfield* (Boston, 1904). This volume contains a portrait of Byfield.

BYFIELD'S ACCOUNT OF THE LATE REVOLUTION, 1689

An Account of the Late Revolution in New-England. Together
with the Declaration of the Gentlemen, Merchants, and In-
habitants of Boston, and the Country Adjacent. April 18,
1689.
Written by Mr. Nathanael Byfield, a Merchant of Bristol in
New-England, to his Friends in London. Licensed, June
27, 1689. J. Fraser.
London : Printed for Ric. Chitwell, at the Rose and Crown in
St. Paul's Church-Yard. MDCLXXXIX.

Gentlemen,

HERE being an opportunity of sending for London, by a
Vessel that loaded at Long-Island, and for want of a Wind
put in here; and not knowing that there will be the like from
this Country suddenly, I am willing to give you some brief
Account of the most remarkable Things that have hapned
here within this Fortnight last past; concluding that till
about that time, you will have received *per* Carter, a full
Account of the management of Affairs here. Upon the Eighteenth Instant, about Eight of the Clock in the Morning, in
Boston, it was reported at the South end of the Town, That
at the North end[1] they were all in Arms; and the like Report
was at the North end, respecting the South end: Whereupon
Captain John George[2] was immediately seized, and about
Nine of the Clock the Drums beat thorough the Town; and
an Ensign was set up upon the Beacon. Then Mr. Bradstreet,[3]

---

[1] For the North End and South End see below, p. 186, note 4.

[2] For Captain John George, R. N., see below, p. 213.

[3] Simon Bradstreet was the last governor under the old régime. Though
he was in his eighty-sixth year, he was chosen head of the provisional government
that was set up after the fall of Andros.

Mr. Dantforth,[1] Major Richards, Dr. Cooke, and Mr. Addington, etc. were brought to the Council-house by a Company of Soldiers under the Command of Captain Hill.[2] The mean while the People in Arms did take up and put into Goal[3] Justice Bullivant,[4] Justice Foxcroft,[5] Mr. Randolf,[6] Sheriff Sherlock,[7] Captain Ravenscroft,[8] Captain White,[9] Farewel,[10]

[1] Thomas Danforth was deputy-governor under Andros; John Richards, Elisha Cooke, and Isaac Addington were members of the council and all represented the "faction" opposed to Andros. Cooke and Hutchinson were selectmen of the town of Boston, and Addington afterward became the first secretary of the colony under the new charter.

[2] Captain James Hill of the militia was a prominent merchant and deacon in Boston. He died in 1720.

[3] Gaol, jail.

[4] Doctor Benjamin Bullivant, apothecary and physician, came to Boston in 1685, and was a justice of the peace and for a time clerk of the council under Andros. Dunton's sketch of him (*Letters*, p. 94) is now known to be of little value. (*Publications*, Colonial Society of Massachusetts, XIV. 256). Bullivant was one of the founders of King's Chapel, the Anglican church in Boston, and served as churchwarden. He afterward returned to England.

[5] Francis Foxcroft, a justice of the peace under Andros, was also a member and churchwarden of King's Chapel. He was one of the "Small Knot of Male Contents" who signed the address to William III. in defence of the Anglican church (*The Andros Tracts*, II. 28–32). After the revolt he remained in the colony and became a judge of the court of common pleas under Governor Dudley.

[6] For Edward Randolph see below, p. 189, note 3.

[7] James Sherlock was a councillor in 1684 and became sheriff of Suffolk County in 1687. After his imprisonment he was sent back to England with Andros. Later he returned to America, going to Virginia, where he became clerk of the council and clerk of the assembly.

[8] Samuel Ravenscroft was captain of an artillery company in Boston in 1679. He became a warden of King's Chapel in 1689, and with Foxcroft signed the address to William III. After the revolt he went to Virginia, where Randolph endeavored to get him a post as comptroller of the customs, stating him to be "an understanding and active man, personally known to Sir Edmund Andros and Lieut. Gov. Nicholson." But his name does not appear on the custom rolls.

[9] Captain William White, one of the new militia officers, commissioned in 1687, was a member of King's Chapel. Dunton's description of him is unusually elaborate and worthless.

[10] George Farwell was a member of the King's Chapel congregation. He was counsel for Randolph in the latter's suit for libel against Increase Mather. He was sent to England with Andros, but returned to New York, where he became king's counsel, and where he served as one of the attorneys who conducted the trial of Leisler (p. 392).

Broadbent,[1] Crafford,[2] Larkin,[3] Smith,[4] and many more, as also Mercey the then Goal-keeper, and put Scates[5] the Bricklayer in his place. About Noon, in the Gallery at the Council-house, was read the Declaration here inclosed. Then a Message was sent to the Fort to Sir Edmund Andross,[6] by Mr. Oliver and Mr. Eyres,[7] signed by the Gentlemen then in the Council-Chamber, (which is here also inclosed); to inform him how unsafe he was like to be if he did not deliver up himself, and Fort and Government forthwith, which he was loath to do. By this time, being about two of the Clock (the Lecture[8] being put by) the Town was generally in Arms, and so many of the Countrey came in, that there was twenty Companies in Boston, besides a great many that appeared at Charles Town that could not get over (some say fifteen hundred). There then came Information to the Soldiers, That a Boat was come from the Frigat that made towards the Fort, which made them haste thither, and come to the Sconce soon

---

[1] Jonathan Broadbent was born in Maryland, was sheriff of New Hampshire in 1671 (Savage), and under Andros served as one of his tax-collectors. He contributed to the erection of King's Chapel. After leaving Boston he went first to New York, where he seems to have held a post as marshal or sheriff (Goodrick, *Randolph*, VII. 406), and then to Virginia, where he commanded a sloop employed by the crown to suppress illegal trade. Benjamin Harrison called him "a man whose character was a sufficient scandal to his employment."

[2] Doctor Mungo Crafford was an apothecary and an attendant at King's Chapel.

[3] Thomas Larkin was also of the King's Chapel congregation, and served as "messenger" or marshal of the council.

[4] Probably Adam Smith, one of the contributors to the King's Chapel fund.

[5] "Scates the Bricklayer" may have been the same as the Scates mentioned in Bullivant's "Journal" (*Proceedings* of the Massachusetts Historical Society, 1878, p. 107), to whom Phips gave a post in the Port Royal expedition. One John Scate is mentioned in the Boston tax lists. There is also a "Richard Keates the bricklayer."

[6] For Sir Edmund Andros see below, pp. 223-227.

[7] Nathaniel Oliver and John Eyre were prominent residents of Boston, belonging to the anti-Andros party. Sewall's *Diary* is full of gossip regarding these Boston men, such as Hill, Winthrop, Eyre, Oliver, Shrimpton, and others, who represented the colonial party against the newcomers. (See p. 177, note 3.)

[8] The Thursday Lecture was an important feature of church life in Puritan Boston.

after the Boat got thither; and 'tis said that Governor Andross, and about half a score Gentlemen, were coming down out of the Fort; but the Boat being seized, wherein were small Arms, Hand-Granadoes, and a quantity of Match, the Governour and the rest went in again; whereupon Mr. John Nelson,[1] who was at the head of the Soldiers, did demand the Fort and the Governor, who was loath to submit to them; but at length did come down, and was, with the Gentlemen that were with him, conveyed to the Council-house, where Mr. Bradstreet and the rest of the Gentlemen waited to receive him; to whom Mr. Stoughton[2] first spake, telling him, He might thank himself for the present Disaster that had befallen him, etc. He was then confined for that Night to Mr. John Usher's[3] House under strong Guards, and the next Day conveyed to the Fort, (where he yet remains, and with him Lieutenant Collonel Ledget)[4] which is under the command of Mr. John Nelson; and at the Castle, which is under the Command of Mr. John

[1] Captain John Nelson was at this time a young merchant and the head of the eight companies of militia. Hutchinson says that he was "an enemy to the tyrannical government of Andros, but an Episcopalian in principle, and of a gay, free temper, which prevented his being allowed any share in the administration after it was settled" (I. 378). Failing to obtain command of the Port Royal expedition, which was given to Phips, he refused to serve as a regular officer, but took part in the war, was captured and sent first to Quebec and afterward to France, not returning for ten or twelve years (*N. Y. Col. Docs.*, IV. 206–211). As nephew and executor of Sir Thomas Temple, governor of Nova Scotia, who died in 1674, he laid claim to the territory of Nova Scotia, a claim that he sold in 1730 to Samuel Waldo of Boston (*Canadian Archives*, 1886, p. cliv).

[2] William Stoughton was one of Andros's councillors, but after the revolution sided with the colonial party, and was rewarded with the lieutenant-governorship (Mass. Hist. Soc., *Collections*, fifth ser., I. 422–423, note).

[3] John Usher, son of Hezekiah Usher, bookseller of Boston, was councillor, treasurer, and receiver-general under Andros. He was lieutenant-governor of New Hampshire, 1692–1696, while his father-in-law, Samuel Allen, was governor, and was reappointed in 1703, serving till 1715. He was always unpopular (Fry, *New Hampshire*, pp. 85–86).

[4] Colonel Charles Lidget, "an accomplished merchant," was one of the founders of King's Chapel. In 1687 he was an assistant judge under Dudley as chief justice. With Nelson, Foxcroft, and other Episcopalians he signed an address in 1690 praying for an assembly. He returned to England but retained his interest in and business connections with the colony until his death in 1698.

Fairweather,[1] is Mr. West,[2] Mr. Graham,[3] Mr. Palmer,[4] and Captain Tryfroye.[5] At that time Mr. Dudley[6] was out upon the Circuit, and was holding a Court at Southold on Long-Island. And on the 21st Instant he arrived at Newport, where he heard the News. The next Day Letters came to him, advising him not to come home; he thereupon went over privately to Major Smith's at Naraganzett,[7] and Advice is this Day come hither, that yesterday about a dozen young Men, most of their own Heads, went thither to demand him; and are gone with him down to Boston. We have also Advice, that on Fryday last towards Evening, Sir Edmond Andross did attempt to make an Escape in Woman's Apparel, and pass'd two Guards, and was stopped at the third, being discovered by his Shoes, not having changed them. We are here ready to blame you sometimes, that we have not to this Day

[1] Captain John Fairweather was one of the selectmen of Boston.

[2] John West came to New York with Andros in 1674. He became clerk of the court of assizes, and town clerk in 1681. Importuned by Andros to go to Boston, he leased from Randolph the secretaryship of the dominion of New England (Toppan, *Randolph*, IV. 155, 231). Randolph entered into this arrangement, which was disadvantageous to him, in order to keep in Andros's good graces (*id.*, 168, 231). It was West not Randolph who carried off to Boston the records and seal of New York, which, however, were afterward returned. Later West became naval officer and deputy receiver in Maryland.

[3] James Graham came to New York with Andros in 1674, and held many important offices there. He was called to Boston by Andros in 1688, and appointed attorney-general. He returned to England in 1690, but finally made his way back to New York and became an influential leader there.

[4] John Palmer was another New Yorker who had served Andros when governor, having been councillor and chief judge of the supreme court. He went to Boston in 1686, and became a judge in 1688. Returning to England with Andros, he wrote an elaborate defense of Andros's government (*The Andros Tracts*, I. 21).

[5] Captain Thomas Treffry was a cousin of Randolph's and through Blathwayt's aunt, Mrs. Thomas Vivian, was a connection of William Blathwayt, the influential auditor general of the plantation revenues and clerk of the Privy Council. Treffry had been an ensign in Lord Bath's regiment in 1685, and was commissioned lieutenant of one of the two companies of regulars sent to New England. When Andros was away from Boston Treffry was in chief command.

[6] Joseph Dudley was president of the council and head of the government, May–December, 1686, councillor and chief justice under Andros, 1686–1689, a member of parliament, 1701–1702, and governor of Massachusetts Bay, 1702–1715. See Kimball, *The Public Life of Joseph Dudley*.

[7] Wickford, R. I.

received advice concerning the great Changes in England,
and in particular how it is like to fair with us here; who do
hope and believe that all these Things will work for our Good;
and that you will not be wanting to promote the Good of a
Country that stands in such need as New England does at
this Day.   The first Day of May, according to former Usage,
is the Election Day at Road Island; and many do say they
intend their Choice there then.[1]   I have not farther to trouble
you with at present, but recommending you, and all our
Affairs with you, to the Direction and Blessing of our most
Gracious God, I remain

Gentlemen,

Your most Humble

Servant at Command,

NATHANAEL BYFIELD.

Bristol, April 29, 1689.

Through the Goodness of God, there hath
been no Blood shed.   Nath. Clark[2] is in
Plymouth Gaol, and John Smith in Gaol
here, all waiting for News from England.

*The Declaration of the Gentlemen, Merchants and Inhabitants of Boston,
and the Country Adjacent.   April 18, 1689.*

§ I.   WE have seen more than a decad of Years rolled away
since the English World had the Discovery of an horrid Popish
Plot;[3] wherein the bloody Devotoes of Rome had in their Design
and Prospect no less than the Extinction of the Protestant Religion:
which mighty Work they called the utter subduing of a Pestilent
Heresy; wherein (they said) there never were such Hopes of Success
since the Death of Queen Mary, as now in our Days.   And we were
of all Men the most insensible, if we should apprehend a Countrey
so remarkable for the true Profession and pure Exercise of the Protestant Religion as New-England is, wholly unconcerned in the Infamous Plot.   To crush and break a Countrey so entirely and sig-

---

[1] *I. e.*, choice, in accordance with their charter, of Rhode Island officers
to act in place of Andros's New England government.

[2] Nathaniel Clark, of Plymouth, was secretary of that colony and a councillor under Andros.   In 1691 he joined with others in an address to the king,
"setting forth our miserable condition."

[3] The Titus Oates Plot of 1678.

nally made up of Reformed Churches, and at length to involve it in the miseries of an utter Extirpation, must needs carry even a Supererogation of Merit with it among such as were intoxicated with a Bigotry inspired into them by the great Scarlet Whore.

§ II. To get us within the reach of the Desolation desired for us, it was no improper thing that we should first have our Charter vacated, and the Hedge which kept us from the wild Beasts of the Field, effectually broken down. The Accomplishment of this was hastned by the unwearied Sollicitations and slanderous Accusations of a Man, for his Malice and Falshood well known unto us all. Our Charter was with a most injurious Pretence (and scarce that) of Law,[1] condemned before it was possible for us to appear at Westminster in the legal Defence of it; and without a fair leave to answer for our selves, concerning the Crimes falsly laid to our Charge, we were put under a President and Council,[2] without any liberty for an Assembly, which the other American Plantations have, by a Commission from his Majesty.

§ III. The Commission was as Illegal for the Form of it, as the Way of obtaining it was Malicious and Unreasonable: yet we made no Resistance thereunto as we could easily have done; but chose to give all Mankind a Demonstration of our being a People sufficiently dutiful and loyal to our King: and this with yet more Satisfaction, because we took Pains to make our selves believe as much as ever we could of the Whedle then offer'd unto us; That his Magesty's Desire was no other then the happy Encrease and Advance of these Provinces by their more immediate Dependance on the Crown of England. And we were convinced of it by the Courses immediately taken to damp and spoyl our Trade;[3] whereof Decayes and Complaints presently filled all the Country; while in the mean time neither the Honour nor the Treasure of the King was at all

[1] The Massachusetts Bay Charter was legally vacated. I agree with Doctor Kimball when he says, "Whether the charter was justly vacated or not is not the question; the method taken was a proper one to use in vacating a charter, and the decree in Chancery stood and was legally binding until reversed by some higher authority" (*The Public Life of Joseph Dudley*, p. 20). On the general situation see Beer, *The Old Colonial System*, part I., II. 312–313. The argument for Massachusetts is given by Deane, *Memorial History of Boston*, I. 369–380.

[2] Dudley's commission for a government by president and council was issued September 27, 1685.

[3] Reference is here made to the more rigorous efforts that were expended to enforce the navigation acts by the royal proclamation of 1675, the new instructions to the governors of the same year, the appointment of Randolph as collector of customs in New England in 1678, and the attempts that Randolph made to check illicit trade.

advanced by this new Model of our Affairs, but a considerable Charge added unto the Crown.

§ IV. In little more than half a Year we saw this Commission superseded by another yet more absolute and Arbitrary,[1] with which Sir Edmond Andross arrived as our Governour: who besides his Power, with the Advice and Consent of his Council, to make Laws and raise Taxes as he pleased, had also Authority by himself to Muster and Imploy all Persons residing in the Territory as occasion shall serve; and to transfer such Forces to any English Plantation in America, as occasion shall require. And several Companies of Souldiers[2] were now brought from Europe, to support what was to be imposed upon us, not without repeated Menaces that some hundreds more were intended for us.

§ V. The Government was no sooner in these Hands, but Care was taken to load Preferments principally upon such Men as were Strangers to and Haters of the People:[3] and every ones Observation hath noted, what Qualifications recommended a Man to publick Offices and Employments, only here and there a good Man was used, where others could not easily be had; the Governour himself, with Assertions now and then falling from him, made us jealous that it would be thought for his Majesties Interest, if this People were removed and another succeeded in their room: And his far-fetch'd Instruments that were growing rich among us, would gravely inform us, that it was not for his Majesties Interest that we should thrive. But of all our Oppressors we were chiefly squeez'd by a Crew of abject Persons fetched from New York, to be the Tools of the Adversary, standing at our right Hand; by these were extraordinary and intollerable Fees extorted from every one upon all Occasions, without any Rules but those of their own insatiable Avarice and Beggary; and even the probate of a Will must now cost as many Pounds perhaps as it did Shillings heretofore; nor could a small Volume contain

---

[1] The first commission to Andros was dated June 3, 1686; the second, which included New York and the Jerseys, April 7, 1688. All these commissions were entirely legal. They established, however, a form of government wholly different from that which had been in vogue since 1630 and one thoroughly disliked by the New Englanders. Probably even a conciliatory and tactful man would have failed to win over the people he governed, and Andros was neither tactful nor conciliatory.

[2] Two companies of British regulars, altogether one hundred men, were sent over under Lieutenants Treffry and Weems.

[3] The New York men were West, Graham, Farwell, Palmer, Captain Francis Nicholson, and Captain Anthony Brockholes. The charge here made is manifestly an exaggerated one; even on ordinary occasions Mather was not given to impartiality of statement, and this was no ordinary occasion.

the other Illegalities done by these Horse-leeches in the two or three Years that they have been sucking of us; and what Laws they made it was as impossible for us to know, as dangerous for us to break;* but we shall leave the Men of Ipswich or Plimouth (among others) to tell the Story of the Kindness which has been shown them upon this Account. Doubtless a Land so ruled as once New-England was, has not without many Fears and Sighs beheld the wicked walking on every Side, and the vilest Men exalted.

§ VI. It was now plainly affirmed, both by some in open Council, and by the same in private Converse, that the People in New-England were all Slaves, and the only difference between them and Slaves is their not being bought and sold; and it was a Maxim delivered in open Court unto us by one of the Council, that we must not think the Priviledges of English men would follow us to the End of the World:¹ Accordingly we have been treated with multiplied Contradictions to Magna Charta, the Rights of which we laid claim unto. Persons who did but peaceably object against the raising of Taxes without an Assembly, have been for it fined, some twenty, some thirty, and others fifty Pounds. Packt and pickt Juries have been very common things among us, when, under a pretended Form of Law, the Trouble of some honest and worthy Men has been aimed at: but when some of this Gang have been brought upon the Stage, for the most detestable Enormities that ever the Sun beheld, all Men have with Admiration seen what Methods have been taken that they might not be treated according to their Crimes. Without a Verdict, yea, without a Jury sometimes have People been fined most unrighteously; and some not of the meanest Quality have been kept in long and close Imprisonment without any the least Information appearing against them, or an Habeas Corpus allowed unto them. In short, when our Oppressors have been a little out of Mony, 'twas but pretending some Offence to be enquired into, and the most innocent of Men were continually put into no small Expence to answer the Demands of the Officers, who must have Mony of them, or a Prison for them, tho none could accuse them of any Misdemeanour.

* He would neither suffer them to be printed nor fairly published. (Note in margin of original.)

¹ Reference is here made to Chief Justice Dudley's unfortunate remark, at the trial of Wise of Ipswich for refusal to pay taxes, "Mr. Wise, you have no more priviledges left you, than not to be sold as slaves." As no general assembly could meet to vote the taxes, levies were imposed by the governor and council. Even town-meetings were forbidden, except for the purpose of choosing officials and collecting such rates as were determined on at the council meetings in Boston.

§ VII. To plunge the poor People every where into deeper Incapacities, there was one very comprehensive Abuse given to us; Multitudes of pious and sober Men through the Land scrupled the Mode of Swearing on the Book, desiring that they might Swear with an uplifted Hand, agreeable to the ancient Custom of the Colony; and though we think we can prove that the Common Law amongst us (as well as in some other places under the English Crown) not only indulges, but even commands and enjoins the Rite of lifting the Hand in Swearing; yet they that had this Doubt, were still put by from serving upon any Juries; and many of them were most unaccountably Fined and Imprisoned. Thus one Grievance is a Trojan Horse, in the Belly of which it is not easy to recount how many insufferable Vexations have been contained.

§ VIII. Because these Things could not make us miserable fast enough, there was a notable Discovery made of we know not what flaw in all our Titles to our Lands;[1] and tho, besides our purchase of them from the Natives, and besides our actual peaceable unquestioned Possession of them for near threescore Years, and besides the Promise of K. Charles II. in his Proclamation sent over to us in the Year 1683, That no Man here shall receive any Prejudice in his Free-hold or Estate, We had the Grant of our Lands, under the Seal of the Council of Plimouth: which Grant was Renewed and Confirmed unto us by King Charles I. under the Great Seal of England; and the General Court which consisted of the Patentees and their Associates, had made particular Grants hereof to the several Towns (though 'twas now deny'd by the Governour, that there was any such Thing as a Town) among us; to all which Grants the General Court annexed for the further securing of them, A General Act, published under the Seal of the Colony, in the Year 1684. Yet we were every day told, That no Man was owner of a Foot of Land in all the Colony. Accordingly, Writs of Intrusion began every where to be served on People, that after all their Sweat and their Cost upon their formerly purchased Lands, thought themselves Freeholders of what they had. And the Governor caused the Lands pertaining to these and those particular Men, to be measured out for his Creatures to take possession of; and the Right Owners, for pulling up the Stakes, have passed through Molestations enough to tire all the Patience in the World. They are more than a few, that were by

---

[1] In the matter of land titles the colonists had a very real grievance. From the point of view of English law, the Massachusetts titles were none too secure, and many of the men in office were land-greedy. There was danger of the imposition of quit-rents, to which the colonists had a deep-seated antipathy (Channing, *History of the United States*, II. 184–185).

Terrors driven to take Patents for their Lands at excessive rates, to save them from the next that might petition for them: and we fear that the forcing of the People at the Eastward hereunto, gave too much Rise to the late unhappy Invasion made by the Indians on them. Blanck Patents were got ready for the rest of us, to be sold at a Price, that all the Mony and Moveables in the Territory could scarce have paid. And several Towns in the Country had their Commons begg'd by Persons (even by some of the Council themselves) who have been privately encouraged thereunto, by those that sought for Occasions to impoverish a Land already Peeled, Meeted out and Trodden down.

§ IX. All the Council were not ingaged in these ill Actions, but those of them which were true Lovers of their Country were seldom admitted to, and seldomer consulted at the Debates[1] which produced these unrighteous Things: Care was taken to keep them under Disadvantages; and the Governor, with five or six more, did what they would. We bore all these, and many more such Things, without making any attempt for any Relief; only Mr. Mather,[2] purely out of respect unto the Good of his Afflicted Country, undertook a Voyage into England; which when these Men suspected him to be preparing for, they used all manner of Craft and Rage, not only to interrupt his Voyage, but to ruin his Person too. God having through many Difficulties given him to arrive at White-hall, the King, more than once or twice, promised him a certain Magna Charta for a speedy Redress of many Things which we were groaning under: and in the mean time said, That our Governor should be written unto, to forbear the Measures that he was upon. However, after this, we were injured in those very Things which were complained of; and besides what Wrong hath been done in our Civil Concerns, we suppose the Ministers and the Churches every where have seen our Sacred Concerns apace going after them: How they have been Discountenanced, has had a room in the Reflection of every Man, that is not a Stranger in our Israel.

§ X. And yet that our Calamity might not be terminated here, we are again Briar'd in the Perplexities of another Indian War;[3]

---

[1] On this point see below, p. 226.

[2] Rev. Increase Mather, agent of Massachusetts in England 1688–1692.

[3] The commentary on Andros's conduct of the Indian war is very disingenuous. Whitmore says: "The accusations of treacherous treaties with the Indians were evidently stories of which a certain use was to be made, but which were not believed by members of the opposition." (*The Andros Tracts*, I. 24.) Andros was a soldier by profession, and he conducted the Indian campaign with skill. See his statement, Mass. Hist. Soc., *Collections*, third ser., I. 85–87. Conditions were much worse after his overthrow.

how, or why, is a mystery too deep for us to unfold. And tho' 'tis judged that our Indian Enemies are not above 100 in Number, yet an Army of One thousand English hath been raised for the Conquering of them; which Army of our poor Friends and Brethren now under Popish Commanders (for in the Army as well as in the Council, Papists are in Commission) has been under such a Conduct, that not one Indian hath been kill'd, but more English are supposed to have died through sickness and hardship, than we have Adversaries there alive; and the whole War hath been so managed, that we cannot but suspect in it a Branch of the Plot to bring us low; which we leave to be further enquir'd into in due time.

§ XI. We did nothing against these Proceedings, but only cry to our God; they have caused the cry of the Poor to come unto him, and he hears the cry of the Afflicted. We have been quiet hitherto, and so still we should have been, had not the Great God at this time laid us under a double engagement to do something for our Security: besides what we have in the strangely unanimous Inclination which our Countrymen by extreamest necessities are driven unto. For first, we are informed that the rest of the English America is alarmed with just and great Fears, that they may be attaqu'd by the French, who have lately ('tis said) already treated many of the English with worse then Turkish Cruelties; and while we are in equal Danger of being surprised by them, it is high time we should be better guarded, than we are like to be while the Government remains in the hands by which it hath been held of late. Moreover, we have understood, (though the Governour has taken all imaginable care to keep us all ignorant thereof) that the Almighty God hath been pleased to prosper the noble Undertaking of the Prince of Orange, to preserve the three Kingdoms from the horrible brinks of Popery and Slavery, and to bring to a condign Punishment those worst of Men, by whom English Liberties have been destroy'd; in compliance with which glorious Action we ought surely to follow the Patterns which the Nobility, Gentry and Commonalty in several parts of those Kingdoms have set before us, though they therein chiefly proposed to prevent what we already endure.

§ XII. We do therefore seize upon the Persons of those few ill Men which have been (next to our Sins) the grand Authors of our Miseries; resolving to secure them, for what Justice, Orders from his Highness with the English Parliament shall direct, lest, ere we are aware, we find (what we may fear, being on all sides in Danger) our selves to be by them given away to a Forreign Power, before such Orders can reach unto us; for which Orders we now humbly wait. In the mean time firmly believing, that we have endeavoured nothing but what meer Duty to God and our Country calls for at our

Hands: We commit our Enterprise unto the Blessing of Him, who hears the cry of the Oppressed, and advise all our Neighbours, for whom we have thus ventured our selves, to joyn with us in Prayers and all just Actions, for the Defence of the Land.

At the Town-House in Boston, April 18, 1689.

Sir,

Our Selves and many others the Inhabitants of this Town, and the Places adjacent, being surprized with the Peoples sudden taking of Arms; in the first motion whereof we were wholly ignorant, being driven by the present Accident, are necessitated to acquaint your Excellency, that for the quieting and securing of the People inhabiting in this Country from the imminent Dangers they many ways lie open and exposed to, and tendring your own Safety, We judge it necessary you forthwith surrender and deliver up the Government and Fortification, to be preserved and disposed according to Order and Direction from the Crown of England, which suddenly is expected may arrive; promising all security from violence to your Self or any of your Gentlemen or Souldiers in Person and Estate: Otherwise we are assured they will endeavour the taking of the Fortification by Storm, if any Opposition be made.

To Sir Edmond Andross Kt.

WAITE WINTHROP.	ELISHA COOK.
SIMON BRADSTREET.	ISAAC ADDINGTON.
WILLIAM STOUGHTON.	JOHN NELSON.
SAMUEL SHRIMPTON.	ADAM WINTHROP.
BARTHOLOMEW GIDNEY.	PETER SERGEANT.
WILLIAM BROWN.	JOHN FOSTER.
THOMAS DANFORTH.	DAVID WATERHOUSE.
JOHN RICHARDS.	

Finis.

LETTER OF SAMUEL PRINCE, 1689

INTRODUCTION

SAMUEL PRINCE, the writer of the following letter, was the son of Elder John Prince of Hull, Massachusetts, and the father of the Rev. Thomas Prince, collector and antiquary and pastor of the Old South Church. He was born in Boston, May, 1649, and, in 1686, married for his second wife Mercy, daughter of Governor Thomas Hinckley. He first resided at Hull and later at Sandwich, and at this time was on a visit to Boston.

Prince's account of the uprising in Boston was sent to his wife at Sandwich to be forwarded to her father, who was the sixth and last governor of the colony of New Plymouth. Prince personally saw many of the events that he describes and so is an authority of first rank. Furthermore, he had no other object in writing than to state briefly and simply the facts as he knew them, and for that reason his narrative stands with that of Byfield as neither a defense nor an apology, but as a reliable picture of the movement. It was written a week before Byfield's account, and so, though covering a shorter period of time, stands nearer to the actual date of the event. Hutchinson printed the greater part of the letter in his *History* (I. 374–377); but he did not know the identity of the author. The letter was printed in full in the *Collections* of the Massachusetts Historical Society, fourth series, V. 192–196, in the Hinckley Papers, a group of manuscripts that had been preserved by Rev. Thomas Prince, whom his grandfather had in a sense adopted and to whom the old governor had imparted his love for gathering historical manuscripts. These papers were bequeathed by Prince to the Old South Church and society.

LETTER OF SAMUEL PRINCE, 1689

BOSTON, April 22, '89.

Honored Sir,

THE consideration of my sending you a blank, wherein only the declaration[1] was enclosed, seems to deserve a check, and constrains me to an apology, not having, at that time, so much as liberty granted me by the messenger to write two or three lines, whereby you might have understood the present state of things, which by this time you are doubtless acquainted withal; but, lest it should prove otherwise, I have now taken the pains to give a brief account.

I knew not any thing of what was intended, till it was begun; yet being at the north end of the town, where I saw boys run along the street with clubs in their hands, encouraging one another to fight, I began to mistrust what was intended; and, hasting towards the town-dock, I soon saw men running for their arms: but, ere I got to the Red Lion,[2] I was told that Captain George and the master of the frigate was seized, and secured in Mr. Colman's house[3] at the North End;[4] and, when I came to the town-dock, I understood that Boolifant and some others with him were laid hold of; and then immediately the drums began to beat, and the people

---

[1] The Declaration printed above, pp. 175–182.

[2] The Red Lion Inn was upon the southeast declivity of Copp's Hill, at the extreme northern part of the North End. It was not far from the Old North Church, the church of the Mathers, who lived near by.

[3] The house of William Colman, merchant, the father of Rev. Benjamin Colman, afterward the pastor of the Brattle Street Church.

[4] The North End was that portion of old Boston lying north of a line drawn from the Long Wharf along what is now State Street to the present Tremont Street and Scollay Square. It included the custom-house, the court-house and jail, the town house, the markets, two churches, and the houses of many of the most prominent citizens.

The South End lay below State Street toward the Fort, and was composed of lanes and open country. The Old South Church and King's Chapel lay nearly on the dividing line, but south of State Street and Prison Lane.

hasting and running, some with and some for arms, Young Dudley[1] and Colonel Lidgit with some difficulty attained to the Fort. And, as I am informed, the poor boy cried very much; whom the Governor sent immediately on an errand, to request the four ministers, Mr. Joylife,[2] and one or two more, to come to him at the Fort, pretending that by them he might still the people, not thinking it safe for him at that time to come to them; and they returned him the like answer. Now, by this time, all the persons whom they concluded not to be for their side were seized and secured, except some few that had hid themselves; which afterwards were found, and dealt by as the rest. The Governor, with Palmer, Randolph, Lidgit, West, and one or two more, were in the Fort.[3] All the companies were soon rallied together at the Town House, where assembled Captain Wintroup,[4] Shrimpton,[5] Page,[6] and

[1] Probably Paul Dudley, prominent in the later history of the colony. Randolph reported that in July, 1686, Joseph Dudley turned out the clerk of the county court to put in his son, then only sixteen years old (Toppan, *Randolph*, IV. 92). If Randolph's statement is to be trusted, Paul Dudley was born in 1670, not in 1675, as is usually stated. As Paul was appointed "a scholar of the house" at Harvard in 1686, it is likely that Randolph is correct, since entering college at eleven and graduating at fifteen would have been unusual even in those days.

[2] John Joyliffe was recorder, treasurer, and selectman of the town of Boston. He died in 1701, blind and infirm.

[3] By the Fort is meant the fortification on Fort Hill, where Fort Hill Square now is. The hill even then had been partly levelled. This important place was the centre of the uprising of April 18. It included the fort and a battery or sconce that formed an outwork of it on the waterside. Andros in 1687 erected there a "palisade fort of four bastions, with a house for lodging the garrison, which is much wanted, till a really fitting fortification can be built" (*Cal. St. P. Col.*, 1685–1688, §§ 1534, 1536). Here on April 18 Andros, Randolph, and others took refuge, but were surrounded by the militia, as the narrative states.

[4] Major-General Wait Winthrop was the youngest son of John Winthrop, jr., governor of Connecticut, and during his early years was an active participant in the military and civil service of that colony. About 1676 he came to Boston, served under Dudley and Andros, after 1689 became head of the militia, and in 1690, when he was forty-six years old, was commissioned major-general.

[5] Colonel Samuel Shrimpton was a prominent landowner, the possessor of Noddle's Island, now East Boston, and a prominent merchant with a large warehouse near the Town Dock. He was also the proprietor of the Royal Exchange Inn.

[6] Colonel Nicholas Paige, captain and colonel of artillery, was a merchant, and a member of the Anglican church in Boston.

many other substantial men, to consult of matters; in which time the old Governor[1] came among them, at whose appearance there was a great shout by the soldiers.

Soon after, the king's jack was set up at the Fort, and a pair of colors at Beacon Hill: which gave notice to some thousands of soldiers on Charlestown side that the controversy was now to be ended; and multitudes would have been there, but that there was no need. The frigate, upon the tidings of the news, put out all her flags and pennants, and opened all her ports, and with all speed made ready for fight, under the command of the lieutenant—swearing that he would die before she should be taken; although the captain sent to him, that if he shot one shoot, or did any hurt, they would kill him, whom they had already seized. But he, not regarding that, continued under those resolutions all that day. Now, about four of clock in the afternoon, orders were given to go and demand the Fort; which hour the soldiers thought long for: and, had it not been just at that nick, the Governor and all the crew had made their escape on board the frigate—a barge being sent for them. But the soldiers, being so near, got the barge. The army divided, and part came up on the back side of the Fort, and part went underneath the hill to the lower battery, or sconce, where the red-coats[2] were; who, immediately upon their approach, retired up the Fort to their master, who rebuked them for not firing at our soldiers, and, as I am informed, beat some of them. One of them, being a Dutchman, said to him, "What the Devil should I fight against a tousand men?" and so ran into the house.

When the soldiers came to the battery, or sconce, they presently turned the great guns about, and mounted them against the Fort, which did much daunt all those within; and were so void of fear, that I presume, had they within the Fort been resolute to have lost their lives in fight, they might have killed an hundred of us at once—being so thick together before the mouths of their cannons at the Fort, all loaden with small shot: but God prevented it. Then they demanded a surrender; which was denied them till Mr. West and another should first go to the Council, and, after their return, we should have an answer whether to fight or no.

[1] Simon Bradstreet; see above, p. 170, note 3.   [2] British regulars.

And accordingly they did: and, upon their return, they came forth, and went disarmed to the Town House; and from thence, some to the close jail, and he under a guard in Mr. Usher's house. The next day, they sent the two colonels[1] to demand of him a surrender of the Castle,[2] which he resolved not to give: but they told him, if he would not give it presently under hand and seal, that he must expect to be delivered up to the rage of the people, who doubtless would put him to death; so leaving him. But he sent and told them that he would, and did so; and so they went down, and it was surrendered to them with cursing. So they brought them away, and made Captain Fairwether commander in it. Now, by this time that the men came back from the Castle, all the guns, both in ships and batteries, were brought to bear against the frigate—which were enough to have shattered her to pieces at once—resolving to have her. But as it is incident to corrupt nature to lay the blame of our evil deeds anywhere rather than on ourselves, so Captain George casts all the blame now upon that devil Randolph;[3] for, had it not been for him, he had never troubled this good people. So, earnestly soliciting that he might not be constrained to surrender

[1] Probably Colonels Shrimpton and Paige.

[2] The Castle was the fort on the hill of Castle Island, in the harbor three miles from the town. This island had first been fortified in 1634, when the colony feared attack from England (Winthrop, *History*, I. 130, ed. in this series). Wait Winthrop was placed in charge in 1686 by Dudley and the council. Andros, after his arrival, built a new fort, with new batteries at the bottom of the hill, and appointed Colonel John Pipon to command. After the revolt Captain John Fairweather took Pipon's place. In 1703 the fortification was reconstructed and a new fort, called Castle William, was built by Colonel Wolfgang Römer.

[3] Edward Randolph was commissioned collector, surveyor, and searcher of customs in New England in 1678, the first royal official in the colony. To him more than to any one else did Massachusetts Bay owe the loss of her charter in 1684. He was appointed secretary of the new government in 1686, and he remained in the colony till he was sent back to England in 1690. He was a zealous and hard-working servant of the crown, who tried to do his duty as he saw it, but he was constitutionally incapable of seeing any other point of view than his own. He was a persistent office-seeker, and always in financial difficulties, and died poor. He was honest, but tactless and unsympathetic, and the people of New England thoroughly hated him. The publication of his correspondence by the Prince Society (in seven volumes) has thrown a flood of light on New England history of this period.

the ship—for, by so doing, both himself and all his men should lose their wages, which otherwise would be recovered in England—giving leave to go on board, and strike the topmasts, close up the ports, and bring the sails ashore; and so they did. The country people came armed into the town in the afternoon, in such rage and heat, that it made us all tremble to think what would follow: for nothing would pacify them but he must be bound in chains or cords, and put in a more secure place;[1] and that they would see done ere they went away, or else they would tear down the house where he was to the ground. And so, to satisfy them, he was guarded by them to the Fort. And I fear whether or no the matter of settling things under a new Government may not prove far more difficult than the getting from under the power of the former, except the Lord eminently appear in calming and quieting the disturbed spirits of people, whose duty certainly now is to condescend, comply, and every way study for peace. So prays the assured well-willer to New England's happiness,

S. P.

Counsellor Clark[2] writ a very grateful letter to Mr. Bullifant, intimating what a faithful friend he had been to said Bullifant, and withal desiring said Bullifant, that if there should news come out of England of a change, which he hoped in God it never would (as to Government), that said Bullifant would do him the favor as to send him word with expedition, that so he might make his escape, living so dangerously in the midst of his enemies, who were even ready to devour him; and the merchants have gotten this pamphlet, and resolve forthwith to print it.—Farewell!

[1] The jail stood behind the court-house on Court Street, not far from the present Old State House.

[2] Nathaniel Clark; see above, p. 175, note 2.

A PARTICULAR ACCOUNT OF THE LATE
REVOLUTION, 1689

INTRODUCTION

AFTER the uprising of April 18, Randolph was lodged in the common jail, whence during the months from May to October he succeeded in despatching by private hands letters to various people, official and otherwise, and in return received replies through the hands of George Monck, landlord of the Blue Anchor Tavern. Among those to whom he wrote letters at considerable length were Sir Richard Dutton, Governor of Barbadoes, Doctor William Sancroft, Archbishop of Canterbury, Doctor Henry Compton, Bishop of London, Francis Nicholson, the Marquis of Halifax, the Lord Privy Seal, William Blathwayt, and the Lords of Trade.

When, toward the end of May, Rev. Robert Ratcliffe, the first rector of King's Chapel, after a somewhat stormy residence of three years in the colony, decided to return to England to solicit aid for the Anglican church in Boston, Randolph gave him a letter of recommendation to the Archbishop of Canterbury, and intrusted him with the delivery of letters and papers to the archbishop, the Marquis of Halifax, William Blathwayt, and the Bishop of London. In his letter to the archbishop he says at the close, "of this Mr. Ratcliffe can give your Grace a good account."

Among the papers in the Lambeth Palace Library is one entitled "A Particular Account of the Late Revolution at Boston in the Colony and Province of Massachusetts." This manuscript was printed by Bishop Perry in his *Historical Collections relating to the American Colonial Church*, I. 53–64, but the name of the author is there declared to be "unknown." Lewis in his *History of Lynn* believes that the writer was Randolph, and there is something to be said in favor of that

view. But a critical comparison of the text with the letters
and narratives written by Randolph at the time discloses such
marked differences of style and phraseology as to render it
impossible that the account should be from Randolph's pen.
The manuscript is not in Randolph's handwriting, a matter
of little importance as it may be a copy. Of more positive
value in determining the authorship is the fact that the writer
was familiar with Byfield's *Narrative*. Randolph could not
have seen this work, either in manuscript or in print, as it was
despatched from Rhode Island and was not printed until
June, at which time Randolph was in jail.

The writer of the *Particular Account* may have been Ratcliffe, though there is no certain and direct evidence connect-
ing him with the authorship. He went to England in July
and probably saw Byfield's *Narrative* after his arrival. The
work shows a good deal of clerical animosity in its references
to the "preachers," to "one Sheapherd, Teacher of Lynn,"
and to the "Professors of the greatest sanctity." Ratcliffe
had suffered at the hands of the preachers of Boston. Intimate association with the Anglican church and communion
in Boston appears from the frequent references to the Church
of England men as the sufferers by the uprising and to the
Anglican chapel as the object of abuse and attack. That the
"Papists" were allowed to go free and the Anglicans imprisoned would naturally rankle in the mind of the rector, while
the "tender kindness" of the Boston people to the Church of
England was not a thing easy for the head of the flock to
forget.

The account was written by one who had "certain knowledge" of the course of events, who was familiar with the
individuals connected with the revolution, and who was able
to add of his own knowledge to that which is contained in
the other narratives. The comment "In like manner Shrimpton showed himself Shrimpton" might well represent the re-

lation which Ratcliffe had with one of his own congregation, who proved a lukewarm supporter in time of need. If Ratcliffe was the writer, it is not impossible that Randolph furnished information for use in the narrative. The facts regarding Andros's expedition and the case of Shepard of Lynn, with both of which Randolph was familiar, may have come from him.

The manuscript was acquired by the Lambeth Palace Library at some time between 1720 and 1763, possibly in the time of Archbishop Secker, who added greatly to the collections there. It is bound up in a volume of miscellaneous papers, and consists of twenty pages, eighteen of which contain the text. The work is well written throughout and is in excellent condition.

A PARTICULAR ACCOUNT OF THE LATE
REVOLUTION, 1689

*A Particular Account of the late Revolution at Boston in the
Colony and Province of Massachusetts.*

THIS Revolution making a great noise in the world, and
being variously reported, I shall with all Sincerity endeavor
to give a brief account thereof.

Who should have thought that in a land of Righteousness
(as the Massachusetts would be accounted), Men should work
wickedness and that Professors of the greatest sanctity should
have anything to doe with Plots and Conspiracys; yet, alas!
this wild design I must lay at the doors of the Preachers and
their Adherents, and it is too notorious, that some who had
sworn to maintaine the Governm't and discover all Plotts
and Conspiracys against the same ought to bee reckoned
amongst the Principall Conspirators. For this was not a
sudden heat, or violent passion of the Rabble, but a long contrived piece of wickedness. A great while travailed they in
Mischief, ere that detestable Monster came forth.

Some few Strugglings it made in January, but two things
prevented the birth: the first was the Governour's longer
stay to the Eastward than they expected, to prevent the incursions of the Indians, and reduce them to their former
obedience. Whilst we[1] in the Sharpest Season of Winter
was endeavouring their Safety and preservation, they in
Boston were Contriveing the Subversion of the Government
and the ruin of the Governour, and with his, the ruine of the
best part of the Colony. The other was this: The People
were not fitted for the faction, in order therefore to prepare

---

[1] The contrast between "we" and "they" does not indicate that the writer
had accompanied Andros on his expedition. It marks merely the distinction
between the Anglican party and the insurgent colonials.

their minds, and draw the ignorant Multitude after them, they scattered abroad many foolish and nonsensicall storys, and pretended wonderfull discoveries of horrid Plotts against the Country, libells alsoe were carried up and down against the Governm't and those in Authority,—how the Governour had confederated with the freemen [French?], Mohoques and other Indians to destroy the Colony and cut off the People. For the confirmation of this, a report was spread abroad of an Indian, whose heart smote him (as the Phrase was), and who confessed the design and for his part he would not joine in it. The English had done him noe hurt, neither would hee doe them any mischief. With these and the like false storys the Country was miserably distracted, and when any came to Town, some secretly told them the same things and others shook their heads and made ugly faces, whereby they concluded all to bee true, which was reported amongst them: So that it was but sounding a Trumpett or beating a Drum, and the Majority of the People was ready to rise against the Governour, who, as they were made to believe, was the great Enemy of the Country.

And that there might be an universall hatred against him, it was whispered about, that the Governour had drawn all the Youth of the Country to the Eastward, on purpose to destroy them, that all the rum they drank was poisoned, and when any were sick, he commanded his Doctor to despatch them. That the Indian war was but a sham, for hee design'd noe evil to the Indians, but the destruction of the Country. That he admitted the Squaws dayly to him; or else he went out and lodged with them, that noe Soldier durst kill an Indian because the Governour had given positive orders to the Contrary.

Whereas never could Man do more to reduce the Indians to obedience or show greater kindness to the Soldiers. These all publickly declared at their return, that hee was a father unto them and took care that they had what was necessary and convenient for them in their Sickness, visited them in their marquees, went to every marquee, tent or lodging, and if he found them uncovered, would cover them, if he found them sleeping with their knee strings bound, would untie them himself, that all the time he was amongst them hee

never spared any labor or paines, but in all things behaved
himself among them like a tender Father in his family.

His prudence against the Enemy was admirable, for he
soe covered the Country that the Indians were not able to
doe any considerable mischief to the Inhabitants, likewise
he blockaded all the Rivers, whereby the Indians were prevented from fishing and hunting; besides all this he routed
them out of their forts and strongholds, whither they concluded the English could never come, took from them their
Stores, many bushels of Indian Corn, their powder, some
pistols and Musquet barrels and about thirty of their Canons,
whereby they were reduced to very great poverty and forct
to the use of their bows and arrows again, soe that in a little
time they must have rendered themselves to his Mercy, or
else have perished for lack of bread and provisions, for the
French, if they had the will, yet were not in a possibility to
relieve their urgent necessitys, being plundered of all their
Stores by the Privateers and as necessitous as the Indians.
So that in all probability that troublesome war was drawing
near to a fair conclusion.

But in this juncture some of the Bostoners[1] understanding
the wants of the Enemy and knowing how to make their advantage of such a time, when for goods and provisions they
could make what returns pleased them best, loaded Vessels
with Ammunition and provisions, cleared them for Bermudas
and other parts, but sent them to the Eastward amongst the
French and Indians, and supplied them with all such things
as they wanted, whereby they put weapons in the Enemy's
hand to destroy hundreds of the King's Subjects and lay the
whole Country desolate.

There are Men now in Town, that can name some of the
Bostoners who were so damnably treacherous and wicked,
yet are reputed great Patriots of the Country and Restorers
of English Liberties and Privileges.

The tales and Scandalous Storys answered the end for which

---

[1] The Bostoners here referred to are David Waterhouse and John Foster,
whose trading activities among the Indians are frequently mentioned in the contemporary correspondence (below, pp. 209, 263) and are specially commented on
later in this narrative.   With them may be classed George Alden, whom Randolph
calls "a great trader with the eastern French" (Goodrick, *Randolph*, VI. 294).

they were invented, and highly inraged the minds of the People against the Governour, insomuch that on his return they were so far from welcoming him home for his good Services, that they were rather for tearing him in pieces.

However lest the design should be abortive, the Heads of the Faction thought it necessary to conceal their Mischief, before they had made triall how ready the People would bee for their Service when called to Action.

In order to do this a false alarum is made in the Town, that a body of Indians was at Spiepond[1] three miles distant from Boston: Therefore what should they doe? All to Arms without acquainting Governour, Colonell, or Captaine, but presently tideings came, there were only six poor Indians a fishing and there was no danger at all; whereupon all was husht, and every one retired to his own house. This gave the heads of the Conspiracy a perfect demonstration of the frowardness of the people.

Hitherto the accursed embryo moved onely in the womb. That it might exceed all other Monsters, it was thought advisable, that it should have not only claws, and teeth and bristles, but alsoe come into the world speaking malicious words, notorious lies, and reproachfull slanders, which could not bee in a more taking manner than by way of a Declaration, which cost much time and no less paines ere it could bee adapted in any tolerable manner for the mouth of the Speaker.

At length comes the 18th of Aprill, the fatal day wherein the Monster was brought forth, and if ever any of that kind forebode evils and calamities this portended noe less than war, fire, surprise, murder, ruine, and devastation of the Country.

Many hands were ready for the Midwifery, as always the Multitude is prone to doe mischief.

About nine in the morning, Green,[2] a Ship Carpenter, with some others of the Same profession, basely and cowardly

---

[1] Spy Pond was near Watertown (Cambridge). The lands that Randolph tried to obtain lay between Spy Pond and Sanders Brook.

[2] Captain George gives the name of the ship carpenter as Robert Small, but as the text mentions others of "the same profession," there is probably no contradiction.

seiz'd Captaine George, Commander of the *Rose* Frigat, just as he came on Shoar about some matters relating to his Ship, which immediately alarmed the whole Town. The Sheriff,[1] hearing the tumult, went to appease the Multitude, whom they forthwith Secured. From him they goe to the Major[2] of the Regiment and demanded his Colours and Drums, who chec't their Insolence and they threatened to shoot him down and forcing themselves into his house obtained at length their demands and confined him prisoner setting Guards before the doors. By this time numbers were gathered together and formed themselves into companys, w'ch were commanded by Nelson, Waterhouse, Foster and others. About ten they were come to the middle of the Town, where they seized Justice Bullivant, Justice Foxcroft, Captain Ravenscroft, and after sometime forc't themselves into Captain White's house whom also they apprehended and with the former conveyed to the prison doors, which they found Shut and the Gaoler would by no means give them admission, whereupon they forc't open the doors, set at liberty those who were in upon execution for debt, and also a Crew of Privateers[3] who were imprisoned for Piracy and Murder, made a new keeper, committed those Gentlemen with many others to his charge, and that they might bee in safe custody set a guard of Musqueteers to prevent all escapes. By eleven, having secured most of the Church of England (who were the only persons sought for), except some few, who were gone to the Governour in the fort, they went to the Council House, and there read the false and slanderous declaration, which had been contradicted in every paper since published, and backt that with a proclamation, that every man should appear in arms on the greatest penalty. Some they forc't to goe with them, others they left to this choice: Either bear arms, or go to gaol. Many for fear bore arms, which detested the action, those who would not joine with them were sent to the Prison.

About 2 in the afternoon the Chiefs of the Conspiracy

---

[1] Sherlock.

[2] Lieutenant Treffry.

[3] The leader of this "crew of privateers" was Tom Pounds. For an account of the crew, their careers, and their fate, see *The Andros Tracts*, II. 54–55, and Drake, *History of Boston*, p. 490.

(prevailing with some easy and good natured persons to subscribe their names for Company), sent a summons[1] to the Governour in the style of Kings' *Ourselves*, telling lies in hypochrisy,
that they knew nothing of the people's takeing to arms, which
was a perfect contradiction to the Declaration and the knowledge of the leading Men of the faction.　For Dr. Winthrop,[2]
whom all along they confided in and design'd for their Generall, had bin with the conspirators of the North end very
early that Morning, to whom the intentions of the people
were very well known, but when the uproar was made, and
they came to his house requesting Him to bee their Commander and lead them, with abundance of Modesty and no
less hypochrisy refused the offer.　But at length pretending
he was wearied with their importunity's, and to doe the Governour a signall kindness, he condescended to accept of the
office, and walk'd before them.

In like manner Shrimpton shewed himself Shrimpton.
When the Goverment sent for Him in the beginning of the
Tumult, the good Man was not at home, but gone over to his
Island;[3] yet all the while was within the walls of his house,
had true intelligence how the number increased, and when
they entred the Town house, was pleased very bodily to appeare
amongst them, and make one of their Council.

The Governour, haveing received the Summons from the
Conspirators, consulted these Gentlemen that were with Him
(who saw the miserable circumstances they were in, for by
this time the rabble headed by their new Captains had drawn
themselves round the fort), It was thought advisable to over-
look all the others and regard only the names of the Council-
lours, who were appointed that very day to meet his excellency
the Governour at the Town house; so that the answer was to
this effect: Seeing the Gentlemen of the Council were assembled, the Governour would meet them according to appointment.

Pursuant to which, leaving the command of the Fort with

---

[1] This summons is printed above, p. 182;　the Declaration is on pp. 175–182.
[2] He had studied medicine and practised it.
[3] Either Noddle's Island (East Boston), which Shrimpton bought from Sir
Thomas Temple in 1670, or Deer Island, which he leased from the town of Boston.
Probably the latter.

Captaine Treffey,[1] the Governour, attended by Mr. Randolph, Mr. Palmer, Mr. West, Mr. Graham, and Mr. Lydgett goes to the Town house. At the door the Governour was received into Custody by Captain Townsend,[2] who very officiously led them up to the Council Chamber, forbidding the other Gentlemen to attend him any farther. The Governour was no sooner entred, but he was smartly check't and reprimanded by some of his own councill. And whilst he was despitefully treated above, the Gentlemen below, who came with him, had their swords taken from them, and were made the Sport of the Multitude. At length they were also commanded up to be the objects of the Council's rage and fury. Shrimpton abused Mr. Graham and Mr. West in the grossest manner, and all their mouths were opened against Mr. Randolph for being soe instrumentall in condemning their charter and making West his Deputy, who answered it was not he but they themselves that destroyed the charter, for he only told what they acted. As to the disposall of his office, they ought not to bee angry thereat, for none was a looser but himself.

After much talk, the Conspirators (who were pleased to call themselves the Council of Safety),[3] told them they were prisoners and demanded the Governour to give orders for the Surrender of the fort, who told them as a prisoner he could not give orders, but if Mr. Randolph pleased, he might goe and acquaint Captain Trefry with his circumstances. Mr. Randolph accepted that employm't; but on his way to the Fort, the Rabble resisted him and some of them threatened to wash their hands in his heart's blood. Not long after the Rabble entered the Fort without opposition, and carried away Captain Trefry prisoner to the Councill, and Nelson was appointed Commander thereof. On this they ordered the Governour and the other Gentlemen to withdraw to Mr. Usher's till they had further considered of Matters. Thither they come, guarded with a full company of Musqueteers, and for

---

[1] Lieutenant Treffry.

[2] Captain Penn Townsend, a prominent resident of Boston, who was at the head of one of the companies of militia, represented Boston in the General Court from June, 1689, to May, 1692, and was speaker, October, 1689–May, 1690, and again in May, 1692 (Mass. Hist. Soc., *Collections*, third series, IV. 289–292).

[3] For the Council of Safety, see below, p. 216, note 2.

the prevention of escapes, Foster was for placing Sentinells on the top of the house that the Prisoners might not run over the walls.

They had not bin long in the house till Waterhouse, another young Captain, came to order them to several prisons. That house was appointed for the Governour, the Common Gaol for Mr. Randolph and the Fort for the other Gentleman.

So passed away the 18th of Aprill. Nothing happened that night worthy of remark, but the Captain to shew his extraordinary care of the Governour came with a Guard of Soldiers to visit him in his Chamber, where he happened to be then in his bed. The Captain understanding this, and desiring to bee sure, would needs see the Governour's face to know whether Hee was really in bed or noe, and that he might not run from him and his guards, was for securing his stockings and shoes.

The next day the violence of the people increased and nothing would serve the Heads of the Faction but the possession of the *Rose* Frigat, and Castle. The ship upon demand was delivered by the Lieutenant, and immediatly stript of her sails; but the Castle caused them noe little trouble, for Ensign Pipon would not surrender it without an order from his Superiour Officer. It was therefore resolved, that they would storm it, and endeavour'd to take it by force. To this end many Boats and other small vessels were prepared for the transportation of soldiers, who had certainly done and suffer'd great mischief, had not Captain Trefry at the request of the pretended Councill of Safety gone down with advice from the Governour to the Ensign; who thereupon followed such measures as the present necessity required. Soe the Castle was delivered and Pipon brought up, and clapt among the prisoners in the fort.

This seemed to please the People and all things were in great quiet. But alas! this was but like a short calm before a destroying hurricane, for about eleven the Country came in headed by one Sheapherd,[1] Teacher of Lynn, who were like

[1] Rev. Jeremiah Shepard was born in 1648, and after a pastorate at Rowley removed to Lynn. He was of great severity and sombreness of character, and frequently in trouble with his congregations. "His dark and melancholy views

soe many wild bears and the leader mad with passion, or
rather drunk with Brandy, more savage than any of the followers. All the cry was against the Governour and Mr. Randolph. The Governour they would have delivered into their
hands or secured in the fort, otherwise they would pull down
the house about his Eares and tear him in pieces.

This scared the pretended Councill of Safety, for they
were like young conjurers, who had raised a Devil they could
not govern. Away they come trembling to the Governour,
and told him the violence of the people and his present danger.
To whom he replied with a smiling countenance, they should
not bee so much concern'd for him, but rather pity themselves,
their wives and children, their posterity and Country, for they
might assure themselves, there must be an account of that
day's uproar, adding withall that whilst he had the Governm't
none of them suffered in person, or Estate, and if they had
raised the Rabble, which they could not govern, it behoved
them to look to it. Whereupon they desired him to goe to
the fort, who answered, he was their prisoner, and must goe
whither they would carry him, and could freely goe at the
head of those who (as they said) were so extremely mad against
him.

At their desires, tho' sick in bed, he gets up and goes along
with them to the Fort, but instead of that outrage w'ch was
pretended, not one of the whole rout opened his mouth against
him.

This done, and Mr. West, Mr. Palmer, Mr. Graham, and
Mr. Trefry sent down Prisoners to the Castle, away goe the
Country people to their respective homes, and our Councill
of Safety take the management of Governm't to themselves,
of which, that they might shew how well they deserved the
name, they first of all recalled all the forces from the Eastward, and left the poor Inhabitants to the severity and cruelty
of the Indians, who a little after came down upon them, destroyed the cattle, plundered and burnt the houses, killed
many and carried others into Captivity. Next they sent

of human nature tended greatly to contract the circle of his usefulness" (Sibley,
Harvard Graduates, II. 267–276). For the grievance of the town of Lynn against
Randolph, see Toppan, *Randolph*, IV. 201, 202, 205.

some considerable men to Pemaquid [1] and those parts, which are far beyond the limits of their Commonwealth, to seize on the Officers of the Army, where, by tampering with and corrupting the Soldiers, at length they accomplished their design and barbarously treated them, tied their hands behind their backs, brought them as the vilest malefactors to Boston, and immediately committed them to Gaol which was all the thanks they had for their winter's labor and service against the Indians.

On this some of the poor Inhabitants out of the Country came to the Councill and petitioned for Succours, otherwise they and their Familys were inevitably ruined; but the Patriots were not at leisure to commiserate their condition, and grant their requests. The next news from those parts gave an account of miserable devastations and ever Since all the posts from the Eastern Country have bin like Job's Messengers, bringers of Evill tidings.

'Tis thought the Bostoners, out of policy, doe not take care to prevent these Mischiefs that they may the easier continue the inhabitants their slaves and keep the Country in extreme poverty, for if rich men settle in those Parts, and the People grow great, they of Boston must of necessity bee low.

These new Governours were hardly warm in their Seats, before the people were extreamely weary of them and their Governm't, and therefore were for erecting a court martiall, or returning to the rules of the old charter. Which being promoted by the Preachers, was carried with a *nemine Contradicente*, so that many of the new upstart Dictators were turned off with a feather in their Caps; the thanks of the Country for their past services.

Many alsoe dislikt Nelson's civility to the Governour and were highly incens'd, that he permitted his friends to come and visit him. And besides this prevented two villains of the

---

[1] Pemaquid was a log fort near the mouth of the Damariscotta River, in Maine. At the head of the garrison was Major Anthony Brockholes, with Lieutenant Weems in charge of the regulars. The fort had been placed under New England by order of the council, June 20, 1686, when the county of Cornwall, in which it lay, was removed from the jurisdiction of New York. The officers seized were Majors Brockholes and Lockhart, Captain Manning, and Ensign Smith. Lieutenant Macgregory and Lieutenant Jordan were taken by their own soldiers, charged with harshness and cruelty.

Guard from their Bloody design of Murdering the Governour; insomuch that they cashired him from his office, and constituted an old, sullen, morose, single eyed hypochrite,[1] formerly a rum-punch maker to the privateers in Jamaica, Captaine in Nelson's place, who sometimes would not suffer the Governour's servants to come near him, nor his Chaplain to visite him, but would search even his very dishes of Meat, lest there should be letters hid amongst them.

Under this close confinem't the Governour laboured till at length the country, weary of the sport, would watch and guard no longer. Whereupon they resolved to send the Governour to the Castle,[2] and turn West into the Common Gaol, and thereby ease themselves of any more watching at the Fort, which some would have immediately razed to the ground, pursuant to which resolve the Governour was carried down to the Castle, and continues Prisoner in the Custody of Captaine Fairweather, who was very respectfull to him, gave him liberty to walk about the Island, on which the Castle is built, and freely admitted his friends to him; but of late there is come forth a peremptory Decree from the pretended Governour, that no Man shall be allowed so much as to visite him, and the Captaine is commanded to straiten his liberty, otherwise they will Nelsonize him, and turn him out of Commission.

Leaving the Governour, I shall shew what has become of the other Prisoners. Mr. White, Mr. Ravenscroft, with many others who were clapt up because they would not bear arms and guard the Governour, after five or six days unjust imprisonment without any warrant, or colour of Law, they would have perswaded to steal (as it were) out of Gaol, paying only their fees, but they refused the kindness and were for standing a tryall, or else would goe out as publickly as they came in. Which at last was granted, after they had been cried about Town to know, whether any person had ought against them. Justice Foxcroft after a long time was admitted bail; Justice Bullivant, and Lt. Coll. Lydgett got out by giving bond for their appearance. Captaine Trefry and Ensign Pipon were

[1] I cannot identify this picturesque gentleman who succeeded Nelson in command of the fort.

[2] Andros was sent to the Castle June 7. Captain Fairweather's account of his treatment of his prisoners is given in The Andros Tracts, I. 174–175.

dismis't by beat of Drum. All the others continue close prisoners, except two notorious and profest Papists, whom they freely dismis't and took care to convey them safe to their own homes. Only the poor Church of England Men continue Sufferers, and can find neither mercy nor common justice.

Thus, Sir, you have a brief account of the detestable design, which was conceived in malice, nourished by falsehood and lies, and brought forth in Tumult and Rebellion, every way odious and detestable. Yet I must add how ugly soever it appears to the world, not half soe horrid as some intended, and as it would most certainly have bin, had the least blood bin spilt in the Revolution. For one of the Preachers was for cutting the throats of all the Established Church and then (said he very religiously), wee shall never bee troubled with them again. Another seriously declared to a Gentl. in person, that if any blood had been spilt, they would have spared none of that Communion. "How," said the Gentleman, "what if a soldier should get drunk, quarrel and fight, must all have Suffered?" The party made answer: "Had there bin any blood spilt, all of that Communion had Suffered." Others affirmed: "It was no more sin to kill such as they were, than to cut off a dog's neck."

I shall presume to give you a signal instance of their tender kindness to the Church of England. On the 16th of May about four in the Morning there happened a fire[1] at the North end of the Town which caused a great Tumult among the Inhabitants. A person of noe mean quality of that Communion, hearing a bustle in the street, opening the Casement looked out at the Window, which a Man full of gray hairs observing, immediately vented his rancour against the Church of England and reviled her Members, adding withall "This is one of their gang hath don the Mischief." Another said, "Wee shall never bee quiet whilst any of the Church of England are left amongst us." The widow woman, tenant in part of the house which was burnt, was of the same Communion, who in the time of the fire prayed the help of the people to save her goods; but received this Religious answer, "Hang the Popish whore, let her and her goods perish." Afterwards

[1] This fire of May 16 is referred to in Captain George's narrative, below, p. 218.

there was a contribution made, and the Man whose house was burnt, had above an hundred pounds given him, but this poor woman, which was a Widow, had two small children and nothing to relieve herself withall, had not so much as a single penny of the whole collection. Here is charity, and such a spirit of Christianity as was never known in the whole world, but N. E.

This is all, Sir, that occurs to my remembrance of the late Revolution at Boston, and I would not have any think mee partial in this narative, because I make no mention of the Governour's cruelty and wickedness, of his great furnace to torment the people in, and his dreadful mines (as some reported), to blow up the Town, as also of his endeavours to make his Escape, his passing two guards in womens apparell, but being at last discovered by his shoes (as the worthy Mr. Byfield reported).

All which storys, Sir, have not the least foundation of Truth, and soe gross and palpable, that wise Men will not credit, and to undeceive the too credulous world (if willing to bee undeceived), I doe declare upon certaine knowledge, are falsehoods, and lies, the Inventions of wicked men spread abroad on purpose to render the Governour odious to his people. Like these are many other aspersions, which are cast upon him, and therefore, I hope, will not bee entertained as Credible by sober and thinking persons, before they have firmer grounds for belief, than the words of some few angry and peevish animals, who, to gratifie their revenge, have learnt this property of the Devil, *fortiter calumniari*, and make no scruple to tell lies for advantage.

Had the Governour written after their Copy, taken directions from the preachers, permitted the privateers to have their wonted resort amongst them, and allowed them freely to break the Acts of Trade, hee had bin the best of men, little less than a reputed God. For the prohibition of these irregularitys made his Government intolerable, which will bee plainly demonstrated from their words and practices since the revolt.

Their discourse was much about their valour and greatness, that now they were a free people, and should the Crown of England send them a Governour, they would not receive him. For they wanted not the assistance of England, neither had England any thing of dominion over them. They had got the Government by the sword, and they would keep it by the sword. If it should come to the worst, they could make it a free port and the Privateers would defend them.

More villanys were committed in Six weeks after the Revolt, than in the whole time of Sir Edmond's Governm't. Houses were frequently broken open and robb'd. Men set at liberty, who were imprisoned on Execution for debt, and known Pirates and Murderers freely discharged the goal. No man safe in person or Estate, noe relief for the greatest injury, or wrong. The Acts of trade were publickly broken, and boats loaden with hogsheads of Tobacco went up the River at noon-day. That they might not plead ignorance in the matter, one of the Gentlemen imprisoned in the Castle desired the Captaine to take notice of it. They sent vessells amongst the French and Indians with Ammunition and Provision, altho' in open hostility against us, who in all likelyhood have with the same powder and bulletts, which they bought of the Bostoners, killed many of their Majestys' Subjects and destroyed the best part of the Country. Fosters and Waterhouse's trading amongst them was the publick discourse of the Town, and that in little more than two months with a small bark they gained £500. Captaine Nicholson[1] found another Bostoner trading amongst them, as he was on his voyage from New York. Two select Companys stole vessells, and went out a privateering, and a third was preparing. There was certaine intelligence that the first had done a great deal of Mischief, and pillaged vessells on the Coasts of Virginia.

A Pirate lay just without the harbour between the Capes, and the *Rose*, Frigatt, would not be permitted to goe out and take him, or so much as to chase him away from the Coast. But the Man of War must lay in the Harbour like an old wreck stript of all her sails and apparell, altho' 20 Thousand pounds security was offered, and the Captaine not allowed so much as to command his Men, but the Pirate at liberty to doe what he listed with the ships on the Coasts.

All this, Sir, is notoriously true, and I can further add many discoursed of sending Ships to Holland and Scotland, and

---

[1] Captain, afterward Colonel, Francis Nicholson was one of the best-known of the colonial governors. See below, p. 321, note 1.

upon very credible information, there is lately arrived in Scotland directly from Boston a vessel loaden with the enumerated Commoditys of the Plantations. And if they shew themselves soe early, what may a Man judge, will be their actings, when they come to be warm in Governm't. Especially if it bee considered, that those who are Lords paramount are the greatest offenders, and some of the chief in Government the very Men, which most notoriously break the Acts of Trade.

LETTER OF CAPTAIN GEORGE TO PEPYS, 1689

INTRODUCTION

CAPTAIN JOHN GEORGE, R. N., was in command of H. M. S. *Rose*, in which Randolph sailed from England, January 20, 1686, reaching Boston, after a tedious voyage, on May 14. Though at first appearing to Randolph as a "very civil person," he soon gave the latter cause to change his opinion, and the later relations between the two men were anything but amicable. George seems to have combined with Dudley to share fees and perquisites that Randolph deemed legitimately his own, and he refused to aid the latter in enforcing the acts of trade or to go to the help of the northern colonies when menaced by the Indians. When on one occasion George did go out after pirates, Randolph reported that his frigate, though "the biggest first rate," was so dull a sailer that all the pirates got away.

From all accounts, George was a swaggering officer, of foul speech and coarse nature but not unlike many of those in the naval service of that time. He listened to Dudley and Andros but to no one else, and was abusive to Wharton, the judge of admiralty, to Randolph, and to Randolph's subordinates. His favorite threat was "to whip them raw," and his men must have been like him, for the council, whose orders he refused to take, once informed him that he must keep his sailors on board at night, since on account of their misdemeanors they would not be allowed on shore after dark. The picture that we get of Captain George is not attractive, though it must be remembered that the evidence is all *ex parte*. Still, in the main, facts uphold Randolph's charges. From 1686 to 1689 the frigate remained in the harbor, anchored off the water front a little way below the Fort, doing nothing. We are not surprised at the captain's complaint that "the worm had seized her and that she would not be able to continue upon this station without a very considerable repair." Nevertheless, there is probably another side to the case, and it is certainly doubtful whether the charge of cowardice can be maintained. After the revolution, early in May, 1690, George sailed with the *Rose* to Piscataqua and rendered efficient service to the northern colonists in their defense against the Indians. From there, on the 19th of the same month, he passed eastward to engage the French off Nova Scotia, and in an obstinate fight on the 24th with a French man-of-war, at "half musket shot" for two hours off Cape Sable, he was killed.

The letter here printed was sent by George to Samuel Pepys, secretary to the Board of Admiralty, and by him despatched to the Lords of Trade, where it was read August 10. With it were enclosed a proposal of sundry merchants for the restoration of the frigate to the command of the captain, and a copy of George's letter to the Council of Safety, making the same request. The original documents are to be found in the Public Record Office, *C. O.* 5 : 855 (15, 15 I, 15 II), and a letter-book copy is in *C. O.* 5 : 905. Abstracts are given in the *Calendar of State Papers, Colonial*, 1689–1692, § 196, I., II.

LETTER OF CAPTAIN GEORGE TO PEPYS, 1689

Capt. George's Letter to the Admiralty.[1]

Rose at BOSTON N. England
June the 12th 1689.

Sir

THIS is the first opportunity I have had of writeing to you since my last of the first of January,[2] which gave you a full account of the condition of his Ma'ts shipp *Rose*, by which I acquainted you that the worme had Seized her, and that she would not be able to continue upon this station, without a very considerable repaire: but since have not had the favour of a line from you nor[3] [for] above Eighteen months before, except the Instructions for the regulateing of Salutes, which hath been punctually Observed.[4]

These last five months this place hath been fill'd with various reports of transactions in England, of the Prince of Orange's Landing, His Ma'tys goeing for France and there died, After which the Prince and Princess of Orange were proclaimed King and Queen of England, but no reasonable confirmation till the arrivall of Two shipps from London, the first the 26th, and

---

[1] This is the original letter. These words written at top in another hand.

[2] George's letter to Pepys, giving a full account of the condition of his vessel, does not appear to be extant. Dr. J. R. Tanner, who very kindly undertook the search for me, reports that he can find no trace of it among the Pepys Papers at Magdalene College, Cambridge, and that Mr. Perrin, librarian of the Admiralty, has likewise been unable to locate it at the Public Record Office, where other captains' letters of that year are preserved.

[3] Altered from "for"; the Letter Book copy has "for."

[4] The regulations here referred to are dated June 22, 1688, and entitled "An Establishment touching Salutes by Guns to be from henceforth observed in his Ma'ys Royall Navy." A copy of this royal order is to be found in the Admiralty Library, MS. 30, and for a copy of it I am indebted to Dr. Tanner and Mr. Perrin. It contains fourteen sections and gives detailed directions regarding the salutes to be fired, in port and upon the high seas, between his Majesty's ships or when meeting foreign ships, upon occasion of the death of an officer, upon embarking or disembarking in foreign ports passengers of position or rank, or when celebrating certain appointed anniversary days. The royal warrant is countersigned, "By his Maj'ts Command, S. Pepys."

the other the 29th of May, Sir Willm. Phipps coming in the
latter, who brought severall proclimations put forth by their
Ma'tys but before this confirmation, on the 18th of Aprill
last, the People of this place and countrey pretending themselves dissatisfied with the Government of Sir Edmond Andros,
rose up in Arms, seiz'd me first, and run me into the common
Goal, by the Instigation of Robert Small my Carpenter, who
had Absented himself from his duty some days before[1] and
had been with the Rebells, and some hours after his Excell'ce
coming downe to sitt in Councill; pretending he had a Designe
to deliver this Government to the French, and the said Carpenter spreading rumours among the People, that at least he
intended to fire the Towne, at one end, and I at the other,
and then with our Gunns from the Friggatt to beat downe the
rest, and goe away in the smoake, designeing for France, w'ch
doubtless will be thought unreasonable to beleive: The Fort
being Surrounded with above Fifteen hundred men was Surrendred, at the same time my Carp'tr went downe to the
Platforme and travers'd severall Gunns against the Frigg't,
and would have fired them, but was prevented by the people:
he proposed severall ways of takeing or burning the shipp, but
not Adherd to; The next day the Governour was committed
prissoner to the Fort under strong Guards, and my Self to
Coll'll Shrimptons house, who was very kind to me in all this
Affaire.

The same day the Castle, about three miles below the towne,
upon an Island, was Summon'd and Surrendred. I was also
sent for to the Councill of Safety[2] as they terme themselves,

---

[1] On April 18, when the uprising took place in the town, a mutiny broke out
on board the frigate. Randolph wrote in December, "Those that made them
[the men of the *Rose*] mutiny before, are as ready as ever to do it again," and one
Jervas Coppindale afterward stated that "when the news of the King's accession
reached New England, Captain George intimated that he would carry the ship
to France, which design was opposed by petitioner and several of the crew"
(*Cal. S. P. Col.*, 1689–1692, §§ 664, 674).

[2] The Council of Safety consisted of Wait Winthrop, Simon Bradstreet,
William Stoughton, Samuel Shrimpton, Bartholomew Gedney, William Brown,
Thomas Danforth, John Richards, Elisha Cooke, Isaac Addington, John Nelson,
Adam Winthrop, Peter Sergeant, John Foster, David Waterhouse, James Russell,
John Phillips, Penn Townsend, Joseph Lynde, John Joyliffe, Eliakim Hutchinson,
Nathaniel Oliver, John Eyre, Jeremiah Dummer, William Johnson, John Haw-
thorne, Andrew Belcher, Richard Sprague, James Parker, Dudley Bradstreet,
Nathaniel Saltonstall, Richard Dummer, Robert Pike, John Smith, Edmund

consisting of the Cheife Gentl'n and Inhabitants of Boston, who demanded of me an order to the Leivet't[1] for Surrendring the shipp, in answer to which I said it was not in my power being a prissoner, nor would I ever be brought to give any such order, and if I should the Lt., who in my Absence was commander and accountable for the shipp, would not Observe them. They told me my Commission was now of no force, and Urged me to take a Commis'n from them and serve the Countrey; I told them my Commis'n was still good till one from the Crowne of England made it Invalid, and that I would Accept of no Commission from them, nor did beleive they durst venture to give me One. They still persisted in theire resolutions of takeing the shipp by force, but I Advised them to the contrary, Assureing them there would be a great slaughter before she could be taken, And that the Kings shipps never did surrender; I also told them If they would lett her ride quietly without molestation, there would be no danger from her, for the Lt. had no Orders to move from that place, nor would the shipp move till Advice from England: but while they were thus discourseing with me, they sent aboard Two or Three men who perswaded the Lt. and company, to strike Yards and Topmasts and declare for the Prince of Orange, w'ch was Immediately done, and presently after they Acquainted me of it and remanded me back to my Confinement. On the 22d of the same an order was sent on board from the sd Councill to the Lt. for the delevery of the sailes, which was accordingly executed, and now remaine in the custody of them: Nor was the Carpenter yet quiett, but procured a marshall to be sent on board from the Councill to demand severall men of the shipps company to come a-shoare, to Testifie against me, which being refused by the Lt. the Carpenter by severall messages sent on board and advised the men to come ashoare, if not with leave by force, for the Councill would take it kindly and would secure them theire wages; w'ch tooke with them and on the first of may at 4 in the morning they left the shipp and went to him, who by his devices and perswasions got them

---

Quincy, William Bond, and Daniel Pierce, thirty-seven in all. The elder Bradstreet was made president, Addington, secretary, and Wait Winthrop, commander of the militia.

[1] Lieutenant David Condon was second in command. In *A Vindication of New England* he is declared to be a Roman Catholic.

to Signe to a paper intimateing my goeing to France without any ground at all, for I am sure it never entred into my thoughts, much less that I should take a resolution thereof, which paper was present'd by him to the Councill, and received with much favour on his side, nor could I gett a Coppy of what was Alleaged against me. I went to the Councill and told them the Ill That might happen to his Ma'tys shipp, by such disorders, and that the Kings Navy was Govern'd by an Establisht Act of Parliament, and was wholy Independant from any Government ashoare, w'ch point they considering advised the men to goe on board againe and Submitt themselves to theire officers, which most of them easily complied with except the Carpenter and half a dozen more who still are in Rebellion; On the 16th of may at 4 in the morning, hapned a fire at the North end of Boston and the report was spread by the sd Carpenter I had caused the Towne to be fired; and raised a great concourse of people which came to my Lodgeing, breakeing open the doors, rudely carrid me away and put me into the Fort prissoner, he at the same time sent two or three boats on board with Arm'd men, and fetch'd the Lt., Officers and men that Sided not with him on shoare, and carried them to the common Goal; where they lay Three days and then by the Councill's Order sent aboard againe, Since w'ch time the shipp hath been more easy. The Carpenter's designe in this last action was to gett a Commiss'n from the Councill to Command the shipp; w'ch he declared was promis'd him of them. Two days after I was released againe from the Fort and tooke the oppertunity to acquaint the Councill that unless they Secured the Carpenter the Kings shipp could not be safe, but they Objected against it and said it could not be done. I have since been assisted by Coll'll Shrimpton in the moveing for the Sailes, but to no purpose. On the 7th Instant there was an Order sent on board to the Lt. requireing him to send Sixteen men on shoare to testifie against me, whose names were therein mentioned, which paper the Lt. sent to me desireing my direction. I sent him word, if I were aboard I could not answer parting with any on such demands from theire Ma'tys shipp. I then went up to the Government,[1]

---

[1] The provisional government lasted until May 2, when a convention of representatives of the towns met and recommended that the old government be resumed. Elections were held, and on May 22 a regular representative assembly

for now they so terme themselves, and acquainted them I thought they would have rather return'd my Sailes then [than] expected what was formerly refused, upon which they told me I should not have my sailes till an Order from England. What they Intend to doe I know not, but threaten to have the shipp further dismantled, but I hope they will be prevented by Speedy Arrivall of Orders from Your hands to returne home. Sir, here is now rideing severall shipps, some bound for London and others for the West Indies, but durst not stirr because there are severall Piratts Attending their goeing out within Eight Leagues of this place, and severall of the *Rose's* men are runn away to them, which gave Occassion to the Merchants to present a paper to the Government, a Coppy of w'ch I heare inclose, but it availeing nothing, this afternoon I wroate a letter to them, a Coppy of w'ch also comes with this, but as yett cannot gaine an answer tho' very much urg'd by me, therefore must refer to the next opportunity w'ch may happen in a fortnight or Three weeks. In the meane time I subscribe my Self

   Sir,
  Your Honours most Obleiged humble servant
        Jo: GEORGE.
The Gunner and Boatsw'n have both declined theire duty and obedience since these troubles.   J. G.

[*Addressed:*] For his Ma'tys Service.
 To the Hono'ble Sam'll Pepys Esqr.,
  Secretary to the Admirallty.
[*Endorsed:*]
 [1.]   N England
      12 June 1689.
      Capt. Georges Leter to the
      Sec'ry of the Adm'lty.
 [2.]   Read the 10 Aug: 1689.
 [3.]   Entred liber 3d } p. 121.
      N England
      B A
      P. 19.

gathered. Executive control was placed in the hands of the same governor and magistrates that had been chosen in 1686, and that were in office when the assembly dissolved on May 21 of that year.

ANDROS'S REPORT OF HIS ADMINISTRATION,
1690–1691

INTRODUCTION TO NARRATIVES OF ANDROS'S ADMINISTRATION, 1690–1691

FEW characters in American colonial history have been the subject of more bitter comment than has Sir Edmund Andros. Writers even to-day speak of him as an oppressor and a tyrant, of his administration as a time of usurpation and absolutism, and of his supporters as minions and henchmen. The vocabulary that does service in describing the Stuart régime in England also does service in describing the régime of Andros in Boston. But the time for unqualified denunciation is past. The writer who still employs the familiar formulae is merely repeating the epithets of contemporary chroniclers who wrote out of the bitterness of their hearts, condemning the policy and methods of a government that was not of themselves. The system that Andros was called on to administer was by its very nature centralized, for it had as its object the consolidating of the resources of a wide territory in the interest of defense and the observance of the acts of trade. Andros did not originate the idea that found application in the "Dominion of New England," neither was it a special Stuart contrivance; it was a phase of English policy that continued to persist even after the Stuarts fell. Andros was merely the agent selected by the authorities in England to put the plan into execution. Our criticism of him must be limited to the manner in which he carried out his trust.

From the point of view of the British government there was ample justification for the experiment. The decentralized system that prevailed in New England may have been beneficial as a seed-ground for future democracy, but it was a failure as far as the commercial welfare of England was concerned. Massachusetts lost her charter in large part because of her persistent opposition to the imperial demands. The colonies wanted all the advantages of independence but they expected England to carry their burdens, and that, too, with only a minimum of co-operation on their own part.[1] When danger arose Massachusetts did not hesitate to apply to the king for aid and protection.[2] To the Lords of Trade New England appeared to be, as it actually was, weak and inefficient. Consolidation meant strength, and strength was required if the laws were to be executed and the colonies protected against attack. A single system, centralized and aggressive, was needed to take the place of the many scattered and loosely organized colonies that were seemingly jealous of each other and quarrelling among themselves, more concerned for rights and privileges than for duties and obligations. The Privy Council was naturally less interested in the political and religious independence that New England had enjoyed for half a century than it was in the imperative demands of the empire itself.

Andros was sent over to establish a strong government. For this purpose he had many qualifications. He was a soldier and had had experience as an administrator. He was loyal, honorable, and energetic, and was not likely to betray the confidence vested in him. He was in the prime of life, forty-nine years old at the time of his arrival in the colony, and was physically competent for the task before him. Having been in New York as governor, he knew something of the conditions that confronted him in America; and, as we may well believe, was in full sympathy with the policy that he was

---

[1] Mather defends New England against this charge in his *Vindication:* see *The Andros Tracts,* II. 23–24.

[2] *Cal. St. P. Col.,* 1689–1692, §§ 797, 798, 802, 807.

commissioned to carry out.   At the same time, to one familiar
with New England, its preachers and saints, he was not the
best man for the place.   He was imperious and impatient, and,
as a disciplinarian, was more than likely to find fault with the
New Englander's haphazard ways of doing things and to ride
roughshod over traditions and prejudices that stood in the
way of the work to be done.   As a soldier, he was not fond of
government by discussion.   When it came to such questions
as censorship of the press, marriage licenses, taking the oath,
organizing justice, and determining titles to land, he would
naturally conform to English law with little regard to previous
practices in the colony; and in his devotion to the Church of
England he was certain to raise an issue involving trouble.
When it came to the actual business of administration he favored Church of England men in his appointments to office,
and called into service a number of New Yorkers whom he
had known at the time of his residence there.   Such men,
though often able and efficient, were, as a rule, wanderers without local attachments and seekers of colonial offices; they could
not but be offensive to the Puritans and their descendants
who had founded in New England a permanent home.

The first two accounts of the administration of Andros
that are here printed represent very different points of view.
The first, written by Andros himself and sent to the Lords of
Trade after his return to England, lays stress upon those fea-
tures that indicate the faithfulness with which he executed
his commission.   Andros told what he had done to carry out
the task intrusted to him and so made clear to the Lords of
Trade how far he was deserving of their confidence.   That
his statement was satisfactory is evident from the fact that he
was acquitted by his superiors of all guilt.

The second account, drawn up by five members of his
council, contains a criticism of the manner in which he had
performed his work, a matter regarding which Andros himself

says nothing. Two of the councillors, Stoughton and Wait Winthrop, were present at nearly every one of the recorded ninety-four meetings; Gedney was present at nearly one third, and Hinckley at nearly as many; while Shrimpton, who entered the council at the end of its career, was present but seven times. These councillors complained that Andros ignored the greater number and governed with the advice of but few, many of whom were strangers to the colony; that he curtailed debate, overruled objections, and displayed extreme harshness in council meetings; that he ignored orders upon which the majority had agreed and put into execution others that the members had not voted on; that he caused meetings to be called unexpectedly and at times when distant members could not be present; and that he forced through measures which a majority of the members wished to defer for fuller discussion.

Our attitude toward these complaints will depend somewhat on our point of view. Discussion was not one of Andros's strong points, and we can perhaps imagine what his answer to the charges might be. Though the council records frequently bear witness to the truth of what the councillors asserted, they also present evidence to show that many of the New England members pursued a deliberate policy of obstruction, and for the work to be done the Puritan's wordiness and love of debate were quite as serious a menace as was despotism.[1] There is nothing to indicate that Andros was despotic; but he was impatient and curt and no doubt cut short many a good argument. Unlimited free discussion has not always been accepted as an unalloyed blessing, even in our own democratic time. Andros probably anticipated some of our modern legislative devices for limiting debate.

As to the further complaints regarding land-titles, quit-rents, and the dispensing of justice there is ample justification

[1] See below, page 249, note.

of them from the side of colonial law and custom, but Palmer in his pamphlet made out a very good case in defending the administration from the side of English law.

The statement of the councillors here printed is, on the whole, a frank and honest attempt to tell the truth as they saw it. That it was the whole truth we cannot believe. A Boston merchant characterized well the Puritan leaders when he said: "They are exceedingly wedded to their own way; a very home-bred people, but exceedingly wise and conceited in their own eyes."

The third account which is here given parallels, to a considerable extent, the narrative which Andros himself furnishes of his administration, though devoting more space than does Andros to the Indian war. The authorship of this pamphlet is not certainly known, but the writer was undoubtedly one of those sent back to England with Andros in February, 1690. The "ten months imprisonment" mentioned on pages 232–233 coincides exactly with the period of imprisonment in Boston, from April 18, 1689, to February 10, 1690. The initials "C. D." are probably alphabetical, concealing the identity of the writer at a time when concealment was desirable. This belief is borne out by an earlier paper signed "C. D.," probably by the same author, and written in reply to one by "A. B.," entitled "An Account of the Late Revolutions in New England." [1] In the preface to the narrative of the councillors, the printed "C. D." pamphlet is called a "scandalous Pamphlet, supposed to be written by an Implacable Enemy of all good men, and a person that for Impudence and Lying has few Equals in the World" (below, p. 240). The reference is clearly either to Randolph or to Dudley, for Andros cannot have written the papers, Palmer published a pamphlet over

[1] *Cal. St. P. Col.*, 1689–1692, §§ 180, 181. The paper by "A. B." was afterward printed in London and has been reprinted in *The Andros Tracts*, II. 191. The first "C. D." paper has never been printed.

his own signature,[1] and West, Farwell, Graham, and Sherlock were not closely enough identified with Massachusetts to have written so intimately of the colony. The mention of the Evangelization Fund points to Randolph, who was continually commenting adversely on this subject (Toppan, *Randolph*, I. 225), but the phrase "our old Charters in New England" would hardly have been used by him, as he was not a New Englander. Furthermore, the style is much better than that employed by Randolph, and a study of his correspondence inclines one to the belief that Randolph was not the writer of the pamphlet.

If we take the two "C. D." papers together, we get a number of fairly definite indications that point to Joseph Dudley as the author. He twice calls the Massachusetts men "my countrymen," and he states that he was "an eye and ear-witness to the Commission which appointed the President and Council for the New Government" in 1686. As the judge before whom Parson Wise was tried, Dudley could well have written "my nearness to the men of Ipswich has made me familiar with the troubles and disturbances there, but how they and their like at Plymouth have been proceeded with I do not know so well." It is quite possible that Randolph had a hand in the composition of the second paper, for it was written after the arrival in England, but that Dudley actually penned the narrative seems demonstrated by the weight of evidence.

Andros's report is to be found among the Colonial Office Papers in the Public Record Office, *C. O.* 5: 855, and is printed in the *Documents relative to the Colonial History of New York*, III. 722–726. The *Narrative of the Proceedings* was printed in Boston in 1691 and reprinted in *The Andros Tracts*, I. 133–147. *New England's Faction Discovered* was printed in London in 1690 and also reprinted in *The Andros Tracts*, II. 203–222. The texts here given of the last two pamphlets are from the rare copies of the first issues in the John Carter Brown Library.

[1] See below, p. 239, note 2.

ANDROS'S REPORT OF HIS ADMINISTRATION, 1690

To the Right Hon'ble the Lords of the Committee for Trade and Plantations.

The state of New England under the goverment of Sr Edmond Andros.

THAT in the yeare 1686 Sir Edmond Andros was by comission under the Greate Seale of England appoynted to succeed the President Dudley and Councill in the goverment of the Massachusetts Collony, the Provinces of Hampshire and Maine and the Narragansett Country, to w'ch was annexed the Collonyes of Rhoad Island New Plymouth and the County of Cornwall.[1]

In the yeare 1687 the Collony of Connecticott was also annexed and in the yeare 1688 he received a new Commission for all New England includeing the Province of New Yorke and East and West Jersey, with particuler order and directions to assert and protect the Five warlike Nations or Cantons of Indians, lying West from Albany above the heads of our rivers as far or beyond Maryland *vizt* Maquaes, Oneydes, Onondages, Caeujes,[2] and Sennekes, as the Kings subjects upon whom the French had made severall incursions, and to demand the setting at liberty severall of them surprized and deteyned by the French, and reparation for sundry goods taken from severall Christians His Majesties subjects in the lawfull prosecution of their trade.

Sir Edmond Andros upon receipt of his Commission went to New Yorke and Albany of which the Indians having no-

---

[1] The county of Cornwall lay east of the Kennebec River and included the district of Pemaquid and the adjacent islands off the coast. Courts were established for the county by the Andros Council in 1687.

[2] Cayugas.

tice, altho' they were then mett in Councill about goeing to Canada came thither, and were setled, and confirmed under his goverment.

He forthwith signifyed to the Gov'r of Canada His Ma'ties pleasure relateing to the Indians, and made demand from him, pursuant to the above orders, and alsoe to quitt a considerable fort which by incroachment he had built at Oniagra[1] in the Senneka's Country southward of the Lake within His Ma'ties dominion, about one thousand miles distant from Quebeck in Canada (notwithstanding all the endeavours and opposition made by the Governor of New Yorke, before the annexation) upon an advantageous pass, neare the Indians hunting places, capable greatly to annoy and awe the Indians and obstruct and hinder the trade with them; That thereupon the Governor of Canada did accordingly withdraw the garrison and forces from the sayd Oniagra and those parts, and did further sig-nifie that the Indians by him taken were sent to France, but would write to the King his master about theire releasement.

The severall Provinces and Collonys in New England being soe united, the revenue continued and setled in those parts, for the support of the government, amounted to about twelve thousand pounds *per annum* and all places were well and quietly setled and in good posture.

The Church of England being unprovided of a place for theyr publique woship, he did, by advice of the Councill, borrow the new meeting house in Boston,[2] at such times as the same was unused, untill they could provide otherwise; and accord-ingly on Sundays went in between eleven and twelve in the morning, and in the afternoone about fower; but understand-ing it gave offence, hastned the building of a Church,[3] w'ch was effected at the charge of those of the Church of England, where the Chaplaine of the Souldiers[4] performed divine ser-vice and preaching.

---

[1] Fort Niagara.

[2] The Old South Church, the third church in Boston, was built in 1672. The congregation of this church seceded from the First Church in 1667–1668 because of more liberal views regarding baptism and the Lord's Supper.

[3] The first King's Chapel, a small, wooden structure, occupied a part of the site on which stood the later churches. (See *The Andros Tracts*, II. 45 and note.)

[4] Rev. Robert Ratcliffe.

He was alwayes ready to give grants of vacant lands and confirme defective titles as authorized (the late Corporation not haveing passed or conveyed any pursuant to the directions in their Charter) but not above twenty[1] have passed the seal in the time of his goverment.

Courts of Judicature were setled in the severall parts, soe as might be most convenient for the ease and benefitt of the subject, and Judges appoynted to hold the Terms and goe the Circuite throughout the Dominion, to administer justice in the best manner and forme, and according to the lawes Customes and statutes of the realme of England, and some peculiar locall prudentiall laws of the Country, not repugnant therto; and fees regulated for all officers.

That particuler care was taken for the due observance of the severall Acts made for the encouragement of navigation and regulateing the plantation trade, whereby the lawfull trade and His Majestys revenue of Customs was considerably increased.

The Indians throughout the goverm't continued in good order and subjection untill, towards the latter end of the yeare 1688, by some unadvised proceedings of the Inhabitants in the Eastern parts of New England, the late rupture with the Indians there commenced, severall being taken and some killed, when Sir Edmond Andros was at New Yorke more than three hundred miles distant from that place; and upon his speedy returne to Boston (haveing viewed and setled all parts to the Westward) great part of the garrison soldiers with stores and other necessarys were imediately sent Eastward to reinforce those parts, and vessells to secure the coast and fishery, and further forces raysed and appoynted to be under the command of Majr Gen'll Winthrop, who falling sick and declineing the service, by advice of the Councill he went with them in person and by the settlement of severall garrisons, frequent partyes, marches and pursuits after the enemy, sometimes above one hundred miles into the desart further than any Christian settlement, in w'ch the officers and souldiers of the standing forces always imployed, takeing and destroying their forts and settlem'ts, corne, provision, ammunicion and canooes, dispersed

---

[1] Twenty-three grants and confirmations are recorded in the extant minutes of the council.

and reduced them to the uttermost wants and necessitys, and soe secured the Countrey, that from the said forces goeing out untill the time of the late revolucion there, and disorderly calling the forces from those parts, not the least loss, damage or spoyle hapned to the inhabitants or fishery, and the Indians were ready to submitt at mercy.[1]

About the latter end of March 1688 Sir Edmond Andros returned for Boston, leaveing the garrisons and souldiers in the Easterne parts in good condition, and sufficiently furnished with provisions and all stores and implyments of warr and vessells for defence of the coast and fishery.

On the 18th of Aprill 1689 severall of His Ma'ties Councill in New England haveing combined and conspired togeather with those who were Magistrates and officers in the late Charter Goverment annually chosen by the people, and severall other persons, to subvert and overthrow the goverment, and in stead thereof to introduce their former Comonwealth; and haveing by their false reports and aspersions gott to their assistance the greatest part of the people, whereof appeared in arms at Boston under the comand of those who were Officers in the sayd former popular goverment, to the number of about two thousand horse and foote; which strange and sudden appearance being wholly a surprize to Sir Edmond Andros, as knowing noe cause or occasion for the same, but understanding that severall of the Councill were at the Councill Chamber where (it being the Ordinary Councill day) they were to meet, and some particularly by him sent for from distant parts also there, he and those with him went thither. And tho' (as he passed) the streets were full of armed men, yett none offered him or those that were with him the least rudeness or incivillity, but on the contrary usuall respect; but when he came to the Councill Chamber he found severall of the sayd former popular Majestrates and other cheife persons then present, with those of the Councill, who had noe suitable regard to him, nor the peace and quiet of the Countrey, but instead of giveing any assistance to support the Goverment, made him a prisoner and also imprisoned some members of the Councill and other officers, who in pursuance of their respective dutyes and stations attended on him, and kept them for the space of ten

[1] See *Narratives of the Indian Wars*, in this series, pp. 186–195.

months under severe and close confinement untill by His Ma'ties comand they were sent for England to answer what might be objected them, Where, after summons given to the pretended Agents of New England and their twice appearance at the Councill Board, nothing being objected by them or others, they were discharged. In the time of his confinement being denied the liberty of discourse or conversation with any person, his own servants to attend him, or any communication or correspondence with any by letters, he hath noe particular knowledge of their further proceedings, but hath heard and understands:—

That soone after the confinem't of his person, the Confederates [took the] fort and Castle from the Officers that had the comand of them, whom they also imprisoned and dispersed the few souldiers belonging to the two standing Companyes then there, as they did the rest, when they recalled the forces imployed against the Indians Eastward (which two Companys are upon His Ma'ties establishment in England,) in w'ch service halfe a company of the standing forces at New Yorke being also imployed, the officers were surprised and brought prisoners to Boston, and the souldiers dispersed, as the remaining part of them at New Yorke were afterwards upon the revolucion there. The other company was, and remained, at Fort Albany and are both upon establishment to be payd out of His Ma'ties revenue there. And the Confederates at Boston possessed themselves of all His Ma'ties stores, armes ammunicion and other implements of warr, and disabled His Ma'ties man of war the *Rose* frigatt by secureing the Comander and bringing her sayles on shoare; and at the same time haveing imprisoned the secretary and some other officers, they broke open the Sec'rys Office and seized and conveyed away all records papers and wrightings.

Those Members of His Ma'ties Councill that were in confederacy with the before mencioned popular Majestrates and other cheife actors in this revolucion, tooke upon them the goverment, by the name of a Councill,[1] who not content with

[1] Stoughton, Wait Winthrop, Hinckley, Gedney, and Shrimpton. W. Brown, the only other councillor who became a member of the Council of Safety, entered the Andros body at the same time with Shrimpton, but attended only three of its meetings.

the inconveniency they had brought on themselves in the Massachusetts Colony, but to the ruine of the poore neighbours, on the twentieth of Aprill gave orders for the drawing off the forces from Pemyquid and other garrisons and places in the Easterne parts, far without the lymitts of their Collony and where the seate of warr with the Indians was, and to seize severall of the officers, and for calling home the vessells appoynted to gard the sea coast and fishery; w'ch was done accordingly, and the forces disbanded, when most of the souldiers belonging to the standing Companys there were dispersed; of which, and their actings at Boston, the Indians haveing notice, (and being supplyed with Amunicion and provision out of a vessell sent from Boston by some of the cheife conspirators before the insurrection to trade with them) they were encouraged and enabled to renew and pursue the warr; and by the assistance of some French who have been seen amongst them and engageing of severall other Indians before unconcerned, increased their numbers, that in a very short tyme severall hundreds of Their Ma'ties subjects were killed and carryed away captive; The Fort at Pemyquid taken; the whole Cuntry of Cornwall, the greatest part of the Province of Maine, and part of the Province of New Hampshire destroyed and deserted; and the principall trade of that countrey, w'ch consisted in a considerable fishery, the getting of masts, yards etc. for the supply of His Ma'tyes navy Royall, and boards and other lumber for the supply of the other West India plantacions, is almost wholy ruined.

By the encouragem't and perswasion of those of the Massachusetts the severall other provinces and collonys in New England as far as New Yorke have disunited themselves, and set up their former seperate Charter,[1] or popular goverments without Charter,[2] and by that meanes the whole revenue of the Crowne continued and setled in the severall parts for the support of the Goverment is lost and destroyed.

The usuall time for election of new Majestrates at Boston comeing on in the begining of May 1689, great controversie arose about the setling of Civill Goverment; some being for a new election, and others that the Majestrates chosen and

---

[1] The colonies referred to are Rhode Island and Connecticut.
[2] Plymouth had no charter.

sworne in 1686 before the alteracion should reassume; the
latter of w'ch was concluded on by them and the pretended
representatives of the severall townes of the Massachusetts,
and assumed by the sd Majestrates accordingly, and thereupon
the old Charter Goverment, tho' vacated in Westminster Hall,[1]
was reassumed without any regard to the Crowne of England,
and they revived and confirmed their former laws contrary
and repugnant to the laws and statutes of England, setled
their Courts of Judicature, and appoynted new officers, and
have presumed to try and judge all cases civill and criminall,
and to pass sentence of death on severall of Their Ma'ties
subjects, some of whom they have caused to be executed.

Alltho in the revenue continued on the Crowne for support
of the goverment dureing his time, the country pay'd but the
old establisht rate of a penny in the pound *per Annum* as given
and practised for about fifty yeares past, the present Admin-
istrators have of their own authority, for not above six months,
raysed and exacted from the people of the Massachusetts Collony seven rates and a half.

Since this insurrection and alteracion in New England [2]
they doe tollerate an unlimited irregular trade, contrary to
the severall acts of Plantations, Trade and Navigacion, now
as little regarded as in the time of their former Charter Goverment; they esteeming noe laws to be binding on them but
what are made by themselves, nor admitt English laws to be
pleaded there, or appeales to His Ma'tie. And many shipps
and vessells have since arrived from Scotland, Holland, Newfoundland, and other places prohibitted, they haveing imprisoned His Ma'ties Collector, Surveyor and searcher, and
displaced other Customhouse officers.

That they sent to Albany to treat with the Indians in those
parts, particularly with the Five Nations, Maquaes etc. and
invited them to Boston; which is of ill and dangerouse conse-

---

[1] The charter of Massachusetts was vacated by decree of the Court of
Chancery, the masters or judges in which sat with the Lord Chancellor in Westminster Hall, the great hall of William Rufus, now a part of the Houses of Parliament. Sometimes the Lord Chancellor heard causes in his own house, but in
the case of the Massachusetts charter the hearing was at Westminster.

[2] In reviewing all the conditions of disunion and weakness that he was expressly sent over to remedy, Andros naturally lays stress on the disastrous con-
sequences of the revolt.

quence, by makeing the sayd Indians particularly acquainted with the disunion and seperate goverments, and shewing them the countrey and disorders therof, as far as Boston, giveing thereby the greatest advantage to the French of gaining or subdueing the sayd Indians and attempting Fort Albany (the most advanced frontier into the country and great mart of the beaver and peltry trade) and of infesting other parts.

The forces raysed and sent out by them the last summer, notwithstanding the great encouragem't they promised of eight pounds per head for every Indian should be killed, besides their pay, proved neither effectuall to suppresse the enemy or secure the country from further damage and murthers; and upon the winters approaching the forces were recalled and the country left exposed to the enemy, who have already over runn and destroyed soe great a part therof. And now by the assistance of the French of Canada may probably proceed further into the heart of the country, being soe devided and out of order unless it shall please His Ma'tie by his owne authority to redress the same, and put a stop to the French and Indians, and thereby prevent the ruine or loss of that whole dominion of New England and consequently of Their Maj'ties other American Plantacions; endangered not only by the want of provisions, but by the many ships, vessells, seamen and other necessarys in New England, capable to supply and transport any force, may annoy or attempt those plantacions; but may be by His Ma'ties authority and comands effectually setled and preserved, and of service against the French or any other Their Ma'ties enemys in those parts, with no greater land force then is necessary to be continued there, and a sufficient revenue raysed to defray the charge thereof, by dutyes and rates, as heretofore hath been practised amongst them and is usuall in other Their Ma'ties plantacions. Humbly submitted by

E. ANDROS.

[*Endorsed* :]
    Sr Edmond Andros's Acco't
    of the State of New England
    under his goverment.
        Recd 27 May. 1690.

NARRATIVE OF THE PROCEEDINGS OF ANDROS, 1691

NARRATIVE OF THE PROCEEDINGS OF ANDROS, 1691

A Narrative of The Proceedings of Sir Edmond Androsse and his Complices, Who Acted by an Illegal and Arbitrary Commission from the Late K. James, during his Government in New England. By several Gentlemen who were of his Council. Printed in the Year 1691.

To the Reader.

THE Particulars mentioned in the ensuing Narrative are but a small part of the Grievances justly complained of by the People in New England, during their three years Oppression under Sir E. A. For a more full Account, the Reader is referred to the *Justification of the Revolution in New England*,[1] where every particular exhibited against Sir Ed. and his Complices, by the Agents lately sent to England, is by the Affidavits of honest men confirmed. If some men find themselves thereby exposed to the just Resentments and Indignation of all true Christians, or true English men, they must thank themselves for publishing such untrue Accounts as that which goes under the name of Captain John Palmers,[2] and that scandalous

---

[1] *The Revolution in New England Justified* (Boston, 1691), by E. R. and S. S. [Edward Rawson and Samuel Sewall], reprinted in *The Andros Tracts*, I. 63–132.

[2] *An Impartial Account of the State of New England : or, the Late Government there, Vindicated. In Answer to the Declaration which the Faction set forth when they Overturned That Government* (London, 1690). This pamphlet is reprinted in *The Andros Tracts*, I. 21–41, and is undoubtedly the ablest of all the papers written in defense of the Andros government. In comparing the four accounts, of which two were written by Andros and Palmer, and two appeared anonymously (though possibly written by Ratcliffe and Dudley), we find so many likenesses and similarities in words used and facts and figures given that it is difficult not to believe in a certain amount of collusion among the writers. Even if unintentional, such agreements would not be surprising under the circumstances.

Pamphlet called *N. E's Faction discovered*,[1] supposed to be written by an Implacable Enemy of all good men, and a person that for Impudence and Lying has few Equals in the World. This which follows, being signed by several Gentlemen of great Integrity, who likewise had a particular knowledge of the things by them related, is therefore of unquestionable Credit. The Design in making of it thus publick, is to vindicate Their Majesties Loyal Subjects in New England, and to give a true Representation of things unto those who have by false Relations been imposed on.

B. N. E.[2] Feb. 4, 1690/1.

HAVING Received from Mr. Addington,[3] by order of the Council and Representatives of the Massachusetts Colony, a signification of their desire, That whereas we were Members of the Late Council in the time of Sir Edmond Androsses Government, we would give some Information of the Grievances and Male-administrations under the same: Upon consideration had thereof, and in answer thereunto, we cannot but own and declare, that not only our selves, but many others in the same station (not now present to joyn with us) were of a long time much dissatisfied and discouraged with very many of the Proceedings and Administrations in the said Government; and had little reason to wonder that so great a number of the People were so too. It might well have been expected that the Governour (not so successful heretofore) notwithstanding the extraordinariness (to say no more) of many Clauses and Powers in his Commission, yea the rather and the more, because thereof, would have cautioned and moderated the Execution of the same: But to our Great Trouble we found it very much otherwise. Many were the things that were accounted Irregular and Grievous therein, far from conducing to the Publick Weal of the Territory, and not a little to the disservice of the Crown, as tending rather to the disturbing and disaffecting of the Subjects here, than to the furtherance of that chearful Obedience, Loyalty, Love and Duty in them, which ought by all good means to have been nourished and

---

[1] See the next piece in this volume.   [2] *I. e.*, Boston, New England.
[3] Isaac Addington, secretary of the colony.

promoted. And of all this unhappiness, we must reckon the first step and in-let to be, that the Governour did so quickly neglect the great number of the Council, and chiefly adhere unto and Govern by the advice only of a few others, the principal of them Strangers to the Countrey, without Estates or Interest therein to oblige them, persons of known and declared Prejudices against us, and that had plainly laid their chiefest Designs and Hopes to make unreasonable profit of this poor People. Innumerable were the evil Effects that from hence were continually growing up amongst us. The Debates in Council were not so free as ought to have been, but too much over-ruled, and a great deal of harshness continually expressed against Persons and Opinions that did not please. The Greatest Rigour and Severity was too often used towards the soberest sort of People, when any thing could be found or pretended against them, their humble submissions were little regarded, and inexorable Persecutions ordered against them, whilst in the mean time the notorious viciousness and profaneness of others met not with the like discountenance, but persons of such a character were put into places of business and trust. The long settled maintenance of the Publick Ministry, even from those that applied themselves to no other way of Worship, but continued ordinary hearers, could not be upheld by any act of Authority providing for the same, and Schools of Learning, so well taken care of formerly, were in most places fallen to decay, and many more such like might be reckoned up. But we shall more especially instance farther in the particulars following, as not the least.

1. And first: It was, as we thought, a great slight put upon the Council, and to the prejudice of the good People of the Territory, That whereas at the Governours first coming a Committee appointed thereunto by himself, and a full Council had with great care and several weeks trouble revised a very considerable number of Orders and Laws collected out of the several Law-Books of these Colonies found by long experience very needful and agreeable to the good of these Plantations, which Laws so Collected and Revised were again presented unto, and upon further advisement approved by the Governour and Council and passed, Yet upon the introducing Mr. West from New York to be Deputy Secretary, they were, for what

causes we know not, totally laid aside, and the People denied the benefit of them. And this Grievance was so much the greater, and a plainer Indication of the severity of some men in their Intended Management of things, because on good deliberation there had also passed an Order of Council, That until the Council should take further order, the several Justices, Town-Officers, and others should proceed according to former Usages, and such Local Laws in the several parts of this Dominion, as are not repugnant to the Laws of England, etc. Yet because by virtue of the said Order some in Authority have proceeded to put forth their power for the support of the Ministry, and some others did justifie themselves in some actions done by them that were not pleasing; hereupon when a discourse only, and some debate thereof, had passed in Council but without any regular determination made, and contrary to the express words of the said Order, it was Entred in the Council-Book concerning it, resolved that the same was only in Force till the next Session of the Council, and so determined as null of it self, and that none presume to act pursuant to such Laws as are or shall be made here.

2. Whereas the Act for the Continuing and Establishing of several Rates, Duties and Imposts was one of the first of so great Moment that came out in Form under the Seal of the Territory, and was publickly proclaimed, we that were present have great cause to remember what trouble and dissatisfaction there was amongst the Members of the Council concerning the same. As that Act was framed and urged upon us, a very considerable number (and we believe we were the Major part) dissented from and argued much against it. And tho the Governor expressed not a little heat and positiveness, alledging his instructions, and held the Council together unreasonably a very long time about it, Yet when we did at last break up we could not imagine that he could take the Bill to be agreed to; Nevertheless it was the next day (to our wonderment) brought in fairly Engrossed in Parchment, and quickly Signed by the Governour without any counting of Voices either then or the day before, which was the more needful because some did continue still to make their objections, others that had spoken against the Bill the day before, declaring their adherence to what they had then said; and many more under so great dis-

couragement and discountenance, as was manifested, sitting
silent, which we are sure in the regular passing of Laws can
never be reckoned for a consent.

3. The Way and Manner used afterwards of proposing and
passing all Laws was very uncertain and unequal, not answerable to the Nature of so great a Power, nor to the largeness of
the Territory that was to be obliged by them, or to the Number of the Councellors appointed therein; for after a little while
there were no set times appointed or given notice of for the
making of Laws, that so the Members of the Council might
attend in a fuller number to be helpful therein. Bills of the
greatest concernment were usually first consulted and framed
in private, and so unexpectedly brought into Council at any
time, and then our work too was often under great disadvantages, not to advise freely and consult about the making of a
Law thought necessary but to maintain a sort of Contest in
opposition to a very inconvenient one, too far promoted and
engaged in already; and above all, there was never any fair
way of taking and counting the number of the Councellors
consenting and dissenting, that so the Majority might be
known in any matter that admitted of any considerable reasonings and debates, by reason whereof both Laws and other
Orders and Resolutions might be set down as passed by the
Council, which ought not to have been. And when it hath been
(as often it was) expresly and earnestly prayed when matters
of greater moment than ordinary were in hand, that the Debate
and Resolution of them might be put off till a fuller Council
of Members from other several parts of the Dominion might
be Convened, such motions were ever disaccepted, and entertained with no little displacency; so that it might be too truly
affirmed, that in effect four or five persons, and those not so
favourably inclined and disposed as were to be wished for,
bear the Rule over, and gave Law to a Territory the largest
and most considerable of any belonging to the Dominion of
the Crown.

4. In pursuance of this way and manner of passing Laws
above expressed, there were two in special that came forth,
which we are sure in fuller and freer Councils would have had
a full stop put to them; viz. First, The Act for Regulating
the Choice of select Men, etc., wherein the Liberty of Towns

to meet for the managing of their Publick Affairs referring to
their Common Lands, and all other their concernments, which
they had enjoyed for so many years, to their great benefit,
was most unreasonably restrained to once a year, and all other
Convening of Inhabitants as a Town Meeting upon any pretence or colour whatsoever, was strictly forbidden: And the
other Act was that intituled, An Act requiring all Masters of
Ships or Vessels to give security, in which there were such
restraints laid upon all persons from Transporting themselves
freely (as their occasions might call) out of the Territory,
That it would have been a meer Prison to all that should be
found therein, and such Bond required of all Ships and Vessels
(extending in the practice even to Shallops and Wood-Boats)
as would quickly have intolerably discouraged, if not ruined
the Trade thereof; and all without any other ordinary general
benefit of the said Act, but the filling some mens Pockets with
Fees: And (as it might be thought from the time of moving
for this Act, which was when Captain Hutchinson[1] was already
gone, and Mr. Mather was known to be intending for England)
the obstructing of such mens going home as were likely there
to make just Complaints, and seek Redress of Publick Grievances; and when this Act had been strenuously opposed in
Council here at Boston, where it was more than once vehe-
mently urged, and as often denied, it was carried as far as New
York, and there an opportunity found for the obtaining of it.

5. The great matter of Properties and Titles to our Lands
is the next to be insisted on. His Majesty that granted the
Charter did fully invest the Patentees with Right to the Soil
throughout the whole Limits thereof, and here on the place,
the Right of the Natives was honestly purchased from them.
The Disposal, Distribution, and Granting of Lands by the
Patentees, who were also incorporated, and made a Body Politick, was in such a plain, ready, easie way, without any charge
to the Planters, as in the Settlement of so large a Countrey
was thought to be most agreeable: And so much of a publick
spirit and design were those Noble Gentlemen, that (though
well they might) they settled not one single Penny of service
or acknowledgment to themselves and Heirs in any of their
Grants, a thing so self-denying and worthy, that few Instances

[1] Elisha Hutchinson.   Increase Mather; see below, pp. 271-272.

can be given of the like. All which notwithstanding, and the Possessions, Descents and Valuable Purchases of so many years that have passed since, The Governour and those he adhered to, resolved and practised to make all mens Titles in effect quite null and void. The purchasing of the Natives Right was made nothing of, and next to a Ridicule. The Enjoyment and Improvement of Lands not inclosed, and especially if lying in common amongst many, was denied to be possession; it was not enough that some men that thought it convenient, and were both willing and able, did take Confirmations of their Lands, the numbers of whom in time might have been a considerable gain to them; but nothing would satisfie unless all in general might be compelled so to do; hence those that refused were declared Intruders upon His Majesty, and put in fear of having their Lands granted unto strangers. Many were Solicited and Encouraged to Petition for other mens Lands, and had a shameful Example set them by some of the chief Contrivers of all this Mischief. When some men have Petitioned for a confirmation of their own Lands, a part of these only was offered to be granted to them, and another part denyed. Nor could any mans own Land be confirmed to him, without a particular Survey of every part and parcel of them first made, the great charges whereof, and of other Fees to be taken, would have been to most men Insupportable: Yea it hath by some been computed that all the money in the Countrey would not suffice to patent the Lands therein contained.

And yet farther, a considerable quit-rent to the King was to be Imposed upon all Lands, though already a constant yearly Tax for the support of the Government had been laid on them.

And for all this most unreasonable vexation to a Laborious and Industrious people, the only Ground pretended was some defects and wants of form and due manner alledged to be in the way of the disposing and conveying of all Lands from the Patentees to the Townships and People here; which whatever it amounted to, might have been easily remedied, either by an application and representation to the King for the obtaining a General settlement of all properties (which would have been highly Worthy and Generous for the Governour to have engaged in, on behalf of the People) or by some other ways that were proposed. But nothing but the way of particular Patenting as abovesaid could prevail. In prosecution whereof all Actions intended upon Informations of Intrusions in His Majesties behalf, or between old Proprietors and new Grantees, must have had their Decision at the Ordinary Courts of Common Law here upon the Place, where matters of Equity and of a Consideration Transcending all ordinary Cases could not have a proper Cognizance and due Influence in the Decision, Determination and Judgment.

6. Though sufficient Courts of Justice were appointed, and held in the several Counties for the Tryal of all Offenders, yet it was too frequent upon more particular displeasure to fetch up persons from very remote Counties before the Governour and Council at Boston (who were the highest, and a constant Court of Record and Judicature) not to receive their tryal but only to be examined there, and so remitted to an Inferior Court to be farther proceeded against. The Grievance of which Court was exceeding great, for hereby not only the Charge was made Excessive upon such persons by the notorious exactions of the Messenger, the Secretaries Fees for Examination, etc., But these Examinations themselves were unreasonably strict, and rigorous and very unduely ensnaring to plain unexperienced men. And the Tryals of several were by this means over-ruled to be at Boston, and not in the proper Counties, and were otherwise so far prejudged as to be rendred less equal.

The Extraordinary Oppressive Fees taken in all matters by indigent and exacting Officers, these were at the first for a long time Arbitrarily imposed and required without any colour of an Establishment of them by the Council. Afterwards a Committee was appointed, to bring in a Table of Fees, that spent a long time without finishing any thing, the reason whereof was because some therein, especially the Deputy Secretary West, insisted upon Fees much more extraordinary than some others could consent to. In conclusion: There was a Table of Fees drawn up to be presented to the Council, and signed by some of the Committee, one of whom (whose Subscription is to this Paper) declaring expresly, that by his Signing he did no otherwise agree, but only that it might be presented to the Council, to do therein as they should see cause, who also when it was so presented to the Council, declared that many of the particulars in that Table contained were unreasonable, and ought to be abated, and of this mind were many others. But the Entry after the usual manner was an approbation thereof.

Lastly, As to those Great Jealousies and Suspicions of Sinister Designs in the Governour as to our Troubles by the Indians, we have to say, That although divers things too uncertain, if not untrue, have been too easily reported and spread concerning him, a practice which some of us have formerly with no little prejudice to our selves discountenanced and born Testimony against; yet there have not wanted some other particulars that might give too great a ground for the same. The principal of them (as far as we have any knowledge of things of that kind) are these:

The Governours Seizing and Taking away the Goods of Mounsieur St. Castine of Penopscot,[1] the Summer before the War broke forth, which thing hath been esteemed not a little to have stirred up and furthered the succeeding Troubles. The Governours not hastening his Return to Boston when these Troubles were actually begun, but lengthening out his Tarrience in places so remote, till the Hostility of the Indians and the great Mischiefs thereof were too far advanced. That during his absence he was not pleased sufficiently to impower and instruct any to act things necessary for the safety of the out Plantations and the Prosecution and Suppression of the Enemy, tho' he had speedy and true Accounts from time to time sent him of all that happened. That all that was done to this purpose in a case of such necessity, either by the Lieutenant Govenour, or by the Justices of Peace and Military Officers in many places, by securing and disarming of Neighbouring Indians, setting up Warding and Watching, Garrisoning several houses for the security of the Inhabitants, especially the Women and Children, in case of sudden Inroads and Surprizings that might be, sending some relief of men to some places that were most in danger, and also what was done by

[1] The Baron de St. Castin was a Frenchman who had established himself among the Indians, on the Penobscot, where now is Castine, Maine. Andros dispossessed him in the spring of 1688.

those Members of the Council that were at Boston in conjunction with the Commander in chief left in the Fort there, who raised and sent some Forces to Casco-Bay, where greatest harms were done—We say, that all that was thus done, was so extreamly disapproved of by the Governour upon his Return back from Albany and New York, and an unaccountable displeasure manifested against all persons that had so acted, and that he was ready to call them to an account as high Offenders for the same, and refused a long time, tho' much solicited, to give any Order concerning the Souldiers sent to Casco, either for the continuance of them there, where they were very necessary, or for their dimission home. Unto all which may be added the Governours sending Messengers, both John Smith the Quaker from Albany, and soon after Major Macgregory[1] to Keybeck,[2] upon such Errands and Business as were not communicated and laid open to the Council. And further, his Relase and setting at liberty sundry Indians that were in hold, some of them known Enemies to the English, and particularly objected against by several of the Council, and that without any exchange of our English Captives then in the Enemies hands.

These are the chief Matters which upon this occasion (without any undue Prejudice against any man, or design to justifie the defects of our selves in the performance of our own shares of duty, but in answer to the desire signified to us as above) we have to set forth, professing truly that by such a state of things as we had the experience and feeling of, The Places that we held were rendred exceeding uneasie to us, and that out of a sincere respect to the Prosperity of these Their Majesties Plantations, we could not but be very desirous that, through the Favour of God and our Superiors, all due Redress might in a good happy season be obtained, and the way of Governing English Subjects in Their Majesties Dominions without an

---

[1] Lieutenant Patrick Macgregory was in charge of the forts at Sagadahoc, Pejepscot (Brunswick), and on the Kennebec. A brief notice of him is given in N. Y. Col. Docs., III. 395. He was an engineer, and Randolph speaks of a map made by him of the region of the Five Nations, and of the French forts from Quebec to the Mississippi. He was killed in New York, in the spring of 1691, when Leisler and Ingoldesby exchanged shots over the possession of the fort (below, p. 391, note 2).

[2] Quebec.

Assembly of the Peoples Representatives[1] banished out of a World for ever.

Boston in New England,
Jan. 27, 1690.[2]

WILLIAM STOUGHTON,
THOMAS HINCKLEY,
WAIT WINTHROP,
BARTHOL. GEDNEY,
SAMUEL SHRIMPTON.

Finis.

[1] The fact that the Andros government was without any representation of the people probably accounts, in largest part, for the dislike the New Englanders had for it. People will endure quite as much "oppression" as is charged against Andros and his council if they are themselves the authors of it. Yet it is hard to see how a representative assembly could have been set up in a region that extended from Maine to the Delaware. Had representative government been tried, and it must not be forgotten that Andros recommended such a trial, the end would inevitably have been rule by the Massachusetts members. In Andros's council delegates from Plymouth were not always present even in the early period, and those from Connecticut and New York appeared only when the council sat in Hartford or New York. There is an undercurrent of self-interest running through all the Massachusetts complaints.

[2] 1691, N.S.

C. D., NEW ENGLAND'S FACTION
DISCOVERED, 1690

C. D., NEW ENGLAND'S FACTION
DISCOVERED, 1690

New-England's Faction Discovered ; or, A Brief and True Account of their Persecution of the Church of England; the Beginning and Progress of the War with the Indians; and other Late Proceedings there, in a Letter from a Gentleman of that Country, to a Person of Quality.

Being, an Answer to a most false and scandalous Pamphlet lately Published ; Intituled, News from New-England, etc.

Honourable Sir,
THO I have but very lately advised you of my Arrival, and given you some short and general Account of the State and Circumstance of Affairs in New-England, at the time I left the place; which I thought might have been sufficient, until I should have the Honour to wait on you personally; but having had the view of a certain Pamphlet lately Published and Intituled *News from New-England,*[1] etc. pretending to give an Account of the Present State of that Country, and finding the same so very fictitious, false and scandalous, published out of a most wicked design to vilifie and traduce some Worthy Gentlemen, who have been better Friends to our Country, than ever the obscure Author thereof was, or knows how to be, and to amuse and perplex others: I could not forbear, out of my Zeal for truth, and the love and value I have for the Peace and Welfare of my Country, to give you the trouble of this Letter, to discover the falseness of the pretended News, and the baseness and ignorance of the Author; who without great difficulty may easily be guessed at, and known by his fruits.

And therefore it may not be amiss to acquaint you, that about two years since, one Mr. J. M.,[2] pretended Teacher of

[1] This pamphlet is not known to exist.
[2] Rev. Increase Mather; see below, p. 271.

253

the Gospel in Boston, privately left that place and came for
London, where of his own authority he set up to be an Agent
for the Country,[1] and used all the art and subtilty he could,
during the Reign of King James, to indear the same into the
affection of F. Peters,[2] Mr. Brent,[3] and Nevil Pain,[4] undertaking as well for himself as us to subscribe to the taking off
the Penal Laws and Tests, to support the Dispensing Power,
and to satisfie his own malice and prejudice (without any ground
or reason) conceived against the then Government of New-
England.

This Man, as it was the Opinion of most sober and considerate Men when I left New-England, so I may very justly
term the Author and Promoter of all our miseries, founded
upon apparent and wittingly devised Lyes and Calumnies, carried on under pretence of Zeal and Piety, insinuated into, and
imposed upon many of the common People, hurrying them into
mischiefs and inconveniencies now sufficiently seen, felt, and
repented of; Him therefore, I will conclude the Author of the
before-mentioned Pamphlet; the falsities whereof I shall now
plainly and briefly detect, to prevent your self and others being
imposed upon by him, as many of my Countrymen and others
have too lately been.

And in the first place I cannot omit to take notice of his
positive confidence to charge a Commission granted in due
Form under the Great Seal of England, for the Government
of one of Their Majesties Plantations, Illegal and Arbitrary;
and that Government a Tyranny, which was by virtue thereof
exercised with a thousand times more justice and lenity, than
when under the pretended Charter, Administration, or Com-

---

[1] Mather had no authority to act as an agent of the colony. He went to
England in the private capacity of one representing the leaders of the old government.

[2] Father Edward Petre, the confessor of James II.

[3] Robert Brent, a Roman Catholic, who having played a conspicuous part
under James II., was charged with high treason and imprisoned, January 14, 1689
(*Commons Journal*, X. 110). Andros says that Brent was the solicitor for Father
Petre and Sir Thomas Powys, the attorney-general, and that he was the inter-
mediary through whom Mather obtained from Powys the opinion that the
Massachusetts charter was illegally vacated.

[4] Henry Neville Payne, a dramatist and pamphleteer who supported the
Stuart cause and after 1689 became involved in conspiracies against the crown.

monwealth Discipline, without any Authority for the same whatsoever; if the Author had been but as well acquainted with the Law, as he was with the Declaration he refers to (and no doubt was the first contriver of), he would have been of another judgment, or at least have conceal'd it until the Opinion of his Superiors had been given therein.

2. That the War with the Indians was begun, as the Author there relates, or that it was ever affirmed by the Indians, that they were encouraged thereto by Sir E. A.,[1] is wholly false; for in the Summer 1688, when Sir E. A. went to receive and settle the Province of New York, then annexed under his Government, it so happened, that a Party of about Nine French Indians fell upon an Indian Plantation at a place called Spectaclepond, near Springfield, on Connecticott River, and kill'd and carried away about Nine Indians, and after coming to a small Village on that River called Northfield, they killed six Christians, and being pursued, fled; the noise of these Murthers soon spread throughout the Country, and notice was given thereof to all the Frontier or Out-parts, advising them to be vigilant and careful to prevent Surprize by any strange or suspected Indians, and soon after this News came to Saco, (a Town and River in the Province of Maine above three hundred Miles distant from the places beforenamed called by that name,) Five Indian Men, and Sixteen Women and Children, who had always lived and planted on that River, were seized on, and sent by Water to Boston, some of whom were so old and feeble, that they were forced to be carried, when ashore, on others backs. On their arrival at Boston, the Lieutenant Governor and those of the Council there examined into the cause of seizing those Indians, and sending them thither; but finding that no Cause was sent with them, nor any ground or reason to hold them in Custody, they returned them to the place from whence they came, to be set at liberty; but before they arrived there, the English near those parts were got to their Arms and Garisons: Other Indians of Ambroscoggen and Kenebeque River, hearing that those of Saco were seized and sent away, forthwith surprized as many of the English in Cascobay and Kenebeque River, saying they intended no harm, but would keep them till the

[1] Sir Edmund Andros.

Indians were returned. Upon the Arrival of the returned Indians, they were sent unto, and a day and place agreed upon when both the English and Indians were to be set at liberty, and all to be composed; but the Indians not coming at the time appointed, the English waited not for them, but were not long gone ere they came, and, by an English Man and two Indians, sent a Letter to the next Garison, importing their readiness to deliver up the English, and to make satisfaction for any hurt or spoil done by them; who from that Garison were Fired upon and ill treated, and not seeing how what they expected could be answered, some of them discover'd other English Men on a Neck of Land, near the place appointed to meet at, and endeavouring to seize some of them, were engaged into a Skirmish, where five of the English were killed and several of the Indians wounded, who presently after in rage killed two of the English Captives. In this manner, and no other, was the War begun; whereupon two Troops of Soldiers were raised, and sent to the assistance of those parts against the Indians, with Provision and Ammunition necessary by those of the Council at Boston, and the Indians first mentioned to be taken, were again sent back and Imprisoned, and all in the absence of Sir E. A. Upon his arrival at Boston, and being informed of the above, and that such Indians were in Prison, a Committee of the Council was appointed to examine, and see what Grounds or Cause there was for their Commitment or Detainer; and the Committee reporting they could find none, those Indians were by order of Council set at liberty, to be sent to the place from whence they were brought if they desired it: As for the mischief said to be sustained by the Inhabitants there, it cannot be imputed to those Indians, for it was either done while they were in custody, or since the Rebellion and Subversion of the Government, from whence begins the date of our Miseries; and I have just reason to believe, the Author was too far concerned therein, as is evident by his directing of his Letters to Simon Broadstreet Esq; Governor of the Massathusets, etc., before it was possible for him to know that he was so, or could have any ground to believe he would be, unless he had contrived or directed it.

3. There was no endeavours used to keep the People ignorant of Affairs in England, nor were any Imprisoned for

dispersing the Prince's Declaration; which was never publickly seen or known to be in New-England, till some time
after the Insurrection: Tho I have heard, that one Winslow
arriving at Boston from Nevis, about the beginning of April
1688, and pretending to shew to several Persons a Written
Copy of the said Declaration, was sent for before a Justice,
and being examined about the said Writing, denied he had
any such thing; and behaving himself contemptuously, he
was committed to Prison; and the next Morning producing
the same Paper to the Justice, he was discharged without any
further trouble or proceeding; and this was all that was acted
in New-England, relating to the Prince of Orange's Declaration; so that there was no grounds or reasons to stir up the
People to Sedition, but only the ambitious desires and wicked
inclinations of their former Popular Magistrates and Members,
to set up their old Arbitrary Commonwealth Government,
that, freeing themselves from the Authority of England, they
might without fear of punishment break all the Laws made
for the encouragement and increase of the Navigation of England, and regulating and securing the Plantation Trade, as is
sufficiently evident by the several Vessels since arrived from
Holland, Scotland, Newfoundland, and other places prohibited
by the Acts of Trade and Navigation.

And that such was their design, to rend themselves from
the Crown of England, will appear by the free and open confession of some well knowing in that Conspiracy; who have
since declared (before Witnesses of undenyable truth now
here in England) that the design of seizing upon Sir E. A. and
subverting Kingly Government in New-England had been
long contrived and resolved on, and was to have been done
the beginning of January 1688,[1] and that those concerned in
the late Revolution were then to have acted the like parts, at
which time was no account of the Prince of Orange's intention
of coming into England known in that Land.

4. It cannot be said, that ever any unlawful Levies of
Money were made upon the Subject under the Government of
Sir E. A., for all that was raised in his time was by virtue of a
law made and practised for about Fifty Years before, which
was continued and confirmed by express command, under the

---

[1] There is no other certain evidence of a conspiracy formed at this early date.

Great Seal of England, for support of the Government, and was but a Rate of one Penny in the Pound, to be annually collected by Warrant from the Treasurer, which those who lately assumed the Government, tho without any Lawful Power or Authority, have so far exceeded, that for about Six Months management, they have caused seven Rates and an half to be levied; and I have since advice that they have ordered Ten Rates more to be exacted.

5. By the Actings and Proceedings of these New-England Reformers, it is easily to be seen, what regard they had to Religion, Liberty and Property, having now had the opportunity to make themselves Persecutors of the Church of England, as they had before been of all others that did not comply with their Independency, whom they punished with Fines, Imprisonment, Stripes, Banishment, and Death, and all for matters of meer Conscience and Religion only: The Church of England, altho commanded to be particularly countenanced and encouraged, was wholly destitute of a place to perform Divine Service in, until Sir E. A., by advice of the Council, borrowed the new Meeting-house in Boston for them, at such times when others made no use of it, and afterwards promoted and encouraged the building of a New Church for that Congregation, to avoid all manner of Offence to their dissenting Neighbors, which was soon compleated and finished at the particular charge of those of the Church of England; whose number daily increasing, they became the envy as well as hatred of their Adversaries, who by all ways and means possible, as well in their Pulpits as private Discourse, endeavour'd to asperse, calumniate, and defame them, and so far did their malice and bigotry prevail, that some of them openly and publickly hindered and obstructed the Minister in the performance of the funeral Rites, to such as had lived and dyed in the Communion of the Church of England:[1] And a most scandalous Pamphlet was soon after Printed and Published by Cotton Mather,[2] Son of the beforementioned, J. M., intituled

[1] Sewall in his *Diary* mentions two funerals conducted according to the Book of Common Prayer, but he records no disturbances. Randolph frequently speaks of "obstructions," but gives no facts.

[2] It was Increase Mather, not his son, who wrote on the "Unlawfulness of the Common Prayer Worship." See *The Andros Tracts*, I. 180.

the unlawfulness of the Common-prayer Worship, wherein he
affirms, and labours to prove the same to be both Popery and
Idolatry, and several scandalous Libels both against the Church
and Government were spread and scattered up and down the
Country, insinuating into the Common People, that the Governor and all of the Church of England were Papists and
Idolaters, and to stir them up to Faction and Rebellion, for
which the said Cotton Mather, and others, were bound over
to answer according to Law; but was superseded by their
Insurrection.   And the Justices having issued their Warrant
for the observation of the 30th of January[1] pursuant to the
Statute, the same was called in and suppressed by Captain
Waite Winthorp one of the Council, who in the Commotion,
appeared the chief Man and Head of the Faction against the
Government, which he twice swore to maintain and support,
and tho at the time of the Revolution most of the Principal
Officers in the Government were of the Independent and Pres-
byterian Party, yet their malice and fury was not shewn to
any of them, but only used and exercised against those of the
Church of England, whom (as well the Governor as other
Officers of the Government, and principal Members of that
Church) they seized and most barbarously Imprisoned.   The
Church it self had great difficulty to withstand their fury, receiving the marks of their indignation and scorn, by having
the Windows broke to pieces, and the Doors and Walls daubed
and defiled with dung, and other filth, in the rudest and basest
manner imaginable,[2] and the Minister, for his safety, was
forced to leave the Country and his Congregation, and go for
England; the Persons Imprisoned were kept and detained,
without any Warrant, Mittimus or cause shewn, and several
of them had their Offices and Houses broke open, their Goods

---

[1] The 30th of January was the day of the execution of Charles I.

[2] It is difficult to get at the truth of this charge.   In addition to the statement made in the text, we have the assertion by the Anglicans that "the deluded
people broke into the church to search for the images they supposed we worship'd."   Mather replied, "All the mischief done is the breaking of a few Quarels
of glass by idle Boys," but Mather's *Vindication* is not convincing, and Whitmore
suspects that the charge had a "basis of fact."   Rev. Samuel Myles wrote in
1690, "Our church is perpetually abused, the windows broken as soon as mended";
and again, "The little chapel for the Church of England . . . is battered and shattered most lamentably already" (*Cal. St. P. Col.*, 1689–1692, §§ 1217, 1239).

and Estates taken away, spoiled, and embezelled: And when application was made to the new assumed Authority, for the benefit of the Habeas Corpus Act, and other Laws made for the Liberty of the Subject, and security of their Property; the same was denyed with this reason given amongst others afterwards there published in Print: that till the unhappy time of Sir Edmund's Government, the Laws of England were never used, nor any Habeas Corpus granted in New-England, and therefore not to be expected then; and about Ten Weeks after their Confinement, several of the Chief Officers were by the House of Representatives voted not bailable, for no other cause or pretended Crimes than for being imployed by the Crown, having therein so faithfully and truly behaved themselves, that none could justly lay any Crime to their Charge. By this means many suffered Ten Months Imprisonment, and others less, being turn'd in and out of Goal, as the Arbitrary pleasure of their New Rulers should be verbally known: In their new Erected Courts, they have publickly declared, they have nothing to do with the Laws of England, and several of Their Majesties Subjects have been not only Fined and Imprisoned by the Arbitrary Will of the Magistrates, without any lawful Tryal by a Jury of their Peers, as the Laws of the Land direct; but for pretended Crimes sentenced to Death, without any lawful Authority or Legal Form of proceedings, and some of them Executed.[1]

6. It is very true, that since the Imprisonment of the Governor, and alteration of the Government in New-England, the whole County of Cornwall, great part of the Province of Maine, and part of the Province of New-hampshire, are over-run and destroyed by the Indians; but the occasion thereof has been by that Insurrection, and the withdrawing of the Forces left in those Parts by Sir E. A. and deserting the Garisons there, which was also the loss of the Fort at Pemaquid, and above three Hundred of His Majesty's Subjects, and notwithstanding the Malice of the Author cannot be the least imputation on

---

[1] Andros made the same charge, above, p. 235. Randolph says: "They have condemned one man to be hanged another burnt in the hand: branded a young woman in the forehead . . . and fined Mr. Cutter," and again, "They have proceeded to exercise the soverain powers: having executed two persons" (Goodrick, *Randolph*, VI. 326; VII. 339).

Sir E. A., who during the time of his Government kept the whole Dominion from injury, save what was done at first by surprizal, as by every honest Man will be confessed, for what was done in releasing the Indians before mentioned was not an Act of Favour but Justice, nor done by him alone, but with advice of the Council, and I can see no reason, why either the Indians or English should be Imprisoned or Restrained of their Liberty without sufficient cause, or why if one Indian commits an Offence, all must be blamed or punished for it, tho they are things too often used and practised by our old Charters in New-England.

Neither were the numbers or quality of those Indians capable of doing such mischiefs, tho the follies and madness of the People since their Revolution have encouraged and provoked many to be their Enemies, and increased their numbers, and no doubt given the French fair advantages to come into their assistance.

The Fort of Pemaquid was burnt by the Indians, and the Guns sometime after fetched from thence, by some of the Forces sent from Boston, and brought thither by them, so that what is mentioned about the Dutch Privateer is wholly false.

7. As to the pretended bloody Fight, said to be between the English and Indians, it was only after this manner: A Party of about three hundred English and Friend Indians, under the command of Captain Benjamin Church,[1] being overnight landed at a Town called Falmouth[2] in Cascobay, in the Province of Maine, the next Morning early a Party of Indians of about two hundred came to attack that place, who meeting with one Anthony Brackett and his two Sons going to his Farm, a little distant from the Town,[3] they Fired and Killed them, and by that alarmed the place; and thereupon a Party was sent to discover, who advised what they were, and that

[1] Benjamin Church was the most conspicuous Indian fighter of his day. He served as captain in King Philip's War and contrived the ambush that resulted in Philip's death. He was commissioned colonel by Governor Dudley in 1704 and died in 1718.

[2] Portland.

[3] Anthony Brackett had a farm at Black Cove toward the point on the west side of Portland harbor. Church's fight there with the eastern Indians is known as the "battle of Brackett's Woods." The account given in the text is quite inaccurate. See *Narratives of the Indian Wars*, in this series, p. 202.

they were very near the Town; the whole number of Men being all called together had Ammunition delivered them, but by reason of the unsizableness of their Guns and Shot, they were forced to beat their Bullets into Slugs, which made it late before they could March to the Enemy, who in the mean time had the opportunity to post themselves advantageously behind Fences, Hedges, Old Trees, etc., and in that manner they engaged; and after about two hours dispute the Indians retreated into a small swamp, and our Forces left them with the loss of Eleven Men, and Seven wounded, of which Five after dyed; but it was not known that one Indian was killed: And this is all we can brag of in that Service, which was only fortunate, in that the Forces were there, when the Indians came to attack the Place, which else probably they would have carried, tho it's believed, had our Forces been ready early to have attacked and pursued the Enemy, some greater advantage might have been gained, but by late advice I am informed that Place is also deserted.

There is little dependence on those we call our Friend Indians, for they are as great Strangers in the Eastern Country as the English, and will not travel or venture farther than they, tho being used to the Woods may be quicker sighted to discover the Enemy. You may perceive the fiery Zeal of the Author and his Correspondent, who will not admit of a charitable Expression or Character of his suffering Neighbours, but after they have been the cause of all their Miseries and Ruine, must expect no other comfort from them than to be accounted and termed Heathenish English Plantations; for which I cannot conceive any reason, unless that many in those Parts have been differently educated from those of Boston, and are of the Church of England, whose Forefathers, for that very cause only, were forced to remove so far to escape the lash of their Persecutors in the Massathusets Colony.

8. We have no reason to brag of our Armies Pursuit after the Enemy, for it was never known that any Party last Summer went twenty Miles from our Settlements (or Place where they had done us mischief) after them, neither, according to the methods taken, would it avail if they had; for tho they knew the Indians are in Arms, and taking all the Opportunities to attack and destroy them, yet no suitable Provision was made

in our out-Towns and Frontiers for their Security and Defence, but after Advice given to Boston of a Town or Settlement being burn'd and destroyed, in about a Fortnights time an Army or Party of about two or three hundred Men would be sent to the Place to see if it were true or not, and whether the Indians did not stay for their coming; which Army of ours usually abide thereabouts till they have eaten and consumed what stock of Cattle or Sheep the Indians had left, and then return home again.

That any Captives escaped from the Indians affirm, that the Indians say they are encouraged by some Gentlemen in Boston vigorously to prosecute the War, is mere Invention, and a most false and groundless Imputation, unless by such Gentlemen in Boston are meant Foster and Waterhouse, two of their own Party, who being of the Conspiracy to subvert the Government, sometime in March, about a Month before the same was put in Execution, loaded a Brigantine with Provision and Ammunition at Boston, and entered her for Bermudoes, but sent her to the Eastward amongst the French and Indians, then in actual War with us, and furnished and supplied them therewith, when the Governor and the Forces were out against them and had reduced them to the greatest want and necessity both for Provision and Ammunition; and soon after the Revolution, that Vessel returned from those Parts with her Loading of Bever and Peltry, which was publickly known and talked, but no notice taken thereof, the grievous effects of which, the Country well knows, and are since very sensible thereof.

The two Captives that last escaped and came to Boston related, that by the Service done by Sir E. A. the last Winter was Twelve-months, against the Indians, they were reduced to that necessity both for want of Ammunition and Provision, that in the Spring following they resolved to come in and surrender themselves at Mercy, which they no doubt had done accordingly, if the Revolution at Boston had not happened, the Forces being drawn off from the Eastern Parts, Garrisons deserted, and they supplied with Ammunition and Provision from Boston, which was the only encouragement they had to renew and continue the War upon us, and has much increased the Numbers of our Enemies.

'Tis true, the Mohawks (tho a small) are a warlike Nation, and have been long Enemies to the French in Canada, and now in War with them; but that no ways affects us in New-England any otherwise than as it is some Diversion to the French; for those Indians that war against us are in a direct opposite part of the Country, remote from them, and can be supplied from Canada, Port-Royal, and Nova Scotia, altho those Mohawks endeavour to obstruct it; and I could never hear any Offer made by them to that purpose, or that they would engage against our Enemies, for we never had any Acquaintance or Correspondency with them, to influence them to our Assistance, they being very remote from Boston, and always under the Government of New-York: but I have been informed by Letters from Persons of good credit at Albany, that when the Agents sent from Boston to treat with the Mohawks, and renew their Peace and Friendship with them, and desire their Assistance, proposed the same, the Mohawks replied, That it was unnecessary for them to come so far to renew their Peace, since to the Indians Knowledge there had been no War between them, and that they had not only by Words, but by Action, manifested their good Heart to the English, particularly to New-England, since they had by means of the Government of New-York engaged themselves in the last Indian War, for their Interest, against the Indians their Enemies, by which means much Christian Blood was saved, altho but little notice of their Service has been taken by those who had the benefit thereof; that they were then in War against the French, and would not increase the number of their Enemies, until they certainly knew that those Eastern Indians assisted the French against them. This is the sum and truth of that Negotiation, which cost us above four hundred Pounds Expence; and what Advantage or Credit we are like to get thereby, all Men may judge.

We of New England (I find) are too apt to boast of what we neither understand nor have any assurance of, and build too much on mistaken Notions and false Grounds, as in this Case of the Indians.

9. The Story about the Mohawks, Jesuits, and Eclipse of the Sun, has not been heard of or acted in any part of New-England, but, as I am informed, is an old Story taken out of

some History of the Spanish Indies, and only inserted by the Author to enlarge his strange News, and fill up his Paper.

But it must be admitted, that with those Mohawks and other Indians several French Priests and Jesuits have dwelt and inhabited, and endeavoured to propagate their Religion amongst them, which is more than any of our English Priests or Teachers have done; for altho by the Piety of our Fore-fathers, considerable Sums of Money have been given, and a Corporation erected for the Evangelizing of the Indians in New-England,[1] a very small progress hath been hitherto made therein; and now scarce any Endeavours or proper Means used at all for their Conversion, tho large Sums of Money are annually sent over and disposed of amongst the Brotherhood, on that pretence, which the Government, or those chiefly con-cerned therein, would do well to enquire after, now there are so many of that Country here capable to give an Account thereof, that so good and pious an Undertaking may be neither neglected nor perverted.

10. It is too true, that great Devastations have been made in New-England by the Indians since the Revolution there, which those that subverted their Majesties Government have been and are the sole occasion of; and that the Fort of Pema-quid, a considerable Frontier next the French, hath been taken, the whole County of Cornwal, greatest part of the Province of Maine, and part of the Province of Hampshire, are destroyed and deserted, besides other Mischiefs in the Massathusets Colony within thirty Miles of Boston; the loss and damage of all which, when I left New England, was not computed at less

---

[1] The Company for the Propagation of the Gospel among the Indians was incorporated by act of Parliament July 27, 1649, largely through the influence of Edward Winslow. At the Restoration the act of incorporation became void and the company defunct, but a revival was effected, through the exertions of Robert Boyle, by order in Council, April 10, 1661 (*Acts P. C. Col.*, I., § 510), the charter passing the seals February 7, 1662. The new title was "the Company for Propagacion of the Gospell in New England, and the Partes adjacent in Amer-ica," shortened in later years to "The New England Company." After the American Revolution the company transferred its operations to New Brunswick and other parts of British America. It is still active, being commonly known as the "Society for Propagating the Gospel in America," but its legal title is that given above. It must not be confused with the Society for the Propagation of the Gospel in Foreign Parts, the well-known S. P. G.

than one hundred thousand Pounds, besides the loss of above three hundred of their Majesties Subjects, and the whole Fish, Mast, and Lumber Trade, and all Out-parts forced to Garisons.

But that so considerable a Force (as is pretended) was sent out against the said Indians, is a Misinformation; for there was not one Man sent from Connecticott last Summer, nor had they resolved to be concerned in the War, tho much persuaded thereto by those of the Massathusets: and when I left those Parts, and for some Months before, there was not a Soldier out; and they have reason enough to apprehend an Attack from the French as well as Indians, in the Spring, so soon as the Rivers are open, and the Snow off the Ground; which (by their present ill Management of Affairs, want of Authority, and the many Divisions amongst them) they will not be in a posture to resist, nor to defend and secure themselves and Country.

11. I did hear before I left New-England, that about sixty Men were ordered to march for Albany from the several Towns on Connecticott River; but whether they were to assist those of Albany against the French, or to reduce them under the Subjection of that Rebel Leslier,[1] (who by the evil Instigation of those of Boston and Connecticott had usurped the Government of New York, which those of Albany always refused to submit to, but continued as they were,)[2] was a great Question, and can only be known by their Fruits and Service.

The base imputation, which the unworthy Author of that scurrilous Paper would cast on Sir E. A. and other Persons concerned in Their Majesties Government, I think are not worth my taking any particular notice of, since both his and their Actions do plainly shew them of whom he so speaks to be Faithful and Loyal Subjects: And from the whole scope of proceedings in New-England, it is most plain that the late Subverters of the Government had no manner of regard to Their Majesty's Interest or Service, but when they had as far as possible ruined and destroyed the same, thought themselves obliged to endeavour their own Security and Preservation, which if His Majesty doth not speedily help by settling of the Government, and giving them further assistance from hence, they are not in a condition to maintain, but will endanger the

[1] Leisler.   [2] See below, p.

loss of the whole Country; As is evident by the farther late advice we have of the French and Indians Incursions upon those parts, the loss of Schenectade,[1] a considerable frontier Town near Albany, and of several settlements on Piscataqua River, with about two hundred more of Their Majesties Subjects killed and carried away Captives, and the several other Parties of French and Indians, we hear are out, designed to fall on other parts of that Country, and feared on Albany it self.

This Sir, is the true, tho miserable State and Condition of that Country, as can be particularly made appear whenever it shall be inquired into, and must pray your Assistance to endeavor a Redress of its present inconveniences, and that we may obtain Their Majesty's favour for a happy settlement, that so considerable a Dominion, on the prosperity of which, depends the Welfare of Their Majesty's other West-India Plantations, may not be ruined and destroyed for want of Their Gracious Protection. Begging your Pardon for this tedious discourse, I presume to subscribe my self,

Honoured Sir,

Your Most Humble Servant,

C. D.

London, Printed for J. Hindmarsh, at the Sign of the Golden Ball, over against the Royal Exchange in Cornhill. 1690.

[1] Schenectady was taken in February, 1690.

INCREASE MATHER'S BRIEF ACCOUNT
OF THE AGENTS, 1691

INTRODUCTION

DURING Andros's administration some of the prominent men of the colony, dissatisfied with the curtailment of their former privileges, determined to appeal to England for relief. Increase Mather, the influential pastor of the Old North Church, was selected to bear to the king, James II., the complaints of the colony, and to obtain, if possible, a restoration of the charter. He was admirably adapted to the task, having served as agent in England only a few years before, while his pleasing address and familiarity with the men and ways of the court at Whitehall were certain to stand him in good stead in the work to be done. He accepted the mission with reluctance, for he was fully aware of its difficulties; but he made no secret of his journey, informing Andros of his plans and openly preparing for departure.

Randolph, however, determined, if possible, to prevent his going, by causing his arrest on an old charge of defamation. A forged letter, purporting to be written by Mather in December, 1683, and containing utterances favorable to the enemies of the crown, had been put in circulation in England, where it had been printed in part by Le Strange in his *Observator*. In a letter sent to some one in New England, Mather had implied that Randolph himself might be the forger, and in consequence the latter had brought an action for £500 damages, but the jury had found for the defendant. Randolph now revived the old charge, on what legal ground is not clear, and brought a new action. On the eve of Mather's voyage he persuaded Justice Bullivant to send an officer to arrest the minister. The attempt failed. Mather, in disguise, withdrew at night to the house of Colonel Phillips, in Charlestown, and thence was taken, by certain young men of his congregation, to Winnisimmet (Chelsea), where he was transferred to the ship *The President* April 7, 1688. After an unpleasant voyage he and his son Samuel landed at Weymouth and reached London May 25.

At London Mather found two of the former Massachusetts assistants, Elisha Hutchinson and Samuel Nowell, the latter of whom had become somewhat notorious as the author of a sermon, entitled "Abraham in Arms," advocating the use of the sword in defending the civil and religious liberties of Massachusetts. With them he joined in a petition to the king, August 10, 1688, presenting certain proposals for the relief of the colony. The petition was brought before the committee of the Privy Council, the Lords of Trade, and the agents were summoned to appear, but before any action could be taken James II. had fled from England, and the old régime was at an end.

Mather now turned to the new government, and through the aid of William Jephson, private secretary to William of Orange and a cousin of Lord Wharton, a friend of New England, obtained an introduction to the prince. With Jephson's aid he and Sir William Phips were able to prevent the despatch to New England of a circular letter, designed for all the colonies, confirming the former governors in their positions. On February 18, 1689, a few days after William and Mary had been proclaimed sovereigns of England, he and Phips sent to the king a petition asking for the restoration of the ancient privileges of the colony. The petition was referred to the Lords of Trade, the membership of which had been changed in 1689, and by them, after consultation with the agents, the decision was reached that a new governor should be appointed for New England and a new charter granted, which, while preserving the rights and liberties of the colonists, should strengthen the dependence of the colony on the crown.

As such a decision was wholly unsatisfactory to Mather, he turned his efforts in a new direction. Sir Henry Ashurst, a good friend to New England, was a member of the Convention Parliament that had met on January 22; and acting under Mather's influence, Ashurst caused a bill for restoring corporations to their ancient rights and privileges to be amended in the house by the addition to the title of the words "and New England and other the Plantations." This bill, reintroduced in the autumn session, was passed January 10, 1690, and sent to the House of Lords. There it reached the committee stage January 23, but such powerful opposition arose to those phrases in the bill which declared the old corporations to have been illegally dissolved that progress was delayed, and Parliament dissolved, February 6, without action. Thus, says Mather, "a whole year's Sisyphean labor came to nothing."

In March two new agents, Cooke and Oakes, representatives of the extreme colonial wing, were sent over from Massachusetts, and a plan was broached of obtaining by legal action a reversal of the decree annulling the charter. But a division of opinion among the agents prevented the prosecution of this plan, which in any case would have failed. No remedy remained except at the hands of the king, and success in that direction required a favorable recommendation from the Lords of Trade and the issue of an order in Council. During the early months of 1690, the Lords of Trade took the business of the colonies into active consideration, and soon made it evident that they were not favorable to a complete restoration of self-government in Massachusetts, but were determined to insist on such a government in New England, New York, and the Jerseys as would enable the people there to carry on defensive and offensive operations against the French.

The situation was one demanding immediate action. Appeals and petitions for and against the charter were coming in from New England, the people of Massachusetts were becoming impatient with Mather because of the delay, and the Lords of Trade were urging the king to make his will known. The arrival of Andros and the others led to lively tilts at the Plantation Office between the agents and their enemies, and the dismissal of the charges against the late governor and his colleagues, because the statement of charges was unsigned, showed that the agents were not acting in harmony. Mather and Ashurst were willing to accept a remodelled government, while Cooke and Oakes were asserting confidently that the king would restore their ancient rights and privileges.

In April, 1690, the Lords of Trade took up in earnest the question of the charter, and from that time until the middle of September, 1691, Mather's efforts were directed to the one great end of obtaining the best terms that he could for the colony. The contest was a vigorous one. The Lords of Trade drew up their minutes for a charter, and Mather replied with objections. Mather presented his proposals and the Lords of Trade rejected item after item, compelling him to give way on many points; but by frequent and determined protest he saved a clause here and there, even after the draught had gone to the attorney general. A passage at arms took place in September over the boundaries, when New Hampshire was made an independent colony, but with the failure of an attempt to obtain rights of coinage for the colony the contest was over. On October 7, 1691, the charter passed the great seal.

In order to defend his course against the criticism which the new charter aroused in the colony, Mather drew up the following account of what had happened in England. Its accuracy is beyond impeachment, as every statement of fact regarding Mather's relations with the authorities in England can be supported by references to the journals of the houses, the acts of the Privy Council, and the journal and papers of the Lords of Trade. As a defense of his own course the narrative is convincing, and as an argument in behalf of the new charter it is a state paper of high rank. With it should be compared Cotton Mather's *Parentator or Memoirs of Remarkables in the Life and Death of the Ever Memorable Dr. Increase Mather*, where the son repeats at somewhat greater length the account that the father here gives of his experiences in London. For a history of the events preceding and accompanying the issue of the charter, Hutchinson's chapter (*History of Massachusetts*, I., ch. III.) has almost the value of a primary source and has never been surpassed.

Mather's *Brief Account* was printed in London in 1691, and reprinted in 1869 by Whitmore in *The Andros Tracts*, II. 271–296. The text here presented is from a rare copy of the original pamphlet now in the John Carter Brown Library.

INCREASE MATHER'S BRIEF ACCOUNT
OF THE AGENTS, 1691

A Brief Account concerning Several of the Agents of New-England, their Negotiation at the Court of England: with Some Remarks on the New Charter Granted to the Colony of Massachusets, shewing That all things duely Considered, Greater Priviledges than what are therein contained, could not at this Time rationally be expected by the People there. London, Printed in the Year 1691.

I MAY rationally suppose that an Account of my Negotiation in England, where I have been attending the great Affair of New-England for more than Three Years, will be expected from me.

When I began my Voyage from Boston for London (which was in April, 1688) New-England was in a very deplorable Condition. He that was then Governour there acted by an Illegal and Arbitrary Commission; and invaded Liberty and Property after such a manner, as no man could say any thing was his own. Wise men believed it to be a necessary Duty to use all Lawful means to obtain some Relief and Remedy against those growing Evils. This could not be done, without first acquainting him who was then in the Throne, with the miserable State of his Subjects in that Territory. No man of common Prudence could be insensible of the Hazard and Danger that would attend his Person and Family, in appearing at Court as a Complainant against a Governour that was King James his Creature.

Nevertheless, being encouraged by many of the principal Gentlemen in New-England, I resolved to venture, tho I perished in the Attempt, rather than to see my Countrey ruin'd.

In June following, I had the favour of waiting on the late King: I must acknowledge he was very kind and Obliging in his Expressions, giving me Liberty of Access in private to him whenever I desired it; seeming to wonder at the things I acquainted him with, and professing that no man in the World should be more ready to relieve the People Interceded for, than he would. Notwithstanding which, nothing was done for them all that Summer. And indeed, good words were as much as any one under my Character had reason to expect in King James his Court.

At the time of the happy Revolution in England, (being introduced by the Right Honourable my Lord Wharton,[1] of whose kindness all New-England has cause to be sensible, his Lordship having upon all Occasions concerned himself for them) I made my humble Addresses to his present Majesty (then Prince of Orange) in behalf of that Countrey. There was a Circular Letter drawn up to be sent to all the Plantations, and in particular to New-England, to confirm those Governours in their Places till further Order. Mr. Jephson (the then Princes Secretary) shewed me the Letter. I assured him that New-England would be undone, if that Letter should come to them. Within a few dayes he told me that he had acquainted His Highness with what I said to him: Who had thereupon Ordered him not to transmit that Letter to New-England,[2] But to all the other Plantations where there were Protestant Governours. This was certainly an happy turn for New-England. How would their Oppressors have insulted over them, had such a Letter come into their hands! I knew that whilest that People enjoyed their Old Charter they prospered wonderfully: But that since they were deprived of the Priviledges therein contained, their ruins were multiplyed; and that the Inhabitants were generally desirous of being resettled as in the days of Old: for which cause I resolved to do what was in me that it might be so.

[1] Philip, Lord Wharton, was a Puritan and an old-time friend of New England.

[2] This circular letter was drawn up "att St. Jameses the 12th day of Jany 1688/9" and signed "W. H. Prince of Orange, By his Highnesses Command, Wm Jephson." Attached to the copy designed for New England and addressed "to Sr Edm. Andros, for Officers Civill and Military, except Papists, to keep their Imploym'ts, etc." is a memorandum in another hand, "Upon the Application of Sr. Wm Phipps and Mr. Mather this Letter was stopped and ordered not to be sent" (C. O. 5 : 905, p. 42).

Whenever I had the Honour of speaking to the King, whether at White-Hall, Hampton-Court or Kensington,[1] I still mention'd the Charter, and always found that the King (although he judged it would be for the Advantage of New-England to have a Governor Commission'd by his Majesty, yet that he) was graciously inclin'd to Restore Charter-Priviledges unto his Subjects in that Territory. Once, at Hampton-Court, his Majesty was pleased to bid me rest assured, that it should be so, if it were in his Power to cause it to be done. I advised with many wise Men about this momentous Affair, whose Judgment was, That the best and most effectual Course would be, to endeavour a Reversion of the Judgment against the Charter of the Massachusets, by an Act of Parliament; and after that, to Petition the King for such additional Priviledges as should be thought needful. I prayed Sir Henry Ashurst,[2] whom I knew to be a worthy Member of the Convention (as well as of this present) Parliament, to concern himself for the good People in that Countrey: Which he did without much intreaty, being of himself forward to do Good: Nor is it possible for New-England ever duely to Recompense him for his sincere Intentions and assiduous Endeavours to serve them. We both of us spake to many of the principal leading Men in that Parliament: The Issue of which was, The Commons of England Voted the Taking away the Charters belonging to New-England (as of those in England) to be Illegal, and a Grievance, and that they ought to be Restored. A Bill was drawn up accordingly, which Passed the House of Commons, and was sent to the House of Lords for their Concurrence, on January the Tenth, 1689.[3] A great Interest, in behalf of New-England, had been made amongst the Lords; but that Parliament being unexpectedly Prorogu'd and Dissolv'd, a whole Year's Sisyphean Labour came to nothing.

When this present Parliament met, it was, for some Rea-

---

[1] The three royal residences.

[2] Sir Henry Ashurst was the son of Henry Ashurst, a wealthy non-conformist merchant of London, who had for many years been interested in the welfare of New England. The Convention Parliament was that of 1689, which had settled the crown upon William and Mary. The present had convened in March, 1690.

[3] 1689/1690. The Convention Parliament ended its sessions on January 27.

sons, thought not adviseable to trouble them with the Affair of New-England. Some Essays were then made, to see if by a Writ of Error in Judgment the Case relating to the Massachusets might be brought out of Chancery[1] into the Kings-Bench. But an unexpected Providence rendred an Attempt of that Nature vain. Never did I see a more signal Hand of Heaven[2] in any Matter, than in Disappointing all Designs, and Frustrating all Hopes for Obtaining the so much desired full Restitution of all Charter-Priviledges, by a Reversion of the Judgment entred against them. There was now but one way left for the Settlement of New-England, sc. To implore the King's Royal Favour.

It was not in the King's Power to Reverse the Judgment against the Old Charter; nevertheless, his Majesty had Power to Re-incorporate his Subjects, thereby granting them a New Charter, which should contain all the Old, with New and more Ample Priviledges.

This, Three[3] of the Agents of the Massachusets Colony Petitioned for; the Right Honourable the Earl of Monmouth condescending to deliver that Petition with his own Noble Hand. After which, through the Intercession of a Great and Worthy Personage, the King was graciously pleased to referr the Affair of New-England to the Consideration of the two Chief Justices, with his Majesty's Attorney, and Sollicitor-General.[4] They Four met three or four times: They were so kind as to give me leave to be present with them at all their Consultations. The Heads of the Charter belonging to the Massachusets Colony, and of that granted to Sir Ferdinando Gorges,[5] were presented in Writing; together with what additional Priviledges we did at present pray for. They all thought there was nothing Unreasonable or Prejudicial to the King's Interest in what was requested. These things were presented

---

[1] The Massachusetts charter had been vacated in 1684 by decree in Chancery upon a writ of scire facias (above, p. 235, note 1).

[2] Probably referring to the differences of opinion among the agents.

[3] Mather, Ashurst, and Oakes. Cooke refused to sign. The date of this petition is not given (Cal. St. P. Col., 1689-1692, § 1276).

[4] The chief justices were Sir John Holt for the king's bench, and Sir Henry Pollexfen for the common pleas. The attorney general was Sir George Treby, and the solicitor general, Sir George Somers.

[5] The charter of the council for New England, 1620.

to the King by my Lord Chief Justice Holt. The King ordered him to present them to the Council; which was done on the First of January last;[1] when they were referred to the Consideration of the Right Honourable the Lords of the Committee for Foreign Plantations.

Immediately upon this, the King began his Royal Voyage for Holland; untill whose Happy Return nothing could be effected as to the Settlement of New-England. In the mean time, I drew up several Reasons for the Confirmation of Charter-Priviledges granted to the Massachusets Colony; which I dispersed among the Lords of his Majesty's most Honourable Privy-Council; and did particularly address my self to the greatest part of them, humbly praying their Lordships Favour to New-England, in a Matter which seemed so Just and Equitable: And had assurance from many of them, that whenever the Affair of New-England should come before the Council-Board, they would do what in them was, that Ancient Rights and Priviledges might be Restored.

Moreover, a Noble Personage did me the Honour to introduce me to the Queen, that so I might have an Opportunity to sollicit Her Majesty's Royal Favour towards her Subjects in New-England. I assured her Majesty, That there are none better affected to their Majesties Government, and that on that account they had been exposed to the Rage of the French, and other Enemies to the present Government in England; and that the King having referred the Consideration of the Affair of New-England to the two Chief Justices, with the Attorney and Sollicitor-General, we only prayed, that what they thought was reasonable, might be granted to us.

The Queen graciously replied, That that was a reasonable Request, and that she hoped it would be done for us, only it could not be done but by the Council. Her Majesty moreover assured me, That she had divers times spoken to the King in behalf of New-England; and that, for her own part, she desired that that People might not only have what was Just done for them, but that something of Favour might be shown to them.—I the rather mention this, that so all New-England may be excited to Pray for so Gracious a Queen.

When the King returned to England, he stayed not there

[1] January 1, 1691.

above a Fortnight:[1] In which time I had twice the Honour to wait on his Majesty in behalf of New-England. The First time I only delivered the last Address from the General-Court at Boston, *viz.* that of Decemb. 16, 1690, and a Petition from many Merchants in London, praying, That Charter-Priviledges might be restored to New-England; and that some Frigats might be sent for the Security of those Coasts. The Second time, I humbly prayed the Continuance of his Royal Favour to his Subjects in that Territory. The King was then pleased to ask me, What I would have to be done for New-England? I humbly put his Majesty in mind of our Old Charter-Priviledges: And that if they should, by his Royal Favour and Goodness, be restored, that would make his Majesty's Name Great in those Ends of the Earth, as long as the World should stand: That none of his Subjects prayed more for his Royal Person, and for the Success of his Arms, than they did: That they were all of them Protestants, and that they differed in lesser Matters from some others, being of those that were called Presbyterians, and Congregational-Men: That his Majesty, in his great Wisdom, had considered the Circumstances of England, and the Circumstances of Scotland:[2] That, according to his Royal Wisdom, he would consider the Circumstances of New-England also; and that such Rulers would not be agreeable to them, as were very proper to the other English Plantations. The King replied to me, That within two or three days he expected a Report from the Committee of Lords for Foreign Plantations,[3] and that he should then see what could be done.

Two days after this, (*viz.* on April the 30th, 1691) it was by the Lords of the Committee proposed to the King, Whether he would have the People in New-England make what Laws, and appoint what Officers They pleased? Or, Whether He would not appoint a Governour of his own, who should have a Negative Voice on all Acts of Government? The King was very inquisitive to know whether he might, without any Breach of Law, set a Governor over that Colony: (For we

---

[1] April, 1691.

[2] In accordance with which he had consented to the establishment of the Presbyterian Church as the State Church of Scotland.

[3] The Lords of Trade.

have a King now that will not Act contrary to Law.) The Lord Chief Justice, and some other of the Council, answer'd, That whatever might be the Merit of the Cause, inasmuch as the Charter of Massachusets Colony, in New-England, stood vacated by a Judgment against them, it was certainly in the King's Power to put them under what Form of Government he should think best for them. The King then said, That he was desirous to promote the Welfare of New-England, as well as of England; and that he believed it would be for the Good and Advantage of his Subjects in that Colony, to be under a Governour appointed by himself: Nevertheless, That he would have the Agents of New-England Nominate a Person that should be agreeable to the Temper and Inclinations of the People there; only that, at this time, it was necessary that a Military Man should be set over them; and that this notwithstanding, he would have Charter-Priviledges Restored and Confirmed to them.

The next day, the King began his Second Royal Voyage for Holland; but an Order of Council was drawn up, intimating, That it was the King's Pleasure to have a Governour of his own Appointing sent to New-England, who should have a Negative Voice in all Acts of Government: And, That the Massachusets Colony should be settled on the same Foundation with Barbadoes, etc. And that a Charter should be prepared accordingly. As soon as I had a Copy of this Order of Council, I went with it to four or five of the Lords of His Majesty's most Honourable Privy-Council: Every one of which said, That as it was worded, it did not (in their Opinion) agree with the King's Expressions or Intentions. Moreover, I caused a Copy of this Order to be transmitted to my Lord Sidney,[1] one of his Majesty's Principal Secretaries of State, then with the King in Flanders; praying, That if that Order, Signed by one of the Clerks of the Council, was not according to the King's Mind, His Majesty would graciously please to signifie his Dis-approbation thereof: But no such Signification ever came.

The Attorney-General, in the mean time, prepared a Draught of a Charter, according to what he took to be the King's Mind, as expressed when his Majesty was last in Coun-

---

[1] Henry, Viscount Sydney, afterward Earl of Romney.

cil. In that Draught, the Free-men (and not all Free-holders) had Power to Chuse the Deputy-Governour and the other General Officers: And the King's Governour had not a Negative Voice allowed him in any Case.

This Draught was presented at the Council-Board on the Eighth Day of June last;[1] when it was by some objected, That by such a Charter as this, the King's Governour would be made a Governor of Clouts; and Order was given to prepare new Minutes, or Heads, for another Draught: Which indeed made the Charter designed to be no Charter of Incorporation, and did deprive the Massachusets of some Essential Priviledges in their former Charter. When those Minutes were agreed on by the Lords, the Secretary of the Committee gave me a Copy of them; with an Order from their Lordships, That if the Agents of the Massachusets Colony were not satisfied therewith, they should bring in their Objections to Mr. Attorney-General. I shewed the Order to the other Agents. Sir Henry Ashurst went with me to the Attorney-General. I expressed my Dissatisfaction, perhaps, with a greater Pathos than I should have done, earnestly protesting, that I would sooner part with my Life, than Consent to the Minutes, or any thing else that did infringe any Liberty or Priviledge of Right belonging to my Countrey. The like I said to some Ministers of State: Who replied, That our Consent was not expected nor desired: For they did not think the Agents of New-England were Plenipotentiaries from another Sovereign State; but that if we declared we would not submit to the King's Pleasure, his Majesty was resolved to settle the Countrey, and we must take what would follow.

I drew up some Reasons[2] against the Minutes proposed; Sir Henry Ashurst joyned with me therein; we argued, That the King had graciously promised a Restoration of Charter-Priviledges to New-England; and that Charter-Priviledges

---

[1] No entry of this important meeting, the turning-point in the controversy between Mather and the Privy Council, appears in the Privy Council Register. Such a draught was, however, presented on June 8, 1691, to the Lords of Trade, and as this body was a committee of the Council (*Cal. St. P. Col.*, 1689–1692, § 17), it is probable that Mather has used the term "Council Board" to mean the Lords of Trade and not the Privy Council properly so called.

[2] These "Reasons" are probably the same as the "Proposals" given in *Cal. St. P. Col.*, 1689–1692, § 1574.

might with as much and more reason be with-held from any or all the Corporations in England which were never legally Restored, as from New-England; with several other Arguments too large to be here inserted. These Reasons we delivered in Writing to the King's Attorney-General, who presented them to the Lords at the Council-Board. I likewise caused a Copy of them to be sent over to the King in Flanders. Moreover, some Great Ones at Court wrote to several of the Ministers of State who were with the King, entreating them to use their Interest with his Majesty, that nothing might be Imposed on New-England, which would be grievous to his good Subjects there.

Some were apt to think, that if the King were in England, we might prevail with his Majesty to signifie his Disallowance of those Minutes which were so grievous to us; and that therefore it might not be amiss to write to the King in Flanders, praying that a stop might be put to any further Proceedings about the Charter, until his Majesty's happy Return to England. I desired a Great Person (whom I knew the Queen had an high Esteem of) to pray her Majesty to write to the King, That he would graciously please to Command that the Charter should Pass, as drawn up by the Attorney-General; or else that it should be Deferred until his Majesty's coming. The Queen was so kind as to do this for New-England. I now concluded that nothing more would be done for some Months.

By continual Attendance on this arduous Affair, I had broken my Natural Rest, and neglected my Necessary Food, insomuch that my Health was greatly impaired: Physicians advised me to recede into the Countrey, and use Mineral Waters for my Recovery.

Before I had been there long, I had (and was surprized at it) notice that the King had signified his Approbation of the Minutes which we were so much concerned about; and that it was his Royal Pleasure that New-England should be forthwith settled accordingly.

Likewise, a very great Man, and a great Friend of New-England, desired a Person of Quality to advise me to take up with what was proposed; withall adding, that if the King were in England, as Matters were now circumstanced, nothing more or better could be expected. I immediately returned to London.

His Majesty's Principal Secretary of State assured me, that he had received such a Signification of the King's Pleasure as has been mentioned; and was pleased to let me see the Letter; wherein it was expressly declared, not only that the King did approve of the Minutes agreed unto by the Lords of the Committee, but that he did by no means approve of the Objections which the Agents of New-England had made against them.

We then resolved however to get as much Good and prevent as much Hurt to the Countrey as possibly might be. A Petition[1] was Signed by Sir Henry Ashurst and my self, praying, That no Property belonging to that Colony, or to any therein, might by the New Charter be taken from them, nor any Priviledges which they had a Right unto: That the Province of Mayn might be Confirmed: Nova Scotia added to the Massachusets: And, That New Hampshire might be put under that Government. As to what concerns Hampshire, we were told, the People there desired to be under any Government in the World, rather than that of Massachusets. Great Opposition was made against what was proposed concerning the Province of Mayn, but at last it was granted; and Nova Scotia, so far as in the Charter is expressed. Just at this time, Letters came to my hand from Plymouth Colony, giving me the Thanks of the General Court there, for that I had prevented their being annexed to New-York, (which was by some Persons of Interest designed above a Year ago:) And intimating, That the generality of People there desired to have a distinct Charter, and be confirmed as a distinct Government amongst themselves: But if that could not be obtained, that then, for the Lord's sake, I would endeavour that they might be united to Boston, rather than to New-York.

When I understood the Charter was finished,[2] and had been read before the Lords, I prayed that I might see it, and

---

[1] This petition was read at a meeting of the Lords of Trade, September 2, 1691 (*Cal. St. P. Col.*, 1689–1692, § 1724).

[2] The second draught of the charter, now in the Public Record Office, shows many erasures, interlineations, and alterations on separate pieces of paper pasted over the original text. Hutchinson prints (I. 412, note) a letter from Elisha Cooke, asserting that William Blathwayt, a clerk of the Lords of Trade and the

carry it to Councel; because there might be some Clauses in
it which their Lordships might have such Reasons suggested
to them, as they would think meet to expunge them, or to add
some Particulars which might be Beneficial to his Majesty's
Subjects in that Colony, and no ways Prejudicial to the King's
Interest, nor yet inconsistent with those Minutes which they
would not suffer to be contradicted. This Request was
granted, only I must return the Copy within a few days: An
Eminent Councellor perused it two or three times, and made
his Remarks on it.

That Phrase of Corporal Oath was altered, that so no
Snare might be laid before such as scruple Swearing on the
Book. A Clause was added, Confirming Grants made by the
General Court, notwithstanding any defect that might attend
the Form of Conveyance, that so Mens Titles to their Lands
might not be invalidated, only for that the Laws which gave
them their Right had not passed under the Publick Seal in
the time of the former Government. Some other Alterations
we prayed for, but we could not obtain them.[1]

The Question now was, Whether we should submit to this
New Settlement? Or, in hopes of obtaining a Reversion of
the Judgment against the Old Charter, signifie to the Ministers
of State, that we had rather have no Charter at all, than such
an one as was now proposed to acceptance? I knew that in
the multitude of Councellors there is safety, and did therefore
advise with many, and with Persons Unprejudiced, and of the
greatest Wisdom and Ability to judge; with Noblemen, Gentlemen, Divines, and Lawyers: They all agreed, that it was not
only Lawful, but, all Circumstances considered, a Duty to
submit to what was now offered. Some said, They were very
weak Men, and unfit to appear as Agents for a Colony, that
should make any Question of it. Others said, That a peremptory Refusal would bring not only a greater Inconvenience,

patron of Randolph, wrote this draught. It is quite possible that he did so, as
such would be the proper business of a secretary of the board, and Blathwayt,
as auditor general of the plantation revenues, probably knew more about the
colonies than any one else in the Privy Council Office; but as there were three
other clerks, the statement cannot be considered proven. Hutchinson accepts
it, however, and Professor Channing follows Hutchinson.

[1] These final objections by Mather are given in *Cal. St. P. Col.*, 1689–1692,
§ 1758.

but a fatal Ruine on New-England; and then Mankind would lay the blame on the Weakness and Wilfulness of the Agents, who when they could not have what they would, ought to submit to what they could get.   The Opinion of the Lawyers was, That such a Passive Submission was not a Surrender, inasmuch as nothing was done under Hand and Seal: Nor could there be a Surrender in this case, since Judgment was already Entred and Recorded against the Old Charter: Nor were the Agents capable of Surrendring, as not being Plenipotentiaries; and that their taking up with this did not make the People in that Colony, in Law, uncapable of obtaining all their Old Priviledges, whenever a favourable Opportunity should present it self; for the World knew, that in a present parting with any of their ancient Rights, they were forced to yield unto Necessity.   I remember, an Honest Lawyer, and a Well-wisher to New-England, told me, That if we were put to our Choice, whether to enjoy our Old Charter (which he was well acquainted with) again, just as it was, or to take up with this, (all things duely considered,) we were not wise if we did not chuse this rather than that.   It was considered, That a Judgment (right or wrong) not in Court of King's-Bench, but in Chancery, standing on Record against the Charter of the Massachusets, whereby it was vacated and annihilated, that Colony was fallen into the Kings Hands; so that he might put them under what Governours, or what Form of Government, he should please.   Their Agents might beg for a full Restitution of all Ancient Priviledges, but they might not either Chuse or Refuse as to them should seem best.   It was considered, That there was no probability of obtaining a Reversion of the Judgment against the former Charter.   We saw it was in vain to attempt to bring it out of Chancery into the Court of King's Bench.   There were thoughts of bringing the Matter into the House of Lords by a Writ of Error in Judgment; but it was believed that no Cursitor[1] would now venture to Sign a Writ of Error; and that if he should, the Lords would not be forward to concern themselves in this Affair.

Although the Archbishop of Canturbury[2] that now is, and

[1] Clerk in the Court of Chancery.
[2] John Tillotson, archbishop 1691–1694, had taken the place of the non-juring Sancroft.

many of the present Bishops, are Friends to New-England, (as well as to all good Men,) and I have cause to acknowledge the personal Respect I have received from many of them: And although a great Interest has been made for New-England amongst the Temporal Lords; nevertheless, when they should understand that the King was desirous to have that Countrey put under another Form of Government, which his Royal Wisdom judged would be better for them than what they formerly enjoyed, the Lords would be very slow in doing any thing that they knew would be dissatisfactory to his Majesty. And if they should see cause to take the Case of New-England into their Consideration, though they would not Justifie the manner of Proceedings, yet when they should hear all that was to be Objected against the Governour and Company, on the Account of their having exceeded the Powers of their Charter in several Particulars, and in a very high degree, they would certainly judge that they had merited a Condemnation thereof. It was also Considered, That the Old Charter was, in more respects than one, very defective: For by that, the Government in New-England had no more Power than Corporations in England have. But those Corporations have not Power in Capital Cases. Both the Judges and Eminent Lawyers have assured me, that though Power was given to Corporations in Criminal, except Capital Cases be particularly expressed, their Power does not reach so far: Nor was there any thing in the Old Charter concerning an House of Deputies, or Assembly of Representatives: Nor had the Governour and Company Power to impose Taxes on the Inhabitants: Nor to Erect Courts of Admiralty, etc. The King's Attorney-General (who is no Enemy to New-England) declared, the two Chief Justices and Sollicitor General concurring with him, That supposing the Judgment against the Charter of the Massachusets to be Reversed, if the Government should exert such Powers as before the Quo Warranto against their Charter they had done, there would now be a Writ of Scire facias issued out against them in Westminster-Hall, and their Charter-Priviledges would undoubtedly be taken from them. And it was Considered, That if the Judgment against the Old Charter had been Reversed by Act of Parliament, the Massachusets Colony would, for all that, have been in a far more miserable Condition than by the present Settlement they are reduced unto: For then the Province of Mayn, as to Government, would have been taken from them, since Government is a Trust that cannot be sold; and Hampshire (which would have been made to extend as far as Salem,) and Plymouth, would have been put under a Governour sent from England; which Governour would have had the Command over the Militia, and the Power of Admiralty, etc., in the Massachusets Colony: So that, in fine, Boston would have been deprived of Trade, and the whole Colony made very insignificant: And if they had exerted Powers necessary for the Supportation of their Government, perpetual Complaints would have been made against them. It was moreover Considered, That if the Agents of that Colony had signified to the Ministers of State, that they had rather have no Charter at all, than this which the King was pleased to grant to them, the Consequence would have been, that they should have had a Governour wholly a Stranger to New-England, and a Deputy-Governour not acceptable to the People there; and many of his Councellors Strangers, and others of them such as were Andross's Creatures; and that this Governour should have had the same Power which the Governours in other Plantations have, to Appoint the General Officers. They are very weak Men that doubt of this; and if they will look no further than their Neighbours at New York and Virginia, they may see Demonstrations before their Eyes sufficient to convince them. It was likewise Considered, That some Persons in London were endeavouring to get a Pattent for all Mines, Minerals, Gums, etc., in New-England: Which Design was, of late, likely to have taken effect, only the New Charter has most happily prevented that which would have been of pernicious Consequence to all that Territory. It was further Considered, That by this New Charter great Priviledges are granted to the People in New-England, and, in some Particulars, greater than they formerly enjoyed: For all English Liberties are restored to them: No Persons shall have a Penny of their Estates taken from them; nor any Laws imposed on them, without their own Consent by Representatives chosen by themselves. Religion is secured; for Liberty is granted to all Men to Worship God after that manner which in their Consciences they shall be perswaded is the most

Scriptural way. The General Court may by Laws Encourage and Protect that Religion which is the general Profession of the Inhabitants there. They may still have Judges, as at the first; and Councellors, as at the beginning, if the fault be not their own. As long as their Principal Magistrates, Judges, Justices of the Peace, are such as will encourage Vertue and Piety, and punish Vice, Religion will flourish: And if they have not such, the fault will not be in the New-Charter, but in themselves; since no bad Councellor, Judge, or Justice of the Peace, can now be imposed on them. These things are as a Wall of Defence about the Lord's Vineyard in that part of the World. The General Court (now that the Massachusets Colony is made a Province) hath, with the King's Approbation, as much Power in New-England as the King and Parliament have in England; which is more than could be said in the time of the former Government there, which had only the Power of a Corporation. The General Court has now Power to impose Taxes upon all the Inhabitants; and to make Laws which shall Incorporate Towns, or Schools of Learning, etc., which by the First Charter they had not Power to do. That Countrey may now expect Protection and Assistance from England, as the Matter shall require, more than formerly. And although there are some things in this New Charter which are not desirable, yet nothing that is intolerable. Take it with all its Faults, and it is not so bad, but that when I left New-England, the Inhabitants of that Territory would gladly have parted with many a Thousand Pound to have obtained one so good. The great fear is, that though at present there be a good Governour (appointed by the King,) who wisheth well to New-England, yet he will quickly be removed, and perhaps an Enemy come in his room. But I am morally certain of it, that if they hearken to the Advice of their best Friends, no Person not agreeable to New-England, in respect of Religion, and the Temper of that People, will be set over them, during their present Majesties Reign, whom the God of Heaven send long to Live and Reign. Yet suppose it should be otherwise: Suppose a Person as bad as Andross (and the New-Englanders think there can hardly be a worse,) should come amongst them, What can he do? He cannot without the Consent of the Council, Chosen by the Representatives of the People, appoint a Sheriff to pack Juries to serve his turn; nor Judges that will act against their Consciences, rather than displease him. Nor can he now send Men out of the Conntrey, without their own consent. Nor can he and his Creatures make Laws, or Leavy Taxes; nor Invade any Man's Property, under pretence that it is the King's; and that they must come to him for Patents, that so they may have a true Title to their Lands and Estates. Nor can he, without violating the Magna Charta of New-England, disturb any Man for his Religion. The King's Governour has a Negative Voice in all Acts of Government; which may be thought a great Infringement of the Peoples Liberty; and indeed, makes the Civil Government of New-England more Monarchical, and less Democratical, than in former Times. Nevertheless, the People have a Negative on him. In which respect, New-England is by this Charter more priviledged than Ireland, and than any English Plantation whatsoever, or than they that live in England it self are. Appeals to England are allowed of by this New Charter; but only in Personal (not in Real or Mixed) Actions, where the matter of difference is above Three hundred Pounds Sterling in value. So that as to Titles of Land there cannot be any Appeal to England, but those Controversies are to have a final Determination in Courts of Judicature amongst themselves. And Laws Enacted by the General Court are to be transmitted to the King for his Royal Approbation: Nevertheless, those Laws, when made, are to be in force as soon as made, until such time as disallowed of by the King: And if within the space of Three Years the King's Disapprobation be not signified, those Laws are to be Perpetual, except by the General Court they shall be Repealed. By the Old Charter, the Governour and Company might not make any Laws contrary to the Laws of England: And such reasonable Laws as are not contrary thereto will no doubt be Confirmed by his Majesty, if the People in New-England be not wanting to themselves as to due Endeavours that it may be so. All these things duely considered, the Best and Wisest Men in England thought that the Persons who were concerned for New-England would do an ill Service for their Countrey, if they should peremptorily decline a Submission to this Settlement, and thereby bring upon themselves that which would be more undesirable.

I must beg leave (for it is a Truth) to say this further, That whereas the People in New-England have not obtained all the Charter-Priviledges which they have at several times Petitioned Their Majesties for; they have more reason to blame themselves, than those of their Agents, who did their utmost to procure every thing for them which they prayed for. Had they at the time of the Revolution entred upon the full Exercise of their Old Charter-Government, and then humbly signified to the King that they had so done; and that they were perswaded, His Majesty, who declared, when Prince of Orange, That Charters and Ancient Priviledges should be restored to the English Nation in general, would not be offended at them on the account of their adhering to what was their undoubted Right, wise Men are of Opinion that they might have gone on without disturbance, until such time as new Complaints should be exhibited against them, on the account of doing things which by their Charter they were never impowered to do. But in an Address to the King, they assure his Majesty, That they had not entred upon the full Exercise of their Charter-Government; but that not having received Directions from England, which they humbly waited for, they entred upon the Government for the Preservation of the Peace, until such time as they should receive an Orderly Settlement from England; which they prayed might be according to their Old Charter, that had been unrighteously taken from them.

Now when wise Men in London saw this: "Will you" (said they) "who are Agents for the Massachusets Colony, refuse to submit to a Settlement of your Government from England, when your Principals have signified to the King that they will do it? Who gave you that Power of Refusal? Has the General Court, in an Address to the King, declared, They have not entred on the full Exercise of their Charter-Government, but that they wait for the King's Pleasure, as to their Settlement; then surely they have not given you private Instructions not to Submit? And if they have not, you cannot answer your Refusal to your Principals, nor to the King, nor to Mankind. Have not your Magistrates caused a new Clause to be added to the usual Oath taken by the Assistants, *viz*. That if contrary Orders arrive from England, that Oath shall

not oblige them to serve as Assistants until the Year be expired?
Shall then their Agents protest against such Orders?"

Such as these have been the Reasonings of wise Men in
London. Moreover, the Government in New-England Peti-
tioned the King to assist them with Frigats, and Supplies of
Arms and Ammunition; which was, in effect, to pray for a
Governour. They could not be so weak, to think the King
would send the one without the other.

When I wrote to this purpose to a principal Person in
Government there, the Answer returned to me was, That I,
and other Persons that were employed as Agents for that
Colony, ought to look on it as the principal thing committed
to our Care and Trust, and that, preferrable to all other things
whatsoever: To endeavour the obtaining Assistance from their
Majesties, against the French, and other Enemies; and that
this was the sence of the generality of the sober People in New-
England. So that if these two came in Competition, either to
have the Old Charter just as it was, or to get Assistance from
England; we were told we should be Unfaithful to our Trust,
if we did not preferr the latter to the former.

Yet further: The Countrey was so impoverished by the
Wars made upon them, as that they could not send a competent
Supply to their Agents for the management of their Affair.

Besides what was sent to me out of New-England, I expended upwards of Two Hundred Pounds of my own Personal
Estate, out of Love to that People. And I did, for their sakes,
borrow of a Merchant in London above Three Hundred Pounds
more, which was Two Years before care was taken for the Re-
payment of it.

The last Year, some who were hearty Well-wishers to New-
England wrote thither, That they must consider, their Life,
their Religion, the Welfare of their Posterity for ever, depended
on a suitable Supply for their Agents that were concerned in
Transacting their great Affairs at Court. This notwithstanding, for more than a Twelvemonth not one Penny was returned:
So that I was necessitated, either to suffer Ruine to come upon
the Countrey where I had spent the greatest part of my Life,
or else must borrow Money again to serve them: Which I did,
and Engaged all the Estate I have in the World for the Re-
payment thereof: This is more than ever any man did before

me, and perhaps more than any Person so Circumstanced as I have bin, will do after me.

And what was I able to do more? I do humbly affirm, That there is not a man in this World, that has done more, nor so much, towards the obtaining of a full Restitution of all Charter-Priviledges to New-England, as I have done. And as to the undesirable Minutes in the New Charter, there is no person living that has manifested his dissent therefrom, or more opposed, or done more to prevent them, than I have: But to reject all the Good therein, because of some things inconvenient, is that which I dared not to be guilty of. As Day and Night have seen it, so I can, and I do appeal to Heaven and Earth, that I have served that People with all Fidelity to the very utmost of my Power.

And now they must give me leave to give them the best Advice I can. I shall not need (for they will do it of themselves) to perswade them to send an Address of Humble Thanks to their Majesties, for their Royal Favour in Restoring Property, and in Conferring greater Priviledges on New-England, than have bin granted to any other English Plantation. And for that their Majesties have been graciously pleased to put the present Government of New-England into good hands. The Person Nominated for Governour (Sir William Phipps)[1] is one that has ventured his Life to serve his Countrey. When Gideon did so, the Children of Israel were desirous that he should Rule over them.[2] The Deputy-Governour, Mr. Stoughton, is one whose worth is known in both Englands. One of more than ordinary Accomplishments, both as to parts Natural and Acquired, and as to Vertue and Integrity. And as for the Twenty Eight Assistants, who are appointed to be of the Governours Council, every man of them is a Friend to New-England, and to the Churches and Interest of Christ therein. To be in the hands of such Rulers is an invaluable Mercy.

---

[1] Sir William Phips was born in 1650 of humble parentage in what is now Woolwich, Maine. He began life as an apprentice to a ship-carpenter, and his most famous exploit was the recovery of sunken treasure off the Bahamas, for which he was knighted. He became the first governor of the province under the new charter. Hutchinson has an excellent characterization of him, I. 396–397, note.

[2] Judges viii. 22.

As for me, whom the Lord Jesus has made use of as an Instrument in his Hand, for obtaining this Mercy for New-England, I desire no Acknowledgment, nor any Reward in the least, for the Difficult and Expensive Service I have for their sakes gone through. Let me wait for my Recompense till the Resurrection of the Just. But if that People be not thankful to God, and to the King and Queen, for what has been done for them, not only the King and Queen, but the Majesty of Heaven, may justly be incensed against them. To be thankful for what is given, is the way to receive more from God and Men.

But let me Propose,

1. That the General Court do, without delay, agree upon a Body of Good Laws. They may make such Laws for the Settlement of the Militia, and for the securing of Liberty to the Subject, as shall be better than their Old Charter. And as to what concerns the Upholding of Religion in that Countrey, there are especially Two things which may be done. The one is, By Laws to Encourage an Able and Faithful Ministry. The other is, To take care that the Colledge be Confirmed in such Hands, as will make it their Concern to Promote and Propagate Vertue and Learning. It was in a special manner with respect thereunto, that I did undertake a Voyage for England above Three Years and an half since. As long as that Countrey lay unsettled, as to the Civil Government, I could not do much for the Colledge; only I prevailed with a Gentleman of my Acquaintance to bequeath a Legacy of Five Hundred Pounds to that Society. And now, in this New-Charter, all Donations or Revenues granted to that Academy are by the King, under the Great Seal of England, Confirmed. I humbly proposed to some great Ministers of State, That a particular Charter might be granted for the Incorporating that School for Academical Learning. Answer was made, That it should be so, if I desired it: But that a better way would be, for the General Court of the Massachusets Colony, by a Law, to Incorporate their Colledge; and to make it an University, with as ample Priviledges as they should think necessary; and then transmit that Act of the General Court to England, for the Royal Approbation; which would undoubtedly be obtained. I look upon this Particular alone, to

be well worth my going to England, and there serving half an Apprenticeship;[1] for that no small Concernment of Religion, and the Happiness of future Generations, are comprehended in this Matter respecting the Colledge.

2. I take it to be good Advice, That Judges, Sheriffs, Justices of the Peace, should be Established throughout the Province, of such as are Men fearing God; and that their Commissions continue, *Quam diu se benè gesserint.*[2]

However it shall be, whether my Counsels be followed or not, or whether my sincere Intentions and unwearied Endeavours to serve New-England find Acceptance with them or no, I have this to comfort my self with, That God has been so gracious to me, as to make me instrumental in obtaining for my Countrey a Magna Charta, whereby Religion and English Liberties, with some peculiar Priviledges, Liberties, and all Mens Properties, are Confirmed and Secured (Allowance being given for the Instability of all Humane Affairs) to Them and their Posterity for evermore.

INCREASE MATHER.

London,
Novemb. 16,
1691.

An Extract of a Letter (Written By some of the most Eminent Nonconformist Divines in London,) Concerning the New Charter Granted to the Colony of Massachusets in New-England.

To the much Honoured General Court Assembled at Boston, in New-England.

Much-Honoured Gentlemen,
We must give this true Testimony of our much Esteemed and Beloved Brother, Mr. Increase Mather, That with inviolate Integrity, excellent Prudence, and unfainting Diligence, he has managed the great Business committed to his Trust. As he is instructed in the School of Heaven, to minister in the Affairs of the Soul; so he is furnisht with a Talent, to transact Affairs of State. His Pro-

---

[1] *I. e.*, half of seven years.
[2] During good behavior. All royal appointees held their offices at the king's pleasure or for life.

ceedings have been with that Caution and Circumspection, as is correspondent to the weight of his Commission. He with Courage and Constancy has pursued the Noble Scope of his Employment; and understanding the true Moment of things, has preferred the Public Good to the vain Conceits of some, that more might have been obtained, if peremptorily insisted on. Considering the open Opposition, and secret Arts, that have been used to frustrate the best Endeavours for the Interest of New-England, the happy Issue of things is superiour to our Expectations. Your present Charter secures Liberty and Property, the fairest Flowers of the Civil State. And which is incomparably more valuable, it secures the enjoyment of the blessed Gospel in its Purity and Freedom. Although there is a restraint of your Power in some things that were granted in your former Charter; yet there are some ample Priviledges in other things, that may be of perpetual Advantage to the Colony.

We doubt not but your faithful Agent will receive a gracious Reward Above; and we hope his successful Service will be welcom'd with your entire Approbation, and grateful Acceptance.

We are,

London,   Your very Humble,
Octob. 17,   And Faithful Servants,
1691.   WILLIAM BATES,   JOHN JAMES,
                 THOMAS WOODCOCK,   SAMUEL ANNESLY,
                 MATTHEW MEAD,   GEORGE GRIFFITH,
                 MATTHEW BARKER,   RICHARD MAYO,
                 RICHARD STRETTON,   ISAAC CHAUNCEY,
                 VINCENT ALSOP,   JOHN QUICK.
                 JOHN HOWE,

The End.

DECLARATION OF PROTESTANT SUBJECTS IN MARYLAND, 1689

INTRODUCTION

THERE is no contemporary account in narrative form of the revolution of 1689 in Maryland, which overthrew the proprietary government and placed the control of the colony for more than two years in the hands of a group of political malcontents. The *Declaration* here printed does not contain a statement of facts but presents rather a series of reasons and motives, drawn up by the leaders of the movement to excuse and explain their action. A satisfactory commentary on these reasons and motives would call for a history of Maryland from 1661 to 1689.

During that period of twenty-eight years, coincident with the restoration of the Stuarts in England, Charles Calvert, son of Cecilius, second Lord Baltimore, and a man of very different type from his father, was governor of the colony. In 1675, on the death of his father, he became third Lord Baltimore and the proprietary. At three different times during these years he was absent from the colony, the government being carried on by deputies, of whom the last was William Joseph, sent by Baltimore from England to serve as president of the council and deputy governor. This absence of the proprietary, particularly in 1689, when the uprising took place, is a factor of importance, inasmuch as Governor Joseph was incompetent to deal vigorously with the revolt.

After 1661 Maryland as well as Virginia suffered from maladministration in government that aroused among the people of the colony feelings of dissatisfaction and discontent. Control of affairs was largely in the hands of the family and relatives of the proprietary; taxes and fees were heavy for a people that were generally poor; a franchise act of 1670 had deprived the landless classes of the right to vote; and the falling price of tobacco created grave uncertainty and much distress. As a rule, the people were ignorant and easily aroused to a belief in their grievances and responded readily to outside influences, whether from Virginia, only a few miles away across the Potomac, or from England, where the conditions antecedent to the revolution of 1688 were certain to find an echo among a people already predisposed to suspicion of their governors.

The accession of James II. to the throne of England; the birth of a son, and the acclaim that accompanied the news of this event in Maryland; the tactlessness and cowardice of Governor Joseph, whose rigid adherence to the Stuart doctrines of divine right and prerogative was strangely at variance with the prevailing sentiment in the colony—all these things gave rise to uncontrolled fears of Roman Catholic domination in Maryland. These fears were increased when, after the flight of James and the accession of William and Mary, the proprietary governor took no steps to proclaim the new sovereigns; and as the rumors of war with France spread, the conviction became fixed that those in authority were designing to carry Maryland over to the side of France. Reports of an Indian war on the frontier of the colony inflamed still further popular sentiment until only a leader was needed to convert sentiment into action.

In July, 1689, the news came that "John Coode was raising men up Potowmack"; by the 27th the insurgents, numbering perhaps two hundred and fifty, had reached St. Mary's, the capital of the province, and, without meeting any adequate resistance, captured the town and the records. A week later Coode and his followers advanced on Mattapany, Lord Baltimore's residence while in the colony and at this time occupied by Joseph and members of the council, which surrendered in order to avoid bloodshed. Thus the malcontents, calling themselves the Protestant Association, obtained control of the government of the province, which they exercised in one form or another for more than two years. From August 1, 1689, until the arrival of Lionel Copley, the royal governor, in April, 1692, Maryland was in the hands of a revolutionary body representing the Protestant interest.

On July 25, 1689, the leaders of the movement issued a "Declaration of the reason and motive for the prest [present] appearing in arms of His Majtys Protestant Subjects in the Province of Maryland." Like other documents issued under similar circumstances, it is a partisan statement, made up of a series of charges against the proprietary government, which inquiry shows to be either without foundation or true only in part. Nevertheless, it is a statement of real historical value, for it is a human document, disclosing the thoughts and convictions of those who took part in the uprising; and it bears an intimate likeness to declarations issued elsewhere to defend other revolutionary movements of this period. As an exposition of actual facts it is of little worth.

Who wrote the paper we do not know. The original document is signed by eight men, John Coode, Henry Jowles, John Campbell, Humphrey Warren, Kenelm Cheseldyne, William Purling, Nehemiah Blakiston, and Richard Clouds, but it is not in the handwriting of any of them. The script is a neat kind of court-hand, apparently that of a clerk, and appears in a number of these Maryland documents. The original Declaration bears two indorsements—due to a second folding of the paper—and it is possible that one of these indorsements, "Declaration for Ann Arundell Countye," is in Coode's own hand. The natural inference is that Coode wrote the paper, but this statement cannot be proved, and the text may have been a co-operative affair.

The other indorsement states that the document was read at the board (of the Lords of Trade) November 22, 1690, and so it must have lain in the Plantation Office for a year before it was formally considered. As the day appointed for the hearing of the case was not November 22, but December 5, and as the copy of the document bears no reference to a reading on that day, I am inclined to think that the text presented on December 5 was not the signed manuscript but a printed copy of it. Some time in August or September, 1689, the manuscript version was slightly emended and printed at St. Mary's by William Nuthead, a fugitive printer from Virginia, who thus issued the earliest known colonial publication with a Maryland imprint. The colony had no press of its own until 1699, when two printing-presses and types were imported. The Nuthead print was sent to England and there reprinted in November or December of the same year. That this printed text was the one read at the meeting of the Lords of Trade on December 5 is borne out by the board minute of January 7, 1691, speaking of "a declaration in print from the inhabitants there" as presented by Lord Baltimore and read at the board (*C. O.* 391:6).

The text here reproduced is that of the London imprint, which differs in but few particulars from the original document. Some of the differences seem to be nothing more than copyist's errors. The original is in the Public Record Office, Colonial Office Papers, 5:718, and the copy of the pamphlet here used is in the Library of Congress.

THE

DECLARATION

OF THE

REASONS and MOTIVES

For the PRESENT

Appearing in Arms

OF

THEIR MAJESTIES

𝔓𝔯𝔬𝔱𝔢𝔰𝔱𝔞𝔫𝔱 𝔖𝔲𝔟𝔧𝔢𝔠𝔱𝔰

In the PROVINCE of

MARYLAND.

Licens'd, *November* 28th 1689. J. F.

A Lthough the Nature and State of Affairs, relating to the Government of this Province, is so well and notoriously known
to all Persons any way concerned in the same, as to the
People and Inhabitants here, who are more immediately Interested, as might excuse any *Declaration* or *Apology* for this
present inevitable *Appearance*: Yet forasmuch as (by the *Plots, Con-*
trivances, Insinuations, Remonstrances, and *Subscriptions,* carried on,
suggested, extorted, and obtained by the Lord *Baltemore,* his Depu-
A   ties,

FIRST PAGE OF THE DECLARATION OF THE PROT-
ESTANT SUBJECTS IN MARYLAND, 1689

From an original in the Library of Congress

DECLARATION OF PROTESTANT SUBJECTS IN MARYLAND, 1689

*The Declaration of the Reasons and Motives For the Present
Appearing in Arms of Their Majesties Protestant Subjects
In the Province of Maryland.*
Licens'd,[1] *November 28th 1689. J. F.*

ALTHOUGH the Nature and State of Affairs relating to the
Government of this Province is so well and notoriously known
to all Persons any way concerned in the same, as to the People
and Inhabitants here, who are more immediately Interested,
as might excuse any Declaration or Apology for this present
inevitable Appearance: Yet forasmuch as (by the Plots, Con-
trivances, Insinuations, Remonstrances, and Subscriptions,
carried on, suggested, extorted, and obtained by the Lord Baltemore, his Deputies, Representatives, and Officers here) the
Injustice and Tyranny under which we groan is palliated, and
most if not all the Particulars of our Grievances shrouded from
the Eye of Observation and the Hand of Redress, We thought
fit for general Satisfaction, and particularly to undeceive those
that may have a sinister Account of our Proceedings, to Publish this Declaration of the Reason and Motives inducing us
thereunto.

His Lordship's Right and Title to the Government is by
Virtue of a Charter to his Father Cecilius, from King Charles
the First, of Blessed Memory. How his present Lordship has
managed the Powers and Authorities given and granted in the
same, We could Mourn and Lament only in silence, would our
Duty to God, our Allegeance to his Vicegerent, and the Care
and Welfare of our Selves and Posterity, permit us.

In the First Place, In the said Charter, is a Reservation of

[1] In 1685 the licensing act of 1662, which had expired in 1679, was renewed
for seven years (1 Jac. II., c. 17, § 15).

the Faith and Allegeance due to the Crown of England [1] (the Province and Inhabitants being immediately subject thereunto) but how little that is manifested, is too obvious to all unbiassed Persons that ever had any thing to do here; The very name and owning of that Soveraign Power is sometimes Crime enough to incur the Frowns of our Superiors, and to render our Persons obnoxious and suspected to be Ill Affected to the Government.

The Ill Usage and Affronts to the King's Officers belonging to the Customs here, were a sufficient Argument of this; We need but instance the Business of Mr. Badcock and Mr. Rousby, of whom the former was forcibly detained by his Lordship from going home to make his just Complaints in England, upon which he was soon taken Sick, and 'twas more than probably conjectured that the Conceit of his Confinement was the chief Cause of his Death, which soon after happened. The other was Barbarously Murthered upon the Execution of his Office, by one that was an Irish Papist and our Chief Governor.[2]

Allegeance here, by these Persons under whom We Suffer, is little talk'd of, other then what they would have done and sworn to his Lordship, the Lord Proprietary; for it was very lately owned by the President himself, openly enough in the Upper House of Assembly, That Fidelity to his Lordship was Allegeance, and that the denial of the one was the same thing with refusal or denial of the other. In that very Oath of Fidelity that was then imposed under the Penalty and Threats of Banishment, there is not so much as the least word or intimation of any Duty, Faith, or Allegeance to be reserved to Our Soveraign Lord the King of England.[3]

[1] "And we do . . . make, create, and constitute him, the now baron of Baltimore, and his heirs, the true and absolute lords and proprietaries of the region aforesaid . . . saving always the faith and allegiance and sovereign dominion due to us, our heirs and successors." From the translation of the charter of 1632.

[2] Lord Baltimore's quarrel with Badcock and Rousby, the collectors of customs, in 1682, had brought upon the proprietary the censure of the Lords of Trade. The statement in the text is not exaggerated. The murderer of Rousby in 1684 was George Talbot, Baltimore's cousin and the "Irish papist" referred to, who as president of the council might be called "our Chief Governor."

[3] In 1684 the proprietary insisted that the members of the assembly take a new oath of fidelity to himself. Four years later Governor Joseph, in a curious

How the *Jus Regale* is improved here, and made the Prerogative of his Lordship, is too sensibly felt by us all in that absolute Authority exercised over us, and by the greatest part of the Inhabitants in the Seizure of their persons, Forfeiture and Loss of their Goods, Chattels, Freeholds and Inheritances.[1]

In the next place, Churches and Chappels (which by the said Charter should be Built and Consecrated according to the Ecclesiastical Laws of the Kingdom of England) to our great Regret and Discouragement of our Religion are erected and converted to the use of Popish Idolatry and Superstition. Jesuits and Seminary Priests are the only Incumbents (for which there is a Supply provided by sending our Popish Youth to be Educated at St. Omers) as also the chief Advisers and Councellors in Affairs of Government, and the Richest and most Fertile Land set apart for their Use and Maintenance;[2] while other Lands that are piously intended, and given for the Maintenance of the Protestant Ministry, become Escheat, and are taken as Forfeit, the Ministers themselves discouraged, and no care taken for their Subsistance.

The Power to Enact Laws is another branch of his Lordship's Authority; but how well that has been Executed and Circumstanced is too notorious. His present Lordship upon the Death of his Father, in order thereunto, sent out Writs for Four (as was ever the usuage) for each County to serve as Representatives of the People; but when Elected, there were Two only of each Respective Four pick'd out and summoned to that Convention,[3] Whereby many Laws were made, and the greatest Levy yet known, laid upon the Inhabitants.

sermon-like speech to the assembly that met in November, 1688, repeated the demand which he emphasized in a second speech made to the two houses in conference. "Refusing allegiance," said Joseph, "implyes rebellion." The reference in the text is to the second speech.

[1] This paragraph means that the proprietary had assumed to himself powers that were the prerogative of the king only.

[2] There is no evidence to show that the proprietary or his government ever discriminated in favor of Roman Catholicism. St. Omer is a town in northern France where was then and is now a seminary for the education of Roman Catholic priests.

[3] In 1678 a law was passed providing for four delegates from each county, but the proprietary refused his consent, and in 1681 issued a proclamation reducing the number to two. The struggle continued for two years and ended in the victory of the proprietary.

The next Session, the House was filled up with the remaining Two that was left out of the former, in which there were many and the best of our Laws Enacted, to the great Benefit and Satisfaction of the People. But his Lordship soon after Dissolved and Declared the best of those Laws, such as he thought fit, null and void by Proclamation; notwithstanding they were Assented to in his Lordship's Name by the Governor, in his absence, and he himself sometime Personally Acted and Governed by the same; so that the Question in our Courts of Judicature, in any point that relates to many of our Laws, is not so much the relation it has to the said Laws, but whether the Laws themselves be agreeable to the Approbation and Pleasure of his Lordship? Whereby our Liberty and Property is become uncertain, and under the Arbitrary Disposition of the Judges and Commissioners of our Courts of Justice.

The said Assembly being sometime after Dissolved by Proclamation, another was Elected and met, consisting only of Two Members for each County, directly opposite to an Act of Assembly for Four, in which several Laws, with his Lordship's Personal Assent, were Enacted: Among the which, one for the Encouragement of Trade and Erecting of Towns.[1] But the Execution of that Act was soon after, by Proclamation from his Lordship out of England, suspended the last Year, and all Officers Military and Civil severely prohibited executing or inflicting the Penalties of the same. Notwithstanding which suspension, being in effect a dissolution and abrogating the whole Act, the Income of Three Pence to the Government by the said Act, payable for every Hogshead of Tobacco Exported, is carefully Exacted and Collected.

How Fatal, and of what Pernicious Consequence, that Unlimited and Arbitrary pretended Authority may be to the Inhabitants, is too apparent, but by considering, That by the same Reason, all the rest of our Laws, whereby our Liberty and Property subsists, are subject to the same Arbitrary Disposition, and if timely Remedy be not had, must stand or fall according to his Lordship's Good Will and Pleasure.

[1] The question of towns had its origin with the Lords of Trade, who desired definite ports for entry and clearance and collection of customs in all the colonies. The dispute between Baltimore and the assembly concerned the controverted point as to who should determine the location of these towns.

Nor is this Nullifying and Suspending Power the only Grievance that doth perplex and burthen us, in relation to Laws; but these Laws that are of a certain and unquestioned acceptation are executed and countenanced, as they are more or less agreeable to the good liking of our Governours in particular; One very good Law provides, That Orphan Children should be disposed of to Persons of the same Religion with that of their deceased Parents. In direct opposition to which, several Children of Protestants have been committed to the Tutelage of Papists, and brought up in the Romish Superstition. We could instance in a Young Woman, that has been lately forced, by Order of Council, from her Husband, committed to the Custody of a Papist and brought up in his Religion. 'Tis endless to enumerate the particulars of this nature, while on the contrary those Laws that enhance the Grandeur and Income of his said Lordship are severely Imposed and Executed; especially one that against all Sense, Equity, Reason, and Law Punishes all Speeches, Practices, and Attempts relating to his Lordship and Government,[1] that shall be thought Mutinous and Seditious by the Judges of the Provincial Court, with either Whipping, Branding, Boreing through the Tongue, Fine, Imprisonment, Banishment, or Death; all or either of the said Punishments, at the Discretion of the said Judges; who have given a very recent and remarkable Proof of their Authority in each particular Punishment aforesaid, upon several of the good People of this Province, while the rest are in the same danger to have their Words and Actions liable to the Constructions and Punishment of the said Judges, and their Lives and Fortunes to the Mercy of their Arbitrary Fancies, Opinions, and Sentences.

To these Grievances are added,

Excessive Officers Fees, and that too under Execution, directly against the Law made and provided to redress the same; wherein there is no probability of a Legal Remedy, the Officers themselves that are Parties and culpable being Judges.

---

[1] Coode himself had been tried for seditious speaking and blasphemy, and probably others of the signers of the declaration had cause to speak feelingly on this point.

The like Excessive Fees imposed upon and extorted from Masters and Owners of Vessels Trading into this Province, without any Law to Justifie the same, and directly against the plain Words of the Charter, that say, there shall be no Imposition or Assessment without the Consent of the Freemen in the Assembly: To the great Obstruction of Trade, and Prejudice of the Inhabitants.

The like excessive Fees Imposed upon and extorted from the Owners of Vessels that are Built here, or do really belong to the Inhabitants; contrary to an Act of Assembly, made and provided for the same: Wherein, Moderate and Reasonable Fees are assertained, for the Promoting and Encouragement of Shipping and Navigation amongst our selves.

The frequent Pressing of Men, Horses, Boats, Provisions, and other Necessaries, in time of Peace; and often to gratifie private Designs and Occasions, to the great Burthen and Regret of the Inhabitants, contrary to Law and several Acts of Assembly in that Case made and provided.

The Seizing and Apprehending of Protestants in their Houses, with Armed Force consisting of Papists, and that in time of Peace; their hurrying them away to Prisons without Warrant or Cause of Commitment, there kept and Confined with Popish Guards, a long time without Trial.

Not only private but publick Outrages and Murthers committed and done by Papists upon Protestants without any Redress, but rather connived at and Tollerated by the chief in Authority; and indeed it were in vain to desire or expect any help or measures from them, being Papists and Guided by the Counsels and Instigations of the Jesuits, either in these or any other Grievances or Oppression. And yet these are the Men that are our Chief Judges, at the Common Law, in Chancery, of the Probat of Wills, and the Affairs of Administration, in the Upper House of Assembly, and the Chief Military Officers and Commanders of our Forces; being still the same Individual Persons, in all these particular Qualifications and Places.

These and many more, even Infinite Pressures and Calamities, we have hitherto with Patience lain under and submitted too; hoping that the same Hand of Providence, that hath sustained us under them, would at length in due time release

us; and now at length, For as much as it has pleased Almighty
God, by means of the great Prudence and Conduct of the best
of Princes, Our most gracious King William, to put a Check
to the great Innundation of Slavery and Popery, that had like
to overwhelm Their Majesties Protestant Subjects in all their
Territories and Dominions (of which none have suffered more,
or are in greater Danger than our selves) we hope[d] and expected in our particular Stations and Qualifications, a propor-
tionable Share of so great a Blessing. But to our great Grief
and Consternation, upon the first News of the great Overture
and happy Change in England, we found our selves surrounded
with Strong and Violent Endeavours from our Governours
here, being the Lord Baltemore's Deputies and Representatives,
to defeat us of the same.

We still find all the means used by these very Persons and
their Agents, Jesuits, Priests, and lay Papists, that Art or
Malice can suggest, to divert the Obedience and Loyalty of
the Inhabitants from Their Most Sacred Majesties, to that
heighth of Impudence, that solemn Masses and Prayers are
used (as we have very good Information) in their Chappels and
Oratories, for the prosperous Success of the Popish Forces in
Ireland, and the French Designs against England, whereby
they would involve us in the same Crime of Disloyalty with
themselves, and render us Obnoxious to the Insupportable Displeasure of Their Majesties.[1]

We every where hear, not only Publick Protestation against
Their Majesties Right and Possession of the Crown of England,
but their most Illustrious Persons villified and aspers'd with
the worst and most Traiterous Expressions of Obloquy and
Detraction.

We are every day threatned with the Loss of our Lives,
Liberties, and Estates, of which we have great Reason to think
our selves in Imminent Danger, by the Practices and Machina-
tions that are on foot to betray us to the French, Northern, and
other Indians, of which some have been dealt withal, and others
Invited to Assist in our Destruction; well remembring the
Incursion and Inrode of the said Northern Indians, in the
Year 1681, who were conducted into the Heart of the Province

---

[1] The charge embodied in this paragraph was common to all the insurrections.
It is here stated rather more wildly than usual.

by French Jesuits, and lay sore upon us, while the Representatives of the Country, then in the Assembly, were severely press'd upon by our Superiors, to yield them an Unlimited and Tiranical Power in the Affairs of the Militia. As so great a Piece of Villany cannot be the Result but of the worst of Principles; so we should with the greatest Difficulties believe it to be true, if Undeniable Evidence and Circumstances did not convince us.

Together with the Promises, we have, with all due Thinking and Deliberation, considered the Endeavours that are making to Disunite us among our selves, to make and Inflame Differences in our Neighbour Colony of Virginia, from whose Friendship, Vicinity, great Loyalty and Sameness of Religion, we may expect Assistance in our greatest Necessity.

We have considered, that all the other Branches of Their Majesties Dominions in this Part of the World (as well as we could be informed) have done their Duty in Proclaiming and Asserting their undoubted Right in these, and all other Their Majesties Territories and Countries.

But above all, with Due and Mature Deliberation, we have reflected upon that vast Gratitude and Duty incumbent likewise upon us, To our Soveraign Lord and Lady, the King and Queen's most Excellent Majesties, in which, as it would not be safe for us, so it will not suffer us to be Silent, in so great and General a Jubile, withal considering and looking upon our selves Discharged, Dissolved, and Free from all manner of Duty, Obligation, or Fidelity, to the Deputies, Governours, or Chief Magistrates here, as such: They having Departed from their Allegiance (upon which alone our said Duty and Fidelity to them depends) and by their Complices and Agents aforesaid endeavoured the Destruction of our Religion, Lives, Liberties, and Properties, all which they are bound to Protect.

These are the Reasons, Motives, and Considerations, which we do Declare, have induced us to take up Arms, to Preserve, Vindicate, and Assert the Sovereign Dominion, and Right, of King William and Queen Mary to this Province: To Defend the Protestant Religion among us, and to Protect and Shelter the Inhabitants from all manner of Violence, Oppression, and Destruction, that is Plotted and Designed against them; which we do Solemnly Declare and Protest, we have no Designs or Intentions whatsoever.

For the more Effectuate Accomplishments of which, We will take due Care that a Free and full Assembly be Called, and Convened with all Possible Expedition,[1] by whom we may likewise have our Condition and Circumstances and our most Dutifull Addresses represented and rendered to Their Majesties: From whose great Wisdom, Justice, and especial Care of the Protestant Religion, We may Reasonably and Comfortably hope to be Delivered from our present Calamities, and for the Future be secured under a Just and Legal Administration, from being evermore subjected to the Yoke of Arbitrary Government, Tyrany and Popery.

In the Conduct of this, We will take Care, and do Promise, That no Person now in Arms with us, or that shall come to Assist us, shall commit any Outrage, or do any Violence to any Person whatsoever, that shall be found Peaceable and Quiet, and not oppose us in our said Just and necessary Designs: And that there shall be Just and due Satisfaction made for Provision, and other Necessaries had and Received from the Inhabitants: And the Soldiers punctually and duely Paid, in such Ways and Methods as have been formerly accustomed, or by Law ought to be.

And we[2] do, Lastly, Invite and Require all manner of Persons whatsoever, Residing or Inhabiting in this Province, as they tender their Allegiance, the Protestant Religion, their Lives, Fortunes and Families, to Aid and Assist us in this our Undertaking. Given under our Hands in Mary Land, the

[1] An assembly was called by Coode for August 22, 1689, and all the counties were represented except Ann Arundel.

[2] The signers of the paper were: 1. John Coode, formerly a minister of the Anglican Church, but latterly a planter, politician, and agitator by profession. He was the nominal head of the movement, but not the real leader; 2. Henry Jowles, a colonel of militia and member of the assembly, and probably the ablest man in the group; 3. John Campbell, a major of militia; 4. Humphrey Warren, a colonel of militia of Charles County; 5. Kenelm Cheseldyne, speaker of the last assembly; 6 and 7. William Purling and Richard Clouds, of whom little else is known; 8. Nehemiah Blakiston, collector of customs, a shrewd not to say unscrupulous man, with an ambition to be governor. He and Coode had married daughters of Thomas Gerrard, while Gerrard Slye, their agent in England, was Coode's stepson. The leaders were Coode, Jowles, Blakiston, and Cheseldyne.

25th Day of July, in the First Year of Their Majesties Reign, Annoque Domini 1689.

God Save King William and Queen Mary.

Published by Authority.

Maryland, Printed by William Nuthead at the City of St. Maries. Re-printed in London, and Sold by Randal Taylor near Stationers Hall, 1689.

A MODEST AND IMPARTIAL NARRATIVE, 1690

INTRODUCTION

THE uprising in New York, though similar in its essential causes to the movements elsewhere, exhibited a degree of personal animosity that gives to it a peculiar coloring of its own. The leading actors on both sides, with the single exception of Lieutenant-Governor Nicholson, who early left the scene, were native New Yorkers and were not only intimately conjoined in the life of the city but were closely related by blood or marriage. Although in Virginia and Maryland, and to a degree in Massachusetts, the revolution took the form of a civil struggle, yet nowhere did the bitterness of feeling cut so deeply into the life of the colony as it did in New York. Families, churches, and neighborhoods were divided against each other. The line of cleavage was not determined by class, race, or religion, though all these factors were at work giving shape to the movement. It was given its final direction by enmities that were personal among the leaders and, among the followers, were born of fear and suspicion on one side and of scorn and contempt on the other.

The leader of the revolt was Jacob Leisler, a German from Frankfort, who had been a resident of the city since 1660. He had been successful as a merchant and wine importer and had added to his wealth and position by a marriage with El- sie Tymans, stepdaughter of Govert Lockermans, niece of Annetje Jans, and widow of a prosperous merchant, Pieter Van der Veen. By this marriage Leisler had entered the social group of the Schuylers, Bayards, Van Cortlandts, and Philipses and had also become involved in a quarrel over property that had created bad blood between himself and the Bayards. He was a man of religious standing, for he became an elder in the Dutch Church in 1670, and he was appointed a captain in the militia in 1684, though he held no important political offices.   There is nothing in his career up to the time of the revolt to stamp him as a dangerous member of the community. He was uneducated and coarse, hot-tempered and violent, and without self-restraint.   Those who praise him would call him "a man of the people," others, a plebeian with all the characteristics usually associated with that term.

It has been customary in the past to speak of Leisler as the leader of the mob or the rabble.   This designation has been largely due to an uncritical dependence upon the assertions of his enemies, such as are here contained in the first two narratives printed.   Certainly among those who accepted Leisler's leadership were a number of unsavory characters, restless and ignorant men, such as the lawless Milborne and the blustering Joost Stoll.   But on the other hand we cannot class with the mob such men as Lodwyck, Stuyvesant, De Peyster, Edsall, Delanoy, and the others who were members of the churches, militia captains, and councillors of the province. The thirteen months of Leislerian government was not a time of mob rule.   Leisler and his associates showed not only vigor of action but also considerable capacity for administration. Leisler may have usurped his functions as lieutenant-governor and commander-in-chief, but in exercising these functions he admitted neither lawlessness nor anarchy.   He organized a government, raised money, made a seal, issued commissions, erected courts, and put down riots.   As commander-in-chief he took up the war against the Indians, fortified the city, appointed military officers, and held courts martial.   As vice-admiral he created a vice-admiralty court and issued letters of marque.   Many of these things he did badly and with no effort at conciliation or compromise, but we have no reason for thinking that at this critical time his enemies would have done any better.

The *Modest and Impartial Narrative* that follows was probably written by Leisler's chief enemy, Nicholas Bayard, perhaps in co-operation with others in New York. As the reader will discern, the narrative is neither modest nor impartial. It closes with Bayard's arrest, which took place probably on January 20, 1690, though the exact date is uncertain. In any case, the note to the reader on page 320 is incorrect in placing that event on the 24th, as Bayard sent a petition to Leisler on that date stating that he had been confined for two days already. We know nothing of the circumstances under which the account was written, but that it was composed at a time when passions ran high is manifest. The *Narrative* has been reprinted, from a copy in the British Museum, in the *Documents relative to the Colonial History of New York*, III. 665–684.

A MODEST AND IMPARTIAL NARRATIVE, 1690

*A Modest and Impartial Narrative Of several Grievances and
Great Oppressions That the Peaceable and most Considerable
Inhabitants of Their Majesties Province of New-York in
America Lye Under, By the Extravagant and Arbitrary
Proceedings of Jacob Leysler and his Accomplices.
Printed at New-York,[1] and Re-printed at London 1690.*

THE Reader is hereby advertised, That the Matters contained in the following Declaration and Narration, were intended to have been presented to the Mayor's Court in New-
York, the 25th of January last past, but that the Fury and
Rage of this Insolent Man Leysler, was grown to that height,
that the day before, by his order, several Persons of Note
were violently seized and divers Houses broken open, so as
it was not thought safe to proceed in such Method. For which
reason it's thought well to publish the same, for information
of all into whose hands it may come, but more especially for
the benefit of our fellow Inhabitants, who are abused by the
false Pretentions of this common Violator of our Laws and
Liberties, as by the following Narrative will plainly appear:
Wherein the Courteous Peruser is desired to take notice, it
hath been our great Care to relate nothing but Matters of
Fact, of which we have substantial Credible Evidences.

The Narrative, etc.

Out of the deep sence we have of the good providence of
Almighty God, in their Majesties happy accession to the Im-

[1] The pamphlet could not have been printed at New York in 1689 or 1690,
as at this time there was no printing-press in the province. Not until April, 1693,
did William Bradford, who had been forced to leave Philadelphia, set up his
press in the city. The printing, if colonial, might have been done at Cambridge
or Boston. There was a press in Virginia in 1680, but it was apparently removed
to St. Mary's in 1683, for the printer, William Nuthead, printed there the *Declaration* of the Protestant Association (above, p. 304).

perial Crown of England, etc., In the first place we, in a most Christian manner, with hearts and hands lifted up to Heaven, give Glory to Almighty God, for this so happy a Revolution, whereof it hath pleased the most High to appear the Principal Author.   In the next place, we cannot but declare and publish to the world our hearty and thankful resentments of the Noble, though hazardous Enterprize of the late Prince of Orange, our most dread Soveraign King of England, Scotland, France and Ireland, Defender of the Faith etc., the Noble Heroe of this Age, for the Protestant Religion, and the preservation of the Laws and Liberties of the English Nation inviolated, manifesting hereby that as in duty bound, so in point of Gratitude, we can do no less than dedicate our Lives and fortunes to their Majesties services, with our most serious and continued prayers for their Majesties long and happy Reign over us, being well satisfied in our own selves, that what our native Land so plentifully enjoys under their Reign, to wit, the Laws and Liberties of the English Nation, we (though inhabiting a remote part of their Dominions) shall share with them in the common Propriety.

In consideration whereof, in all humble and obedient manner as Dutiful subjects to their Majesties, and well wishers to this their Province of New York, we can do no less than in the presence of God, and to the world, declare our abhorrence and dislike of the unreasonable, Illegal and Arbitrary proceedings of some Men inhabiting with us in this their Majestys Province who have usurped Authority over us.

Against all such proceedings of theirs hereafter faithfully and impartially set down and against them, as the Actors thereof, we do hereby publickly declare and protest.

Now to the end that the Reasonableness of this our Protestation may appear unto all to whose hands it may come, we count ourselves obliged to give a brief recital of the case of our Late Lieutenant Governour Francis Nicholson,[1] for the more peaceable quiet and satisfactory governing this their Majestys Province.

To obviate all suspicion of Jealousies that might arise in

[1] Francis Nicholson, destined to become one of the best-known of the royal governors in America, was at this time twenty-nine years old and holding his first colonial office as lieutenant-governor under Andros.

ill affected turbulent spirits, our said Lieutenant Governour by and with the consent of so many of the Council as here resided (upon the whispering of the late happy change) did convene together,[1] with the Mayor, Aldermen and Common Council men of the City of New York, with all the Commission Officers of the Militia of this City and Country; at which convention our said Lieutenant Governour proposed to admit of part of the Train-bands of this City and County to take their turns of watching and warding within their Majesties Fort under their own Officers; And further offered, with the advice and consent of his Council, Civil and Military Officers, there met and assembled, that the Customs formerly paid by the Inhabitants of this Province should still continue, only with this alteration, that whereas formerly it was expended and laid out in defraying of the charges of the Government, and Soldiers in pay in the Garrison, it should thence forward be imployed in the fortifying and putting this City in a posture of defence against a foreign Enemy, on which the welfare and safety of this Province so much depends.

In pursuance of the same an order issued forth from the said convention, signed by the Lieutenant Governour, his Council, the Mayor and Aldermen of this City, and most of the Commission Officers of the Militia, none shewing so great a dislike to it as Jacob Leysler, one of the Captains of the Train bands of this City, who at that time had a Ship loaden with wines, the customs whereof amounted to upwards of one hundred pounds; the payment of this he utterly refused, alledging, The Collector, being a Papist, was not qualified to receive it, denying the then power to be legal; but whether for that or his own private interest let the impartial judge.

The turbulent mind of this person not being satisfied in denying the payment of the usual Customs, though appointed for the use aforesaid, he sets himself upon inventing ways how he might overturn the Gov't which was then peaceable and quiet. The first thing he falls upon was to stir up and animate the people of the East end of Long Island[2] to advance with

[1] April 27, 1689. Minutes of this session and of subsequent sessions are printed in the *Collections* of the New York Historical Society, 1868, pp. 272–290.

[2] Leisler had nothing to do with the uprisings in eastern Long Island, where the towns, eager for union with Connecticut, were stirred to action by news

sufficient force to take possession of the Fort, lest it should be in danger of being delivered up to a Foreign Power; this readily took with them whose minds were already heated by the example of Boston in clapping up of our Governour Sir Edmund Andros, and after some consultations amongst themselves, they put forward in a Hostile manner increasing as they came along the Island, until they were so far advanced as the Town of Jamaica, being then about eighty in number, whence they halted, and sent up three[1] of their principal leaders to discourse the Lieutenant Governour, who upon their coming convened his council, the Mayor and Aldermen of this City, and the Commission Officers of the Militia of City and County, into which Convention the Persons sent were admitted, where after some long debates they seemingly went away satisfied, at least so far as that they and the men accompanying them returned home to their own Townes and habitations, without doing the least hurt or damage to any.

This stratagem failing our Masanello[2] Leysler, in a short time after a Rumour was spread amongst the quiet Inhabitants of this City, of a horrible design there was of murdering them, their wives and children, as they were worshipping of God in the Dutch Church within the Fort, and the Sunday prefixed, when this cruel act was to be accomplished; Captain Leysler in the mean time instigating and stirring up the Inhabitants to self preservation against this imaginary design, which so far prevailed with part of the Inhabitants as that the Friday before the Sunday markt out by this report for the pretended massacre, they rose in a hostile manner; the first

---

from Boston. Their *Declaration* is dated May 3, and on the 10th the eastern insurgents reached Jamaica, three weeks before Leisler seized the fort in New York. The first Leisler letter to the Long Islanders was that requesting the counties to choose delegates for the meeting of June 26 (*Huntington Records*, II. 32), and the first communication designed "to stir up and animate the people of the east end of Long Island" was dated as late as September 1.

[1] Captains Matthew Howell of Southampton, John Wheeler of Easthampton, and Ebenezer Platt of Huntington. With them went Captain John Jackson of Hempstead.

[2] Masaniello or Tomaso Aniello; see p. 31, note 1. The use of this term as applied to Leisler by Bayard and Chidley Brooke in their correspondence (*N. Y. Col. Docs.*, III. 661, 757) furnishes a clew to the author or authors of this "modest and impartial narrative."

who appeared in arms were some under Leyslers Command who (as a plot was laid) went to the House of their Captain, and threatened to shoot him if he did not head them. This no ways surprized the courageous Captain; a substantial reason why, himself being the sole contriver of it: Yet whether prevailed most, the want of valour, or the apprehensions, if he should miscarry in this bold attempt, the Country would be destitute of one so fit as himself to command, we leave the judicious to determine.

However it was it seemed not good unto this Champion to venture himself, but commits the conduct of his Men unto one Stoll,[1] famous for nothing, unless his not being worth a groat; up marches Stoll with his brisk followers, and to the Fort gates they draw near, where they met with a very civil Gentleman, one Hendrick Cuyler,[2] left[3] under Captain Abraham Depeyster,[4] who commanded that part of the Train bands, who by turn had the Guard in the Fort that day; this Persons civility was such that it's hard to determine whether Stoll and his party without were more desirous to enter, than he within was ready to open the Gates to them. In fine, entrance they had with great acclamations and joy on both sides, that so meritorious a design was not prevented

How far this valiant Lieutenant Cuyler, in this base act of his, hath answered the Law of Arms or the trust reposed in him, we will not now determine; but sure we are, the season they took for accomplishing this their unmanlike contrivance, doth

[1] Ensign Joost Stoll, a dram-seller, played an aggressive part in the early history of the revolt. He was sent to England in August, 1689, and proved an ill-chosen ambassador. His pretentious ignorance undoubtedly prejudiced the court party at Whitehall against the Leislerian cause. Stoll was afterward (1692) indicted for treason, but discharged.

[2] Hendrick Cuyler, lieutenant in De Peyster's company, seems to have been a baker. He it was who, in dispute with Nicholson regarding the placing of a sentinel at the fort, drew from the lieutenant-governor the unfortunate remark that rather than see things going as they were "he would set the town on fire." It is significant that neither of the anti-Leislerian accounts here printed makes mention of this dispute or contains any reference to Nicholson's remark. The incident is mentioned in the third narrative (below, p. 380).

[3] Leftenant, lieutenant.

[4] Abraham De Peyster, a prominent native New Yorker, and a "gentleman of figure" in the province. As a Leislerite he had a stormy career in the years following the revolt.

not a little add to their crime, it being of that juncture of time when our Lieutenant Governour and conventment (whereof we have before made mention) were consulting for the more orderly quiet and peaceable Governing this their Majesties Province, who at this sudden change were startled, and acted what was left in their power, publickly protesting against this rude Action, and the Actors thereof.   By this time their great Champion Leysler being well assured all danger and hazard was over, he most couragiously Girds on his Sword, Marches stoutly up to the Fort, in order to his carrying the Game he had so fairly begun, where he is joyfully received, and a consultation immediately held, how they should obtain the Keys of the Fort, which the Lieutenant Governour had in Custody, being in the City Hall, where he was in consultation as is already hinted.

The evening approaching, Captain Lodwick[1] and his Company advances to the Fort to mount the Guard, as his turn was; some time after his being in the Fort, nothing would satisfy the Tumultuous Multitude, but that three or four files of men must be sent under the Command of William Churchill,[2] Sergeant to Captain Lodwick, to fetch the keys from the Lieutenant Governour (a fitter person for such a Message could not be sent than this Churchill, infamous for his mutinous and turbulent spirit).   With much Insolence this impertinent impudent fellow rushed into the room where the Lieutenant Governour was, and demanded the keys; the Lieutenant Governour commanded him to call his Captain, who was prevailed with to come, hoping thereby to appease the people, unto whom the Lieutenant Governour delivered the keys, and Captain Lodwick returning to the Fort, the expectations of the multitude being answered, after publishing Ja. Leysler Colonel, all leave the Fort to Captain Lodwick and his Company, who stayed their usual time and it was then agreed upon amongst the Captains, that each should take his

[1] Charles Lodwyck came to New York in 1684, and resided there as a merchant for sixteen years.   He was an Englishman with a Dutch name, a captain in the train-band, and a Leislerite.   In 1692 he wrote a description of New York that was read before the Royal Society.

[2] William Churcher played the part of marshal for Leisler, making frequent arrests at the head of a file of musketeers.   He was a bricklayer.

turn to reside in the Fort as Chief, till their Majestys pleasure should be further known.

The Lieutenant Governour, his Council and Convention aforesaid, taking into their serious considerations, what danger the Moneys was in, paid by the Inhabitants of this their Majestys Province as well for Customs as Publick Taxes, which at that time was secured in the Fort, The said convention agreed upon and ordered the Moneys should be removed to the House of Frederick Phillips[1] one of the Council, a man of known credit and the most considerable for Estate in their Majesties Province.

This was concluded on the day our Usurper Leysler, by his Instruments, seized the Fort, being the 31st day of May last past. But to no purpose was this agreement of the convention; for those who had made themselves masters of their majesties Fort were resolved to command the Money too, being the sum of seven hundred seventy three pounds, which they peremptorily denied the removal of, when demanded by the Lieutenant Governour, in pursuance of the order aforesaid. How they have disposed of this Money, is not our present business to enquire; we leave that until the happy arrival of a Governour Legally commissionated from the King.

The Fort being thus in possession of the Captains of this City, by turns, all the violence used for severall days was that upon the arrival of any Vessel, great or small, a file of Musqueteers were sent on board, the Masters and Passengers carried to the Fort, and the Letters taken from them, some whereof were open'd, and publickly read amongst the People.[2] Never the like known in this place, under any former English Governor.

This is too little to satisfy the unsatiable Ambition of this

---

[1] Frederick Philipse, we are told, was the son of a Bohemian Hussite refugee in Holland. He lived at Bolsward in Friesland as a carpenter's apprentice, and went to America during the period of Dutch control in New Amsterdam. He became one of the richest men in New York, and in 1698 was spoken of as "one of the most ancient inhabitants and greatest trader to Albany." His part during the revolt reflects little glory upon either his courage or his public spirit. He and his wife figure also in the *Journal of Jasper Danckaerts*, in this series.

[2] Four such cases are mentioned, John Dishington and Nicholas Gerrets from Barbadoes, Philip French and Nicholas De la Plaine from Boston. The arrests were generally made by William Churcher.

Great usurper, Leysler, who could not content himself with
the station nature had fitted him for, and placed him in, but
his soaring, aspiring mind aiming at that which neither his
birth nor education had ever qualified him for, to wit, to be
their Majesties Lieutenant Governor of this Province, making
no matter of conscience how illegally he attained thereunto
whether by usurpation or otherwise. It being his turn to
command in chief in their Majesties Fort the third day of
June past, he caused an Alarum to be beat, that he might
accomplish his wicked designs, the intent of this hubhub being
only to ensnare those of the Inhabitants, who till that day
had kept themselves clear of these actions.

The Inhabitants unanimously appeared in Arms that day
to stop the mouths of their Gainsayers, and were headed by
their Colonel Nicholas Bayard,[1] though many of them were
sensible it was only a sham Alarm, as it afterwards proved.

They being all drawn up on a plain before the Fort, and
no appearance of an Enemy, Colonel Bayard gave command
to that Captain whose turn it was to work on the Fortifications
of this City, that he and his Company should repair thither;
and to the other Captains he gave command that they should
dismiss their men. But this not answering the end of those
who were made privy to the design of Leysler, they march
into the Fort, without their Captains, who stayed so long on
the plain, until they were told, If they went not in, the Commonalty would pull down their Houses and they would be
in danger of their lives.

To prevent which, they followed their Companies (instead
of leading them) into the Fort, where a Paper[2] was prepared

[1] Nicholas Bayard, a prominent resident and office-holder since 1664,
though connected with Leisler by marriage (his brother having married a sister
of Leisler's wife), was a bitter and persistent opponent, despising Leisler as a
plebeian. The latter returned the sentiment in full measure, hating Bayard as
a grandee and causing him to be seized and confined in irons. Later, when the
Bellomont administration restored the Leislerites to power, Bayard was charged
with treason and condemned to death. The sentence was not carried out. He
is supposed to have been the author of this *Narrative*.

[2] A "Declaration of the Inhabitants Soudjers belonging under the Severall
Companies of the Train Band of New York" is printed in O'Callaghan's *Doc.
Hist. N. Y.*, II. 11, dated May 31, 1689. The reference in the text, however,
seems to be to another *Declaration* drawn up June 3 (*N. Y. Col. Docs.*, III. 639).

to be signed by every one, the contents being, That with their lives and fortunes they would defend the Protestant Religion and keep the Fort for King William and Queen Mary, until their Majesties further orders.

This being done, Leysler begins to think himself sure of his point. Gabriel Munveil, one of the Captains of the Train Bands, well considering the ill effects that such proceedings would produce, wisely procures his discharge from the Lieutenant Governour and no more appeared amongst them. The rest of the Captains continued their command, more, as we are ready to believe, to do what in them lay to prevent mischief, and check the insolence of this proud usurper, whose immoderate desire after greatness and dominion over his fellow subjects so far infatuated him as that upon all occasions (especially if any strangers present) he hath publickly made his boasts, how he contrived and laid the whole design as is before related.

The next Invention of Leysler was to animate and stir up the People to the choice of Committee men, upon pretence of writing a letter to the King in behalf of the Country, and to consider the Reparations of the Fort, which was of absolute necessity. However legal this Company of Men assembled were (who afterwards termed themselves a Committee of safety)[1] we leave till a fitter time to dispute. But we cannot pass by the method of being chosen, which we are sure was altogether illegal and disorderly, there being not one third part of the Inhabitants of this their Majesties Province that condescended thereunto, nor was it ever intended by Leysler

---

[1] The commission appointing Leisler captain of the fort is dated June 8, that appointing him commander-in-chief is dated August 16. Both are signed by ten men styling themselves the Committee of Safety. But the abstract of proceedings of the "Committee of Safety," which first sat on June 27, when moderator and clerk were chosen, and dissolved August 15, when the decision was reached to send Stoll to England, mentions thirteen names, only seven of which are the same as those attached to the commissions. Van Cortlandt, writing on July 9, speaks of eighteen members from nine towns, but gives the names of only two. In one or two instances we meet with the names of men spoken of as members of this committee which are not on the lists (e. g., William Cox, N. Y. Col. Docs., III. 602). Thus the actual membership of the committee is in doubt, but it is clear that Albany, Suffolk, Ulster, nearly all of New Jersey, and eastern Long Island were not represented.

they should, lest by that means his expectations should be frustrated. In fine, a Company of these men Elected by the far least number of the Inhabitants, coming together in the Fort, two of them indeed with more honesty and a clearer discerning than the rest, perceiving that the main drift was to set up Leysler and make him Commander in Chief, fairly and wisely withdrew themselves, and after the first time appeared no more amongst them.

The fruits of this unsafe Committee, as we have cause sufficient to call them, was to make Leysler Captain of the Fort, requesting of the other Captains of the City that they would yield him their assistance when desired.[1]

Now begins this Usurpers greatness, which he is no ways wanting in improving (with the assistance of his Committee men) in all the illegal Arbitrary Acts man in so short a time could be guilty of. His working brain stands not still with Commanding the Fort, nor were his desires fully answered thereby; Nothing less than Lording and domineering in all Causes (Eclesiastical, Civil and Military) will satisfy this Man, who was and is much alike qualified for them all.

The Laws and Liberties of the English Nation (with which we have good cause to judge he is little acquainted) he thinks no crime to violate, not regarding the Noble example of the late Prince of Orange, our now most renowned Soveraign King William, who for the prevention of the violation of our Laws and Liberties hath so eminently appeared to the end they might be preserved in their due channel.

This our proud Usurper, finding the sweetness of an arbitrary Power agreeable with arbitrary mind, deems it a fault in any, who objected the Law against his illegal proceedings. Upon all such occasions he would angrily answer, "What do you talk of Law? the Sword must now rule." As if that which was judged so hainous in our Native Land would be deemed meritorious in these parts of their Majesties Dominions.

Our Neighbouring Colony of Connecticut being full of disorders amongst themselves, albeit they had assumed their former Government, a General Court of that Colony sitting,

---

[1] At this juncture Nicholson left the colony. He planned to leave New York on June 10, and Leisler made no effort to detain him, as the Massachusetts men did Andros. He did not actually sail till the 24th.

take upon them to send two persons to discourse those who (by usurpation) had taken possession of their Majesties Fort of this Province.

Information being given unto the Mayor, Aldermen and Common Council of this City, met and assembled at the Mayor's House[1] the 22nd June last past, that Major Gold and Captain Fitz[2] were sent by Connecticut Colony, with orders to proclaim their Highnesses, Prince and Princess of Orange, King and Queen of England etc., That Board requested Alderman William Merrit[3] to go to the Fort where those two Gentlemen were, and desire the favour of them to come to the Mayors House, which he accordingly did and they complyed with the request. Being come to the Mayors House he signifies to them the information was had of their coming to this place with directions to proclaim King William and Queen Mary, and desired they would acquaint them what orders they had for it, that so they (of this City) might be ready to shew their forwardness to act in the same with such Honour and Splendor as the occasion required.

Major Gold and Captain Fitz answ'd, They came upon no such account but came to the Persons that had the Fort in Custody, to discourse about some particular matters from their General Court; and that they did not know before they came from home but that the King had been already proclaimed here. That when they came to town, going to the Fort, as they were sent, they having the Proclamation about them, Mr Jacob Leysler desired them to let him have the use of it to Proclaim the King and Queen here.

The Inhabitants being in Arms to this intent, by beat of the drum, the Mayor and Aldermen of this City (though not

[1] After May 31 the mayor and aldermen met at the house of Stephen Van Cortlandt, the mayor. Sessions must have been omitted while Van Cortlandt was in Albany (August–September) but were resumed early in October after his return. The last meeting was on October 8. On the 14th a Leislerian mayor, Peter Delanoy, was installed. He was elected by the citizens of New York, acting under instructions from the Committee of Safety. The writer of this *Narrative* (below, p. 337) evidently deems the "election" a farce.

[2] Major Nathan Gold of Fairfield and Captain James Fitch of Norwich.

[3] Alderman William Merritt was an old-time skipper and merchant and the lessee of the ferry to Long Island. His son, William Merritt, was afterward mayor.

thought worthy to have any notice of it, till after they were
proclaimed at the Fort) went to the City Hall to attend the
Solemnity.   Which being performed, Leysler desired the Mayor
and those with him to go up to the Fort and drink the King
and Queens health, which they shewed their readiness to do.
No sooner were they come into the Fort, though by invitation of Leysler himself, but he tells them, The people were so
much incensed against them, that it would not be safe for
them to continue long there, and gave them his friendly advice to be gone.   An entertainment not unlike the Person
that gave it.

Their Majesties being proclaimed in this Province and a
printed Proclamation coming to the hands of the Mayor and
Aldermen of this City, That all Justices of the Peace and
Sheriffs should continue until further order except Papists;
they caused the same publickly to be read, requiring the Inhabitants to take notice thereof accordingly.[1]   This madded
our proud Usurper, being averse to nothing more than a civil
Government, which he knew must needs curb and be a check
upon his Insolency.

Therefore to prevent this he gives his malicious spirit the
full swing and endeavours afresh to enflame the common people, by branding of those who were in commission of the Peace
with being Popishly affected, for no other reason than that
they would not join with him in violating all our Laws and
Liberties.   His envious malicious mind could not have vented
itself in a more pernicious Falshood than this; for upon due
Examination it will be found that not one Papist or Popishly
affected throughout this their Majesties Province were in Commission of the Peace, and that many whom he hath thus
wickedly scandalized have always been of far greater Reputation both in Church and State than himself.

The malice of this Mans spirit hath been so general against
all that would not say as he did, that the Dutch Ministers[2]
of the Reformed Churches within this Province have not escaped the lash of his inveterate tongue.   Nor hath his endeav-

[1] This proclamation was issued on the same day, February 19, with that
ordering the colonies to proclaim their majesties (Brigham, *Proclamations*, pp.
146–147).

[2] For the ministers, see below, p. 367, note 1.

ours been wanting to create the same disorders and confusion in Church as he hath already done in Government.

How far what is already related evinceth this Usurper Leysler to be an Enemy to and infringer of the Laws and Liberties of the English Nation, we leave to the Judgment of the impartial. Yet lest all that he hath hitherto acted were not sufficient to declare his averseness to the Laws and Liberties of the free born subjects of England, he further proceeds to action. And

On the 25th day of June last past, going into the Custom House, where was present Commissioners appointed by the Lieutenant Governours, Council, Mayor, Aldermen and Common Council of this City, Mr Paulus Richards, Mr John Haynes, and Mr Thomas Wenham, Merchants of this City, who were authorized by the convention aforesaid to receive the usual customs paid by the Inhabitants of this their Majesties Province, and the same to keep until orders came from their Majesties. The reason why this convention took upon them to authorize the Gentlemen above mentioned was the particular recommendation of the Lieutenant Governour, considering the circumstances of Matthew Plowman,[1] Collector, and that he was not qualified as their Majesties Proclamation, bearing date the 14th February 1688 directeth.

This violator of our Laws and Liberties going into the Custom House as is above hinted, abuses the Gentlemen then present with scurrilous Language peremptorily demanding of them, By what Authority they sate there? To whom they modestly replied, That when he satisfied them what power he had to examine them they would return him answer, but in the mean time desired him to go out of the Custom House, where then he had no business.

In a little space after, this Usurper comes the second time, with his Power, which power which was neither the Laws of England nor this Province, nor yet a Legal Commission, but a Company of Men with Swords and Guns (according to his usual maxim, The Sword must rule and not the Laws) and by

---

[1] Matthew Plowman was appointed "collector" by James II. in 1687. His duties were to collect all the proprietary and royal revenues and differed materially from the duties of the regular collectors of customs appointed by the Treasury to collect the plantation duty only.

force of Arms turns them out of the Custom House. In which violent action of this usurper Colonel Bayard narrowly escaped with his Life, who hath wisely ever since absented himself, lest by the instigation of this malicious Man he might be murdered unawares.

The next exploit this violent Leysler falls upon is to fulfil a promise he was heard to make in the beginning of our Troubles, That in two months time he would do all the English Rogues business for them so that two of them should not be seen to walk together. In pursuance whereof on the 14th day of August he sends severall Armed men, with no other warrant than their Swords and Guns, to the House of Mr Thomas Clark,[1] a Merchant in this City, who at that time was under some indisposition of body, which they no wayes regarded nor the intreaty of his Wife (then big with Child) who begged of them not to be so rude, his Children being frightened. They replyed, They mattered it not, if they were all killed. And in a violent manner they carried this Free born subject of England and free man to the Fort, where Leysler lays to his charge a Paper delivered by him unto the Committee, but principally that he should say, The next time the Drum beat an Alarm he could raise four hundred men. For no other reason is this free born subject of England confined a close prisoner in the Fort, without any Warrant of Commitment wherein the cause of his confinement ought plainly and especially to be set down as the Law directs; neither was there any due process of Law against this their Majesties subject, thus arbitrarily debarr'd of the liberty of his person. By which this Usurper hath made the greatest breach and Inroad upon the Laws and Liberties of this English Nation, that was possible for him to do, as the Gentlemen learned in the Law, both by Study and practice, have sufficiently demonstrated by sound and solid arguments, That the violation of Mans Person is a crime of a deeper dye and higher nature than that of his Estate, for as much as nothing in the world is so near and dear to a Man as the liberty of his Person.

This Villanous Userper Leysler not regarding the great care and pains of the Supream Powers of England met and assem-

---

[1] "Thomas Clark was brought in to answer for a paper reflecting on the Committee and was secured." (Committee of Safety minutes, August 14.)

bled in Parliament, for these many years past, to preserve the
Subjects Liberties unviolated and to that end, how many excellent Acts have passed which are as so many Walls and Bul-
warks against all Arbitrary Usurpers, who though for a time
may flourish and meet with applause by their deluded followers, it's not probable can terminate in any thing less than
utter confusion and Destruction to themselves, and shame and
Ignomy to their beguiled Abettors only made use of as so
many tools for the better accomplishing their own wicked ends,
who then are to be laid aside and new favorites taken in.

Nothing seems so consentaneous to this abuser of our freedom and Liberties, as the French Kings maxim (*Sic Jubeo Sic
volo*), who by birth we are ready to believe may claim the
greatest share in him, or at least by his actions be equally
scorning, with that proud Tyrant, to give any other reason for
his Arbitrary Actions than his own unlimited will and pleasure.

The many abuses particular persons have met withal, by
having their goods taken from them, without either warrant
or legal proofs, would be too tedious here to insert. Upon all
such occasions the Actors being demanded, By what warrant
they committed this violence? they would usually answer (clapping their hands upon their Swords) "Here is our warrant."

The keen edge of this mans malice could not be taken off
by his cruelty to one of them, whose ruin he had before avowed,
but he goeth on to fulfill his wicked promise. And

On the 16th day of August past causeth another Alarm,
to that end and purpose, as some of his own party were heard
to say, some days before it happened, That shortly there would
be an alarm in order to the taking hold and securing some not
well affected to their Actions, which were such as this violent
Leysler intended as the subjects of his unbridled envy. And
accordingly in a violent manner, by force of Arms, these following persons were dragged to the Fort, to wit, Mr William
Merrit,[1] Mr Jacob Dekey, Mr Brandt Schuyler,[2] Mr Philip
French, and Mr Robert Allison, Merchants and considerable

---

[1] Son of Alderman William Merritt, mentioned above.

[2] Brandt Schuyler was a brother of Peter Schuyler, first mayor of Albany.
He was doubly related to Stephen Van Cortlandt, as each married the other's
sister, and all were connected by marriage with Leisler, whose wife, Elsie Tymans,
was Van Cortlandt's cousin. Brandt Schuyler and Jacob De Key were elders in
the Dutch Church.

traders in this City and Province, Mr John Merrit son to Mr William Merrit, Mr Edward Buckmaster,[1] Mr Derrick Vanderburgh,[2] who were committed the same night of the Alarm, without either warrant or legal Process.[3]

The next day Captain John Tuder,[4] meeting with the Courageous Lieutenant Cuyler, upon some words between them was in like manner dragged to the Fort, as his fellow Citizens were the night before.

Mr Thomas Clark after some days Imprisonment was brought to that weak condition, that he was more like to die than live, and was carried home in a Sedan, by order of his Gaoler Leysler.

Also Mr John Merrit, after twenty four hours confinement, himself being ill, his Wife much indisposed, and his only Son lying on its death bed, had his liberty.

Alderman William Merrit, the Grandfather of this Child, greatly desiring to see it before dead made application to his cruel Gaoler, Leysler, for leave to visit the Child, offering any security he should demand for his return thither, or if he pleased to send a guard of his Soldiers with him he would satisfy them for their trouble; but nothing could prevail with this Barbarous Man, who resolved to keep the said Merrit with the others before named during his own will and pleasure close prisoners in the Fort, which continued for twenty one days, and then were set at liberty, as yet being strangers to their crimes that deserved so severe punishment.

On the twenty fifth of August comes to this place one Mr Jacob Milborne[5] from England, as he gave out; we are

---

[1] Edward Buckmaster was a tavern-keeper.

[2] Derrick Vandenburg was a mason who had been one of those engaged to repair the fort before the revolt.

[3] Leisler gives his account of these seizures in his letter to the king (*N. Y. Col. Docs.*, III. 615–616) and in the memorial of June 24, 1690 (*id.*, 739, 740–748). If the evidence is to be trusted, and it bears the mark of reliability, these men were arrested for taking part in a riot, the most considerable of the period, in which Leisler was attacked and was apparently in danger of his life.

[4] Captain John Tuder was an English attorney in New York. He defended Philip French, who had been arrested for destroying, or threatening to destroy, proclamations posted by the Committee of Safety.

[5] Jacob Milborne, Leisler's son-in-law, was born in London in 1648, the son of a London tailor. According to reports, he was early convicted of clipping coins and was shipped to Barbadoes. About 1663, he was sold as an indentured

obliged to mention his name by reason of the great part he acts in our future troubles. This mans affected ambiguous way of expressing himself renders him unfit for the conversation of any but the vulgar, who in this age are so apt and ready to admire and applaud that they understood not. This persons decayed fortunes were such that not unlike a Man ready to be drowned, letting go a sure hold, catches at a twig, so he in like manner relinquisheth his old acquaintance and friends, and joins with our Usurpers whom he revives by telling them, That in the middle of May last he was in England, where all things were settled by the common voice of the people in peace, under King William, who was an elective King and had submitted his Regal power wholly to the people, so that it was now become a maxim, *Vox Populi est vox Dei*, and the King was only a Servant to his Subjects. By this our Usurpers were encouraged in their old manner of reasoning, when objected against their illegal proceedings, What Law or warrant they had to back them in their Actions? They would always reply, "By what Law, warrant, or Commission did the Prince of Orange go into England, and act as he hath done? And how do you think King William can take that amiss in us who have only followed his example?" The very rehearsing of this Disloyal comparison is sufficient to cause an abhorrence and detestation in every Loyal Subject.

The next fruits of this Milbornes News is, that the Committee of Safety, as they termed themselves, take upon them to give forth an order to the inhabitants of this their Majesties Province, signifying: That whereas several Inhabitants had already turned out their old officers, they should proceed in election of Civil and Military Officers in the several Counties of this Province. Some Counties accordingly did, by the appearance of small numbers, turn out the Justices of the peace

---

servant to a Hartford man, with whom he remained until 1668, when his term having expired he went to New York. There he engaged in various employments, on one occasion getting into trouble with Andros, by whom he was imprisoned. He afterward sued Andros in England and recovered £45 damages (below, p. 347). He had a brother, William Milborne, a Fifth Monarchy man, equally restless with himself, who at one time lived in Bermuda, where he made trouble for Governor Cony. Fleeing from the island about 1684, this brother went to Boston, where he became a Baptist preacher, "the great ringleader of the Rebellion," according to Randolph.

and Military Officers, and choose new. A method never formerly allowed of under any of our Kings reigns, it being always granted to be the undoubted prerogative of the King to Commissionate his Justices of the peace and Military Officers. However when we are better satisfied that it hath been his Majesties gracious will and pleasure to seperate this branch of his prerogative and bestow it on the poeple, we shall readily show our thankful reception; but till then, we think it the duty of all Loyal Subjects not to appear in such elections.

The 29th day of September being the time appointed for the choice of Aldermen and Common Council-men, in a charter of Priviliges granted to the city by Colonel Thomas Dungan, when Governour of this Province,[1] accordingly the Inhabitants met in the several wards and chose as usually, no ward being attended with so much disorder in their Election as that whereunto Captain Leysler belonged; who its evident resolved right or wrong to have his Son in Law, Robert Walters, to be returned Alderman for that ward. The method he took for doing it was thus: coming into the place where the Inhabitants were assembled in order to their choice, he finding the vote was like to be carried against his Son Walters, in the first place he objected against Captain Anthony Brockholst's Vote, a considerable freeholder of that Ward, his being a Papist; and afterwards says, "I vote for my son Walters, my son Jacob Votes for his brother Walters, and my son Walters votes for himself, that's three, put them down"; By this means was his son Walters returned for that Ward.

The usual day of publishing[2] the Mayor, Sheriff, Town Clerk, Aldermen and Common Council of this City for the succeeding year was on the 14th day of October, the birth day of the late King James; in the mean time comes forth an order from the Committee impowering all the Protestant freeholders of this County, on the   day of October to elect Mayor, Sheriff and Town Clerk, at which election the far greatest Number of the Inhabitants not appearing (well knowing that by the express words of the Charter, that power was solely reserved in the Governours breast to appoint these three

[1] Governor Dongan's charter of 1683 to New York City.
[2] Leisler's proclamation publishing the names of the officials is given in the *Doc. Hist. N. Y.*, II. 35.

Officers) the least Number of the Inhabitants in pursuance of
the Order aforesaid, met and assembled together, and by
majority of voices chose one Peter De Lanoy Mayor, Johannes
Johnson Sheriff, and Abraham Governour, Town Clerk,
against which persons we object not so much, as the method
of their being chosen; neither shall we be offended if it shall
please his Majesty to add unto our former priviledges this
likewise. The Gentlemen named being thus chosen were
published on the customary day.

By this time Mr Milborne recovers of a fit of sickness that
had hitherto rendered him incapable of acting anything else
but affording his chamber advice, which upon all occasions
was consulted by our usurper Leysler; now being restored in
great measure to his former health, he vigorously joining with
this usurper and his unsafe committee a notable piece of service is immediately assigned him by them, which was to go
up to Esopus and Albany in order to the bringing those Counties in the same condition and disorders as they had done
this and the Neighbouring Counties near adjacent. In pursuance hereof, he goes on board a sloop and sails forward to
Albany with fifty Men, who had listed themselves as Volunteers to assist that place, if occasion were, against the
French. Upon his arrival there, by the great care, conduct
and prudence of Peter Schuyler, Mayor of that City, assisted
by the Recorder, Aldermen, Common Council and Military
officers, the designed purposes of this dark politician were
happily frustrated so that he returns back to this place under
some Disappointment.

The eighth day of December arrives *per via* Boston one
Riggs[1] with two pacquets from his Majesty, King William,
whereby we hoped to have had deliverance from the usurpation, Slavery and cruelties of Leysler, but our expectations
were soon at an end. The Superscription of the Pacquets
begin thus, "To our Trusty and well beloved Francis Nicholson Esquire our Lieutenant Governour of our Province of
New York in America, or in his absence, to such as for the
time being take care to keep the peace and Administer the
Laws of our said Province." [2]

[1] For John Riggs, see below, p. 362.

[2] Similar orders, similarly worded, were sent to Massachusetts, July 30, 1689,
and to Maryland, February 1, 1690. In Massachusetts the order was received

This infringer of Laws and Liberties Leysler peremptorily assumes the Pacquets to himself; saying, He was the Man to whom they were directed in the Lieutenant Governours absence. But upon what pretence he deems himself the person, except it be for his breach of the peace, and obstructing the due course of the Law ever since he hath possessed himself of the Fort, Arbitrarily and illegally ruling by the Sword, is sufficiently evidenced to the unbyassed Reader by the foregoing lines.

Frederick Phillips and Stephen Van Cortland, both of the Council, and left in Trust by the Lieutenant Governour for the keeping of the peace and legally Governing of this their Majesties Province, which they carefully and honestly would have discharged the Trust reposed in them, if they had not been prevented by this Violator of our Laws and Liberties and that with more renown and Reputation to their Majesties as well as the better satisfaction of their Liege People inhabiting this their Majesties Province,

The two Gentlemen of the Council before named, being sent for to the Fort, by the request of Mr John Riggs (the Pacquets being by him at that time not delivered) they signified to Leysler and those present with him, That they were ready to observe such Orders as his Majesty had given in his Pacquets to his Lieutenant Governour, then absent, from whom they, together with Colonel Bayard, had instructions to keep the peace and administer the Law of this Government, which they always were ready to have fulfilled, if had not been obstructed.

At this our Usurper rages, and vents his passion in his usual Billingsgate Rhetorick, calling them popishly affected, Dogs and Rogues, and bids them immediately go out of the fort, for they had no business there. A strange entertain-

and acted on by the revived charter government. In the case of Maryland, the packet was intrusted to Nicholson, who was going to Virginia as governor, and he in doubt wrote to Maryland asking to whom he should deliver it. He finally sent it to the General Convention, chosen April, 1690, and its receipt was acknowledged by the Grand Committee, appointed by the Convention, consisting of Jowles, Blakiston, and twelve others. In New York, Bayard and Van Cortlandt had no legal claim to the order, as they were but councillors of a defunct government, the Dominion of New England, and at best could act only with a quorum of five present. As New York had no legal government, Leisler was probably doing as much as any one to preserve the peace.

ment to them, who for these many years past have always as Councillors Officiated under the several Governours of this their Majesties Province, and at that time those who were left in trust by their Majesties Lieutenant Governour. However seeing there was no remedy but patience (this violent usurper resolved still to Govern by the sword) they quietly went to their own homes.

Their Majesties Pacquets being thus assumed by our Usurper, he immediately abuseth his deceived Abettors by affirming to them, He had received a Commission to be their Majesties Lieutenant Governour, and that all their Actions were well approved of. This readily gained credence with the vulgar, who are too apt and willing to be beguiled by their Popular leader. From this time forward he assumes the title of Lieutenant Governour, and according to the Instructions given in the Pacquet, he swears some, who were of his Committee of Safety before, to be Councillors now, as also some few more of the Inhabitants, much alike unto these Persons, neither of the highest rank nor reputation, but such as our Usurper was well assured were for his turn. This being done they proceed to action.

N B. On the 16th day of December an order comes forth Entituled, "By the Lieutenant Governour and his Council,"[1] signed underneath, Jacob Leysler.

The contents as followeth:[2]

By the Lieutenant Governour etc. and Council.

Whereas there is an Act of Assembly dated One Thousand Six hundred eighty three, Entituled, a continued Bill for defraying of requisite charges of the Government, and many of the Inhabitants of this Province notwithstanding they have subscribed to comply with the same, have disputed it when required thereunto,

---

[1] The councillors were eight in number, Delanoy, Staats, Jansen, Vermilye, Beekman, Edsall, Williams, and Lawrence—French, English, and Dutch. Each was a man of substantial merits, and occupies a prominent place in the family history of the province. The council was named on December 11, 1689, and kept a record of its meetings, but the book is lost.

[2] This extract and the extracts that follow are from the Charter of Franchises and Liberties for the colony passed by the abortive assembly that met under Dongan, October 17, 1683. As the charter was disallowed by James II., it had no binding force on the colony.

These are therefore to give Notice unto all persons, within this Province, that the Customs and excise settled by the said Act, hath and doth still remain good and of full force, and that the Collectors and Receivers thereof are empowered to do their duty therein; all persons being hereby strictly required to obey the same as they will answer the contrary at their peril. Given under my hand at Fort William the Sixteenth day of December 1689.

JACOB LEYSLER.

This order of the pretended Lieutenant Governour and Council, being set up in all the public places of this City, did not a little alarm the considerate Inhabitants, who thereby clearly saw the willingness of this Usurper and his abbettors to enslave them and their posterity, so that he might command their purses. A strange change in a little time! For this Leysler, in the beginning of our troubles, was the first man that disputed the payment of the Customs, consulting with several of the Inhabitants, how these Arbitrary Impositions might be pulled down. Further, how contrary this order of our Usurper and abbettors, is to their own so often repeated maxim (That whatsoever was acted by a Papist Governour, or under his authority, was *ipso facto* null and void and of no effect in Law.) If there yet remain any candour or Ingenuity in this violent man and his abbettors, it will be more honourable for them publickly to recant so plain an error, than still to persist in it, for we pray of the unbyassed Reader, what else is the intent, purport and meaning of this Order, but to enforce a Law made by a Papist Governour and under his authority, which by their own argument is void in itself, so that they must either own this their dark unintelligible Oracle hath much deceived them in this point of Politicks, or its evident to the World they have assumed upon themselves a Power to levy Taxes, Customs and benevolences upon the Inhabitants of this their Majesties Province, without and contrary to their own consent, notwithstanding the many wholsome Laws that have passed under the several Kings Reigns in the Realm of England, made for the preservation of the same; as also contrary to a particular branch of that Act which their order hath reference unto, that in express words says thus, That no aid, Tax, Tollage, Assesment, Custom, Loan, Benevolence or imposition whatsoever shall be laid, assessed, imposed or levied on any His Majesties Subjects within this Province, or their Estates, upon any manner or colour of pretence, but by the Act and consent of the Governour, Council and representatives of the People in General Assembly met and assembled.

Now to the end we may further make out to the world the unreasonableness as well as the illegality of this, we cannot omit to advertise the Impartial reader, That in the year 1683 arrived at this Province Colonel Thomas Dongan, appointed his Majesties Governour under his Royal Highness the Duke of York, the Lord Proprietor of this Province, who in a short time after his arrival here according to particular instructions given him by his said Royal Highness, did issue forth writs to the several Counties within this Province for the Electing of Members to serve in General Assembly, which accordingly was done and the same were convened and begun their first Session on the   day of October, and the first Act which passed this Session was that their order refers to, wherein our Representatives wisely provided against the critick Lawyers of this Age, who too nicely distinguish betwixt the Kings subjects inhabiting within the realm of England, and those inhabiting his Dominions abroad, denying the latter the priviledges confessed to be the undoubted birthright of the former, upon which our said Representatives prudently in the first part of that Act endeavour to secure unto themselves and posterities what was the birth-right of every free born subject of England. This being done, they continue this Act for the defraying of the necessary charges of this Government, which begins thus,

"The representatives of his Royal Highnesses Province of New York, convened in General Assembly, Have, for and in consideration of the many gracious and Royal favours expressed and extended to the Inhabitants of this His Province; and also for the bountiful confirming and reserving to them and their posterity, the rights and Priviledges, Liberties and Immunities before recited and expressed and for the better defraying of the necessary charges and expences of this Province"

How far this Act is binding upon the Inhabitants of this Province, will further appear, by duly considering another clause of this very Act which runs thus,

"That all Bills agreed upon by the said Representatives or the Major part of them shall be presented unto the Governour and his Council for their approbation and consent; all and every which said Bills so approved of and consented to by the Governour and Council shall be esteemed and accounted the Laws of this Province, which said Laws shall continue and remain in force until they be repealed by the Authority aforesaid," that is to say the Governour, Council and Representatives in General Assembly, by and with the approbation of his Royal Highness, or expire by their own limitations.

Now that this act of the Assembly, in a strick sense, cannot be allowed to be a law of this Province and so not binding upon its Inhabitants, we humbly offer these reasons:

First, For that by the Authority aforesaid this act never was assented unto, the approbation of His Royal Highness being always wanting, who was so far afterwards from approving of it, that he utterly disallowed the same, and that first by a Letter to his Governour Colonel Thomas Dongan, and afterwards coming to the Imperial Crown of England he publickly disallowed that Act by sending over a Commission under the broad seale of England to the said Colonel Dongan, to be Captain General of this Province and with seven Councillors to govern the Inhabitants thereof, any five of which Councillors made a Quorum and the Majority of that five with the Captain General were empowered to make all laws. A method contrary to what the afore recited Acts prescribe.

Secondly, Our second Reason why this Act is no ways binding on the Inhabitants of this Province, is that the Customs, Impositions and Excises granted unto his then Royal Highness, his Heirs and successors, in the said Act were given in consideration of his said Royal Highness Confirming to the Inhabitants the Charter Priviledges making up the first part of the said Act, which never was enjoyed by the Inhabitants nor confirmed to them but the contrary as is proved.

Thirdly, For that hitherto wee are ignorant of any Law either made within the Realm of England or this their Majesties Province by which the Inhabitants thereof are obliged to pay unto his Majesty the Custom and Excise set down in the before recited pretended Act of Assembly.

When any such Law is produced, those of us who have

signed to pay unto King William the Customs due unto him, when legally demanded, shall readily comply; but until that be done, we cannot see those Notes given by several of us for peace and quietness sake (importing no more than what is above written) are any ways obligatory.

However, when it shall please Almighty God a Governour arrives to this Province from King William, we are ready to submit this point as well as all other Abuses and irregularities done unto us, then to be decided in a Legal way and manner. To a Governour so arriving, we shall not be backward to assist, either with our persons or Estates, for the more orderly and peaceable Governing this Province and defraying the Public Charges thereof in such a way and manner as shall be Legally agreed on.

On the 23d December about seven or eight a Clock in the Evening, Jacob De Key Junior, son to Jacob De Key already mentioned, with Cornelius Depeyster son to the widow Cornelis, both lads, were violently carried away to the Fort by force of Arms without *Mittimus* or Legal process, alledging they had defaced and torn down the order of the pretended Lieutenant Governor and his Council, which upon a due examination will evidently appear, was standing several hours after their committment. How sollicitous this cruel usurper is to vent the fury of his rage against both young and old is evident to all by the illegal confinement of these two lads for no other cause but his own arbitrary will and pleasure.

The same Night an Indian Slave belonging to Philip French was dragged to the Fort and there Imprisoned.

The next day Mr French, falling in amongst some of Leyslers crew, resented the injury done unto him by the illegal detaining of his Slave so highly that some of the standers-by immediately went and informed against him, so that in a short time after as the said French was walking in the publick streets of this City about his lawful affairs, John Burger Serjeant to this Usurper Leysler, attended with six Musqueteers, lays violent hands on him and tells him he was his Prisoner and to the Fort he must go. Mr French replyed, "not unless you carry me," which accordingly they did, in the nature of a dead Corpse, though living, where he soon meets with the Entertainment of a close imprisonment.

Some hours after the Commitment of this his Majestys Subject, by his own particular request, Captain John Tuder and Mr James Emet, both allowed Attorneys of this Province, made application to his Gaoler Leysler for a copy of his *mittimus* in order to their taking such care for their clients enlargement as the Law allowed of, and directed unto; All the answer they obtained at that time was That he could do nothing without advising with his Council and they should meet in the Evening when they might re-attend. This they carefully did though to little purpose; for they were denied entrance into the Fort that Evening several times; nor could they be admitted to speak with their Client, so that near twenty four hours were expired er'e this Usurper saw cause to deliver the following papers which for the readers satisfaction, we shall here recite *Verbatim.*

Fort William, Decr 24th Anno 1689.
Whereas complaint is made to me, That Mr Philip French hath in a most insolent manner contemned this Government, threatening to tare off (if it had not been already done) the Proclamation for continuing his Majesties Customs and Excise, according to an Act of Assembly, etc., although it was forbid all persons at their peril,

These are in his Majesty King William's name to will and require you to bring the said French before me and Council, to answer for the same.

Given under my hand and seal the date abovesaid.
JACOB LEYSLER.
To Sergeant John Burgher, and his assistants.

At a Council[1] held in New York the 24th of December, Anno 1689.

PRESENT—Lieut. Governour,   Mas. Cuyler
Samuel Edsall,   Benjamin Blagg
Thos. Williams,   Jno Van Coussenkeven
Hendrick Janse   Alderman

Whereas Philip French hath behaved himself very contemptuously against the Lieutenant Governour and Council, as by Evidence taken before him doth appear, and continueth in the same, being examined before them,

[1] This list shows some changes since the council was first named. "Janse" should be Jansen, and "Coussenkeven" Couwenhoven.

Ordered, That the said French be forthwith committed to safe custody within Fort William, till further consultation in this matter.

A true Copy, Examined by

JACOB MILBORN, *Secretary*

Now whether the reason of this Usurpers deferring the delivery of the warrant and Order of the Council, above described, may not rationally be construed, as some do, that the warrant directed to Serjeant John Burger and his assistants was written several hours after Mr French's being close prisoner, or not, is a question we shall not now insist on.

The Warrant and Order of Council above written coming to the hands of the before named Attorneys, on the behalf of their Client they apply themselves afresh to the pretended Lieutenant Governour and Council sitting on Christmas Day in the Evening, to whom they signified, That having perused the warrant and order of Council by which Mr Philip French was committed close prisoner within the Fort, they found nothing contained in either, but what according to the known Laws of England as well as this Province was Bailable, and for that end and purpose they appeared before them on the behalf of their Client, to offer Bail to the value of Twenty Thousand Pounds if desired, for his appearance in any Court of Record within this County, there to abide such Determination as by Legal process should be made against him, for or by reason of the charge alledged against him in the aforesaid warrant and order of Council. All the Arguments used by these Gentlemen of the Law no ways prevailed with this cruel Leysler, and his nominal Council, whom he is making use of as his Tools for the better cloaking of his own arbitrary Illegal actions and intentions. It seems as if this usurper were of the same opinion with some Soldiers in Plutarch's time, who wondered any would be so importunate as to preach Law and Moral Reason to men with swords by their sides, as if Arms knew not how to descend to rational Inquiries. All the satisfaction given to this so lawful demand of Bail on the prisoners behalf, was only some small diversion, Our late upstart Statesman, Mr Milbourne, now advanced to the Secretaries Office by his new made Lieutenant Governour, was pleased to afford them by dropping now and then his wonted obscure sentence, asking the Prisoners Council, Whether they would submit the determination of their Clients cause to the Lieutenant Governour and Council? Who thereupon modestly enquired in what capacity they sat there whether Military or Civil? Answer was made by Melborne, Both. The uncertainty of this reply as well as its unreasonableness, yielded fresh matter to argue upon, all which centered here, that our dark politician demanded, How they would help themselves, or by what means they would be relieved? To whom it might have been fitly replyed, In the same way and manner as you, not many years past, recovered forty five pounds by a legal course, against Sir Edmund Andros, for nine hours false Imprisonment. For notwithstanding the many endeavours used by our Usurper to quash the various reports coming to us many ways of a Governour hastening from his Majesty for this Province, we are not discouraged in our expectations of and well wishing for his safe arrival, and then we doubt not but to see some of our Usurpers receive the just demerits of their illegal Arbitrary doings.

The 4th of January Captain John Tuder, by particular warrant from Mr Philip French, applied himself to the Mayor of this City with the Kings writ of Habeas Corpus returnable to the next Mayors Court, which was the 7th of the same Month. This writ so signed by the Mayor was safely conveyed to Mr French and by him delivered to his keeper, who forthwith acquainted the head Goaler Leysler therewith, who immediately ordered the windows where the said French was confined to be nailed up and that a more strict watch should be kept over him as if the cruelties already exercised towards this free born subject of England were not sufficient, who hitherto hath been denied the access of his friends and acquaintance, no not so much as his Counsellors at Law admitted to come near him, a usuage more cruel and barbarous than the most notorious Fellon, Traytor or Rebel commonly meet withal.

The 7th day of January being come and the Mayors Court sitting, Mr John Tuder dilligently attended it, expecting to have met his Client there, by virtue of the aforesaid writ; waiting a considerable time and no appearance of Mr French he informed that Court, That the Mayor was pleased on the 4th Instant to sign his Majesties writ of Habeas Corpus for the bringing the body of the said Mr French together with the cause of his Committment before that Court, where he was ready to argue on the behalf of his Client the matter of Law that might arise; but seeing he was disappointed by the aforesaid writ being disobeyed, he should take upon him to open to the Court the nature of the said writ which (said he) is a writ granted in the subjects favour to prevent the illegal detainure of any of the Kings Subjects falsely Imprisoned, so that a violation of this kind was a crime of the deepest dye, and every subject was nearly concerned therein. none knowing whose turn it might be next to have their Liberties subjected to the Arbitrary will and pleasure of this Man (Leysler).

Also, to the Bench he directed himself in this manner, "You who are the Mayor and Aldermen for the time being of this City and so consequently the Patrons thereof, it behoves you to take care, the Ancient Liberties and freedoms of this City be not infringed and that its Inhabitants be not in this manner dragg'd, by a Marshal force, to the Fort, and there kept close prisoners."

Our Usurpers Oracle Milborne, being present in the Court, after a long continued Silence, Learnedly expressed himself thus; "I do affirm to this Court that Mr French is none of the Kings Subjects," without giving any further reasons. At which the standers by hissed and some publickly charged him with being the principal Actor of our present troubles.

On the 12th January certain advice coming to this place of a Ship designed to this Port, whereof one Prents was Master, being struck on some Rocks near New London, and Mr French being chiefly concerned in the Loading, was forced to submit to this proud usurper and to Petition him by the Title of Lieutenant Governour who had before menaced him, if he would not give the Title of Lieutenant Governour he would put him where he should never see the face of Man more. To prevent which and the exigency of his affairs at that time he gratified the Ambitious Humour of this man Leysler and thereby obtained his Liberty, upon his and Mr Thos. Winham's entering into a recognizance of five Hundred Pounds to the King, for the said French his good behavior during twelve months and a day from the date thereof.

To return again to our account of the two lads first Im-

prisoned. Cornelius Depeyster, by the humble petition of
his Mother, was set at Liberty. Jacob De Key is still under
confinement albeit his enlargement has been much endeavoured
by his Master, Mr John Barbary,[1] a considerable Merchant
in this City, who went to his Goaler Leysler and offered Two
Thousand Pounds security for his Mans appearance to answer
a legal process against him, to which end and purpose a copy
of his *Mittimus* hath divers times been demanded, but could
not be obtained, nor no bail would be taken; nothing will serve
this proud usurper Leysler nor release this Lad, but his parents
sending in a Petition, directed to Jacob Leysler, Lieutenant
Governour and his Council, wherein they must beg forgiveness
for faults they are ignorant of their sons being guilty of. A
strange and unheard of method, to force people to pay Homage
to his person ! Children must be taken from their Parents,
Servants from their Masters, Husbands from their Wives,
Masters from their families, and all this on no other acc't
than their denying to give this proud usurper Leysler a title
that no way appertains or belongs to him.

And we dare this proud man to produce, if he can, any
actions against those Inhabitants he most maliciously Char-
acterizes as Popishly affected so much savouring of Popery as
these we charge him with, and are ready to prove against him
when a convenient time and opportunity presents.

For we pray the unbyassed reader, what is the difference
betwixt bloody Bishop Bonner's Coal-hole,[2] and this cruel un-
merciful Usurpers Dungeon and Bullet-hole, the former being
fitted and prepared for the poor Protestants, that would not
idolize their consecrated Wafer, this latter for the quiet Inhabitants of this their Majesties Province who cannot in their
conscience ascribe that Honour to him, which is only the right
of the King to infer upon him and then its time enough for
his subjects to obey.

The 13th January this Usurper Leysler sends under the
command of Lieu't Churchill[3] twenty soldiers over to Long

[1] John Barberie was a French Huguenot merchant and an elder in the
French Church.

[2] See Foxe's *Book of Martyrs;* Bonner was the persecuting bishop of London
in Queen Mary's time.

[3] William Churcher, above, p. 325, note 2.

Island, the next day they came to Jamaica, where they in a violent manner by force of arms broke open the House of Mr Daniel Whitehead, one of his Majesties Justices of the Peace appointed by our Governour Sir Edmund Andros, and being entered into the house they in like manner aforesaid brake open several chests and boxes, but found not what they looked for, and so returned the next day without doing any more mischeif as we yet hear of.

On the Sixteenth of January the Publick Post Mr John Perry, setting out from the House of Colonel Lewis Morris[1] towards Boston, was not advanced on his way above a quarter of a mile before he was laid hold on by a warrant from our Usurper Leysler, and brought back to this place—New York —with his Letters which were opened and perused at the will and pleasure of this arbitrary Man, who its plain and evident unto all that are not wilfully blind, hath made it his contrivance how to ruin the Inhabitants, and hinder the Prosperity of this Province, ever since his taking upon him to Govern by the Sword, which he hath in great measure affected, by his continual breach of the peace, and obstructing the due course of Law and Justice. But lest this was not sufficient, he resolves to destroy, as much as in him lies, the Commerce and Trade of this Province. A more ready way than this could not have been taken by him for that purpose, to obstruct and hinder advice, which is acknowledged by all to be the Life of Trade; for how can this be given or received, where intercepting Mens private Letters is become so modish with our pretended rulers, as that they are so far counting it a Crime, as by their Action they deem it a virtue.

Before we draw to a conclusion of this our Declaration and Narration, which is already swelled beyond its intended limits, we cannot omit transcribing two other branches of the pretended Act of Assembly, they seemingly make such a pudder[2]

---

[1] Colonel Lewis Morris was a Quaker, and the house here mentioned was in Westchester, upon what afterward became the great estate called Morrisania. Leisler deemed the place a convenient rendezvous for his opponents, and acknowledges that he stopped Perry, "a letter carrier," and obtained from him several letters, "whereby," as he wrote to the Bishop of Salisbury, "your Lordship may perceive the horrible devices they can invent," among others "a plot to massacre them (us) on New Year's Day" (N. Y. Col. Docs., III. 656–657).

[2] Pother.

about, which upon an impartial Enquiry (allowing it to be an Act binding, though that we cannot do, for the reasons already given) these our usurpers will be found the greatest violaters thereof. The branches we think fit to insert are these following *Viz.*

That no free man shall be taken and imprisoned, or be disseized of his free hold or Liberty or free Customs, or be outlawed, or exiled, or any other ways destroyed, nor shall be passed upon, Adjudged or Condemned, but by the lawful Judgement of his Peers and by the Laws of this Province.

Justice nor right shall be neither sold, denied or deferred, to any man within this Province.

That in all cases whatsoever, Bail by sufficient surety shall be allowed and taken, unless for Treason or felony, plainly and especially expressed and mentioned in the warrant of Commitment.

How far these our Usurpers Actions evince their little regard unto the pretended Act of Assembly, except it be to that part which would bring Greast to their Mill, let the unbyassed judge.

This arbitrary proud person Leysler having thus far exalted himself above his brethren disdains to own his very kindred unless they will entitle him Lieutenant Governour, nor will he free them from his Bullet-hole on any other terms.

A plain demonstration of this he hath given by his late carriage to Mr Lucas Keerstead,[1] who after the usual manner was forced to go to the Fort; when he came before this Usurper, he softly applies himself thus to him, "Cousin Leysler what is your will and pleasure?" At this he flies out in a great rage, "How dare you call me Cousin!" Then he spoke to him by the name of Captain, but that would not do, and he was told, that if he gave him not the title of Lieutenant Governour he would be put among the Bullets. To avoid which, he gave him that title, and was then suffered to go home.

I'ts strange this violent man Leysler, who otherwise is so Publick, should be at a stand, when this plain question is put to him, "Who gave you this Name!" Why doth he not answer, as in truth it is, "My Godfather Mr Milborne, and his assistant vain glory, together with my God-Mother Ambition,

---

[1] Lucas Kiersted.

who have engaged on my behalf, that I should cleave to the Infernal Prince and his works, Hug and embrace all the pomps and vanities of this wicked world, and as I had hitherto been, so I shall continue a faithful servant to that black prince of the Air, as long as the many headed beasts the rude multitude would stand by me."

To sum up all, we readily submit the decision of this question to the considerate peruser of the foregoing lines, whether those branded by Leysler as King James his men,[1] or himself and his rude crew, deserve that title most?

Sure we are, that upon a serious perusal of the Declaration Entituled, *The Declaration of the Lords Spiritual, and Commons Assembled at Westminister Die Martis* 12 *February* 1689, Several articles therin exhibited against the late King James and declared illegal are and have been most notoriously committed by this Usurper and his abettors, some whereof we shall here insert and set down as in the said printed declaration Vizt.

That levying money for or to the use of the Crown, by the pretence of prerogative without grant of Parliament for longer time or in other manner than the same is or shall be granted, is illegal.

That excessive bail ought not to be required, nor excessive fines imposed, nor cruel and unreasonable punishment inflicted.

That this arrogant man Leysler is palpably guilty of both these branches before recited we prove thus, *Viz.*

That by his instruments he hath and doth exact (by pretence of Prerogative and for the use of the Crown) Customs Impositions and Excise never granted to the Crown; which that he might the better accomplish, he hath taken upon him to erect a Court of Exchequer, consisting, as members of the said Court, *viz.* Samuel Edsall, Benjamin Blagg, Johanis Provest, Hendrick Jansen, John Cowenhoven who began their session on the 20th January; the 18th of the same month several of the Inhabitants received summons to appear at this

---

[1] Leisler deemed these men "factious disturbers and rioters, who treated your Majesty's government with great scorn and contempt." He characterized William Nicolls, son of the former secretary of the province, Matthias Nicolls, as a most dangerous person, who had written him an anonymous letter threatening "every one who wears the hated name of Leisler with poniard, poison, or pistol" (*Cal. St. P. Col.*, 1689–1692, § 672).

unusual Court on the day above said, to give their reasons
why they would not pay the monies they were indebted to the
King for Custom.

The persons so summoned unanimously made choice of
Mr Thomas Clark to appear for them, who went to the Fort
where this Court was sitting, and being admitted he first en-
quires, whether any there had a Commission from King William to be Baron of his Exchequer?[1] And if any, that his
Commission might be publickly read and afterwards proceeded
to shew the unreasonableness of their demands; but all to
little purpose, the Court proceeding to enter Judgements
against the Inhabitants for whom he appeared, only giving
them eight days time to consider, whether they would volun-
tarily pay their (illegal) demands, which otherwise would be
levied upon them by distress.

About 4 oClock in the Afternoon of this day, was in some
measure verified an expression our Usurper not long since was
pleased to utter to a person of good reputation in this Province
who enquiring of him By what power he did such Actions?
To whom he answered, That he was invested with such a power,
as in a little time he could command the Head of any man in
the Province, and it would be forthwith brought him. Something like hereunto was this day fulfilled; for giving command
to William Churchill and several Soldiers with him, assisted by
several of the Inhabitants of this City, namely Abraham
Brazier, Abraham Clomp, Wil Tomber, and divers others, they
go to the House of Colonel Nicholas Bayard and by force of
Arms entered the same, breaking open several doors and locks,
in order to the seizure of the said Colonel Bayard, whom (as
some of them said) they were ordered to take dead or alive.
Colonel Bayard for his own security had left his own house and
was gotten into his Neighbours, near his back-side, *viz.* one
Mr Richard Elliot a Cooper, whose house in like manner by
Churchill and his Attendants was broken open, where they
laid hold of Colonel Bayard and in a most abusive manner
dragg'd him to the Fort. In this riotous tumult was stoln
out of the house of the said Elliot three silver spoons.

But the unlimited will of this violent rapacious Usurper
was not yet satisfied with the taking and imprisoning Colonel

[1] The judges of the Court of Exchequer in England were called barons.

Bayard, nor his malice thereby fully answered, for in like manner he vents his fury against Stephanus Van Cortlandt, late Mayor of this City, whose house likewise was broken open and most of his doors and Locks spoiled though they were frustrated of their design, by his escaping out of their cruel hands for that time.

Also Mr William Nicols was laid hold on by the men of Breuckle[n][1] at the Ferry-house on Long Island, and was brought over in the Evening and carried to the Fort. The next morning the Ferry man was in like manner brought to the Fort, where these three subjects of their Majesties are illegally imprisoned, and with whom how barbarously they intend to deal, Time will best discover.

We shall end this our Declaration and Protestation narratively set down by naming the principal authors of our principal miseries, which are these following, *vizt.*

Jacob Leysler	Thos. Williams
Jacob Milborne	Jno Cowenhoven
Samuel Edsall	Benj Blagg
Dr Geo Beckman of Flackbus[2]	Hend'k Jansen
Peter De Lanoy,	Hend'k Cuyler
Dr Samuel States	

Against whom we wait a fair opportunity legally to proceed. Dated in New York 21. Jany A. D. 1690.

Finis.

---

[1] Brooklyn, originally named from Breuckelen in the Netherlands.
[2] Vlacke Bos, Flatbush, on Long Island.

A LETTER FROM A GENTLEMAN OF THE CITY OF NEW YORK, 1698

INTRODUCTION

THE two accounts that follow cover, though in briefer fashion, the ground traversed by the *Modest and Impartial Narrative* and continue the story to the close of the insurrection and the execution of Leisler and Milborne. The hasty execution of the two leaders divided the people of city and province into two antagonistic parties that remained unreconciled until the rise of a new generation and new issues brought peace to the colony. During the administrations of Sloughter, Ingoldesby, and Fletcher, 1691–1698, the anti-Leislerian party was in the ascendant. Though Fletcher, on his arrival in 1692, was greeted with "demands of reperation for Leslier's bloud and soe suddaine a storm" as to surprise him, and though in the same year he was ordered by the Privy Council to release the remaining prisoners and in 1694 by Parliament to restore the confiscated property, he nevertheless identified himself with the hostile party and made strenuous efforts to keep all Leislerites out of office and power. He was not an amiable man himself, and his administration was marked by corruption, intimidation, and factional rule.

In the year 1695 leading Leislerites, Jacob Leisler, jr., and Abraham Gouverneur, brought to the attention of the Lords of Trade the miserable state of the province. As their charges seemed to be confirmed by other complaints from the colony and by reliable witnesses heard at the Plantation Office, the board finally decided to recommend the removal of Fletcher and the appointment of the Earl of Bellomont in his place. Though Fletcher declared that "as to the complaints given in against me, I thank God I have a clear and undisturbed mind and shall be able to vindicate myself," he and his anti-Leislerian councillors, Nicholas Bayard, William Nicolls, William Pinhorne, and Chidley Brooke, met frequently at his lodgings and there concocted measures for defense and means whereby to influence public opinion against the Leislerian cause. A month before Bellomont's arrival in April, 1698, at a formal council meeting, they approved the printing and circulating of a letter "found at the printers" which contained "nothing but truth." This paper, entitled *A Letter from a Gentleman of New York*, was written probably by the Scottish secretary of the council, David Jamison, at the request of Bayard, Nicolls, and Brooke, and was printed by William Bradford in 1698. It repeats in simpler and more direct fashion the earlier denunciations of the Leislerites, calling Leisler "a vile usurper," his allies men "of mean birth, sordid education, and desperate fortunes," and his followers "poor, ignorant, and senseless folk." Bellomont thought it "calculated to put this Town and Country into combustion," as it probably was. A reply was immediately draughted and printed in Boston, entitled *Loyalty Vindicated*, which answers point by point the charges made in the *Letter*. The author is not known, nor is there any clue in the paper itself to his identity. He was clearly an Englishman, not a Dutchman, but beyond that nothing can be definitely stated. The Boston imprint is suggestive, in view of the support given to the Leislerites by the opponents there of the governor, Joseph Dudley, who had presided at Leisler's trial in New York. Of the three accounts here printed this is the only one that presents the Leislerian side of the case.

The *Letter from a Gentleman of New York* was reprinted in 1849 in the *Documentary History of the State of New York*, II. 425–435, octavo ed., and again in 1887 in *Collectanea Adamantæa*, vol. XXII. (Edinburgh). It is here reprinted from a rare copy of the original Bradford print, in the New York

Public Library. The *Loyalty Vindicated* was reprinted in the *Collections* of the New York Historical Society, 1868, pp. 365–394, from a copy of the original in the possession of the society. The text here reproduced is that printed in the *Collections*.

A LETTER FROM A GENTLEMAN OF THE CITY OF NEW YORK, 1698

A Letter From A Gentleman of the City of New-York To Another, Concerning the Troubles which happen'd in That Province in the Time of the late Happy Revolution.
Printed and Sold by William Bradford at the Sign of the Bible in New-York, 1698.

Sir;

I CANNOT but admire to hear that some Gentlemen still have a good Opinion of the late Disorders committed by Capt. Jacob Leysler, and his Accomplices, in New-York, as if they had been for His Majesties Service, and the Security of that Province; and that such Monstrous Falshoods do find Credit, That the Persons before in Commission, and did labour to oppose and prevent those Disorders, were Jacobites, or Persons ill affected to the Happy Revolution in England. But it has been often the Calamity of all Ages to palliate Vice with false Glosses, and to criminate the best Actions of the most Virtuous and most Pious Men. So that Truth and Innocency, without some Defence, has not proved at all times a sufficient Bullwork against malitious Falshoods and Calumnies. Wherefore I shall endeavour to give you a true and brief Account of that matter, as I my self have been a Personal Witness to most of them.

It was about the beginning of April, 1689, when the first Reports arrived at New-York, that the Prince of Orange, now his present Majesty, was arrived in England with considerable Forces, and that the late King James was fled into France, and that it was expected War would be soon proclaimed between England and France.

The Leiut. Governour, Francis Nicholson, and the Council, being Protestants, resolved thereupon to suspend all Roman

360

A
LETTER
From A
Gentleman
OF THE
City of New - York
To Another,
Concerning the Troubles which happen'd
in That Province in the Time of the late Happy
REVOLUTION.

Printed and Sold by *William Bradford* at the Sign of the
Bible in *New-York*, 1698.

TITLE-PAGE OF "A LETTER FROM A GENTLEMAN OF
THE CITY OF NEW YORK," 1698

From an original in the New York Public Library

Catholicks[1] from Command and Places of Trust in the Government, and accordingly suspended Major Baxter from being a Member of Council and Captain of a Company at Albany, and Bartholomew Russel from being Ensign in the Fort at New-York, they both being Papists, who forth-with left their Command, and departed the Province.

And because but three Members of the Council were residing in New-York, *viz.* Mr. Frederick Phillips, Coll. Stephanus Cortlandt, and Coll. Nicholas Bayard, all of Dutch Birth, all Members, and the two last, for the space of near thirty Years past, Elders and Deacons of the Dutch Protestant Church in New-York, and most affectionate to the Royal House of Orange, It was Resolved by the said Lieut. Governor and Council, to call and conveen to their Assistance all the Justices of the Peace, and other civil Magistrates, and the Commission Officers in the Province, for to consult and advise with them what might be proper for the Preservation of the Peace, and the Safety of said Province in that Conjuncture, till Orders should arrive from England.

Whereupon the said Justices, Magistrates and Officers were accordingly convened, and stiled by the Name of The General Convention for the Province of New-York; and all matters of Government were carried on and managed by the major Vote of that Convention.[2]

And in the first place it was by them agreed and ordercd, Forth-with to fortifie the City of New-York.

And that for the better Security of the Fort (since the Garrison was weak, and to prevent all manner of Doubts and Jealousies) a competent Number of the City Militia should keep Guard in said Fort, and Nicholas Bayard, Coll. of said Militia, recommended to give suitable Orders accordingly.

And that the Revenue should be continued and received

[1] There were four prominent Roman Catholics in New York at this time, Anthony Brockholes, Jervas Baxter, Bartholomew Russell, and Matthew Plowman. Dongan reported but "few Roman Catholics" in his day, and this statement seems to be borne out by his attempt "to erect a Jesuit College upon cullour to learn latine. . . . Mr. Graham, Judge Palmer, and John Tuder did contribute their sons for some time, but no boddy imitating them the collidge vanished" (*N. Y. Col. Docs.*, III. 415; *Doc. Hist. N. Y.*, octavo ed., II. 23).

[2] It will be noticed that this "General Convention" was not a general assembly and in no sense represented the people of the province.

by some Gentlemen appointed by that Convention, for Repairing the Fort, and Fortifying of the City; but against this Order Capt. Leysler (who as a Captain was a Member of that Convention) did enter his dissent, with some few others.

It was also recommended to said Coll. Bayard to hasten to fortifie the City with all possible speed, who upon the Credit of the Revenue did advance what Money was needful for Materials, And by the Assistance of the Militia Officers, and daily Labour of the Inhabitants, had the same finish't before the end of May, excepting Capt. Leysler's Quota.

About the middle of May the Ship *Beaver*, John Corbit Master, being ready to sail for England, the Lieut. Governour and Council sent in her by Mr. John Riggs,[1] and in several other Ships that soon followed, Letters to the Earl, now Duke, of Shrewsbury, then Principal Secretary of State, and to the Lords of the Committee for Trade and Plantations, wherein they signified their rejoycing at the News of his Royal Highness the Prince of Orange, now his present Majesties, arrival in England, in order to Redress the Grievances of the Nation, and giving a particular Account of the state of Affairs of this Province, and that they would endeavour to preserve its Peace and Security till Orders should arrive from England, which they humbly prayed might be hastened with all possible speed. Which said Letters were most graciously received, and answered[2] by his Majesties Letter, bearing date the 30th of July, 1689.

But against Expectation it soon happened, that on the last day of said Moneth of May, Capt. Leysler having a Vessel with some Wines in the Road,[3] for which he refused to pay the Duty, did in a Seditious manner stir up the meanest sort of the Inhabitants (affirming, That King James being fled the Kingdom, all manner of Government was fallen in this Province) to rise in Arms, and forcibly possess themselves of the

[1] John Riggs had been an ensign under Andros in Boston. He sailed from New York on May 18.

[2] There is nothing to show that the royal letter, which is printed at the end of this narrative, p. 371, was an answer to the letters of the lieutenant-governor and council. As we have already seen, the form of address is similar to that used in the letters sent to Massachusetts and Maryland (above, p. 338, note 2). The councillors are not named, nor are they the persons necessarily addressed.

[3] Road = harbor.

Fort and Stores, which accordingly was effected whilest the Lieut. Governour and Council, with the Convention, were met at the City Hall to consult what might be proper for the common Good and Safety; where a party of Armed Men came from the Fort, and forced the Lieut. Governour to deliver them the Keys; and seized also in his Chamber a Chest with Seven Hundred Seventy Three Pounds, Twelve Shillings, in Money of the Government. And though Coll. Bayard, with some others appointed by the Convention, used all endeavours to prevent those Disorders, all proved vain; for most of those that appeared in Arms were Drunk, and cryed out, They dis-own'd all manner of Government. Whereupon, by Capt. Leysler's perswasion, they proclaimed him to be their Commander, there being then no other Commission Officer amongst them.

Capt. Leysler being in this manner possest of the Fort, took some Persons to his Assistance, which he call'd, The Committee of Safety. And the Lieut. Governour, Francis Nicollson, being in this manner forced out of his Command, for the safety of his Person, which was daily threatned, with-drew out of the Province.

About a week after, Reports came from Boston, That their Royal Highnesses, the Prince and Princes of Orange were pro-claimed King and Queen of England. Whereupon the Council and Convention were very desirous to get that Proclama-tion, and not only wrote for it, but some of them hearing that two Gentlemen were coming from Connecticut with a Copy of said Proclamation, went out two days to meet them, in expec-tation of having the Happiness to proclaim it; but Major Gold and Mr. Fitz, missing them, having put the Proclamation into Capt. Leysler's hands, he, without taking any Notice of the Council or Convention, did proclaim the same, though very disorderly, after which he went with his Accomplices to the Fort, and the Gentlemen of the Council and Magistrates, and most of the principal Inhabitants and Merchants, went to Coll. Bayards House and drank the Health and Prosperity of King William and Queen Mary with great Expressions of Joy.

Two days after, a printed Proclamation was procured by some of the Council, dated the 14th of February, 1688, whereby their Majesties confirmed all Sheriffs, Justices of the Peace,

Collectors and Receivers of the Revenues, etc., being Protestants; which was forth-with published at the City Hall by the Mayor and Alder-men, accompanyed with the Council, and most of the chief Citizens and Merchants. And pursuant thereunto the Collector, Mat. Plowman, being a Papist, was forth-with suspended by the Convention; and Coll. Bayard, Alder-man, Paul Richards, Capt. Thomas Winham, and Lieut. John Haynes, Merchants, were by them commissionated and appointed to collect the Revenue until Orders should arrive from England. Whereupon those Gentlemen were sworn by Coll. Cortland, then Major[1] of the City, they being the first in this Province that took the Oathes to their Majesties appointed by Act of Parliament, instead of the Oathes of Allegiance and Supreamacy.

But as soon as those Gentlemen entered upon the Office, Capt. Leysler with a party of his Men in Arms, and Drink, fell upon them at the Custom-House, and with Naked Swords beat them thence, endeavouring to Massacree some of them, which were Rescued by Providence.[2] Whereupon said Leysler beat an Alarm, crying about the City, "Treason, Treason," and made a strict search to seize Coll. Bayard, who made his escape, and departed for Albany, where he staid all Summer, in hopes that Orders might arrive from England to settle those Disorders.

The said Capt. Leysler, finding almost every man of Sence, Reputation, or Estate in the place to oppose and discourage his Irregularities, caused frequent false Alarms to be made, and sent several parties of his armed Men out of the Fort, drag'd into nasty Goals within said Fort several of the principal Magistrates, Officers and Gentlemen, and others, that would not own his Power to be lawful, which he kept in close Prison during Will and Pleasure, without any Process, or allowing them to Bail. And he further publish't several times, by beat of Drums, That all those who would not come into the Fort and sign their hands, and so thereby to own his Power to be lawful, should be deemed and esteemed as Enemies to his Majesty and the Country, and be by him treated accord-

[1] Mayor.
[2] The four men were turned out by Leisler, and Delanoy was appointed in their place, June 25.

ingly. By which means many of the Inhabitants, tho' they abhor'd his Actions, only to escape a nasty Goal and to secure their Estates were by fear and compulsion drove to comply, submit and sign to whatever he commanded.

And though Capt. Leysler had at first so violently opposed the collecting of the Revenue, alledging it unlawful, as soon as his Wines were landed, and that he got into some Power, he forth-with set up for himself the collecting of said Revenue by Peter d' Lanoy, allowing him a great Sallary, and all the Perquisits of that Office.

Upon the 10th of December following returned the said Mr. John Riggs from England, with Letters from his Majesty and the Lords, in answer to the Letters sent by the Lieut. Governour and Council above recited, Directed, "To Our Trusty and Well-beloved Francis Nicholson, Esq; Our Lieutenant Governour and Commander in chief of Our Province of New-York in America, and in his absence To such as for the time being, take care for the Preservation of the Peace, and administring the Laws in Our said Province." Whereby his Majesty approved of the Proceedings and Care that had been taken by said Lieut. Governour and Council for the Peace and Safety of the Province, with further Power and Directions to continue therein till further Orders. Which said Letters the said Mr. Riggs designed to deliver on the following Morning to the Gentlemen of the Council, to whom they properly did belong, being an answer to their said Letter; but was obstructed therein by said Leysler, who sent a party of his Men in Arms, and brought said Riggs to the Fort, where he forced said Letters from him, though some Gentlemen of the Council, that went the same time to the Fort, protested against it, but he drove them out of the Fort, calling them Rogues, Papists, and other opprobious Names.

Soon after the Receipt of said Letters, said Capt. Leysler stiled himself Lieutenant Governour, appointed a Council, and presumed further to call a select Number of his own Party, who called themselves The General Assembly of the Province,[1] and by their advice and assistance raised several

[1] This "General Assembly" was the same as the "Committee of Safety," for which see p. 328. One Pieterson testified that "about a month after [June 10] a Committee of the representatives of the said province in the nature of a General

Taxes and great Sums of Money from their Majesties good Subjects within this Province. Which Taxes, together with that 773*l.* 12*s.* in Money, which he had seized from the Government, and the whole Revenue, he applyed to his own use, and to maintain said Disorders, allowing his private men 18*d. per* Day, and to others proportionably.

On the 20th of January following Coll. Bayard and Mr. Nicolls had the ill fortune to fall into his hands, and were in a barbarous manner, by a party in Arms, drag'd into the Fort, and there put into a Nasty place, without any manner of Process, or being allowed to bayl, though the same was offered for said Coll. Bayard, by some of the ablest and richest Inhabitants, to the Sum of Twenty Thousand Pounds, either for his appearance to answer, or depart the Province, or to go for England; but without any Cause given, or Reasons assigned, laid said Coll. Bayard in Irons, and kept him and Mr. Nicolls close Prisoners for the space of fourteen Moneths, where they, with several others, that had been long detained Prisoners, were set at Liberty by Governour Slaughter.

And whilest he kept those Gentlemen in Prison, he quartered his armed Men in their Houses, where they committed all manner of Outrages; And to give one Instance of many others, A Party of twelve Men were quartered at the House of Coll. Bayard, with directions to pillage and plunder at discretion, which was bought off with Money and plentiful Entertainment. But the same day, when that party had received their Money, another party came in with Naked Swords, opened several Chambers and Chests in said House, and did Rob and carry away what Money and other Goods they found.[1]

At the same time Coll. Bayard and Mr. Nicolls were taken, strict search was made for Coll. Cortlandt, but he, with several other Gentlemen, having made their escape, were forced to leave their Families and Concerns, and remain in Exile, till relieved by the arrival of Governour Slaughter.[2]

It is hardly to be exprest what Cruelties Capt. Leysler and his Accomplices imposed upon the said Prisoners, and all

Assembly was held," and Jacob Leisler, jr., in 1695 spoke of the body that appointed his father captain of the fort and commander-in-chief as "the Assembly."

[1] Bayard estimated his losses at £200.

[2] Sloughter arrived March 19, 1691.

others that would not own his Power to be lawful. Neither
could the Protestant Ministers in the Province escape their
Malice and Cruelty; for Mr. Selyns, Minister of New-York,
was most grosly abused by Leysler himself in the Church at
the time of Divine Service, and threatned to be silenced, etc.
Mr. Dellius, Minister at Albany, to escape a nasty Goal, was
forced to leave his Flock, and fly for shelter into New-England.
Mr. Varick, Minister of the Dutch Towns on Nassaw-Island,
was by armed men drag'd out of his House to the Fort, then
imprisoned without bayl, for speaking (as was pretended)
Treasonable words against Capt. Leysler and the Fort; then
prosecuted, and decreed by Peter d' Lanoy, pretended Judge,
without any Commission or Authority, To be deprived from
his Ministerial Function, amerced in a Fine of 80*l.* and to
remain in close Prison till that Fine should be paid; yea, he
was so tormented, that in all likelyhood it occasioned and
hastened the suddain Death of that most Reverend and Religious Man. The French Ministers, Mr. Perret and Mr.
Dellie, had some better Quarters, but were often threatned to
be prosecuted in like manner, because they would not approve
of his Power and disorderly proceedings.[1]

None in the Province, but those of his Faction, had any
safety in their Estates; for said Capt. Leysler, at will and
pleasure, sent to those who disapproved of his Actions, to
furnish him with Money, Provisions, and what else he wanted,
and upon denyal sent armed men out of the Fort, and forcibly
broke open several Houses, Shops, Cellars, Vessels, and other
places where they expected to be supplyed, and without any
the least payment or satisfaction, carried their Plunder to the

[1] Rev. Henricus Selyns was minister in New York and Brooklyn, 1660–1664.
In the latter year he went to Holland but returned in 1682 and remained minister
of the Reformed Dutch church in New York until his death, in 1701. Rev.
Godfrey Dellius was minister of the Dutch church in Albany till 1699. Leisler
presents his case against him in a letter to the Earl of Shrewsbury (*N. Y. Col.
Docs.*, III. 753). Rev. Rudolphus Varick was the minister of the Dutch church
on Long Island, 1686–1693. He was imprisoned for five months by Leisler for
speaking treasonable words. Rev. Mr. Pieret founded the French church in the
colony in 1687. He was its pastor until 1690. Rev. Mr. Daillé was the French
colleague of Domine Selyns. All of these ministers, except Domine Varick,
were opposed to Leisler from the beginning and evidently sought to influence
their congregations against him. Varick afterward joined with them.

Fort; all which was extreamly approved of by those poor
Fellows which he had about him, and was forced to feed and
maintain; and so he stiled those his Robberies with the
gilded Name and Pretence, That it was for their Majesties
King William and Queen Mary's special Service, though it
was after found out, that whole Cargo's of those stolen goods
were sold to his Friends in the City, and Shipt off for the
West Indies and else where.

In this manner he the said Leysler, with his Accomplices,
did force, pillage, rob and steal from their Majesties good
Subjects within this Province, almost to their utter Ruin, vast
Sums of Money, and other Effects, the estimation of the
Damages done only within this City of New-York amounting,
as by Account may appear, to the Sum of Thirteen Thousand
Nine Hundred and Fifty Nine Pounds, besides the Rapines,
Spoils and Violences done at Coll. Willets[1] on Nassaw-Island,
and to many others in several parts of the Province.

And thus you may see how he used and exercised an Exorbitant, Arbitrary and Unlawful Power over the Persons and
Estates of his Majesties good Subjects here, against the known
and Fundamental Laws of the Land, and in subvertion of the
same, to the great Oppression of his Majesties Subjects, and
to the apparent decay of Trade and Commerce.

In this Calamity, Misery and Confusion was this Province,
by those Disorders, enthrawled near the space of two years,
until the arrival of his Majesties Forces, under the command
of Major Ingoldsby, who, with several Gentlemen of the Council, arrived about the last day of January, 1690/1, which said
Gentlemen of the Council, for the Preservation of the Peace,
sent and offered to said Leysler, That he might stay and continue his Command in the Fort, only desiring for themselves
and the Kings Forces quietly to quarter and refresh themselves
in the City, till Governour Slaughter should arrive; but the
said Leysler, instead of complying, asked Mr. Brooke,[2] one of

[1] Captain Thomas Willett was at the head of the Long Island militia. His
name survives in Willett's Point.

[2] Chidley Brooke came to New York in the *Beaver* with Ingoldesby and the
soldiers, January 25, 1691. His later career as collector, receiver-general, and
naval officer forms an interesting chapter in the history of provincial New York.
He was suspended from office by Bellomont in 1698.

his Majesties Council, Who were appointed of the Council in this Province? and Mr. Brooke having named Mr. Phillips, Coll. Cortland and Coll. Bayard, he fell into a Passion and cry'd, "What! those Papist Dogs, Rogues! Sacrament! if the King should send Three Thousand such I would cut them all off"; And without any cause given, he proclaimed open War against them. Whereupon they, for Self-preservation, protection of the Kings Forces and Stores, and the safety of the City, were necessitated to perswade to their assistance several of their Majesties good Subjects then in Opposition against the said Leysler, with no other intent, as they signified to him by several Letters and Messages, but only for self-security and Defence; yet notwithstanding, the said Leysler proceeded to make War against them and the Kings Forces, and fired a vast Number of great and small Shot in the City, whereby several of his Majesties Subjects were killed and wounded as they passed in the streets upon their lawful Occasions, tho' no Opposition was made on the other side.

At this height of Extremity was it when Governour Slaughter arrived on the 19th of March, 1691, who having publish't his Commission from the City Hall, with great signs of Joy, by firing all the Artillary within and round the City, sent thrice to demand the surrender of the Fort from Capt. Leysler and his Accomplices, which was thrice denyed, but upon great Threatnings, the following Day surrendered to Governor Slaughter, who forth-with caused the said Capt. Leysler, with some of the chief Malefactors, to be bound over to answer their Crimes at the next Supream Court of Judicature, where the said Leysler and his pretended Secretary Millborn did appear, but refused to plead to the Indictment of the grand Jury, or to own the Jurisdiction of that Court; and so after several hearings, as Mutes, were found guilty of High Treason and Murder, and executed accordingly.[1]

Several of the other Malefactors that pleaded were also found Guilty, and particularly one Abraham Governeer for Murdering of an Old Man peaceably passing along the Street, but were Reprieved by Governour Sloughter, and upon Coll. Fletcher's arrival by him set at liberty, upon their Submission and promise of good Behaviour.

[1] On Leisler's trial, see below, p. 392.

Sir, All what is here set down is True, and can be proved and justified by the Men of greatest Probity and best Figure amongst us. If I were to give a particular Narrative of all the Cruelties and Robberies perpetrated upon their Majesties most affectionate Subjects in this Province, they would fill a Volumn: There was no need of any Revolution here; there were not ten Jacobites in the whole; they were all well known, and the strictest Protestants, and men of best Figure, Reputation and Estates were at the Helm, it may plainly be perceived by the several steps and measures were followed at that time, and by their Letters to the then Earl, now Duke of Shrewsbury, and to the Lords, and the Kings Answer thereunto. The Copy of which Answer, and some other Papers worthy of your perusal, are inclosed.

So soon as Governour Sloughter arrived, an Assembly was called, which upon the 18th of April, 1691, did present an Address to his Excellency, signed by their Speaker, together with the Resolves of that House, which when you are pleased to read, gives the Conclusive Opinion and Judgment of the General Assembly of this Province, of all those disorderly Proceedings, for which those two have suffered Death, and their Sentence was since approved by Her Majesty, of ever blessed Memory, in Council.

Many worthy Protestants in England, and other parts of the world, being sincerely devoted to his Majesties Interest, have yet notwithstanding (unacquainted with our Circumstances, and not duely apprized of the truth) been more easily induced to give credit to the false Glosses and Calumnies of byassed and disaffected Persons from this Province. But in my Observation, most Gentlemen that have come hither so prepossessed, after some time spent here have been thorowly convinced of their Mistake, and that those men who suffered Death, did not from pure zeal for their Majesties Interest, and the Protestant Religion, but being of desperate Fortune, thrust themselves into Power, of purpose to make up their wants by the Ruin and Plunder of his Majesties Loyal Subjects, and were so far engaged in their repeated Crimes, that they were driven to that height of Desperation, had not the Providence of Almighty God prevented it, the whole Province had been Ruined and Destroyed.

I have put this in writing at your Request, to assist your
Memory, and leave it to his Excellency Coll. Fletcher, and your
own Observations, to enlarge upon the Characters of those
Persons who have been the greatest Sufferers in the time of
those Disorders, and of their Patience and Moderation since
your arrival; also, of the Disaffected, and the Causes which
you have frequently observed to hold this Province in Disquiet
and Trouble.   Notwithstanding all which, and the frequent
Attachs of the French and Indians upon our Fronteers, this
Province has not lost one foot of ground during the War, but
have had considerable Advantages upon the Enemy, which,
under God, is due to the prudent and steady Conduct and
great Care and Diligence of Coll. Fletcher, our present Governour.

You have been an Eye Witness, and have had Time and
Experience enough to enable you to inform others in England,
which if you will please to do, I doubt not but it will gain Credit,
and be an extraordinary piece of Service to this Province.   I
am,

Sir,

Your Most Humble Servant.

New-York, December 31,
1697.

The King's Letter.

William R.

Trusty and Well-beloved, We greet you well.   Whereas We
have been given to understand by Letters from you, and others the
principal Inhabitants of Our Province of New-York, of your Dutiful
Submission to Our Royal Pleasure, and readiness to receive from Us
such Orders as We should think requisit for settling the Peace and
good Government of Our Province of New-York, We have thought
fit hereby to signifie unto you, That We are taking such Resolution
concerning the same as may tend to the Wellfare of Our Subjects,
Inhabitants there.   And in the mean time We do hereby Authorize
and Impower you to take upon you the Government of the said
Province, calling to your Assistance, in the Administration thereof,
the principal Free-holders and Inhabitants of the same, or so many
of them as you shall think fit, Willing and Requiring you to do and
perform all things which to the Place and Office of Our Lieutenant
Governour and Commander in Chief of Our Province of New-York
doth or may appertain, as you shall find necessary for Our Service,

and the good of Our Subjects, according to the Laws and Customs of Our said Province, until further Order from Us. And so We bid you Farewell. Given at Our Court at Whitehall the 30th Day of July, 1689, in the first Year of Our Reign.

By His Majesties Command,

NOTTINGHAM.[1]

Was Superscribed,

To Our Trusty and Well-beloved Francis Nichollson, Esq; Our Lieut. Governour and Commander in Chief of Our Province of New-York in America; And in his Absence, To such as for the time being take care for preserving the Peace and administring the Laws in Our said Province of New-York in America.

[1] The Earl of Nottingham was one of the two secretaries of state, the other being, as mentioned above, the Earl of Shrewsbury.

LOYALTY VINDICATED, 1698

LOYALTY VINDICATED, 1698

Loyalty Vindicated from the Reflections of a Virulent Pamphlet called [A Letter from a Gentleman of New York, concerning the troubles which happened in that Province, in the time of the late happy Revolution] wherein the Libellous Author falsely scandalises those Loyal Gentlemen, who couragiously threw off the absolute Slavery that Province then lay under : and Declar'd for His present Majesty, the Protestant Religion, and the English Laws.

ALTHOUGH to name but the Authors of this Pamphlet, to give account of the time, manner, and design of its Publication, would sufficiently confute it, and were it all Truth, take away its Credit, Yet I shall first by plain proof of Fact and Reason, disabuse whom it may have imposed on; and then expose the Seducers themselves whose corrupt minds gave birth to this *Ignis fatuus*.

I know the Authors have triumph'd, that their Libel hath not hitherto been answered, but they will have but little cause, when they consider it required some time to recover the damp and stunn given to honest minds, by the late corrupt Government of New York that publisht it : and some time will always be naturally taken up for the exults of joy, that truth and honesty will now have their turn of being protected by Authority.

It was with great dread known, that the late King James was bound in Conscience to indeavour to Damn the English Nation to Popery and Slavery, and therefore no wonder (since he made such large steps towards it in his Kingdom's) that he took a particular care of this Province, of which he was Proprietor, and at one jump leapt over all the bounds, and Laws of English Right and Government; and appointed a Governour[1] of this Province of New York, who (although he was a

---

[1] The reference here is to Governor Thomas Dongan, 1682–1688.

375

person of large indowments of mind yet) gave active Obedience
to his Prince without reserve; and accepted of a Commission
now on record in the Secretarys Office, giving him power with
consent of any Seven of his Council to make Laws and to
raise Taxes (as the French King doth) without consent of the
People, (for the Council are no body, but whom [he] pleases to
name, and therefore could represent nothing but the Kings
pleasure). Hereby the will of the Prince became the Law;
and the estates of the subjects became the Kings property.
And this Governour and Council were the tools to inslave
their Country, who pursuant to their Commission did make
Laws and Assessed Taxes accordingly, without any Representatives of the People, as appears by the Records of the Council
book.

This French Government being thus (by Commission) introduced, it was natural that Papists should be employed in
the highest Trusts; such as the Council, the Revenue, and the
Military Forces; and since no Law was left alive to make them
unqualifyed, therefore this obedient Governour admitted
major Brockholse and major Baxter into the Council, Matthew
Plowman to be Collector of the Revenue, and said Baxter and
Russel to Command Military Forces; all professed Papists to
assist in making Arbitrary Placats, and forcing obedience to
them from a Protestant free People.

This was the condition of New York, the Slavery and
Popery that it lay under, until the Hand of Heaven sent the
glorious King William to break those chains, which would
otherwise have fetter'd all Europe. And these were the
reasons that moved the Gentlemen concerned in the Revolution of New York to be early in shaking off their Tyrants, and
declaring for their Deliverer.

These things premised do make way for the answer to the
bold Assertions of the Libeller, who had the Author Printed
the Letter ten years before, viz. the time of the Revolution,
he would have come under the penalty of spreading false News,
which he in particular knows,[1] in Scotland is call'd Leesing,
and deserves the death call'd the Maiden.[2]

---

[1] An allusion to the Scottish origin of David Jamison.

[2] The Scottish Maiden was a kind of guillotine, with an axe dropping in
grooves from a height of about ten feet.

In the third page which is the first of the Letter, he declares that Jacob Leisler and his accomplices committed great disorders in the Revolution. And was ever Revolution made without them? What, must the noxious humours of the body natural be loosned and put a float, and very often with pangs and gripes, before the Medicament can officiate the discharge? and must not the body politick suffer a Convulsion to pluck up Spiritual and Temporal Tyranny that was taking root in it? But I pray explain yourself, was not the Revolution it self the greatest disorder that could be given to you and the Jacobite party? and therefore you need not admire nor wonder that all those that have a good opinion of the Revolution, have so likewise of Jacob Leisler, and other early Instruments of it in this Province: Nor is it a wonder that it should be credited, that the persons then in Commission in New York were Jacobites, and persons ill affected to the Revolution (which now the Libeller dare not say otherwise than call happy) for their very Commissions from King James were expresly contrary to Law, and their persons unqualified to serve in any Capacity in any English Government and so that as Jacobites (*i. e.* obeyers of King James's Arbitrary Government) and as Papists they must naturally be ill affected to the happy Revolution in England, and implacable Enemies to the well wishers thereof in New York. The proof of this appears by the Printed account of the State of the Government of New York, attested by the Records of Sir Edmund Andross, Coll. Nicholson, Matthew Plowman, major Baxter and Bartholomew Russel's Commissions; which are Evidence undeniable and point blanck contrary to the Testimony of the Libeller, who calls himself a personal witness. But the Author was safe at the time of Publishing the Letter, for it was when the Province lay under the calamity (more then in any other age) of Licensing this Letter, which gives Authority for the palliating of Vice with false glosses, and of criminating the Actions of the most Just and Virtuous and pious persons, and when Truth and Innocency were strip'd of all defence against the malice, falsehood and calumny of Col. Fletcher, and his complying Council.

We are told the Lieutenant Governour and Council were Protestants, and perhaps they were; and so were Friend,

Perkins, Jefferys, Herbert, Bishop of Chester, and Brian Haynes the player;[1] therefore that is no infallible Test that they were well affected to the Revolution, if they had no other. But they resolved Thereupon to suspend all Roman Catholicks from Command and places of trust in the Government. Well resolved, though they did not perform it, as the Libeller afterwards owns. But what means the word "Thereupon"? *i. e.*, King James was fled into France, the Prince of Orange was Armed with considerable Forces in England, and by consent and voice of the Nation declared their Deliverer and King: and since King James could not stand by them, and the Arbitrary Commissions he had given them, and Old England would be sure to Command New-York: *Thereupon* they, etc. No thanks to them for their Thereupon. Besides if I am not mistaken, the execution of their Illegal Commissions (which they held as long as they could) and their fear of exasperations they had justly given to the People, by being Voluntary slaves to King James his Will, and Authorised to make all under them to be likewise so: (as the Devils would have all men Damn'd with themselves.) For these reasons these faint resolves were made and ill executed. But we do not find that *Thereupon* they declared for the Prince of Orange, or the Protestant Religion. No, these Gentlemen had submitted so intirely to such a blind Obedience to their Prince as (notwithstanding their Profession) was never practis'd by any Christians, but the Papists; and think to hide their nakedness by the fig leaf of turning a single Papist out of the Council, just as their Master King James did, when the Prince of Orange was landing, the Nations hearts alienated from him, and his standing Army likely to run over to the Prince: *Thereupon*, he restored the Charters of Corporations, and Magdalen Colledge

---

[1] Sir John Friend, a wealthy brewer of London, was avowedly a Protestant, but at the same time a friend and ally of James II. He was executed in 1696. Sir William Parkyns, son of a London merchant, was engaged in the plot against William III. in 1696. He was executed with Friend in that year. Judge George Jeffreys, chief justice of the king's bench under James II., was the well-known judge of the Bloody Assizes. Sir Edward Herbert succeeded Jeffreys as chief justice of the king's bench. Thomas Cartwright, bishop of Chester, though an Anglican, was favorable to Roman Catholicism, upheld the policy of James II., and fled with him to France. Brian Haynes was connected with the Popish Plot and the trial of Titus Oates.

of Oxford,[1] and declared to call a free Parliament: Just with the same good will as these New York Thereuponmen. But it is notoriously false and known to be so by the Inhabitants of New York, that Thereupon these disbanded Papists forthwith left the Province: For Baxter stay'd here several Moneths, not knowing whether it was a real Revolution or no; and Russel stay'd and dyed in New York, but Plowman continued fix'd in the greatest Trust of Collector of the Revenue, being intrusted by the Protestant Lieutenant Governour and Council with the sinews of War in his management, who would be sure as a strict Papist to employ it in the service of a Protestant Revolution, from the same good affection with themselves.

To proceed, this Libeller names three Dutch Gentlemen of their Council, and tells you, that but two of them were most affectionate to the Royal house of Orange, although Mr. Phillips (I believe) had the same affection with the rest: but the Libeller never tells you, that any of them were pleased that the Prince of Orange, had rescued from ruine our English Laws, Liberties and Protestant Religion, and was become a Royal English King: which was but a small reward to Him for the Blessing it gave us: he only tells us, that as Dutchmen they loved the Royal house of Orange: So I presume the late King James doth, being tyed by blood thereto,[2] although he wishes him far enough from England. I suppose those Dutch Gentlemen will give the Libeller few thanks for his remarks on them. He adds, that the said Lieutenant Governour and Council Convened to their Assistance all the Justices of the Peace and Civil Magistrates, and Military Officers. But they had quite forgot the English Constitution of calling the Representatives of the People: and whereas several of this Convention were the Persons that were pitched upon, and thought fit by the then Arbitrary Government to have Commission, Office and Power to enslave the subject, No wonder the People did not think themselves safe in their hands, to be managed by the major Vote of such a Convention.

Neither was the first thing they ordered, *viz.* Fortifying the City of New York, any wise satisfactory; since it was most proper that those persons who gave occasion for a Revolution,

[1] See Macaulay, *History*, chapter VIII.
[2] Mary, wife of William III., was the daughter of James II.

were most probable to make themselves strong to oppose it. And therefore Coll. Bayard, made Coll. of the Militia by King James, was most liable to obey and execute King James's order, and an unsure Security for the Fort; Especially having so often declared in Words, and Letters, under his own hand to Mr. West, etc., That those who were in Arms for the Prince of Orange were Rebels. But it is absolutely false, that Coll. Bayards industry fortifyed the Fort; for Capt. Leisler opened the Well, which was closed up; he it was ordered the Batteries, that were made about the Town, he mended the Breast works of the Fort, as likewise the Platforms, and Powder Room, all which were in a miserable Condition: and these great works took up near a Twelve Moneths time, with Vigorous application and industry of the Inhabitants, after Bayard was out of the Power of betraying the Fort, which could never have been defended in the posture he kept it, with no Well open, nor any covering for it, defence or security for their Ammunition. Besides when the Militia Forces were on guard in the Fort, the Lieutenant Governour in Passion altered their Orders given by their Officers, and told them, if they gave him any farther trouble he would set the City on fire. This prooved by the Depositions of Albort Bosch and Henry Coyler. And for their own sakes they appointed and continued the Revenue, as being very useful for men of any design: which makes nothing for their cause.

It matters not what Letters were sent home by the Lieutenant Governour, for it is plain neither Governour nor Council would declare for the Prince of Orange, pretending they wanted Orders; No, they wanted good will; for without Orders this Libeller pretends they turned out Baxter and Russel out of Commission. I wonder how they dared to go so far, and no farther. But no body but themselves know or care whither they wrote or no, for it signifyed nothing, except to excuse themselves from declaring till an answer came, and they knew who was uppermost. I suppose they had a mind to stay to see who got the better in Ireland, before they would declare.

A Lying building must have a lying foundation, and therefore the Libeller says, That Capt. Leisler, unwilling to pay the Duty of his Wines, stirred up the People to Rebellion. The case was thus, the Popish Collector Plowman was then con-

tinued in Office, and Capt. Leisler did, even with him, make
entry in the Custom house for his Wines, and ingaged to pay
the Customs to such as should be legally qualified to receive
them, which the Papist Plowman was not.

And now the people being exasperated by the delay of the
Governour and Council to declare for the Prince, the greater
body of the Militia with their Officers did Seize on the Fort,
and did send and demand the Keyes from the Lieutenant
Governour; and since they had taken the Government on
them, they did Seize what Publick Moneys they could find;
and took the Seven hundred Seventy three Pounds from Coll.
Nicholson, which with great prudence they did Expend for
the safety and defence of the Revolution: nor were the People
Drunk or Mad: for no Man, Woman, or Child, was hurt by
them even in the very Convulsion of changing the Government;
nay the very Papists then in Office, and others who were justly
suspected of designs of betraying the Country to King James's
faithful Allie, the French King, had not a hair hurt, except
by the fright their own guilt occasioned; and these Revolu-
tioners must either be very sober or loving in their drink, or
these Jacobites had never scap'd being Dewitted[1] by a sufficiently provoked People, who had the Power, but more grace
than to use it.

False Assertions without proof are sufficiently answered
by denying them. This northern forehead answers himself:
for the Libeller says, the people cry'd out that they disowned
all Government, and in the next line tells you, they proclaimed
Capt. Leisler their Commander. But I suppose, he gives the
contradiction as a proof of the Peoples being drunk; to be
against all manner of Government, and choose a Governour
in the same breath. 'Tis likewise notoriously false, that no
other Commission'd Officer was amongst them: for most of
the Officers of the Militia of the City joyned therein: But
had it been true, then Capt. Leisler as the only Commission
Officer ought to Command them; and they were just and sober
in their choice, as well as prudent in their Trust of so good
and faithful a Person. But the fact of this was false, for
Capt Leisler. though instrumental in shaking off the Tyran-

---

[1] A reference to the murder of the Dutch statesmen Jan and Cornelis De
Witt by the infuriated populace of The Hague in 1672.

nical Government, did not believe he had a Title to govern longer than the Peoples Resolutions were known; and therefore, circular Letters were carryed by Coll. Depeyster and Capt. De Brayn to the several Counties; whose Freeholders chose their Representatives, who being met appointed Capt. Leisler Commander in Chief under their Hands and Seals, and appointed several to be of his Council, under the name of a Committee of Safety to preserve the Publick Peace of the Province: who did it so effectually, that those divested of the Governing power had no other harm done to their persons; and the late Lieutenant Governour was permitted to withdraw himself whither he pleased. And here I must remark that he fared much better than Sir Edmund Andross at Boston, who was made close Prisoner and sent home to England, and yet no man was Executed or attainted there for that act of Loyal Violence.

Boston having proclaimed King William and Queen Mary, and New York Fort and Government possess'd by Loyal Leisler and his party, and the Lieutenant Governour withdrawn out of the Province, then the Libeller saith, That the late Council and their Convention of Justices of the Peace and Officers, had a great mind to proclaim the King and Queen, whom they never had declared for, and we must take his word for it: but he owns the Loyalists did proclame them, but saith, it was very disorderly. I observe whatever made for the Revolution, or against the late King James, is very displeasing to the Scribler: For when the People took the Government out of their Arbitrary betrayers hands, he saith, they were drunk or mad; and now the proclaiming of the King and Queen was very disorderly, in neither of which he gives one instance: But thank God, they were proclaimed, and their goodness will pardon small disorders which were the effects of Loyal Zeal, Although the Jacobites will never forgive them for it. Some of which Council and Magistrates went to Coll. Bayards house and drank and rejoyced that Leisler had done what they never could have the heart to do, nor made one step towards. And we may know what kidney these drinkers were of, by whose Wine they drank: For Coll. Bayard having been a complying tool all King James's Arbitrary Reign, you shall judge of the rest by his opinion of the happy

Revolution, in his letter to Mr. West of the 14th of January 1689/90, Wherein he calls them Philistines, calls Leisler and his Loyal party, the Arch Rebel and his hellish crew, wishes he had a sufficient number to suppress the Rebels, calls them usurpers of the Government, and Sir Edmund Andross, his Excellency, and calls his friends Loyal, and the whole tenour of the Letter is to keep up King James's title, to admit his Commissions of Government to be of force, to brand all that declared for the Prince of Orange with the black name of Rebels; by which he owned King James was still in his heart, and had he power equal to his will, would have kept him still on the Throne, and therefore we may judge of his and his Companies joy, on this occasion, and whose Health they drank: which, eight years after, they tell us was King William's and Queen Mary's.

His Majesties Proclamation to confirm Sheriffs, Collectors, etc. in their Offices being Published, the Convention removed Matthew Plowman a Papist from being Collector, but this is now when Capt. Leisler had rescued the Government, was possess'd of the Fort and had proclaimed King William and Queen Mary. Then the Convention (who had done none of these things and were angry at those who did) they removed a Papist from his Office, about the middle of June, who was permitted by them to act above two Moneths from the time that the Lieutenant Governour and Council resolved to remove Papists from Offices; which (as the Libeller in the first page of his Letter saith) was the beginning of April: they kept him in as long as they could, and now to mend the matter, they put others in his place of the same principles as to King James, of which the famous Bayard aforementioned was the Ringleader. And the Libeller brags, that they were the first in the Province that took the Oaths to their Majesties, appointed by Act of Parliament: It may be true; but it is as true, that they were the last and backwardest to assist in the Revolution, or declare for the Prince of Orange, which they never did; but afterwards pursued to death those that had done it. They were indeed most forward to take Oaths, when they were to gain by them, and to have the fingring of the Revenue. For the carrying of the purse they will deny their old Master King James; not out of hatred to him, but love to Money; being bound by solemn Oath to be true to their own interest; which Oath binds them closer than any Oath of Allegiance.

These worthy Commissioners of the Revenue sate in the Custom-house, but Capt. Leisler with the Inhabitants who had possession of the Government and Fort, demanded of them by what Authority they pretended to act; who refusing to give Capt. Leisler any Account they offered to turn him out of the Custom-house by force; on which tumult (made by three Jacobites) a guard of Inhabitants from the Fort came to defend their Captain. And the People in the Streets were so enraged at Coll. Bayard (who they knew was as inveterate as any Papist against the Revolution) that they certainly had tore him to pieces, had not the good temper of Capt. Leisler been his protector, who was the only person capable of saving him in that extremity, and favored his escape, and let him live to have afterwards a hand in the Murdering his deliverer: So that the Violence of Armed men and naked Swords, beating the Commissioners from the Custom-house, was very modestly done, for no man was hurt, not so much as a skin broke of those who deserved the halter; but they are still alive; some of them to watch another occasion to betray their Country, when they can get a Popish King of England to assist them.

Captain Leisler finding several Papists and false Protestants in the Town, like a prudent Officer kept good guards, sent parties to prevent any Conspiracy they might make to resume the Government, and to preserve the Peace, which was dayly attempted to be broke by declaring for King James, and his Governour Sir Edmund Andross, and denying the Authority of the People, and Capt. Leisler intrusted by them, on which it was wisely done of Capt. Leisler to secure in the Fort those whom he found so troublesome to the publick Peace, and as the heads of them he Imprisoned the afore-mentioned famous Coll. Bayard and Mr. Nichols, but without barbarity they were confined, and not in a nasty Goal, but in handsome lodgings, such as now are thought proper for the Captain of the Guard, the Store keeper and the Secretary of the Province to lodge and keep Office in. It is true that Coll. Bayard was put in Irons, as he well deserved for his aversion to the Revolution, disturbing the Peace, and attacking Capt. Leisler (then Commander in Chief) in the open Street, as appears by several credible Oaths. Nor could it be safe to admit such fire brands to Bail; and therefore they were kept close from doing mischief, which is the part of all good Governments to do, and was most necessary in this Revolution.

Captain Leisler with the Committee of safety (appointed by the Representatives of the Freeholders of the several Counties of the Province) having published their Declaration for the Prince of Orange, the Protestant Religion, and the English Laws and Liberties, they thought it prudent to discriminate the Well affected from the Enemy, and therefore Summoned all the Inhabitants of the City to the Fort, to sign their names to such a Declaration as owned the Authority of the Prince of Orange. And the refusers must justly by him and all mankind be deemed Enemies to the Revolution, to His Majesty, and their Country. And is this a crime to know the Sheep from the Goats, or to take all Reasonable methods for the safety of the then Government: but the Libeller is angry at every prudent step was taken, nor is he satisfyed, although it is above Seven years since he was gorg'd with their innocent blood which he had a hand in shedding.

It is notoriously false that Capt. Leisler opposed the Collecting of the Revenue; indeed he was not willing a Papist should run away with our Protestant Kings Money, nor did he think it safe in Bayards, etc. hands. But the Committee of safety (and not Capt. Leisler) appointed Mr. De Lanoy (in whom they durst confide) to that trust, who received no Customs until December following, when his Majesties orders arrived; till then he took only notes from the Merchants to pay the Customs when demanded. And 'tis well known that Mr. DeLanoy gave a fair and true Accompt of his Receipts and payments of the Customs to Governor Slaughter: whereby it appears he had expended five hundred Pounds of his own Money above the Money of the Revenue, for the Kings Service and the support of the Revolution; which Money is not repaid him to this day through the iniquity of some Jacobites afore-mentioned, who crept into power, and who have thereby gratifyed their revenge on men of greater sense and Loyalty than themselves.

On the tenth of December one Riggs brought his Majesties Letters which were delivered to Capt. Leisler, as they ought according to their direction; for Coll. Nicholson (to whom they were first directed) had withdrawn himself out of the Province, and in his absence the Letters were directed to such as for the time being took care for the preservation of the Peace and Administring the laws; which was none other but Capt. Leisler, who was appointed thereto by the Representatives of the Freeholders of the several Countyes of the Province and had the Command of the Fort; nor could those who called themselves of the Council be intituled thereto, for they were the Persons that were made use of in the late Arbitrary and Tyrannical Government, to the over-turning of all Laws, and Civil Rights, and who gave Occasion for the Revolution in New York, and did never declare for the Prince of Orange.

These Letters from His Majesty fully confirming Capt. Leisler in the Government, whereto he was chosen by the People's Representatives, he indeavoured to execute his trust faithfully, and on such an Emergency it was the greatest wisdom and prudence to find Money to support the Government, which he did as regularly as the time would permit, by and with the consent of the General Assembly of the Province fairly chosen by the Freeholders; which this seducer falsely insinuates were only Selected and Appointed by Capt. Leisler. And by and with their advice and consent Taxes were raised and properly applyed. And 'tis observable the Libeller tells us, that Capt. Leisler applyed these Sums to his own private use, and yet the very next words tells us, it was to maintain said disorders, allowing private men Eighteen Pence *per* day: by disorders he means the Government reposed by the People and confirmed by King William in Capt. Leisler which had disordered and routed the former Slavery the People lay under; for it was disorder to none but Papists and Jacobites. And the Eighteen pence a day was for the private use of the private men to whom it was paid, for their subsistence in defending the Government: and their defence was indeed of private use to Capt. Leisler, as comprehended in the Publick general good thereof: But the Revenue was not sufficient to defray so great a charge, had not Capt. Leisler expended great Sums out of his own private Estate, as others concerned with him likewise did, for which he was repayed with a barbarous Death, through the means of men who will never venture their Lives or Estates to serve their Prince, Country, or Protestant Religion.

Nor could Coll. Bayard and Mr. Nichols complain of their aforementioned confinement in the Fort, since they would fly in the face of Government, and give such vent to their invenomed passions as appears by the Record of their Committment, and Coll. Bayards confession in his Petition to Capt. Leisler.

But it is point blanck a lye, nor was it ever, or can be proved that Capt. Leisler gave directions to any man to plunder Coll. Bayards house, nor was any thing of that sort done by his order to any house, but Commands given to the contrary, and the Souldiers were compelled to restore what could be made appear they had forcibly taken from any man. Even so small a matter as a Hat taken out of the house of Mr. Lambert, was restored to him.[1]

Coll. Cortland and others might leave their houses and families, but they would have had no occasion for so doing had they peaceably and quietly minded their own affairs and submitted to the Government; for all such had no manner of disturbance given them, but were protected.

The Protestant Ministers, the Libeller saith, could not scape Capt. Leislers Malice and Cruelty: I am afraid those Ministers he mentioned, were Popish Trumpets, to Preach up the damn'd Doctrins of Passive Obedience and Non Resistance, and to noise in our Ears with their accursed breath, that we ought patiently to hold our Protestant Throats to be cut by the Command of a Popish King: and when Capt. Leisler with his friends had taken hold of that wonderful Deliverance offered immediately from God to Redeem His People from Slavery upon Earth, and Popish Damnation in Hell, to have false Priests of Baal get up, and use their wicked Eloquence to make the People believe a lye, even in the house of the God of Truth, and from the Pulpit, to tell these Captains

---

[1] Dennis Lambert was one of those who took part in the so-called assault upon Leisler, June 6, 1690. A witness deposed that he saw "Lt Govr Jacob Leisler encompassed by several persons and saw Dennis Lambert have hold of the sd Lieut. Govrs sword by the hilt . . . and that Robert Alison lifted up his cane (intended as the Dept thought) to strike the sd Lt Govr" (N. Y. Col. Docs., III. 741).

of our Temporal Salvation to their faces, that being faithful to their God, their Country, and their Laws, in the defence of the Holy Protestant Religion, and the Rights and Liberties of English men, and their thankful declaring for the most glorious Prince upon Earth their Deliverer: was the blackest of Treason and Rebellion. Such Apostasy and base Treachery hath deserved, and often met with severer rebukes than the friendly Verbal admonition given by Capt. Leisler to the blind Seer, and had nothing of the Malice and Cruelty in it of the Libeller, who wrote so false a Pamphlet: and so the other time-serving Priests (who were Protestants shooing horns to draw on Popery) might have been more quiet, and left the result of the Revolution to Divine Providence, and not pass such hard Censures as to attaint blood and accuse of Rebellion, all that would accept of Gods deliverance from the two greatest plagues of mankind, Popery and Slavery. But I hope they have repented and will be saved, otherwise whilst they Preach to others they themselves will be cast away.

'Tis true Capt. Leisler sent to the Merchants of the Town to supply the Garrison with Provisions and other necessaries, and sent without distinction to all People who had Stores;[1] otherwise the Garrison might have perished: but he honestly gave them Credit in the Kings Books, and they have since (for the greatest part) been satisfyed; and Capt. Leisler (as he ought) did order forcibly to break their Ware-houses open, where they were refractory, and refused on so great Emergency to afford support to the Government; but exact Accompts were kept of all such goods, and Entries made in Books kept for that purpose; so that it was not plunder, (as the Libeller falsely calls it) but they were to be satisfyed, and paid for the same. And I believe it was never known in the Memory of man, that ever a Revolution, or change of Government, was more regular: or where Military power would not force Victuals where it was denyed them, when they wanted it: and therefore it was for the special Service of King William and Queen Mary, to keep alive those that were the only persons in that Province who declared early for Them, and owned Their Authority. Nor can any proof upon Earth be brought

[1] Leisler seized large quantities of pork and other provisions for which claims were afterward presented to the Sloughter government. Bellomont passed an act paying for them, but the Privy Council disallowed it (*Acts, Colonial*, VI. 19–20).

(except such as the Libeller) that one Farthings Value of goods was ever converted to the private use of Capt. Leisler, or Transported by him to the West Indies, but the imposture of the whole book depends on such positive falsehoods.

The Accompt of Thirteen Thousand nine hundred fifty nine Pounds of damages done the Province is made up by the Libeller himself; for no man living, of truth, hath ever demonstrated that Capt. Leisler or his friends ever made pillage of any man's Estate, but I believe the Libeller reckons that he and his Jacobite party had so much damage by the Revolution, which they might Arbitrarily have extorted from the King's good Subjects, if it had not happened. Good damages! which I am glad of with all my heart. At this rate pray what damages had the Popish Clergy of England and Ireland, by King Williams hindering their being restored to Abbys, Monasterys, and Peter Pence; but it is better that the Jacobites should suffer damage of their Estates and Lives too, than an English Protestant People should have the damage of loosing their Laws and Religion, their Properties and their Souls. And as for Coll. Willets losses, which the Libeller magnifies, he could not put a particular Value on them, they were so small. Had they been considerable he would since have made a particular complaint, to have reparation, which he never did, nor had occasion for; but had he been ruined he would not have been pittyed by good men, because he so far forgot that he was an English man and Protestant, that he Executed an Illegal Commission,[1] and raised Forces to destroy all those that declared for our Deliverer, that we might return to our Vomit, which was a Dog trick in him.

And thus the Libeller expatiates on Capt. Leislers Arbitrary proceedings over his Majesties Subjects, Persons and Estates, against the fundamental Laws of the Land; but he should have considered that all the fundamental Laws of the Land were wholly subverted and trampled upon by the Hellish, Popish, Arbitrary Government, Established by King James's Commission; so that Capt. Leisler found no fundamental Laws to transgress; and was forced in discharge of his

---

[1] Reference is here made to Willett's acceptance of an order from Ingoldesby to raise troops on Long Island in January, 1691. Thomas Clark, Daniel Whitehead, and others accepted similar commissions.

trust from the People, and by and with the consent of those appointed by their Representatives, to use these violent methods which Heaven gave him the power to make use of to restore those fundamental Laws, which were abolished by tools of the same temper with the Libeller.

Major Ingoldsby, a Captain of a foot Company, arrives near two years after, saith the Libeller, "And with several Gentlemen of the Council sends to Capt. Leisler, that for the preservation of the Peace he might continue to command in the Fort, until Coll. Slaughter's Arrival, and only desired that major Ingoldesby and the Kings Souldiers might be permitted to quarter, and refresh themselves in the City: but instead of complying, he in passion told Mr. Brooke, on his acquainting him, that Mr. Phillips, Coll. Bayard, Coll. Cortland were of the Council, that they were Papist Dogs, and if the King should send Three Thousand of them, he would cut them off; and without cause Proclaimed open War; on which said major Ingoldesby perswaded several of the Inhabitants to joyn with him merely for self preservation. On which several great and small Shot from the Fort killed and wounded several of His Majesties good Subjects, who made no opposition."

This whole Paragraph I shall shew to be the greatest complication of Iniquity, and fit to be the production of a Monster begat by an Incubus on a Scotch Witch, who had kindled his malice against Truth from the flames he put to the holy Bible,[1] thereby to become the Adopted Son of the father of Lyes.

For major Ingoldesby, having no Commission, nor Authority to Command, on his Arrival took on him the Title of Commander in Chief, usurp'd a shew of Government, calling a Council, and Issuing peremptory orders, as appears by the Records of the Council Book:[2] nay, quite contrary to the

[1] See below, p. 398.
[2] Professor Channing thinks that Ingoldsby had a commission authorizing him to exercise supreme power as commander-in-chief, but whether from the king or by deputation from Sloughter he does not say. It is difficult to believe that if Ingoldsby had had such a commission, he would have failed to show it to Leisler. I have been unable to find any trace of a royal commission, even of the customary sign manual, appointing Ingoldsby lieutenant-governor; whereas Governor Sloughter in his letter to Lord Nottingham states that the vessels bearing Ingoldesby and the soldiers parted from him at sea "without any direction or allowance." There seems to be no doubt but that Ingoldesby had nothing more than his captain's commission, as the text says.

Romantick Account of the Libeller, he sent a demand under his own hand, which I have seen, wherein he acknowledges Capt. Leislers offer to him of his own Houses in the City for the Accommodation of himself and Officers, and to appoint fit Quarters for the Souldiers; which major Ingoldesby under his hand denyes to accept of, saying, he demanded the Fort from him, which unless Capt. Leisler would deliver up to him, he would esteem him as an Enemy to King William and Queen Mary. I have likewise seen Capt. Leislers Letter to Major Ingoldesby, full of Civility and true Reason, wherein he acquaints him, that he held the Fort and Commanded by Virtue of a trust reposed in him by the People, and confirmed by His Majesty, and assuring him, that if he had any Commission from His Majesty, or any Instruction or Order from Coll. Slaughter appointed Governour of the Province, on his producing it, The Fort should be immediately delivered to him, but desired to be excused from resigning his trust, till he found one qualifyed and authorized to receive it from him. But this was not satisfaction to major Ingoldesby, who was prevailed with to take the Government on him in opposition to Capt. Leisler, and as Governour in Chief (although never impowered by King or People) he issues orders to the several Counties to be ready to attend and assist in opposing Leisler and his party with Arms; which was the proclaiming open War; and pursuant thereto he sends his Rounds in the night, and ordered or permitted his Rounds at all hours to pass the guards and centrys on the Walls of the Fort, and not to make answer, but by reproachful Language, when challenged by them, in order to provoke the drawing of blood, and ingaging the People in a Civil War: and farther, major Ingoldesby ordered all the men under his Command to wear Marks[1] on their Arms, to distinguish them from those who joyned with Capt. Leisler.

During this Revolution and Civil War, I am told not above two persons were killed,[2] which happiness attended the moderate temper of Capt. Leisler and the Committee of Safety, who could not be raised to punish the Insolence of the Tory party, suitable to what they gave just occasion for.

Soon after, *viz.* in March, about a Month or five Weeks

---

[1] The "Marks" were white scarfs tied around their left arms.

[2] One of those killed was Lieutenant Patrick Macgregory.

after major Ingoldesby's usurpation,[1] Coll. Slaughter Arrived, who Summoned the Fort late at night, and, contrary to the Libellers assertion, it was never denyed to be delivered: but the delivery suspended till next Morning, it not being proper (according to Military Rules) to deliver a Fort in the night, and then it was Surrendered by Capt. Leisler, who waiting on the Captain General Coll. Slaughter, instead of thanks for the faithful Service he had done His Majesty in defending the Fort and Province from the French (our professed Enemies) and the Treachery of Papists and Jacobites amongst ourselves, was immediately by his order Seized with Mr. Milbourn, and others of the Loyal party, and bound over to answer at the next Supream Court of Judicature; where Capt. Leisler and Mr. Milbourn pleaded to the Jurisdiction of the Court, That whereas he was in possession of the Government by the choice of the People, and confirmed in it by the Kings Majesties Letters, that he was not bound by Law to answer for his Mal Administration in Government, to any Court or Authority, but to His Majesty, who had intrusted him: but this was overruled by the Violence of the Court, without reason or Law, and as Mutes they were found guilty of High Treason and Murder; and although a Reprieve was granted them by Coll. Slaughter, untill His Majesties pleasure should be known in the Matter: yet the Violence of the Jacobite party (of which sort were most of Capt. Leislers Judges and Officers of the Court)[2] was such that they gave no rest to Coll. Slaughter, untill by their Importunity they prevailed with him to sign the Dead Warrant. And they were Executed accordingly. So that the representation of the matter, with an account of their Reprieve, reached His Majesty at the same time with the account of their Execution and Death. So fell Capt. Leisler and Mr. Milbourn, men of known Integrity, Honesty

[1] The period of Ingoldesby's "usurpation" was from January 29 to March 19, 1691.

[2] Joseph Dudley presided at the trial. The other justices were "Thomas Johnson, Esqre, Sr. Robert Robinson, Knt, Chidley Brooke, William Smith, William Pinhorne, John Laurence, Esqrs, Capt. Jasper Hickes, Maj. Richard Ingoldesby, Col. John Young, and Capt. Isaac Arnold," constituting the court of oyer and terminer commissioned by Sloughter, March 26, 1691. The trial began on March 31 and continued on the 1st, 6th, 8th, and 15th of April. Ten prisoners were tried, each separately, and each was allowed counsel. The

and Loyalty, and by a pretended course of Law, contrary to all Law, condemned, where their Judges were most of them violent Enemies of the happy Revolution, and therefore resolved to revenge themselves on these Gentlemen who were the most Early and Zealous Instruments of it; and who had first expended great part of their Estates, and then suffered Martyrdom for King William and Queen Mary, their Religion and Laws. The proofs and papers referred to in this account remain in the hands of Mr. Jacob Leisler, only son of Capt. Jacob Leisler, the Martyr to Jacobite Revenge. The proof that Capt. Leisler was legally Governour of New York, That major Ingoldesby was but a bear Captain of Foot, and had no other command in that Province, nor authority to demand the Fort from Capt. Leisler; The proof that Capt. Leisler did as a good Subject deliver the Fort to Coll. Slaughter upon demand, and his Justification, is immediately expressed in the Act of Parliament of England which reverses their Attainders, and restores their Families in Blood and Estate.

So that this is the full and true account of this Tragedy: New York lay under the Curse of an absolute Gover ment by King James's Commission to Sir Edmund Andros; the people took courage on the first News of the Revolution in England, and shook off the Oppressors, and declared for the Prince of Orange; the Lieutenant Governor, the Council, and Justices of the Peace, which met and call'd themselves a Convention (being Officers constituted by King James) would not declare for the Prince of Orange; Wherefore the people did not think themselves safe in their hands, but Seized upon the Fort, and chose Capt. Leisler Commander of the Fort until Circular Letters had procured a return of Representatives of the Free holders of the several Counties of the Province, who on their meeting making a Declaration for His present Majesty, did under their Hands and Seals constitute Capt. Leisler Com-

petit jury, selected from a panel of forty-eight names, acquitted two, Delanoy and Edsall, and found eight guilty, Leisler, Milborne, Gouverneur, Beekman, Coerten, Williams, Vermilye, and Brasier. Leisler and Milborne refused to plead and were condemned as mutes. On the 17th the eight were sentenced to death. Leisler and Milborne were hanged on May 16, Sloughter having signed the death-warrant, after the consent of council and assembly, which convened on April 9, had been obtained. The other six were returned to prison, but released the next year by order in council, dated May 13, 1692.

mander in Chief until the Kings pleasure should be known; and likewise appointed him a Council, by the name of a Committee of Safety. And in these Persons the Government was lodged, who proceeded to support themselves by the most moderate methods could be devised.

The Lieutenant Governour hereupon withdraws out of the Province, major Ingoldsby Arrives with Authority over none but his Foot Company, and yet demands the Fort, which Capt. Leisler durst not deliver to him without betraying his Trust both to the King and People; major Ingoldsby usurps the Title of Commander in Chief, he Issues Orders and Warrants to the People to rise in Arms to assist him to wrest the Fort out of Capt. Leislers hands, and provokes Capt. Leislers men in the Fort to Acts of hostility, by which means one or two men were accidentally killed. Coll. Slaughter Arrives, demands the Fort, which was surrendered to him immediately; the Persons of Capt. Leisler and Mr. Milbourn are Seiz'd, and soon after brought to Tryall; their plea to the Jurisdiction of the Court (which could not by Law try them for Mal Administration in Government) violently over ruled, and they Condemned as Mutes, for High Treason and Murder; they were Reprieved until His Majesties pleasure should be known; and notwithstanding the Reprieve, the Warrant of Execution Signed, and they Executed.

But the Enemies to King William, and consequently to these Gentlemen, had not sufficiently gratified their malice, by these mens innocent blood: but they labour in England to get a justification for themselves, and a confirmation that the said unjust Judgment was according to Law; and when His Majesty was in Flanders and several Ministers of State were in place and trust in the Committee of Trade, which His Majesty hath since thought fit to remove from His Council and their Offices, a report was obtained from the Committee of Trade affirming that these Loyalists were Condemned and Executed according to Law.[1] But however the said Committee represented their Sons as fit objects of Her Majesties mercy, to be restored to their Fathers Estates; which

---

[1] The order in council of March 11, 1692, based on the report of the Lords of Trade of the same date, declared that Leisler and Milborne "were condemned and have suffered according to law."

Her Majesty was graciously pleased to grant. And these malignant Confederates so far prevailed with the Assembly of New York to compliment and flatter their new Governour, Coll. Slaughter, as to pass several Votes against the whole proceedings of the happy Revolution, and to excuse the barbarous Severity of the Illegal Condemnation and bloody Execution which he had ordered. And this was the State of the Case until the Parliament of England took the matter into their Consideration, and the honorable the House of Commons in the Sixth and Seventh year of His present Majesties Reign appointed a Committee to examine all parties in relation to Capt. Leislers Execution, where they were heard by their Council at Law, and where Mr. Dudley (who formerly applyed to get Money by Magistracy and Government in New England, and set up for a Judge in matters of Blood in the Tryal of Capt. Leisler at New York) was heard to make his defence, where his Cobb-Webb Eloquence was too thin to put a vail over so black an Action, as created horrour in the minds of that Honorable and Numerous Committee; who reported the matter fully to the House, and thereupon an Act of Parliament passed the Royal Assent, wherein His Majesty, the Lords, and Commons of England do recite the Legality of Capt. Leislers Authority, and justifie his proceedings in the Government, and more especially his refusing to deliver the Fort to major Ingoldesby, being the Fact for which he was Condemned; and do absolutely reverse the Attainders and restore the Blood and Estates of Capt. Leisler, and those persons Condemned and Executed in New York; which Act of Parliament is Printed at the end of this Treatise.[1]

And now after all, it being about Eight years since these men dyed, when the Grave and Time should have so buryed the Persons and Memories of these good, but unfortunate Persons, that no Revenge should have room to desire a farther

---

[1] The act of Parliament reversing the decree of the court of oyer and terminer and removing the attainder was passed in 1695 (6–7 William III., c. 30, private acts). By this act "the several convictions, judgments, and attainders" were "repealed, reversed, and declared null and void." Chalmers tells us that one of the agents for Massachusetts, Constantine Phipps, framed the bill, and we know that the other agent, Sir Henry Ashurst, was chairman of the committee that reported it favorably to the House. Bellomont, the later pro-Leislerian governor of New York, was also one of the committee.

gratification, and when the Annimosities between those of a Dutch extraction (who are the most numerous, Loyal and Sober Subjects of that Province) and the few English (who were most averse and backward in the Revolution, but violent and bloody in the Execution of Capt. Leisler, as well as the most dissolute in their Morals) in this Province, had time to cool, and might by a good Government have been wholly heal'd, After all, I say, to have this fire again blown up, to open these Wounds and to open the Graves of the Dead, to disturb the Living, was such an artifice of the Devil as must give a more than usual abhorrence in good minds; which leads me to give an account of the Occasion, the time, manner, and design of the Publication of this fire brand call'd *A Letter*, and withall take some notice of the supposed author.

It is evident in New York, and will soon be made appear to His Majesty, that the late Government of New York under the Administration of Coll. Fletcher[1] was a perfect sink of Corruption. And although he was exalted to that Government from a poor mean refugee of Ireland; yet he soon forgot the hand that raised him, and to satisfy his Soul, his Idol Gain, he made a fast friendship with the few Papists, Jacobites, and dissolute English of New York, who had opposed the Revolution and revenged themselves on Capt. Leisler; and who, to be supported in their hatred to the Loyal Williamites, and connived at in their open breach of all the Acts of Trade, found great advantage to reward Coll. Fletcher's friendship by Presents from themselves, and gifts from Pirates; and complyed with him, and consented to all things proposed to them by him; to the squandering of the Kings Revenue and (to the great dishonour of the King) destroying all conveniences of a Succeeding Governour; and disposing of all the Lands in the Province, that not one Inch is left to be given in reward to any who may by their Services to His Majesty deserve, or to incourage new Settlers, and that in such quantities as will wholly make it impossible ever to People the Province; giving to one man Seventy Miles in length, and to several Fifty, Forty and Thirty Miles in length, and several Miles in breadth; with many other unjust, gross Mal Administrations.

---

[1] The years 1692–1698, when Fletcher was governor, were a period of anti-Leislerian supremacy.

On this bottom Coll. Fletcher joyned in the mortal hatred
to the lovers of the Loyal Leisler; and when several condemned
to dye for their motions in that Revolution were ordered by
Her gracious Majesty of Sacred Memory to be discharged,
Coll. Fletcher did it as an act of grace of his own, and told
them that although he released them yet he could call for them
when he pleased, and hang them. And some time after told
them, That they dealt worse by him than the Lepers cleansed
by our Saviour, some of which returned to thank him, but none
of them ever did, meaning none of them had given him a
wicked Bribe or reward which he was used to receive. These
Truths Mr. Beekman and Mr. Gouverneur will attest. Coll.
Fletcher likewise paid that disregard to the Act of Parliament
of England, (Reversing the Attainders and restoring Capt.
Leisler and others condemned in Blood and Estate) that he
refused the Widow Leisler to be repossessed of her Estate;
nor had she that justice done her, during Coll. Fletchers
Government, nor untill my Lord Bellomont granted her a
Writ of Possession; which was a year and half after she was
Entituled to it by Act of Parliament in England, Reprinted at
New York. He likewise wholly discouraged the generality
of those who were active in the Revolution, putting few or
none of them into Office, or Employment, and wholly adhering
to those that gratifyed his Vanity, Pride, and Covetousness.
For which in return he gave them countenance in all matters,
as well as connivance at their unlawful Trade.

His Majesty having appointed the Earl of Bellomont
Governour of New York (whose great Honour and Justice
Coll. Fletcher both knew and dreaded) some considerable time
passed between his Patents being passed, and his beginning
his Voyage, which Coll. Fletcher took the advantage of,
therein to contrive methods so to divide the People of the
Government that in Publick disorder he himself might escape
having strict Scrutiny made into the Corruptions of his Government; he therefore not satisfyed with crushing the Loyalists,
during his Government, was resolved to assist the Publishing
this Libel, which might give such an Account of the Revolution of New York, as should Exasperate to the highest degree
all that were concern'd in it, and at the same time assured his
Jacobite party, that it was necessary such a book should be

Licensed, to possess the strangers who came with my Lord, with such falsehoods as were useful to their party; my Lord being, as he feared, inclined to favour whoever was well inclined to the Loyalty of Leisler. So that, as is supposed, one Mr. Jamison[1] was employed to frame this Libel, who was Clerk of the bloody Court that Condemned Leisler; a person most in the graces of Coll. Fletcher, who was in Scotland condemned to dye for Atheism and Burning the Bible, and was banished to New York; where he was by Contribution freed from being a Servant, and permitted to teach School, and being somewhat a Scholar, and having good natural sense, made the use of his wicked parts to teach Blasphemy, and Atheism, and to ridicule Sober Religion, till he got a Reputation amongst the dissolute Church of England men, whose Liturgie he then would and still doth gabble over with great seeming devotion and uplifted eyes a few hours after he had been Blaspheming Christianity; but his form of saying the Common Prayer sufficiently recommended him to Coll. Fletcher, so that the Secretary Clarkson[2] was prevailed on to make him his Deputy for a Hundred Pounds a year Rent; and Coll. Fletcher gave him Fifty Pounds per Annum Salary out of the Kings Revenue as Clerk of the Council, and through all his Government made use of his vile Service, and afterwards recommended him to the Earl of Bellomont, as one of the honestest men in the Government; although at the same time he knew the said Jamison was actually marryed to two Wives then living. This man so qualifyed was intrusted to do this piece of Service, but 'tis believed the aforementioned Coll. Bayard gave him some assistance in furnishing him with some Materials, and without doubt, according to orders, no falsehood was balk'd that could serve the cause, and so this Libel was hammered out, in which there is scarce a Paragraph, but what contains one or more Scurrilous Untruths, which are delivered with an Highland

[1] David Jamison was a Scotsman who had come over as a redemptioner in 1685. He became the master of a Latin school and afterward studied law and became clerk of the council under Governor Fletcher. He was removed from office by Bellomont.

[2] Matthew Clarkson went to England with Joost Stoll in August, 1689, but took no part in Stoll's mission. He became secretary of the province under Fletcher and was removed from office by Bellomont.

modesty and peremptorily affirmed to be truth without any proof, on purpose to Vilify the Transactions of the Revolution, and Massacre over again the Reputation of those, whose persons were murdered Eight years before for their Loyalty, and withal [with all] the Villany proper to persons who hate the present Government are added to this Account some Servile Votes of the Assembly of New York made to flatter their new Governour Coll. Slaughter, who signed these Loyalists Warrant for Execution, and likewise is Printed an order or report (God knows how obtained) of the Committee of Trade for Justifying the said Condemnation and Execution. But this Libeller, contrary to his duty to truth, allegiance to His Majesty, and respect to Laws (for he could not hide his Virulency to the present Government) takes no notice of the Act of Parliament of England Reversing the Attainders of these Condemned Gentlemen, which gives the Lye to his whole Libel, Justifies Capt. Leisler as Lawful Governour of New York, and in full effect expresses that he was basely Murdered, contrary to all Law and Reason, for doing his duty as His Majesties Lawful Governour of New York; which is the sence of the words of the said Act. But the Libeller did as he was ordered, and the book raised the flame it was designed to raise, and was carryed to the Press by Mr. Brook, who although a Refugee from Ireland and preferred by King William to be Collector and Receiver General of the Customes and Revenue of New York, and a new-comer thither, took upon him to be one of the bloody Judges of this Royalist; but is since for betraying his said Trust and neglect of his duty suspended from all his Employs, even that of being Judge, and one of the Council, by the Right Honorable the Earl of Bellomont, who was his Security for his Collectors place to the Commissioners of the Customs of England, but could not bear his treachery to that Trust which he himself had been Instrumental to advance him to. And Mr. Wilson,[1] late Sheriff of New York, a hot headed despicable fellow, who to serve the Tory party, contrary to his Oath, made a most false Return of Assembly men to serve for the Counties of New York and Orange in the last Assembly. For which palpable breach of his Oath

---

[1] Ebenezer Willson, captain, merchant, and sheriff of New York, was also removed by Bellomont.

and Trust, His Excellency the Earl of Bellomont with consent of the Council suspended him from being Sheriff of New York. But when this Libel was so midwived to the Press by the Kings Collector[1] (who was likewise one of the Council) and this foresworn Sheriff, Then Coll. Fletcher calls the Council where 'tis proposed (as appears by the Minute of Council) that a book being found at the Printers, giving an Account of the Revolution of New York and contained nothing but Truth, 'Tis resolved *Nemine contradicente,* that it should be Printed. But who were the Council who consented to this great piece of Service to His Majesty? Why Coll. Fletcher, who is supposed to have given orders for its being Written, Coll. Bayard of whom enough is said plainly and truly, Mr. Brook who carried it to the Press and was one of Leislers Judges; Mr. Pinhorn, another of Leislers Judges (who is since removed by His Excellency the Earl of Bellomont from being Judge and of the Council, for speaking most Scandalous false and reproachful words of His most Sacred Majesty King William, and for protecting and concealing in his house a Popish Priest) and some other Enemies of the Revolution. So that (to omit the false sordid flatteries given to Coll. Fletcher, which are impertinently added by the Libeller) it is apparent that there was a wicked conspiracy, by this book to give distraction (by Printing it just before the Earl of Bellomont's Arrival at New York) and thereby to divide the People and so to disturb Affairs under his Government, that there should be no time or opportunity of quickly inquiring into the Corruptions of Coll. Fletcher's managements.

This was the time and design of its Publication, these the qualities of the supposed Authors, and of the Persons who carryed it to the Press, and after this manner (by Coll. Fletcher and the afore mentioned of the Council) it was permitted to be Printed; so that it is no wonder, that this book was a Mine Sprung from Hell to blow up the Peace of this Province, when so many Sons of Belial in Office and Authority joyned in its Contrivance and Publication, who must keep to their nature and not stick at any plain falsehood (although it fly in the face of the King, Lords and Commons of England, and

[1] Chidley Brooke was king's collector. Under Fletcher he was both collector and naval officer.

Truth itself) that may Exasperate and raise a flame, and if possible Murder over again those Martyrs for their Loyalty, Capt. Leisler and Mr. Milbourn, who were barbarously Executed for bravely Asserting the Rights and Liberties of Englishmen against Popish and Arbitrary Government; and for their Early and Sincere Affection to His most Sacred Majesty King William, whom God send long to Reign.[1]

[1] In the original pamphlet the text is followed by a reprint of the "Act for reversing the Attainder of Jacob Leisler and others." This act is printed in the *Documentary History of New York*, II. 435–437, octavo ed.

INDEX

403

Winthrop, John, the elder, *History*, 189 n.

Winthrop, John, jr., 187 n.

Winthrop, Major-Gen. Wait, 169, 172 n., 182, 187, 187 n., 189 n., 201, 216 n., 231, 249, 259.

Wise, J. C., *The Early History of the Eastern Shore of Virginia*, 66.

Wise, Rev. John, trial of, 178 n.

Wiseman, Samuel, 79 n., 104.

Witchcraft, 18, 111.

Woodcock, Thomas, 297.

Yong, Capt. John, 97.

Yonge, S. H., *The Site of Old Jamestowne*, 70 n., 136 n.

York County, Va., 83, 85 n.

York Fort, 62.

Young, Col. John, justice, at trial of Jacob Leisler, 392 n.